Poverty Scholarship:
Poor People-Led Theory, Art, Words, and Tears Across Mama Earth

LISA "TINY" GRAY-GARCIA, DEE GARCIA,
AND THE POOR MAGAZINE FAMILY

Published by POOR Press
Oakland, CA
© 2019
Cover art by Asian Robles
Book design by Isa Knafo
ISBN: 978-1-7329250-0-7

Dedicated to mi hijo Tiburcio, my beautiful sisStar comrade, Poverty skola Laure McElroy, my beautiful OG Poverty skola Mama Dee, and all the houseless, disabled, indigenous, bordered, incarcerated Mamas, for without whom there would be no we.

A Note from the POOR Press Linguistic Liberation Team

As you read this beautiful POOR Press book, please understand that as a colonized and oppressed peoples in poverty, we do not speak the colonizer's languages with academic precision. We resist linguistic domination by writing and speaking and creating. There will be typos and different uses of language. These are our voices, our art, and our resistance narratives. Read them with love and spirit in your hearts. Decolonize your mind one page at a time.

The photos in this book are of varying quality and size, and we chose to include them as they are. We believe this honors poverty scholars and the realities of poverty journalism. It was more important to preserve the photos as documentation, rather than leave them out. Wherever possible we tried to use high-resolution photos, or improve the quality of smaller ones, but some images could not be improved or re-shot. We believe the book is better because these images are included.

Tiny (aka Lisa) Gray-Garcia is the author of the main narrative throughout this book. Where others' work appears, their names appear with the title of their piece.

Acknowledgements

First, I would like to thank my mama, without whom there would be no me. Ghetto Fabulous OG poverty skola Dee, who created the first shorter version of this text in 2003 when everything was truly falling apart for us. As a poor unhoused single mama with her daughter, and then as part of a poor- and indigenous-people-led movement, intrinsically and unabashedly enmeshed in both our survival and, every so often, thrival, she was by my side. I love you and miss you so much, mama.

To the Solidarity Family of POOR Magazine, for being such hardcore redistributors and community reparators, who made this book possible with their linguistic domination skills and loving time and work. Shout out to Lex Horan, Jess Hoffmann, Roan Boucher, and other Solidarity Fam revolutionaries Savannah Kilner, Toby Kramer, Cecilia Cissell Lucas, Yael, Ro Seidelman, Mara Chavez-Diaz, Cathy Rion Starr, Marlee and Paul Blasenheim, LT, Claire Urbanski, Julian Wade, Cynthia Beard, Jessica Rosenberg, and Jessie Spector.

To Isa, Sandra, Laura Guzman, Ibby Grace, Corbett, and everyone else for making this PeoplesText possible.

To mi hijo Tiburcio, for being the best Sun in the world. To sis-STARS Corrina Gould, Fuifuilupe, and Loa Niumetolu for loving me and Tiburcio and the whole POOR family through the worst time of our organizational and personal lives and for being hardcore poverty, indigenous warriors and land/ocean liberators.

To my loving and beautiful brother, Leroy Moore, without whom this book could not have happened.

To Auntie Gerry, for being such a strong loving poverty skola and lifelong warrior; to mi hermanos y hermanas, Muteado Silencio, Aldo, Bruce Allison, Sue Ferrer, Norma, Dee Allen, Diallo McLinn, Jeremy Miller, La Mesha Irizarry, Bilal Ali, Ingrid DeLeon, Vinia Vanessa Castro, Kathy Galvez, Gloria Esteva, Julio Chavez, Teresa Molina, and anyone else I missed. To fellow welfareQUEENs and poverty skolaz, Vivian Flaherty, Queennandi, Jewnbug, Laure, Auntie Frances, Tenika Blue, Tracey Bell-Borden, Audrey Candy Corn, Martrice, Al Osorio, Pearl Ubungen, Jose Cuellar, Xochi Maez Valdez, Jean Ishibashi, Diana Viellman, and so many more.

To Auntie Teresa and Utopia and Kim Robles, for being the best cousins and aunties; to Tony Robles, for opening his doors to us when we were unhoused. Again.

To Uncle Al Robles and Bill Sorro, elder revolutionary poverty skolaz that this poverty skola had the blessing of knowing.

To Kimo, Tyray, Queena, Daione, Bella, Tristen, Amir, Zair, Aselah, Alex, and Amun Ra, for being the best youth skolaz a mama teacher could ever know.

To Elaine Katzenburger, for giving me the original channel of access to make my first book, Criminal of Poverty, possible.

To Iris Canada, Ron Likkers, Elaine Turner, Lola McKay and all the other poverty skola/elders who died behind the violence of eviction, displacement and gentriFUKation.

To every lavaplatero (dishwasher), street artist, street performer, trabajadora, day laborer, domestic worker, shoe-shiner, panhandler, street-corner newspaper seller, recycler, sex worker, underground economic strategist, waitress, waiter, mama, daddy, abuela, abuelo, who are always working, always teaching, and always sharing their love, time, sweat, and poverty scholarship.

Contents

TINY (AKA LISA) GRAY-GARCIA *is the author of the main narrative throughout this book. Where others' work appears, their names appear with the title of their piece.*

2
LINGUISTIC DOMINATION, LANGUAGE SUPREMACY, AND THE MYTH OF ILLITERACY

3
MEDIA: POVERTY JOURNALISM, "I" JOURNALISM, REVOLUTIONARY AND REAL MEDIA BY POVERTY SKOLAZ

4
ART AND CULTURAL WORK

5
POOR PEOPLE-LED EDUCATION, WE-SEARCH, AND INFORMATION VS. INSTITUTION-LED AKKKADEMIA, RESEARCH, AND DESTRUCTION

6
LIBERATING THE POOR BODY OF COLOR FROM HELLTHCARE, POVERTY PIMPS, AND SOCIAL WORK

7
UNDERGROUND ECONOMIC STRATEGIES, UNRECOGNIZED WORK, AND SURVIVAL WORK

8
DEFAULT COLONIZERS, 21ST-CENTURY MISSIONARIES, AND OUR OWN POOR PEOPLE-LED MOVEMENTS

9
HOMEFULNESS:
A POOR PEOPLE-LED SOLUTION TO HOMELESSNESS

10
COMMUNITY REPARATIONS AND REVOLUTIONARY GIVING: MOVING AWAY FROM PHILANTHRO-PIMPING AND THE NON-PROFIT INDUSTRIAL COMPLEX

11
LIBERATION, DECOLONIZATION, AND BUILDING POOR PEOPLE-LED SELF-DETERMINATIONS

"Thank you, Grandmothers and Grandfathers, for the circles that you bring together in all of the creations of our humble work that is done on behalf of the ancestors. We thank you for the opportunity to work together with amazing people that you place in our paths. Thank you for opening our eyes and ears and hearts to the work that you want us to do. Thank you for the blessings of bringing us all together at this time to share these words with others that may be touched by the work that we have embarked on as a way of life. Thank you for the continued blessings. We ask that we are able to continue to touch people's lives, to work together to make a better world for the next seven generations. Oooooh."

— PRAYER BY CORRINA GOULD
(CHOCHENYO / KARKIN OHLONE)

Introduction

The notion of poverty scholarship was born in the calles, prisons, street corners, community centers, welfare offices, shelters, kitchen tables, assembly lines, tenements, favelas, projects, and ghettos—all the places people don't look for educators, experts, leaders, researchers, lecturers, linguists, artists, creative thinkers, writers, and media producers.

Poverty scholars are the people usually silenced: incarcerated, criminalized, displaced, homeless, disabled, marginalized, sorted, separated, and extinguished.

Poverty scholarship can be found in community newsrooms and indigenous news-making circles; impromptu writing workshops in welfare-office waiting rooms; reviews of a neighborhood's sources of free food; reporting about what's going on in the streets by people who live there; and poetic autobiographies of struggle.

Poverty scholars are told our knowledge is not valid or legitimate. Our speech is improper; our work and our choices, criminal; our words, inept. Our languages, writing, thinking, and art are deemed invalid by a process I call linguistic domination—a complex battery of tests and studies developed and promoted by formal institutions of learning that have gained power, authority, and legitimacy through their wealth and privilege, and through white supremacy.

Formal institutions of learning were launched by wealthy people with access to land stolen from indigenous peoples. With their wealth and privilege, the formal institutions have been able to buy their legitimacy and position their forms of knowledge as the only knowledge that is valuable and important, therefore cornering the entire "market" of education. To keep their incredibly imbalanced market share, formal institutions of learning have a stake in the ongoing repression, destruction, and silencing of informal institutions of learning and of poverty scholars.

In relation to formal institutions of learning, we poverty skolaz are valued as subjects of research, surveys, curriculum, and study. Our situations and struggles are developed into complete degree programs, and graduates of these programs are fed into jobs in the ever-hungry nonprofit industrial complex, prison industrial complex, welfare system, and/or academia—all sites that use our struggles as a rationale for their existence. Our art is considered quaint or fetishized as "outsider" or folk art. If we don't ascribe to or have access to formal education, if we don't master its complex system of language, we are called "at-risk" and/or learning-disabled and/or speakers of an "invalid" tongue such as Ebonics or pidgin. Our writing is called mediocre and our research is deemed invalid. We are only deemed important as the subject of other people's research.

For the last fifteen years, I have been teaching, innovating, and developing complex curriculum based on my own poverty scholarship: the knowledge I've gained from my struggle to survive and care for my family in an underground economy, on welfare, or with nothing, all the while making media and art and doing research that has been continuously deemed invalid by those with institutional power. I have worked tirelessly—in multi-racial, multi-lingual, multi-generational groups of poverty skolaz from all corners of Pachamama—to promote the expertise, creativity, literature, media, solutions, and research of silenced mamas, daughters, sons, fathers, grandfathers, tías, tíos, abuelitos, abuelitas.

Poverty skolaz' schools are everywhere. Our teachings are essential, haphazard and immediate, fluid and static. We are your mama, your cousin, your elders, your corner-store owner, and your recycler. Our research is based on our lives and our experiences; our solutions come from our vast knowledge of what works and what can work. Our visions are based on the dreams of our ancestors, our elders, and our youth. Our languages are many (albeit mostly of the colonizers' tongues, while we strive to move back to our indigenous, pre-colonized complex forms of communication).

With this book, I hope to insert poverty scholarship into its proper place. Our crucial knowledge should be recognized and understood. My hope is not to destroy, dismantle, or disrespect formal institutions of learning. As indigenous peoples, we don't work to destroy and oppress, silence and contain; rather, I hope that we, the poverty skolaz, can begin to engage in a dialogue with institutional scholars from a place of mutual understanding and respect between equal parties creating and promoting the knowledge, art, dreams, and thinking of all peoples. I hope that through this sharing we can be truly in relation with each other.

You can't audit a course in the skool of hard knocks.

—TINY

1

Poverty Scholarship 101

Anthropology
Ethnography
Psychology
The study about us
Without us

Our spirit
Our cultures
Our traditions

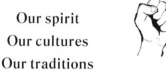

Through your lens
Fetishized
Researched
Studied

Deconstructing our struggle
Figuring us out
while our communities are dismantled
and left in rubble

Funded by fellowships
Acquired with academic privilege.
Linguistic domination gifts
Long ago parsed out to the sorted and separated
who excelled in amerikkklan school systems,
formal institutions of learning,
the myth of inclusion
and the cult of independence

How you gonna take photographic essays of gente pobre
in Nicaragua, Arkansas, and Bangladesh
But not give them so much as a slice of your
Privilege,
equity
and access

How you gonna fly
Back to your lands
Your publishers
Your nests
With warm feelings
of 21st-century colonizers,
our stories
and a good grade on your thesis
and final tests

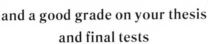
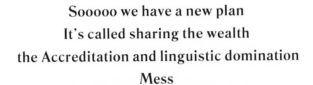

Sooooo we have a new plan
It's called sharing the wealth
the Accreditation and linguistic domination
Mess

Flipping the hierarchy
Of who is an expert,
who is a scholar
Who does the picture-taking, story-making
And who gives the tests
Mamalaure, Jewnbug, Gloria, Teresa,
Queennandi, Marlon, Tony, Bruce, Jasmine,
Tiburcio, Vivian, me, so many more,
and gente pobre the world over...
hold the knowledge, of survival, struggle,
thrival to create a new kind of fellow-ship,
a sister-ship, brother-ship
and Mama-Ship

that is rooted in all of our gifts
It's a new non-colonizing,
non-hierarchical,
equity sharing tip
its called poverty scholarship

—TINY

"I'm here for the writing group." She didn't look up, her deep brown eyes tired from too many nos and far too many almosts.

"Welcome to your house," I said, and offered her a seat. She sat down. Her eyes remained focused on our broken-tile floor.

It was the first day of one of POOR Magazine's core programs, the Po' Poets Project. We began with our trademark slam-bio exercise, which teaches folks to use their biographies of struggle with poverty, racism, houselessness, disability, or incarceration to introduce their scholarship through poetry.

My Name is A. Faye

A. FAYE HICKS

> My name is A. Faye
> I am a Lady of the Shelters.
> I am a student and teacher of Life
> In Indoor shelter living and Outdoor cardboard shelter living
> I have met Hundreds of People
> Most with Tragic Stories.
> Jailhouse, Sickness . . . Mental and Physical
> I am all alone
> Yet not alone!
> Sheltered in the Wings of Heaven!!!!

After Ms. A. Faye aced this exercise and many more, she became, like all of our students, a co-teacher and co-leader of the infamous Po' Poets Project. She eventually became our first Po' Poet Laureate.

The cover of a book of A. Faye Hicks's poetry, called The Poor Nation. A. Faye wears a floral dress and a red hat, and stands with one hand on a large globe, a small smile on her face. The book was published by POOR Press in 2004, with graphic design by Diallo McLinn.

What Is Poverty Scholarship?

There are many things that I, a poverty scholar, can teach you but, in reality, no more or less than any of the poverty skolaz you see — or more likely don't see — every day in your cleaned-up, cleaned-out, gentrified, and redeveloped cities, neighborhoods, streets, and parks. Houseless families, poor youth of color, migrant workers, panhandlers, sex workers; sitting, dwelling, camping, soliciting work, convening: I am them, they are me.

We are in a revolutionary struggle to remain alive, to thrive, or to just barely survive while battling the looming jaws of poverty, the criminal injustice system, the Po'Lice, the welfare system, and gentrifying landlords. We are in struggle to not be lied about, incarcerated, mythologized, and misconstrued; to be truly listened to, heard, and recognized for the deep scholarship we all hold.

But the one thing this poverty scholar *must* teach you is to rethink your notions of scholarship itself.

Who is considered a great scholar? How is scholarship attained? How is greatness honored?

What barometer do we use to assess this scholarship?

Through the perspective of my own extreme struggle with poverty, landlessness, incarceration, and criminalized and unrecognized labor, I began to realize a very different notion of scholarship. I have witnessed and shared in the struggles of my elders', ancestors', and families' oppression under generations of racism, poverty, violence, and displacement. The love, interdependence, and indigenous values taught and practiced by my mama, a disabled, poor, African/Taino/Roma and Irish single parent, have fostered a scholarship based on lived experience, struggle, survival, and resistance. This is the scholarship of poverty.

This scholarship has a new canon with new designations for greatness. Survival itself — through extreme poverty and crisis, houselessness, migration, racism, disability, incarceration, and/or substance use — is what you need to qualify as a poverty scholar. Conversely, a person who only holds a degree from a formal institution of learning but no poverty scholarship would be considered unqualified to write, lecture, or legislate on issues that impact communities in poverty without the collaboration, inclusion, and equitable involvement of a poverty scholar.

The recognition of poverty scholarship enables folks in struggle to truly liberate ourselves from the shame and shackles of both self-imposed and societally perpetuated otherness. It enables all people to redefine knowledge as not just one fixed notion, but many things, with many potential curricula, teachers, voices, research models, and mediums. This scholarship resists linguistic domination through a revolution of language. It is filled with music, theater, love, food, dreams, eldership, spirituality, visual art, stories, poetry, graffiti, and hip-hop.

This scholarship enables us poverty skolaz to re-envision ourselves as liberators of ourselves, our families, our communities, our elders, our cultures. It allows us to delink ourselves from middle-class media makers, missionaries, social workers, nonprofit industrial complexes (NPICs), and nongovernmental organizations (NGOs), and their controlled systems of housing, education, service provision, art making, and care-giving.

This redefinition of scholarship enables us to clearly see the ways we are silenced and separated from our own solutions, resources, and voices. It allows us to return to our own people-led liberation.

You are a scholar on your own experience, no matter what it may be. If your experience is in poverty and race, in a capitalist racist white supremacist society, then you are a race scholar. If you're a young person, in poverty or not, you are a youth scholar. If you are an elder, you are an elder scholar. The word *scholar* is usually associated with formal institutions of education; in an act of resistance, we reclaim it as applicable to lived institutions of learning. Scholarship as we're defining it comes from lived experience.

As we recognize and honor our cultural, linguistic, ancestral, and indigenous scholarship, we can decolonize ourselves from and challenge formal institutions of education, media, and research. We can begin a new relationship based on sharing equity, knowledge, and resources among all peoples.

Poverty skolaz in suit jackets lead a group of young people with class privilege on a "gentriFUKation tours r us" tour through colonized Ohlone land named after the colonizers who stole it: "the Mission district" of San Francisco. These tours exist to document the theft of stolen spaces, and to reclaim them through memories, images, lives and dreams, re-inserting ourselves in the stolen landmarks and reclaiming what little of us might still be left.

Deconstructing the Privilege of Writing:
The Birth of POOR Magazine

"Writing, reading, thinking, imagining, speculating. These are luxury activities, so I am reminded, permitted to a privileged few, whose idle hours of the day can be viewed otherwise than as a bowl of rice or a loaf of bread less to share with the family" —TRINH T. MINH-HA, *WOMAN, NATIVE, OTHER*

On my personal journey through the violence of poverty and marginalized other-ness into a new recognition of scholarship, I was exposed to the revolutionary writings of Trinh T. Minh-ha, who breaks down the privilege of thinking and writing itself. This was my truth, my struggle: I was a houseless child who had to drop out of school in the sixth grade to support my family. I did not have the time away from earning a loaf of bread; I did not have the paper; I did not have a computer. Most importantly, I did not even have the privilege of an organized life, the privilege of knowing what I would be doing from one moment to the next.

The formally understood "signs" of scholarship, such as writing, researching, critiquing, and publishing in one of the dominant (aka colonizers') languages, require privilege. These signs afford people the ability to be integrated, heard, and recognized.

I would not have been able to express my writing, my ideas, my solutions, my poverty scholarship, without the innovative intervention of a civil rights attorney who provided me with what I call revolutionary legal advocacy in 1993. I was facing jail time and several thousand dollars' worth of fines for the sole act of being homeless and poor. My "crime" was "habitating in a vehicle or sleeping/living in a vehicle"—a crime, like the act of sitting, standing, or sleeping while poor, that relates to racist and classist stereotypes of people in poverty in the United States.[1]

"What can you do?" was the attorney's simply stated opening question when faced with the chaos and poverty struggle that was me. His name was Osha Neumann, and he ran a nonprofit organization that practiced advocacy and civil rights law for homeless youth and adults. At the time, I had no concept of myself as a writer or journalist: I wholeheartedly believed the many welfare case workers, landlords, and creditors who had said I was incapable of anything except "leeching off society." But, quite tentatively, I expressed to him that I could write. He crafted a scenario in which my court-mandated community service would be to write an essay on some issue related to poverty under his supervision; it would be an act of advocacy journalism. He arranged a weekly check-in/critique appointment and created a timeline for me to follow. This afforded me the privilege to write, to think, and established my vocation as a writer, turning my unrecognized street scholarship into a documented, understood, and "heard" tract.

This moment with Osha is what I have forever since referred to as the first miracle or the first intervention. Unlike most advocacy meted out to people through low- or no-cost attorneys or public pretenders (public defenders), his help was not tied to fifty-six-page proof-of-income forms or psychiatric evaluations or assessments of the true severity of my situation, nor was it rooted in NPIC-esque patronizing behavior, timelines, grant guidelines, or system constraints. Rather, he began and ended his advocacy with a real, horizontally-formulated question rooted in respect for a human being, no matter who they are, or what they are doing or going through.

This first "intervention" was one of a series of small but revolutionary moments in which my mother and I were exposed to revolutionary skolaz in Afrikan studies, Raza studies, and women's studies. We began to realize and transform the deadly sorrow of our life and struggle in the context of a larger struggle of peoples in poverty across Pachamama.

In 1996, while still in the struggle of survival, my mama and I, and many other landless poverty skolaz from the United States, Central and South America, and Africa launched POOR Magazine out of a tiny office in the Tenderloin district of San Francisco. POOR Magazine is a poor-people-led/indigena-people-led organization dedicated to revolutionary media access, people-led education, and art.

In POOR Magazine's first year, we launched street-education programs, which we called Extreme Outreach workshops. These were writing and art workshops in group homes, jails, Supplemental Security Income (SSI) offices, welfare offices, homeless shelters, and the streets and parks where folks were sitting, sleeping, working, and dwelling. In that first year, I began to formulate the notion of poverty scholarship, which was inducted into POOR's core practices. We had the clear realization that it was not enough for us to just write our stories. If we were truly going to de-silence our individual and collective voices, us poor folk had to flip the power of media, voice, and authorship to actively demand inclusion and access. By any means necessary.

Revolutions of Poverty Scholarship

From a peasant poet.
I was born here in the bush
I have always lived a trabaiá,
In my poor modesty,
I could not study

— PATATIVA DO ASSARÉ, "THE THRUSH AND THE HAWK"

Patativa do Assaré (1909–2002) was an indigenous, revolutionary poet, organizer, and artist of the gente pobre in rural Brazil. Through his poetry and poverty scholarship, he led thousands of people in poverty to resist the oppression of the rich landowners. Patativa used his poetry to tell the stories of himself and his people: poor farmers struggling with substance use, landlessness, and oppression. He critiqued academia and recognized his own poverty scholarship.

Throughout history/herstory, in every favela, shelter, school, farm, jail, community center, open mike, and hip-hop club across the globe, there are countless poverty skolaz. Some are known, but many are unknown. Working in groups or as individual artists, they use the word to translate oppression and seed people-led revolutions. These poverty skolaz include The Last Poets, brother Malcolm, ken moshesh, The Watts Prophets, Ghetto Brothers, The Welfare Poets, the welfareQUEENs, Piñero, Piri Thomas, Avotcja, Tato Laviera, Wanda Coleman, and Mutabaruka.

In San Francisco's Manilatown in the 1970s, Al Robles used poetry in collaboration with fellow Pilipino elders to actively resist eviction and displacement.

Amandla, a poor-people-led movement of rhythm, chant, and dance, drove the resistance to apartheid in South Africa.

Across the globe, poor people create and distribute street newspapers that center their voices and stories. Hip-hop and street musicians in poverty drive people-led consciousness and lead micro art-businesses, selling tracks and spitting scholarship on street corners and in favelas, projects, and homemade studios, representing multiple voices of media resistance.

At POOR, we have created the Po' Poets Project, a multi-generational, multi-racial, multi-lingual group of over forty-five poets and artists who speak on poverty, racism, disability, and oppression. *All the scholarship is created by people who experience that oppression every day.* We create poetry in support of actions and protests, and as a form of media to respond to the violence of poverty, evictions, and displacement of poor peoples of color locally and globally. We created the Houzin' Project, a literary and visual-arts resistance project on houselessness, gentrification, and displacement. And in 2003, we launched POOR Press, the book-publishing arm of , to resist, infiltrate, and break open the closed channels of publishing access.

The revolutions of poor-people-led cultural work can be personal and collective. It provides healing for all peoples to speak and create. Poetry, music, and theater can speak, educate, and transform awareness and communities in a way that linear speechifying can't touch. From the Ghetto Brothers to The Welfare Poets, from the '60s to the '90s to the present, poets in poverty in the United States and beyond have used their poetry to speak truth to power and domination.

Fetishization versus Integration: The Roots of Other-ness

The so-called legitimate models of service provision, social work, advocacy journalism, academia, and activism only serve to fetishize and separate poverty skolaz more. They attempt to "help" poor people as opposed to truly integrating us; hold us up as examples of failure instead of recognizing our innovation; talk about, rather than talk with, us; and sympathize rather than empathize. All of these positions have nothing to do with recognizing our scholarship, listening to our solutions, or truly hearing our voices.

The process of true integration and true recognition of poverty scholarship occurs in many ways.

In media, for example, a story written about poor people facing the end of their welfare benefits in Alameda County, California, would be co-authored by homeless poverty skolaz in Alameda County, California. A story on youth "crime" would be authored or co-authored by youth skolaz who have been Po'Liced and harassed.

In service provision, it would mean that community-based poverty, race, and disability scholarship would lead the discussion on social service, school, and health-care systems. Poverty skolaz would truly be listened to. We wouldn't be dismissed with racist and classist terminology such as "the homeless people," "the illegals," "the youth," "the drug users," "the crazies," or "the bums," as though we were tribes walking the earth. Our solutions would be based on real access to equity and a roof, such as sweat-equity-based permanent housing, free and extensive legal services, and free community mental-health care. Schools that truly integrate families and community would be established in place of schools that implement the racist and classist mandates of programs like No Child Left Alive.

In activism, it would begin with understanding that there is elitism in middle-class-led revolutions that silence and exclude poverty, race, disability, elder, and youth skolaz. In order for U.S. activism to be redefined to be truly cross-class and cross-cultural, poverty skolaz and indigenous skolaz must lead the resistance movements against globalization, environmental racism, and economic injustice. These movements must come from and speak to the direct experience that we poor folks are having with our work sites, our neighborhoods, our children, and our civil and human rights. For us to lead revolutions, the revolutions must include different forms of support, care-giving, voices, and actions.

In academia, it would mean that truly grassroots poverty, race, disability, and youth skolaz are integrated into teaching and learning. Community models of teaching and learning would be recognized, and poverty, Native, youth, and elder skolaz would be credited for the teaching they are already doing in communities and neighborhoods. Our books, libraries, and media would not be written and held by publishing companies who intentionally exclude poor people who don't have channels of academic access.

Finally, this poverty scholar can teach you many things — no more or less important than the things that can be taught by all of us struggling to survive and thrive in an increasingly criminalized, stratified world — but one of the most important lessons is to rethink who you consider a scholar and what kind of recognition, understanding, access, and privilege that consideration affords.

The Poor Nation
A. FAYE HICKS: THE PO' POET LAUREATE OF POOR MAGAZINE

The PEOPLE are being Scattered
shuffling along with blankets, backpacks, shopping
bags & pushing carts

No more Unity in the poor Nations
Park benches uprooted—shopping carts over-turned, homeless people unjustly
arrested
Police circling around like VULTURES, camouflaged as Human Beings
The sick living in doorways, & behind cardboard boxes.
Bathrooms locked, water fountains denied
This is a sad state. Thought the tired so-called Bag Lady
Alone, Mental Faculties sorely tested, Weakened by a gnawing hunger.
From her womb, Misery was etched upon her copper tone belly
She paused to rest for a moment
Dark eyes glazing into the distant skies
Pondering the next move

Remembering the Peaks of her non-existence
An old Lady at Eighteen
Birds flying in formation, overhead
Dark clouds floating, silently in shapes of nightmares
Her only safe shelter the Blazing Sun, capturing her attention
If only I had a Star to wish upon or Something I can get some energy from.
She stepped upon the wet, well-cut lawn of a Californian City Hall
Its dampness drinking in & nourishing her being
Her breast painful from unused Mother's Milk
Sticking to her dress, Ragged around the edges of her soul.
Its wetness the Morning Dew or Her Deluge of Tears
Coming from deep within an inner well.

THE POOR POOR NATION

Ah, The grass, so soothin to her wiggling toes. COMFORT
Half worrying about Police Surveillance
Knowing she was on Public Property
Not daring to rest
Because a trespassing ticket would dip off into her Funds?
The gold nail polish on her sunburnt toes glinting magically
Spiraling undrugged thoughts upward seeking
A hole in the Bushy Hedges?
Dare she rest? A Haven?
Her curled into a Tiny Ball! Her hide-away bed The City Hall
With its Black & Gold Dome, warrin against a winter sun
A King's Ransom, Battling against the principles of the Homeless Nation
Unnatural Flags, wavin in the Beautiful Breezes, Compromising Life
One Nation Under God?
YO! YES
The power hungry god!
The prestigious god!
The Greedy Gut god!
And the bloodthirsty one!
Ah, Knowing, she sighed,
Better get a move on
There is no rest for my weary Bones here.

***

After months of writing and workshopping with A. Faye, I realized that she must be honored as the first Po' Poet Laureate.

"This is a poem I wrote for homeless mothers." One day A. Faye handed my mama two pages of moist and slightly crumpled notebook paper, wet from her endless nights sleeping alternately outside in a doorway and in a local shelter. On the papers were carefully handwritten letters in pencil, *A Poem for Mamas*, sweeping across the top of the first page. I watched my mama and A. Faye look at each other slowly, exchanging that look of hurt and healing, a look between women who have suffered and survived, and suffered again.

My mama read the poem, her head moving slowly up and then ever so slowly down, like a distant runner moving through the desert, an "uh huh" and "oh yea" lingering at her lips. And then my mama looked up from the paper at A. Faye. My mama's wide, full, beautiful, always ready, rarely happy lips parted, a smile rumbling in its beginning. This smile culminated in a crescendo of teeth and dimples and lips and sparkling eyes, a smile reserved only for fellow skolaz like A. Faye, who made my mama know why she should keep on fighting her own personal struggle.
"This is beautiful," she whispered, "just beautiful."

My sixth-grade formally educated self had never heard of a poet laureate. Even the word *laureate* seemed filled with other-ness, cloaked in the concrete walls of institutional silence. And like all of these distinctions, spaces, and categories of recognition, it felt completely inaccessible to me and my fellow skolaz. This inaccessibility angered me, and it depressed me, and ultimately I was inspired to change it up.

As I did more research, I noticed that the word *prolific* was always associated with the poets who were chosen to be laureates. They were almost always connected to institutions of higher learning. It was not until a few years later, when I was blessed to meet the amazing devorah major, poet laureate of San Francisco, and Amiri Baraka (whose laureate title was snatched from him because he didn't hold a purported master's degree), that I realized that there were some amazing community skolaz who became poet laureates. So, working on the fixed idea that academia owned the esteemed notion of laureate, I decided it needed to be redefined, remixed, and bestowed upon the amazing and prolific A. Faye.

A. Faye Hicks, a mama, a houseless, African-descendent scholar with a PhD in poverty, was most definitely a prolific poet, so prolific and so inspiring in her work that she had to be the first of the Po' Poet Laureates. Like all poet laureates, she used her poetry to speak on, illustrate, and create commentary about almost everything in life. Unlike most poet laureates, no large academic institution published her work, awarded her recognition, or gave her an honorary degree. She was a poet of the people in the truest sense. Her work spoke about women in homeless shelters, about being Black and poor, about being a mother, about being a disabled elder without health care in the richest country in the world, about the lies of service provision and social work, and the myth of charity. Her work spoke about herself and all of us poverty skolaz and all of the poverty skolaz before and since, struggling to stay alive and warm and fed.

Poetry Scholarship in Action

> *"They are making us wait all night in a long line out on the street, and even then we don't get a bed."* —A. FAYE HICKS

When A. Faye spoke, sometimes she got mad at you, herself, the world, or all of the above, and she would storm out of the room. There was probably some DSM category that a psychiatrist would happily apply to her "personality disorder." To me, she was a po' poet, an elder who had suffered racism and poverty her entire life, and was very understandably pissed off.

In 2004, when POOR Magazine was only alive in theory, squatting office spaces while I stole diapers and cold cuts from various big-box stores to survive, A. Faye came and pronounced that she wanted to write about the scandal of the Care Not Cash (Proposition N) system in San Francisco. Our new mayor, Gavin Newsom, came into office having gained votes from his promise to "clean up the homeless problem." This is a favorite battle cry of desperate legislators in need of a base and confident in the results of beating the drums of low-level fascism to gain a following among a voting U.S. public who equate "cleanliness" with the lack of people and things in an environment. Care Not Cash was based on New York mayor Rudy Giuliani's pogrom against poor people. It converted their welfare into pay for a shelter bed, and built up constant and focused policing of poor people who dared to convene, sit, or lie in public places.

Barricades at the Door: An Insider Poetry-Journalism Report on Prop N's Premature and Illegal Implementation

A. FAYE HICKS, PNN'S SHELTER CORRESPONDENT
REPRINTED WITH PERMISSION FROM POOR MAGAZINE
24 SEPTEMBER 2003

Thursday Morning TV news, finally daylight

I stretch my aching bones after a night in the
homeless shelter
Ah, what's this I hear? The Homeless in San Francisco

Getting served coffee while waiting for a bed

Who spreads these rumors

I began to question myself
Did not I spend the Night at the Shelter?

The one with the Barricades in the Lobby,
Yes I most certainly did

First you have to be buzzed In!
Yeah people stopped yammering and banging on the door

Not because a solution has been found

But because no one was answering the door unless
you had a ticket

You ring and ring the bell!
Where am I on this Computer

There are no beds, No such Luck

And I can't get inside for comfort!
The Rumors they spread!

I guess I have to inhale my coffee

Along with the Cold Night Air!

***

A. Faye and I proceeded to create a series of undercover poetry-journalism pieces based on her insider observations in the shelter. Each day for almost six months, she would come in and write a piece. Her work focused on the complete and utter abuse of disabled elders within the Care Not Cash system, the overt patronism, the day-to-day system breakdown, and the ways that other poor people were treated and destroyed by this horrible "new" program. The pieces launched a column on PoorNewsNetwork (PNN). We worked closely with our allies—Coalition on Homelessness, People Organized to Win Employment Rights (POWER), the Lawyers' Committee for Civil Rights, and others—on a series of investigative-journalism pieces that were used to speak truth to power by all the people fighting the takedown of our meager sources of support and the silencing of our voices.

The mayor eventually won his fascist campaign against the people of San Francisco, but the first-person poetry journalism of A. Faye Hicks, myself, and many of the PNN poverty skolaz, was instrumental in bringing transparency and resistance to the Care Not Cash implementation process. It also helped launch multiple checks and balances within the system. A shelter-monitoring committee was established, including some poverty skolaz and advocates who have an impact on legislative decisions affecting poor folks caught in that system. And poverty skolaz like POOR's own Charles Pitts used their new understanding of the Sunshine Ordinance, a San Francisco policy aimed at providing access to public records and open meetings, to extract truth from the politricksters in local and national government agencies. The people were truly heard.

Sorted, separated, segregated, occupied—
intimidated
silenced before we speak,
teach, or write—
because we talk in tongues
considered dumb
—not right—
not proper and
therefore permanently kept an outsider.
They call it linguistics,
we built our own languages
they missed it
these are our tongues—our songs—
long ago written,
already sung—
from our elders—from our young—
indigenous cultures culled
from years past—
always put last—
stolen—beaten—taken down—
this theft is our legacy—
from a racist genocide called missionaries, formal education,
and occupation
perpetuated throughout herstory
the loss of our myths and stories, language and glory. . .
Pidgeon, ebonics, nawat, zulu, tagalog, urdu, masagua
Take your pick
we have created complicated alphabets—
u get paid with fellowships to study, learn, archive and re-do
And then sort us out with your tests
When we dont / cant wont speak like the man—
u call us illiterate—
at-risk—

—TINY, EXCERPT FROM LINGUISTIC DOMINATION—DA POEM

2

Linguistic Domination, Language Supremacy, and the Myth of Illiteracy

Linguistic Domination

From the GED to the *New York Times*, linguistic domination is used to exclude, shame, silence, segregate, disempower, and destroy voices speaking indigenous languages. Meanwhile, proficiency in the colonizers' tongues affords access, space, resources, and power to a much smaller group of people with race, class, and/or educational privilege.

Across Pachamama (Mother Earth), linguistic domination has aided and abetted the colonization efforts of missionaries, social workers, service providers, academics, and media makers.

The teaching of "the man's language" was integral to the so-called civilizing of indigenous peoples across the globe, from Turtle Island (North America) to Australia.

Before Spanish colonization, many different indigenous groups—including the Lenca, Maya Chortí, Maya Pocomam, Cacaopera, and Nahua Pipil—lived in what is now El Salvador.

Today, almost all of the indigenous people in El Salvador speak only Spanish. Not many Lenca, who live in the eastern El Salvador and western Honduras, still speak their traditional language, Potón Lenca, though a few texts in this language have been published.

Spanish colonizers not only violently seized control of the land the Lenca lived on and set up systems that exploited both land and people, they also decimated the indigenous language and culture. Over centuries of horrific colonial violence, indigenous people feared that they would lose their lives if they spoke their traditional language or maintained indigenous customs. To survive, many began speaking the colonizers' language and practicing Catholicism, restricting traditional practices to the privacy of their homes.

The near-complete destruction of the indigenous peoples' native tongue enabled the colonizers' sanitized lies to be perpetrated on generations of children. It allowed young people to be sorted and separated and forced to learn the colonizers' history and language. Finally, excellence in the colonizers' tongue became the only barometer for success as well as a dire survival technique.

However, the Lenca have maintained the memory of their pre-colonial history and their resistance to the Spanish through oral tradition. They "have instituted programs with universities and community councils to preserve and promote their heritage, history, health, and human rights," as reported by Minority Rights Group International. The Lenca have even claimed a slice of the airwaves in western Honduras with a high-power AM station called "La Voz Lenca."

For peoples of color in the US, and indigenous peoples from other parts of Pachamama who have migrated to the US due to imperialist wars, globalization, or theft of land and resources (and subsequent poverty), linguistic domination plays out in the demand that all peoples must speak the one language of the English-speaking colonizer.

The English language is used as a way to "weed out" all but a few students who can master not only the master's language but the dominant way of thinking and living. English-language domination is implemented both covertly and overtly through language testing, curriculum development, English-only mandates in schools, and racist laws like Arizona's SB1070, which includes the demand that all peoples must speak the language of the colonizer and nothing else.

When the No Child Left Behind (Alive) Act became law in 2002, mandatory standardized testing of all public-school students was codified into US federal law, locking into place a deadly obstacle for poor children and children from cultures that don't speak, think, or act like the people who write these tests and shape these laws.

These institutionalized forms of silencing dictate what — and whose — words and information is considered legitimate, who and what is funded to create media, and who is considered an expert, a media maker, a communicator.

Linguistic domination is full of oppressive processes of defining "literacy" and naming the "correct" language and who speaks it "right," understands it "completely," and has the "skills" to teach on it. Reeling from the realization of this violence and destruction, I began to teach on the idea of linguistic domination, a concept I started developing while working on racial justice in education policy at an organization called Justice Matters. It was the only formal J-O-B this poverty skolar has ever held, and within it I witnessed the impact and fallout of linguistic domination in US skkkools. I began researching the original theft from indigenous peoples of their native alphabets and dictionaries. I reached out to other indigenous skolaz and community members to find out what, if any, active resistance to this domination was occurring on Turtle Island.

As I researched, I discovered there weren't a lot of post-colonial communities doing this as part of a public curriculum or academically documented process. But resistance is happening—both at the formal/institutional level, and more informally, at the grassroots level, in communities, in pop culture, and elsewhere.

Language Resistance

Ebonics

Notwithstanding the institutionalized attempts at silencing, destroying, and linguo-colonizing everyone's speech and knowledge-exchanging to one limited linguistic option, language resistance has infiltrated our limited vocabulary through the rabbit-hole of pop culture, the thriving by-product of a consumerist society. Through the revolutions of Hip Hop, Rap, and Spoken Word, there has been a beautiful recognition, embrace, and, sadly, eventual corporate co-opting of Ebonics, a language with many nuances, versions and dialects. A language full of art, poetry, beauty, and rhythm. A language arguably born from diasporic roots in a multitude of US African-Descendent, Caribbean, and indigenous African peoples from the Mother-Land.

Dr. Ernie Smith helped coin the term "Ebonics" — a combination of "ebony" and "phonics" — in 1973. The powerful Dr. Smith has led the charge to de-criminalize and de-racialize African peoples in relation to their language differences and the ways those differences impact learning, speaking, and racism. He makes the connection between the phonetics of slave-descendent people and several distinct indigenous African languages. He argues that by recognizing Ebonics as a distinct language with its own unique phonetic roots we can change the course of our children's education.

Dr. Smith was a major player in the debate that took place in the Oakland Unified School District in 1996 to recognize Ebonics as a language. This resolution would have resisted hundreds of years of linguistic domination by declaring Ebonics its own language that deserved to be taught, studied, and maintained. But the massive controversy that erupted led the school district to withdraw the resolution.

Denying that Ebonics is its own distinct language means that the language and learning ability of African-descendent peoples remains observed and judged from the Western-colonized language of English. This lens leads to ghetto-ization, allowing for the facile determination of African-descendent children as illiterate, learning-disabled, or in need of special education. For African-descendent children, it also creates the soul-crushing dissonance of seeing and understanding yourself through the eyes of someone who not only doesn't understand you or recognize your beauty, but in fact holds hate and disrespect for you, your people, and your voice of origin.

If Ebonics were *truly* recognized in public education, workplaces, and beyond, as we do at the liberation school POOR Magazine launched called Deecolonize Academy- where we honor it, embed and incorporate into all our Decolonized English and Herstory curriculum, we would experience a tectonic shift in relation to our children of African descent. It would be a shift of love, appreciation, and honor led by culture and consciousness. It would make obsolete so many of the systems that exist to incarcerate, hate, marginalize and displace generations of young skolaz across Amerikkka.

Indigenous Language Recognition and Preservation at the UN

Another institutionalized language-resistance effort is the inclusion of indigenous-language preservation and recognition in the UN Declaration on the Rights of Indigenous Peoples. Article 13 of the Declaration states, "Indigenous peoples have the right to revitalize, use, develop and transmit to future generations their histories, languages, oral traditions, philosophies, writing systems and literatures, and to designate and retain their own names for communities, places and persons." Article 14 goes on to say, "Indigenous peoples have the right to establish and control their educational systems and institutions providing education in their own languages, in a manner appropriate to their cultural methods of teaching and learning."

Language Resistance Is Everywhere

In 1995, the Alaskan K-12 public school system formally adopted an indigenous-based curriculum for teaching indigenous youth. Indigenous dialects are integrated in much of the project-based learning, which is taught by native elders from different nations in Alaska.

One of the more public recent acts of language resistance was launched by Bolivian president Evo Morales. Since he took office in 2006, Morales has deconstructed the domination of the indigenous people (who are the majority population of Bolivia) via the colonizers' language (Spanish). Morales has insisted that the Bolivian congress use the indigenous Quechua language of the peoples, and he has worked for inclusion and official recognition of indigenous languages in school curricula. Other resistance efforts include Hawaiian peoples who teach their native languages as part of an indigenous curriculum, and efforts by Taino peoples or Caribbean Indians (my Nation) who have created dictionaries of lost Taino languages. There is also an academically documented case of the "Miami language" revitalization process launched with Miami indigenous peoples.

The Wampanoag People: Language Reclamation

"Hi, I am Hartman Deetz. I'm Wampanoag. We are the native peoples who first encountered the pilgrims and for the last ten years I have been learning my native language."

Hartman Deetz spoke in POOR's Indigenous News-Making Circle about his tribe's work to reclaim their indigenous language. This process has been called language revitalization, language renewal, or language regeneration, but because this process is rooted in the colonization of indigenous peoples, I am prone to using the most political term for this act of resistance: language reclamation.

It was through POOR Magazine's own indigenous We-Search that I began to find out about Deetz and the Wampanoag peoples. I had told multiple family members and indigenous compañeros that I was trying to connect with language-resistance efforts. Then I heard from one of my sisters in resistance, Mari Villaluna, who co-founded POOR Magazine's Indigenous Peoples Media Project. She had met Deetz through another Native friend. The people-led education sharing was launched.

Hartman explained to our News-Making Circle that tribal member Jessie Littledoe had launched the language reclamation project 20 years ago, working off of one crucial document: a Bible.

"Because we had the misfortune of being one of the first peoples contacted by the European missionaries, who believed that the best thing to do for native peoples was to teach us how to read and write, one of the first books that was ever printed in the US was a bible that was completely translated into Wampanoag," Hartman told us. Hartman went on to explain that when Jessie Littledoe began the language reclamation project, only a few people spoke a little broken Wampanoag. But with the help of the Bible and countless letters, deeds, and other documents, they were able to piece together a workable alphabet and begin the process of re-learning what was stolen from them.

It is our goal at POOR Magazine to teach our children what still exists in our ancestral memories—what the late POOR family member Uncle Al Robles used to call our collective spirit and the deepest places in our collective souls.

Linguistic Resistance in Our Communities

For poverty scholars, the most important work is already happening in our own communities, our minds, our souls, our mouths.

As young people of all colors try to emulate, learn, and practice linguistic resistance — and corporations viciously co-opt their brilliance — new and different words and ways of using words are created, used, and dreamt every day, outside of the rigid Western Canon. No philanthropimped, Akkkademia-inspired, culture-stealing research studies, magazine features, or documentaries need be launched. The process is fluid and filled with people talking, dancing, speaking, singing, b-boxing, crumping, and breaking.

As revolutionary litero-theorists re-writing our herstories and designing our own non-poverty-pimped systems of housing, education, care-giving, and media-making, together we can practice, create, re-shape, deconstruct, and challenge the power of linguistic domination.

As peoples emerging from diasporas of oppression—slavery, poverty, globalization, racism, struggle, disability—as peoples de-colonizing our minds from capitalism, scarcity models, and the like, our new/old "voices" can be birthed from our anger, our protest, our chants, our songs.

We can create new language, or carefully listen to and dream on our cultures' and ancestors' ways of communicating.

Poverty skolaz resist the kkkolonizers' notion of literacy every day—the idea that we cannot speak publicly, research, develop curriculum, or create media because we haven't mastered the master's language, the language of the same master that perpetrated the destruction of our cultures and languages

Educated Ghetto Gurrl

JEWNBUG
REPRINTED WITH PERMISSION FROM *POOR MAGAZINE*
16 FEBRUARY 2011

BORN IN A PLACE
CONDITIONED FOR DEATH
RAISED ON GOVERNMENT CHEESE
PARENTS TARGETED TO BE DOPE FIENDS
HOUSELESS N HUNGRY
SOCIETY WANTS ME TO BE IGNORANT
BUT AIN'T NO DUMMY
GOT WIZE TO THA MIZEDUCATION
OF YO SURVEILLANCE
PROJECTS
PUBLIC SKOOLS
PRIZONS
US MILITARY ENLISTINGS
NEVER ASSIMILATING OR LISTENING
STAY THUG LIFE
RESISTING
RISING TO THA TOP
SINGING GHETTO SUPASTAR!
CONSCIOUSNESS
CULTIVATED UNDERGROUND
CAN'T AFFORD YO BRAND NAME LABELS
MAKING MY FASION TALK OF THA TOWN
REBEL WITH A CAUSE

SPEAKING OUT AGAINST
YO POLICIES, PROTOCOLS, LAWS
PROHIBITED MY NATIVE TONGUE
PIGEON
SLANG
EBONICS
U AINT MY GOD
N I AINT YO SON
SPEAKING TOO LOUD TOO FAST
CAUSING LYRICAL WHIPLASH
I SMASH ON U
U THINKING U MORE DIGNIFIED
CUZ I ROCK A SHOELACE FO A BELT ON SUM JEANS
PLEASE!
U PUT ME DOWN
THEN CAPITALIZE ON MY SWAGGER
LIKE, "THAT'S HELLA GHETTO"
I DON'T PLAY THO
NO DIPLOMATIC TACTFUL RAGE
STRAIGHT UP IN YO FACE
U LABEL ME
TROUBLE MAKER
THAT'S CODE FOR
TRUTH TELLER
FO REAL FOR REAL
NO FAKER
I KNOW TRU ESSENCE OF SUCCESS
DESPITE THE MESS
OF YO CIVILIZED VEST
MY INTEREST TO DO MORE THAN SURVIVE
MANIFEST
CAME WHEN I HELD MY HEAD HIGH
WITH NO SHAME
YEA I'M FROM THE GHETTO
N I'M DOING BIG THANGS
EDUCATED GHETTO GURRL
SHE WAS KUNG FU FIGHTING
SHE WAS ALWAYS WRITING
EDUCATED GHETTO GURRL
PUTTIN WHOLE SOCIETY ON TRIAL
N BRINGING THEM TO THEIR KNEES

English-Language Domination Becomes Voces
de inmigrantes en resistencia

Linguistic domination intersects with criminalization, colonization, racism, and exploitation when migrant peoples from Central America, South America, and the Caribbean are excluded, silenced, and abused by employers, service workers, media producers, and educational institutions because they speak other colonizers' languages, not English.

English-language domination happens in overtly racist acts like English-only legislation across Amerikkka. It also happens in more covert and complicated ways: language services in schools are given as a budget crumb to migrant Raza families like some kind of benevolent gift by kkkolonizer schools, causing resentment in other poor families of color who are barely receiving an education in the stripped-down schools of 21st-century Amerikkka. And this domination happens alongside corporate media's use of the word "illegal" to speak about migrant peoples.

Holding all of these struggles, POOR Magazine's migrante and indigenous poverty scholars launched "Voces de inmigrantes en resistencia," a series of journalism workshops with migrante mothers and fathers in poverty. In 2008, Voces was instrumental in bringing poverty, race, disability, and migrant skolaz before the FCC to speak on net neutrality.

EXCERPT | **Palabras de Resistencia en los Medios/
Words of Media Resistance**
GUILLERMO GONZALEZ AND GLORIA ESTEVA / PNN

Gloria was up next to speak. "We at POOR News Network/PNN publish articles written by the 'Voces de inmigrantes en resistencia' on the internet. We also work with KPFA, *El Tecolote*, *The SF Bayview*, and other sources of published media around the Bay. I know you're not really interested in that, but I am here to say that we have a right to be informed. We have a right to any and all information published on the net. The information from PNN, and other organizations like us who are trying to spread the truth, is published on the net. We, the people at POOR News Network, have the right to be heard."

Her voice captivated everyone's attention. As she spoke and I translated, I noticed that every pair of the FCC representatives' eyes were focused on this strong, immigrant woman's presence. And how could they not be completely captivated?

As the one-minute time-limit bell rang the whole audience rose up and demanded that Gloria be allowed to finish. "I just want to say that although we are at the lowest link of our economy and our society, we still have the right to be informed. Because even though we don't make enough money with our meager jobs to pay the internet fees and the costs of computers, our truth should still be heard. Our truth is asking the scientists and all the righteous people of this world, why it is that poor people exist? Our answers are not what the books tell us, but the truth that we publish at POOR Magazine. We are working people that are contributing to the economic prosperity of this country and we have a right to be heard!"

Los Viajes: A Literary Anthology

Por un año y medio Prensa POBRE ha conducido talleres de arte y escritura, bilingües y multi-generacional gratis en refugios, escuelas, y centros comunitarios con sabios de la pobreza y emigración de todo el mundo, para ser incluidos en esta antología imprimida y grabada, llamada *Los Viajes*. *Los Viajes* introduce un lente nuevo sobre la emigración y la inmigración de la gente a través de la Pacha Mama, informado por la Declaración de las Naciones Unidas sobre la Gente Indígena.

La siguiente historia de "Chispita" es un extracto de las muchas historias de viaje de gran alcance incluidas en *Los Viajes* — una antología literaria de la resistencia.

For a year and a half POOR Magazine conducted free bilingual, multi-generational art and writing workshops in shelters, schools, and community centers with migrant poverty scholars from across the globe to be included in the audio and print anthology *Los Viajes*. *Los Viajes* introduces a new lens on migration of peoples across Pachamama, informed by the UN Declaration on Indigenous Peoples.

We launched *Los Viajes* to ensure that the Spanish-language voices of poverty scholarship, which had been silenced by English-language domination, would not only be heard but would actually lead the conversation on migration and false borders. We self-published *Los Viajes* with the poetry, prose, and art written in both English and Spanish, but with Spanish always printed first, challenging the English-speaking reader.

The following story of "Chispita" is an excerpt from the many powerful journey stories included in *Los Viajes*—a literary anthology of resistance.

De Oaxaca, Mexico ...

CHISPITA
REPRINTED WITH PERMISSION FROM
LOS VIAJES: A LITERARY ANTHOLOGY

Aquí estoy. Sentada en todo lo que tengo, una banca pública, viendo a mi niño Jesús con lágrimas en sus ojos. Le duele mucho, se puede ver. Sus ojitos me miran pidiendo ayuda, trato con todo mi ser no mostrar en la cara desesperación, y es imposible evitar que las lágrimas rueden por mis mejillas tan abundantes como cascadas. Yo volteo hacia arriba por ayuda, y veo que los pasillos se hacen interminables, las bancas crecen al tamaño de paredes, y las luces fluorescentes casi me ciegan. Oigo los pasos de miles de gente, siento el temblor de las turbinas, y miro las caras de todas estas personas. Todos contentos, se van de vacaciones, o quizás visitan a su familia. Todos arrastran equipaje y saben por dónde van. Todos menos yo.

"Ma, Ma"
"No llores Chui, ya casi vienen por nosotros."

¿Dónde estarán? Ya son cuatro horas y todavía no llegan. Chui está muy grave y necesitamos ayuda. Veo sus ojos y hay tanto dolor. ¿Qué hago? Han pasado horas desde que comimos algo pero ya se me acabo la lana. ¿Qué hago? Duérmete Chui, duérmete.

Nunca hubiera pensado que un aeropuerto en Tijuana me pudiera dar tanta angustia. Mi nieto y yo estamos a miles de millas de casa y ya sólo queda continuar con nuestro viaje, pero mi cuerpo se estremece al momento de pensar que no vamos a sobrevivir. Mi Chui ya estaba enfermo cuando nos subieron al avión para acá, y su condición sólo empeora. Ya le llamé a mi contacto que nos dijo que pronto nos iban a recoger, pero eso hace cinco horas.

"Señora. Señora. Despierte, Señora.."
"¿Sí?"
"¿Eres Chispita?"
"Sí." Finalmente llegaron! "Chui, despiértate."

Subimos a un van y nos llevaron a una casa cerca de la frontera. En pocas horas se llevarían a Chui—que estaba aún más pálido—para cruzar en coche. Ha llegado la hora de despedirnos. Me duele muchísimo que se lleven a mi nieto, pero si se queda aquí, en esta casa conmigo, de seguro se morirá. Chui no quería irse, y mucho menos despedirse de mí. Sus ojitos nublados me miraban y lloraban. Nos abrazamos fuerte, y yo le prometí que pronto nos volveríamos a ver, y también vería a su mamá. El abrió sus brazos y me abrazó una última vez. Lo metieron a un coche y se fueron. Su manita y su rostro no dejó de voltear hasta que desapareció en la carretera.

En ese momento, parada allí en esa calle, todas mis preocupaciones y miedos se manifestaron en mi cuerpo en un río de lágrimas. Lloré y lloré hasta que la dueña de la casa salió y me abrazó.

La Noche De Fiesta

Después de una semana de que se llevaron a Chui, Amalia, la dueña de la casa, me dió un regalo de sorpresa, un vestido de fiesta.

"Muchas gracias por el vestido, Amalia, pero, ¿cuándo me voy a vestir tan bonita? ¿Acaso vamos a ir a una fiesta?"

"Es tu vestido de despedida... y de entrada."

"Despedida y entrada? Cómo?"

"Bueno, te despides de mí, y entras a los Estados Unidos para reunirte con Chui. Mañana, te van a venir a recoger unos compas míos. Todos van a estar vestidos para una fiesta. Van a llegar a la frontera, y van a caminar sobre el puente hacia una fiesta en los Estados Unidos. Así de fácil."

***

Amalia me acompañó al coche, nos despedimos, y nunca la volví a ver. En el coche había un silencio incómodo flotando entre los dos hombres, la mujer que estaba a la par mía. Yo sé que sabían que yo era la más nerviosa del grupo. Se acercó la mujer. "No se preocupe, señora, nosotros estamos en más peligro que usted. Juré no hacer esto nunca, pero su niño me conmovió y deseo que pronto este con él. Esa enfermedad sí es curable. Dios le va ayudar."

Cuando llegamos a la frontera, todas las luces, los coches, los retenes, y el puente me recordó en mi estómago que yo no estaba lista. Corrí al baño para vomitar, pero no salió nada. Sentía como que estaba flotando sin control en un mar tormentoso de todas mis preocupaciones y temor. En medio de esta tormenta oí que entró alguien al baño. Era la mujer.

"¿Qué pasa, Gloria? Todos te estamos esperando. Mira, no te preocupes, hay tanta gente pasando ahorita y a ninguno de ellos los pararon. No más tienes que pensar y creer que vas a una fiesta. Ponte en ambiente de fiesta y no te van a parar."

Me concentré en lo que tendría que hacer para estar junto a Chui. Tendría que actuar como una dama de fiesta que la única preocupación en su mente es verse bella, y divertirse. Tendría que actuar como que en las últimas semanas de mi vida, incluyendo esta noche, casi no me matan. Tendría que actuar como si no tuviera un nieto enfermo que dependía de mi al otro lado de esta frontera. Tendría que actuar como si no fuera yo.

No se cuánto tiempo me tardé en ese baño porque mi realidad en esos momentos fue como que si estuviera mirando una película de suspenso, en la cual yo era la artista. Antes de salir del baño, sí recuerdo pidiéndole a Dios que me ayudara en ese momento.

Salí del baño con una sonrisa y con un paso que casi bailaba. Yo iba a una fiesta y estaba muy emocionada. Pasé cerca del grupo, y casi no me reconocían, hasta que logré ver a la mujer y en sus ojos esos destellos de bondad que siempre nos damos las mujeres. "Gracias," le dije, y continué actuando. Caminamos en el puente hacia las oficinas de inmigración riéndonos y gozándonos. Cinco pasos antes de llegar al poste donde estaba el agente de inmigración, mi risa se paró.

Empecé a pensar en Chui, y sabía que si yo no tenía éxito al cruzar esta noche, estaría solo con esos tremendos dolores. Sentí que me desmayaba al pensar que me detendrían. Uno de los hombres del grupo me vió que caminaba más lenta y con la cabeza abajo. Estaba a dos pasos del poste. El tiempo se congeló, y voltió a ver el hombre. Su sonrisa me recordó que íbamos a una fiesta. Ví que ya habían pasado a la mujer y al otro hombre; ahora sólo faltábamos nosotros. Un paso del poste. El tiempo se congeló otra vez. El agente nos dio una mirada de pies a cabeza. Yo traté de sonreír... y no desmayarme.

Volví al poste. Miré hacia el agente, y no sabía si todavía me estaba sonriendo. Sin quitar la mirada, nos dio una seña con su mano, una seña que nos comunicó que continuemos. El tiempo se congeló una vez más. Este momento de mi vida nunca lo voy a olvidar. Lo hice. No sentía mi cuerpo. Solo sentía mi alma saltando en mi corazón, y salió de mi cuerpo en forma de lágrimas.

No me recuerdo mucho más de esa noche. Pero ahora que me recuerdo, sí era una noche de fiesta, para mí. Mi alma gozaba que pronto estaría apoyando a Chui. Mi alma gozaba ya que en este país, tendría la oportunidad de seguir luchando para mantener a Chui sano. Mi alma gozaba porque esa noche, en la frontera de Tijuana, tuve la fuerza de sobrevivir, y es con esa misma fuerza que hasta hoy he sobrevivido en este país.

ENGLISH TRANSLATION

Here I am. Sitting on all I have, a public bench, watching my child, Jesus, with tears in his eyes. It hurts him a lot, it shows. His little eyes stare at me asking for help. I try with all my being to not show desperation on my face, and it is impossible for me to avoid the tears that roll down my cheeks as abundantly as cascades. I turn my head upwards seeking help, and I notice how the hallways become endless, the benches grow the size of walls, and the fluorescent lights almost blind me. I hear the footsteps of thousands of people, I feel the tremor of the turbines, and I stare at faces of all of those people. All of them happy, they are going on vacations, or maybe to visit their family. They all drag their luggage and they know where they are going. Everyone except for me.

"Ma, Ma."

"Do not cry, Chui, they are almost here for us."

Where can they be? It has been almost four hours and they still do not arrive. Chui is in very critical condition and we need help. I see his eyes and there is so much pain. What can I do? Hours have passed since we last had something to eat but I have run out of cash. What can I do?

"Sleep Chui, sleep."

Never did I think that an airport in Tijuana could ever give me such anguish. My grandson and I are thousands of miles from home and continuing our journey is the only thing that is left, but my body shakes at the moment when I consider that we might not make it. My Chui was already very ill when they put us on the plane headed here, and his condition only worsens. I already called my contact that told me that they would soon be here to pick us up, but that was five hours ago. Perhaps we will stay here the whole night, in the airport of Tijuana.

"Señora. Señora. Wake up, Señora."

"Yes."

"Are you Chispita?"

"Yes." Finally! They arrived! "Wake up, Chui."

We get in a van and they take us to a house near the border. In a few hours they would take Chui, who looked even paler, to cross by car. The time had come for us to say goodbye. It hurts me so much when they take my grandson, but I know that if he stayed with me in this house he would surely die.

Chui did not want to go, and much less to say goodbye to me. His blurry eyes stared at me and cried. We hugged tightly and I promised him that we would see each other again, and that he would also see his mom. He opened his arms and gave me one last hug.

They put him in a car and they left. His little hand and face did not stop turning towards me until they disappeared on the highway. In that moment, standing there on that road, all of my worries and fears manifested themselves in my body as a river of tears. I cried and I cried until the owner of the house came out and gave me a hug.

The Night of the Party

After the week that Chui was taken, Amalia, the owner of the house, gave me a surprise gift, a party dress. At first, I did not know why she had given me a surprise gift, and I almost forgot to give her thanks, almost.

"Thank you for the dress, Amalia, but when am I going to get dressed up so pretty? Or are we actually going to a party?"

"It is your dress of farewell, and of entry."

"Farewell and entry? How?"

"Well, you will say farewell to me and enter the United States to reunite with Chui. Tomorrow several friends of mine will come to pick you up. All of them will be dressed for a party. They will arrive to the border, and they will walk along the bridge to a party in the U.S. It is as easy as that."

When we arrived at the border, all of the lights, the cars, the check points, and the bridge reminded me in my stomach that I was not ready. I ran to the bathroom to throw up but nothing came out. I tried and tried to throw up and nothing but saliva would come out and I felt even dizzier. The last time I tried to vomit, I did not even feel that I was stepping on the firm ground, I felt as if I was floating without control, in a tumultuous ocean of all my worries and fears. In the midst of all this torment I heard someone come into the bathroom. It was the woman.

"What's going on, Gloria? Everyone is waiting for you. Look, don't worry, there are so many people passing right now and none of them were stopped. You only have to think and believe that you are going to a party. Get in a party going mood and they will not stop you."

I concentrated on what I had to do to be with Chui. I had to act as if I was a lady going to a party, whose only concern was to look beautiful and have fun. I would have to act as if the last few weeks of my life, including this night, did not almost kill me. I would have to act as if I did not have an ill grandson that depended on me on the other side of that border. I would have to act as if I was not myself.

I am not sure how long I took in that bathroom because my reality in those moments was as if I was watching a suspense movie, in which I was the actress. Before leaving the bathroom, I do remember asking God to help me in that moment.

I came out of that bathroom with a smile and with a step that almost danced. I was going to a dance and I was very excited. I walked close to the group and they almost did not recognize me until I was able to see the woman. Her eyes sparkled with the type of kindness that women always give each other. "Thank you," I told her, and I continued acting. We walked on the bridge towards the immigration offices, laughing and having a good time. Within five steps of reaching the post where the immigration agent was, my smile stopped.

I began to think of Chui, and I knew that if I did not succeed in crossing that night, I would only be left with those horrible pains. I thought I would pass out at the idea of being detained. One of the men in group noticed that I walked more slowly and with my head down. I was two steps from the post. Time froze and I turned towards that man. His smile reminded me that we were going to a party. I saw how the other woman and man had already passed and now we were the only ones left. The agent gave us a look from our feet to our heads. I tried to smile, and I did not faint.

I looked towards the agent, and I did not know if I was still smiling. Without removing his stare, he gave us a sign with his hand, a sign that communicated that we continue. Time froze once again. I will never forget this moment in my life. I made it. I did not feel my body. I only felt my spirit jumping in my heart, and come out of my body in the form of tears.

I do not remember much more about that night. But now that I remember, it was a party night for me. My spirit rejoiced that I would soon be there to support Chui. My spirit rejoiced that I was already in this country. I would have the opportunity to continue fighting to keep Chui healthy. My spirit rejoiced because on that night on the border of Tijuana, I had the strength to survive, and with that same strength, I have survived in this country till this day.

EXCERPT | **Crossing Pains**
NuBe−F.C.
REPRINTED WITH PERMISSION FROM
LOS VIAJES: A LITERARY ANTHOLOGY

Ni Nehua Mixtli
I am Indigenous
Native son to Nuu Saavi and Yaqui Abuelas y Abuelos, Tatas y Nanas
I am Queer
My gender fluid without compromise sung to the origins of pipe carriers, Hamblecha ceremonies,
Nuu Saavi Mezcal
And
Nixtamalli Maiz
I am a Migrant powerful and strong like an eagle in the sky oh so high. I fly with my ancestors and my vision incorporates my revolutionary love
I am a Survivor of sexual abuse, homelessness, patriarchy, sexism, homophobia from all sides of my borders, and many others. I cross often.
I am Brave, my wisdom incorporated in Mexica and Dine Songs.
I am a Xol@ east los brought who decided to owe it to my gangsta'

cousins to keep the tradition of pocho ebonics and xicano slang.
Enlisted with oldies and cruising down Whittier blvd or Santa
Ana Nights. With the mentality of my home, my hood, my love
everywhere I go.
I am a painter and my acrylics are designed to blister and caress my
ancestral memory.
I am an eternal lover and my song speaks to Ix Chel the Luna.
I love too much. I bleed. I sing. I rejoice. I torment. I relief. I climax.
I am reborn. I die. I live. I love.
I am a child of the Moon. She guards my spirit through two spirit
medicine. Through Xicano aesthetics. Through African dreams.
Through Spirit.
I am son of Yemaya and Ochun.

I am crossing everytime I leave the door, speak in front of privileged
folks, dare to speak about my sexuality or my love, dare to read a
book in an institution, kiss my family, make love, fuck, organize,
paint a mural or a canvas, walk down my hoods with confidence
and a swagga', cuando voy por pan dulce y como de las dudas de mi
masculinidad, every time I live in a corrupt system. I am resistance.

Breathe.
Hunger.
Pain.
My Ama In Pain.
Felt death's whisper.
Sed.
Sol.
Too Hot.
My Ama In Pain
Crusty feet.
Sores.
Blisters.
My Ama in Pain.
Soñaba que caían gotas de Tepache Y bolillos de miel.
My Ama in Pain.
Ellegua se burlaba
Tezcatlipoca Cantaba
My Ama in Pain
In Yemayas arms lleguéé.
Y en el mar gozé
Pain was lost hope was gained.

…So now,
They rename us,
To
Members of the lodging tribe,
And
Remove us from the land
For having to sleep
There

—KEN M.,
ELDER, POVERTY AND RACE SCHOLAR
AT POOR MAGAZINE

3

Media:
Poverty Journalism, "I" Journalism, Revolutionary and REAL Media from Poverty Skolaz

It began on stiff plastic chairs in the corner of the welfare office in Oakland. There were only four of us. Some of us were hungry, many of us were hungover, all of us were disgruntled and depressed. We were waiting, small paper tear-off numbers crumpled in our pockets, to be called in for our welfare-worker evaluations. A perfect setting for a writing workshop, I decided.

Within sixty minutes (while still in waiting), we had created a body of powerful work, not necessarily linear, none of it word-processed, much of it scribbled on the backs of old General Assistance (GA) evaluation forms, assessment letters, and termination letters. We wrote about houselessness, disability and eviction, loss and racism, loss and poverty, and loss, period. We wrote about living on the street and in doorways, shelters, and cars. We wrote about addiction to crack, meth, and alcohol. We wrote and spoke about jobs had, then lost; people and families held together and torn apart by systems, institutions, gentrification, and displacement. We wrote about the violence of poverty and racism in amerikkka.

We also wrote about resistance. And scholarship. And beauty and art and love. And revolution. We knew that we weren't defined by our poverty, our color, our disability, our crisis. We weren't the lies told about us, created without talking with us. We were mothers and fathers and uncles and aunties. We were artists and laborers and chefs and designers and singers and poets.

We created journalism about what was happening to us. We proactively worked to change what was happening to us. We launched constitutional lawsuits, demanded appeal hearings, protested the mayor and Board of Supervisors. We fought Po'Lice harassment of ourselves; the murder of our children of color; the violence in our homes, shelters, and communities. We began working on visionary change projects, rethinking the original theft of our resources, our cultures, and our lives.

What Is Media? A Poverty Scholar's Definition

Media is survival. Media is herstory. Media is your story, the story of your mama, your grandmother, your grandfather, your aunties, uncles, children, babies, family, friends, community, ancestors. Media is "I" journalism, poetry journalism, hip-hop journalism, gossip, chisme, talk-story, song, ritmo, beatz, conversating, spoken word, rants, chants, screams, phone calls, letter writing, advocating. Media is the story told by the houseless man living with a mental disability, screaming on the corner about someone who hurt him so many times, so many years ago. Media is the stories taught to indigenous children by their abuelitos y abuelitas, grandmamas and big mamas about slavery, struggle, and survival by any means necessary.

Media is visual art: murals, photographs, drawings, graffiti, posters, flyers. Media is the pictures drawn on plantation walls by incarcerated brothers and sisters. Media is the sides of milk cartons and backs of cereal boxes.

Media is books, newspapers, radio, video. Media is communication, public or private, dangerous or safe. Media is truth and media is lies, depending on who is making it. For poor people, media is sacred. Media is a tool for survival, thrival, resistance, and revolution, to resist the lies told about us, not with us, for us, not by us. Media is our voice being heard, recognized, seen, and listened to.

"I" Journalism Versus Lie Journalism

P-O-O-R Skolaz til we die
The Revolution Begins with "I"

At POOR, we began to develop a new genre: "I" journalism, or revolutionary poverty journalism. We created the tagline "The Revolution Begins with 'I'," refuting the myth of journalistic objectivity and Eurocentric notions of "legitimate" media.

What we weren't creating was more "other" journalism, the typical journalism in which our voices—the voices of houseless people, poor youth of color, disabled folks, elders, and incarcerated peoples—are captured, reworked, over-dubbed, and barely included. Paul Boden, a formerly houseless poverty scholar who does revolutionary organizing around housing with the Western Regional Advocacy Project, calls typical, otherizing journalism about poor peoples "faces" campaigns. "Faces" campaigns involve corporate and independent media producers talking at us, and creating useless cover stories based on our lives and fronted by "beautiful" images of our broken bodies for voyeuristic consumption.

"I" journalism is power. "I" journalism is truth. "I" journalism is transparency, empathy, interdependence, and love. "I" journalism means not just re-porting but sup-porting—because speaking on issues of poverty, racism, ableism, criminalization, eviction, and oppression requires either personal experience or deep love, support, personal action, and accountability. "I" journalism requires that we write openly from each of our individual truths on the issue, person, or community we are writing on.

"I" journalism runs counter to everything we are taught in formal institutions of learning about journalism, which mandates the separation of writer from subject to allegedly create a "balanced" and fair report.

But what is actually created is a story separated from the truth, what I would call "lie" journalism. A story written in the third person removes the writer from any accountability to what they create and how they actually relate to, connect to, or disconnect from the story. "I" journalism holds the writer personally accountable for their writing, and therefore for their actions around the issue or struggle. This process of engagement is rooted in our connection to each other and our collective thrival, rather than connection to profit or corporations.

Too Dangerous to Ride

DELL'TRIANNA DAVIS, POOR NEWS NETWORK YOUTH MEDIA SCHOLAR
REPRINTED WITH PERMISSION FROM POOR MAGAZINE
25 JULY 2011

On Saturday, July 16, a nineteen-year-old young man, Kenneth Harding, from Seattle, Washington, came to San Francisco at the wrong time. He rode a transit vehicle to Bayview-Hunters Point's Palou Station only to exit and have an encounter with two police officers about paying his $2 fare.

Harding ran from being detained and was shot from the back multiple times, causing him to bleed to death at the scene. This shooting took place in broad daylight by San Francisco police in front of kids, family, and friends near the Joseph Lee Community Center. And sadly, this is not the exception. Police encounters that turn ugly happen all the time to residents of the Bayview, like me.

Police say Harding fired at them first—and maybe even shot at himself—which they say justified their shooting at Harding. What we hear and read says that the officers were fired upon, but people of the Bayview say that was a no-go; Harding only ran from the transit station to resist citation inquiries.

As Harding lay there at the scene, there was no emergency ambulance treatment for as long as thirty minutes. Police stood there for several minutes with guns on Harding only to watch him bleed to death.

Lately, the public transit inspectors have been taking their jobs a little too seriously, but only in the poor communities, causing public humiliation to those short on fare. Once, I was short on fare and had no transfer to show the inspector, which led to me receiving a citation. While the authorities wrote my ticket, they ignored my voice and searched and rambled through my belongings, only to find no ID—which I had already said I didn't have.

Riding public transportation is getting dangerous. I'm afraid for the residents of my community because of how the police mob the buses, supposedly looking for people short on fare.

The police are unaware that we, as a Black community, do see the way they view our young men—seeing them as slick-dressed boys—which is why the police must hear us say, "Stop killing our brothers and sisters because being poor is not a crime!"

(Revolutionary) Media Advocacy Versus Media Missionary Work

Corporate media often frames stories about us "poor people" as media advocacy, implying that they are helping us by reporting on us.

These acts of so-called media advocacy result, at best, in otherizing, criminalizing, and stereotyping us. At worst, they lead to our incarceration, deportation, and eviction, and the demolition and displacement of our homes, schools, and neighborhoods. To add an "if it bleeds, it leads" aspect to these stories, they are labeled media "exposés" and "investigative reports."

Charles Dickens' first book, *Sketches by Boz* (1836), portrayed the people of London's tenements, prisons, pawnshops, and streets. While this book was (and still is) perceived by many as a social critique that described the otherwise "forgotten" peoples of the city, it's an early example of "objective" journalism in which the reported-on community is stripped of agency and framed as in need of privileged people's charity. Dickens' style, called literary positivism, meant writing about poor people as "interesting" and fetishized objects, portraying them as crazy, dirty, ugly, lacking. This kind of writing was crafted to make privileged people seem like the saviors of poor people, as if the poor people Dickens wrote about would never have been able to survive without the benevolence of rich people.

To me, the poor families living in tenement houses are obvious heroes of survival: they raised six or seven children in cramped apartments with no heat, in conditions where most humans couldn't survive. But instead of focusing on the agency, the heroism, the beauty, the power of poor peoples' survival, Dickens could only see them as people who needed to be saved. Authors like Dickens thought they were documenting facts and therefore revealing objective truths, without understanding that they were missing a huge part of the story: the voices of poor people. And, as is often the case, the writers built careers on it, with little to no responsibility to the people they wrote about.

A few decades later, Danish American journalist Jacob Riis wrote a series of articles about the filthy conditions of New York tenement dwellers. Riis could have written an exposé on the slumlords who owned these buildings. Instead, he focused on the poor people, portraying them with no agency and their situation with disgust. This series has been framed as a journalistic "victory" because it resulted in the demolition and closure of thousands of "substandard" homes where poor immigrant families were living. But the truth is, "media advocacy" exposés by benevolent, liberal, middle-class writers like Charles Dickens and Jacob Riis—who received all kinds of positive press for their work—resulted in the demolition of the affordable, albeit small and cramped, homes of thousands of poor immigrant families.

Justified by this kind of framing, in the 1930s, New York mayor Fiorello La Guardia ordered the sudden demolition of the tenements where poor folks were living, as if this "slum clearance" would help them. Instead, thousands of poor peoples were forced to scatter to empty land with no money or resources to build houses or purchase land. Many children and families were forced out of downtown New York, and the places where the demolished homes used to stand were replaced with factories and sweatshops where poor people worked in dangerous conditions for almost nothing.

In the 1990s, Sheriff Joe Arpaio of Maricopa County, Arizona, got into bed with devil-opers who wanted to turn the downtown Phoenix area into a yuppie-loft paradise. Local corporate newspapers ran an "exposé" of the "horrible" conditions of hundreds of Single Room Occupancy hotels, so horrible that the only solution was to demolish them all. After the controlled demolitions of over 5,000 rooms of poor people's housing, the sheriff began his criminalization and incarceration campaign against now-houseless Phoenix residents. The neighborhood was now "safe" for yuppies who would buy new lofts there only if no one was on the streets outside. This same kind of racist and classist criminalization and hate-for-profit was later focused on im/migrant residents of Phoenix.

Since newspapers have been printed and pictures have been taken, there have been exposés, photojournalism spreads, and "shocking" series depicting the conditions, the homes, the barrios, and the lives of poor peoples locally and internationally, consistently absent of our voices and perspectives.

These acts of "media advocacy" are so deadly and so full of lies and propaganda that they should be renamed media missionary work, colonizing peoples and destroying cultures and communities, one story at a time.

In the late 1990s, a series of "media advocacy" pieces were filtering through corporate media about all the nice doctors providing "free check-ups" to poor peoples in California communities. One such story, called "Health care fair helps poor Latinos: 'Su Salud' an annual Central

Valley event," published in the *San Francisco Examiner* on July 22, 1996, profiled a doctor whose health fair had received an award from George Bush. The doctor was portrayed as a savior to the helpless poor peoples who "appreciated" his wonderful benevolence.

But that's not the real story. In the 1990s, there was a systematic movement to dismantle many forms of health-care provision and create a monolithic system of corporate HMOs. The HMOs were deeply leeching the U.S. health-care system, infiltrating public programs like Medi-Cal and Medicaid, and building the corporate medical industrial complex that exists today. Payouts to doctors working with public programs got even lower than they already were, further discouraging treatment of poor people.

While HMOs were stripping individual doctor visits under Medi-Cal and Medicaid, and closing poor-people health clinics at a clip, they were offering up the savior doctor as the "answer." He would travel to poor communities and offer "free" check-ups at health fairs. Articles like "Su Salud," celebrating these savior doctors and never centering the voices of the poor people who had to wait in long lines at crowded fairs to see them, supported the creation and entrenchment of the giant, profit-based health-care industry we are struggling with today.

Using "media advocacy" to perpetuate the silencing and displacement of poor peoples can also be seen in the coverage of real-estate developers like the Lennar Corporation. Since the 1990s, Lennar has been trying to buy up and "redevelop" land in Bayview-Hunters Point, one of the last majority-Black neighborhoods in San Francisco. Lennar has been publicly slammed in forums like the *Bay View*, a Black-owned independent newspaper, for ignoring the environmental impacts of building on a Superfund site (the Hunters Point Naval Shipyard) and for pushing "development" plans that would displace long-time Bayview-Hunters Point residents. To counter the negative press they were receiving, Lennar bought ad space in the *Bay View Newspaper*—sometimes directly across from an article calling out the corporation's "development" plans—to promote themselves as an asset to the community. In corporate media, Lennar rarely, if ever, paid for advertising because corporate newspapers would regularly run "news" stories about Lennar's latest condo developments, telling the story as if this engine of displacement and gentrification was doing a public service to the community. The lies of corporate media advocacy are plenty, as long as millions of dollars flow freely from the public-relations departments of corporations to support their creation.

Globally, lies are promoted and reported on to perpetuate stereotypes of the helpless, voiceless, savage, terrorist-leaning poor peoples from Haiti, Afghanistan, Mexico, and beyond. Media depicts the poor and indigenous peoples reported on as having no agency, self-determination, or solutions of their own, only "surviving" by the grace of the godly empire of the U.S. and Western Europe, the International Monetary Fund, and the benevolent and kind NGOs. For example, after the devastating earthquake in Haiti in 2010, mainstream media outlets were all too ready to depict poor people there as helpless, violent, and in need of endless amounts of aid from richer nations—yet they were rarely willing to talk about the massive debt that has hung over Haiti ever since its 1804 revolution made it the first Black republic in the world. "Media advocacy" only extended to media coverage that would allow certain kinds of "aid"—in the form of neocolonial NGOs and military units—to flood the country, always in the best interests of nations in the Global North.

EXCERPT | **The Mayor's Back Door: Lennar's Toxic Condo Plans**
BRUCE ALLISON
REPRINTED WITH PERMISSION FROM POOR MAGAZINE
25 JULY 2009

After getting the fifth degree from a security guard who wanted to know more about me than my own parents, I got approved to go into 1095 Market Street, a seven-story building with only six or seven companies in it. (Also the site of POOR's previous office, which we were unceremoniously gentrified out of!)

I walked into environmental action non-profit Green Actions' headquarters for an interview with POOR Magazine family friend, and long-time Bayview activist and powerhouse, Marie Harrison. We had a half-hour interview about Lennar, the nuclear dumpsite, and biohazards, all of which are located in Hunter's Point. The area where Lennar Corporation is planning to build low-income housing has been capped five times due to toxic and nuclear leakage.

As my interviewee explains, "Newsom and his auntie gave Lennar a 3-million-dollar loan," and magically Newsom's brother-in-law got a job in Lennar's executive ranks. This area is so toxic that the Navy has lost all records of how much has been dumped there. It goes back to WW2 when Fat Man and Little Boy were assembled there, and parts that weren't used were dumped into the water. Letterman Hospital in the Presidio also has records of animal parts being dumped there after experiments.

This historically was a mixed-use area. Through WW2, you had a Japanese fishing colony and a hunting lodge in Hunter's Point. During

WW2, a building was there for working people, which is presently the ghetto; this building was originally for shipyard workers and their families, and was to be torn down at the end of the war. Now it's the Evan's Street/ Candlestick projects.

The housing set aside for the people who paid money for it will be three ten-story towers that will be put in Hunter's Point, where presently low-income people are living.

As a sixth-generation native of this city, and an elder, my city has been robbed and raped by many corporations and agencies, with Lennar and the San Francisco Redevelopment Commission as their partner in crime. The redevelopment commission is the back door the mayor uses to do this dirty work without leaving his fingerprints on it.

Media Missionaries and the "Independent" Media Mythos

Many independent media producers partake in media missionary work as well, but the pimping is more nuanced and covert. It appears to the world as "great journalistic work," with people receiving awards and fellowships to make photo essays and author journalistic series on poor peoples across the globe, without ever sharing the wealth, access, resources, or fellowships with the "subjects" of the stories or exposés.

Thousands of well-meaning U.S. and European journalists practice what Black psychology calls a trans-substantive error: making a judgment about a group of people, culture, or community based on your cultural deep structure, not theirs.

Take the famous case of Brad Will, a white indie-media journalist from the U.S. who was killed while reporting on the Oaxacan revolution in Mexico in 2006. I mean no disrespect to his family or his memory, but when Brad Will went to Oaxaca to report on the revolution, a lot of revolutionaries told him not to come. The revolution was full of subtleties that he didn't understand. Oaxacan teachers were not only striking for better pay but also to protest corporate-owned, Eurocentric education policies and mandates that erased pre-Columbian history and indigenous educational values. And like the U.S. FBI operation COINTELPRO, which in the 1960s and '70s derailed and crushed the Black Panthers, the American Indian Movement, the Brown Berets, and countless other revolutionary organizations, infiltrators in the Oaxacan revolution had lain deep tendrils of wrongness that an outsider could simply never understand. But in a very western style of "getting the story, no matter what," filled with the arrogance and daredevil-ness that is so emblematic of western cowboy-esque journalism, Brad Will went anyway.

Will was killed by any number of possible covert operatives, and the revolution in Oaxaca raged on.

There are other cases like Brad Will's. Euna Lee and Laura Ling were young womyn journalists who worked for Al Gore's online journalism endeavor Current TV. In 2009, they were caught by North Korean police and incarcerated after accidentally crossing the border from China while seeking an exotic "exclusive" story. I don't blame them; I do, on the other hand, hold Al Gore accountable, as he should have known better and counseled them not to go. It is because of the privilege of these journalists that their crossing of international borders was depicted as an "honest mistake." As in the case of Brad Will, the media about Euna Lee and Laura Ling never questioned their right to travel freely in search of a dangerous, "exciting" news story.

There is deep tragedy in these stories. But they are also examples of the carte blanche access that people from the U.S.—from the empire— depend on in their movements across Pachamama. Even though they were conscious, progressive people, there was no analysis in the media of whether it was okay for them to be in these places, and why they felt entitled to such freedom of movement that most of us can never take for granted.

Mostly, in all of these cases, I blame the arrogance of U.S. peoples to constantly act in this colonizing way – acting as though everything is open to them, as though they deserve "access" to everything, no matter what the culture or the protocol of the land or the peoples is. They are infused with the concept of "independence," drilled into the roots of U.S.-Ayn Randian capitalist education that makes them think, "We know what's right, and We Deserve the Truth."

Really? But what is the truth? And how do peoples who have been raised without eldership, respect of land, ancestors, spirit, and indigenous herstory know what the truth is?

Taking Back Our Voices: Media Production by Any Means Necessary!

> *"She is barely literate — how can you call her a reporter?"*
>
> *"I think, due to his literacy issues, it will be almost impossible for him to do any media."*
>
> *"This isn't real journalism…"*

I was told countless times, by countless different people, that that neither I nor any of my fellow poverty skola reporters, writers, producers, editors, and poets should be able to write, broadcast, report, interview, or blog.

What all of these well-intentioned, caring service providers, educators, legislators, media producers, and even activists failed to realize is that they were perpetuating the exclusion of the very voices, feelings, and scholarship they purported to care about, judging us by their standards of literacy and their standards of knowledge transmission.

How do poor mothers, low-income youth of color, migrant workers struggling to keep two or three jobs just to survive, disabled elders, and people struggling to keep a roof over their heads produce media? How do poor people who are actively lied about and stereotyped de-silence their collective voices? How do people who have been told they "can't write well" become journalists? How do people who have been told they can't speak clearly become radio and TV broadcasters? How do peoples who have been repeatedly silenced, barely quoted, only referenced, racialized, criminalized, and so often talked at, rather than talked with, become truly heard, become authors and producers of their own stories?

The answers to these questions reveal the deeper question: who controls, owns, and has access to the microphone, the camera, the laptop, and the pen?

These remain the most important questions for the few truly poor-people-led, indigenous-people-led media groups that exist: from the mama revolutionaries who took over a television news station as part of the people-led resistance of Oaxaca in 2006, to the street-newspaper movement in the United States, which began as a micro-business option in poor-people-hating places like San Francisco and Florida, to the non-FCC-sanctioned neighborhood/poor-people-led radio stations like Radio Favela in Brazil and Radio Zapatista in Chiapas, to Tribal Radio stations across amerikkka, to the *Block Report* to the *SF Bay View* to KPOO to POOR Magazine/PoorNewsNetwork and PeopleSkool.

Because indigenous communities and poor peoples have been so consistently spoken about, not spoken with; talked at, never consulted; fetishized and deconstructed, some revolutionary grassroots groups have said "no" to the reporting on our communities, struggles, and resistance movements. In many cases, this means intentionally protecting our voices from both corporate and independent reporters who practice the traditional voyeuristic model of journalism.

For example, a few years ago I met a well-funded white photographer who had been traveling the world doing photo essays. He told me that, in 2009, he traveled to South Korea to cover the labor strikes organized by a group of South Korean farmers. When he said that he wanted to cover their story in western media, they asked him to leave. They didn't want him in their meeting, covering their stories. They wanted him to go home.

He didn't understand; he thought he was "helping." As people who are otherized and spoken for, we sometimes make a decision to not talk to reporters as an act of resistance.

We at POOR Magazine practice eldership and ancestor worship in our indigenous news-making circle/community newsroom, which empowers all members of the community equally, as media producers, thinkers, and skolaz. We have launched countless poor-people education projects like PeopleSkool/Escuela de la Gente, which teaches people in struggle how to become media producers and provides stipends, childcare, and meals throughout the process. We create art and media projects that value the scholarship of poverty that poor people already have, like Voces de In/migrantes en Resistencia, Revolutionary Worker Scholar profiles, PoorNewsNetwork, The Poetas POBREs Project, Indigenous Peoples Media Project, the welfareQUEENs, and our people-led, not institution-led, research project, We-Search Camp.

El Tecolote and the *Bay View*, reporting on corporate greed, gentrification, racism, poverty, and more, struggle year after year to publish their beautiful papers rooted deeply in our communities so that the workers, the elders, the small businesses, and all our gente can stay connected and informed on issues happening to our communities locally and globally. The *Block Report* consistently speaks for and with incarcerated, profiled, and silenced youth and adults in Black communities from Hayward to Haiti.

We poor people and people of color media producers and artists are here. We have always been here.

Profile of the San Francisco Bay View
NATASHA REID

The San Francisco Bay View is a newspaper that, curiously, interests itself with broadcasting the news. The real news. Without agenda. If there is an agenda, it's the empowerment of Black people and all oppressed peoples to not only hear the truth about politics that directly affect them, but to stand up and fight against injustice.

Their purpose is simple: To bellow out the counter-arguments to governments who insist on lying about the true objectives that drive their imperial wars; to international organizations who seek profits under the guise of "humanitarian aid," for example in Haiti; to expose domestic issues that the corporate press cast their shadow of propaganda over— police brutality, mass incarceration, and the demobilization of Black folks in American society. The Bay View fights propaganda with truth, tirelessly counter-attacking the demonization of people of color in the corporate media that serves to justify thug-like criminal actions committed by our agents of law and order.

It is a newspaper with a mission—a mission that is spearheaded by a couple of bulls that cannot be tranquilized. Two website hacks and a bullet through the window of the Bay View editor and publisher's bedroom window — both likely attempts at gagging the "radical" newspaper — failed. Completely. It seems that there's nothing that can stop this newspaper from doing what it is that a newspaper likes to do: tell the news.

They have a big heart and lots of room for eager voices. I'm a Black Zimbabwean, raised in Scotland, with the dream of becoming a writer, and perhaps even an influential one. When I heard about the Bay View, I found it remarkable that such a paper could exist. When I emailed the editor to find out if there was any room for an extra voice, she all but came to Scotland to get me herself. They are keen to connect with people who share dreams and visions of, well, world peace, and can find a role for anybody to play.

They aren't afraid to get their hands real dirty: they will roll around with depleted uranium, NATO-assisted genocide of Black Libyans, African land grabs...the list goes on.

They're not afraid to show support for their community: they have made a lot of noise about the asbestos-contaminated shipyard that is located in their local neighborhood—Bayview-Hunters Point—that has left residents with deadly health conditions while the City of San Francisco turns a blind eye.

They're not afraid to show support for comrades with a cause: they supported the prisoners in solitary confinement in California from day one of one of the largest hunger strikes to ever take place in the United States, by directly communicating with prisoners and their families and spreading the word far and wide. They are solidarity soldiers, here, quite simply, to stand alongside the united community of the politically oppressed, and add some decibels to their outcry.

For a newspaper that is accustomed to fearlessly fighting battle after battle, the caring and compassionate nature of the folks behind the print, who read all of their mail (much of it from prisoners), is almost paradoxical. One minute, they're denouncing politicians, police officers, and corporate-press publishers, with fangs snarled; the next minute, they're signing up new prisoners for free newspaper subscriptions, delighted at the thought of giving prisoners something to look at in their cells.

The Bay View lives for the community, with freedom from political and corporate interests. If it was up to them, there would be no Bay View newspaper. If there were no battles to be fought, no government lies to expose, no oppression of Black and Brown people—then the paper would cease to exist. And gladly so! Their purpose is not to line their pockets with hard cash, or anybody else's for that matter. Their sole purpose is to make the paper redundant by creating much-needed balance in society.

So that's it, ladies and gentlemen. That's what the Bay View is all about. I've been here for three months now and feel spoilt with the luxury of freedom of speech. It's the kind of thing I never realized I didn't have until I had it. And it's not only speech, but freedom of thought, too. Because in today's society, the way people think has become so controlled that you don't even notice it until you are in an environment that encourages free thought. I'm writing this as my last assignment at my desk in the Bay View office before flying back to Scotland. I am raring to come back and continue my part in this roaring engine in the very near future. A luta continua!

Troy Anthony Davis and Useless Leadership: A Black Agenda Radio Commentary

JARED BALL
REPRINTED WITH AUTHOR'S PERMISSION
ORIGINALLY PUBLISHED ON BLACK AGENDA REPORT
28 SEPTEMBER 2011

Editor's note: Troy Davis was a Black man convicted of killing a police officer in Georgia in 1989. Though significant evidence suggests he was innocent, Davis was murdered by the racist criminal–legal system of the state of Georgia on September 21, 2011. Democracy Now!, a Pacifica Radio news program anchored by Amy Goodman, provided extensive coverage of the hours leading up to Davis's execution.

The grotesque spectacle of Georgia's final execution of Troy Davis may have been politically useful to the pretenders to the mantel of Black leadership, but in the end, the mis-leadership class proved useless to Troy.

Not long after the four-hour additional torture imposed on Davis by the Supreme Court, and after the final word came that Troy was dead, I got a phone call from an angry friend. He began by asking, "What is the value in electing or investing support in leadership that cannot stop even this? What is the value in investing support behind these so-called 'movements' that benefit useless leadership more than the people they claim to be moving for?" And then he said, "Troy was definitely a better man than me."

"Word?" I asked. "That's my word," he said. He took a breath to calm himself and went on. "First of all, his last words were praise to his supporters and all those gathered around the world. Then he had words of encouragement for the family of the cop he didn't kill. No way, man. I would have been of no use." That line struck me. "What do you mean, 'no use'?" I asked. "Everyone knows he didn't do it," he went on. "Everyone knows it and yet they all use him while he dies, in convenient fashion." "Convenient fashion? That's deep, my man," I said. "Did you watch the coverage on Democracy Now! last night?" he asked. "Every minute," I said. "Then you know what I mean. The cop's family got polite support from a man from whom they gained closure; the activists got praise from a man they were too soft to save; and Amy Goodman's people got love for doing what they should have been doing for at least ten years."

"You saw their coverage, right?" "Yes," I said. "Then you noticed how it is on the night Troy is killed that they gave more attention to his case than during the entire twenty years of his incarceration. And how often do they talk about the associated issues of mass Black imprisonment?" "Okay," I said. But he went on, increasingly angered, "What you saw was spectacle. Amy Goodman used his death like CNN used Desert Storm, you heard her say, 'and we are the only ones here covering the moment.' Just like CNN, she was locking up ten more years of support from the Left as the major media." "She didn't do some good with the coverage?" I asked, sounding like the people I usually refer to as soft. "Whatever good she did was useless to Troy and the rest of us. And look what she did the next day — went right back to her real top stories, Israel and Palestine and mainstream-journalist book writers."

"But that wouldn't have worked with me," he went on. "Because I would have used my last words to tell them to go home, go back to the stories you prefer. I don't want to become a fundraiser for you. You didn't tell my story enough or in ways to get your audience to get me out. I am about to die, anyway, so to me, you are useless. In fact," he said, with even more venom in his voice, "I would have told everyone gathered out front, everyone listening to whatever media was covering me, that they should go become a problem, the kind of problem that keeps me alive or gets me out. Make them storm-trooper cops need that gear they brought to the rally. Tell them that I won't be the only one to transition tonight. But don't use me to add to your phony activist credentials. If indeed 'we are all Troy Davis,' then we should all be prepared to die tonight."

He noticed my silent discomfort. He sensed my fear of my own politics. But he was angry and relentless. "My last words would have been to spread out, break those ranks, and let Sharpton, Brock, and Jealous know, no more show-time for you and the God you keep praising as all 'capable' when he can't keep me from the poison. Your God is useless. We don't praise the same one, if we praise one at all. My God wouldn't let me and mine suffer while others use that suffering to enrich and reposition themselves." "I feel you," I said. "And it was even more infuriating to listen to them apologize for Obama's inability to inter—" I could not even finish the sentence.

"Obama's uselessness was so evident and emblematic," he interrupted. "A Black president, a Black attorney general, a Black Supreme Court justice, two Black men on the Georgia parole board, all the Black civil rights glitterati, and still nothing could be done. It is final proof, if we still needed it, of the uselessness of what is called 'leadership'."

I agree but only wish I had the courage to say it myself.

Community Newsroom (Sala Comunitaria), or Indigenous News-Making Circle

POOR Magazine's indigenous news-making circle/community newsroom (sala comunitaria) is where we redefine news as art, poetry, talk-story, prayer, and music, where we redefine who is a news-maker, and where we decide what the news will be, together, as a family, in a non-hierarchical circle. This is the process for all of PNN's news about youth, adults, and elders in poverty, locally and globally.

> *"No yo crucé a la frontera—la frontera me cruzó a mi/I didn't cross the border—the border crossed me…Soy Muteado Silencio, poet, reportero and co-teacher, indígena purapecha who migrated to Estados Unidos from Michoacán, México, with my mother."* — MUTEADO SILENCIO

We sit together. Dreams, fear, trauma, and hope co-mingle with sage and candlewax. Our lips form visions, our eyes leak despair. We sit together, we lisp, murmur, sing, pray, and think. We sit together.

Each session of POOR Magazine's indigenous news-making circle begins with a prayer for the indigenous Ohlone ancestors whose land we are standing on in Turtle Island; for all the displaced, evicted, incarcerated, and Po'Lice-murdered ancestors who were here before us; and for all of our children still to come.

> *"I am Johnny. I am a Black man in amerikkka. I have struggled with racism, profiling, and struggle for my whole life. I am a recycler. I am a reporter. I am houseless."* — JOHNNY X.

Young folks, elders, ancestors, and adults speak, share, spit, sing multi-lingual gossip, art, tears, rants, poetry, beats, chants, love, hugs, and, most of all, our own "I" stories of houselessness/landlessness, racism, eviction, Po'Lice harassment, gentrification, profiling, criminalization, migration/immigration, oppression, and resistance.

"Yo soy Ingrid DeLeon, de Guatemala, mamá soltera de cuatro niños . . ."

— INGRID DELEON

The first news we create together in newsroom is what we call bio news. Whoever they may be, each person who enters our sacred circle of non-colonized media and care-giving is empowered with the mic to tell a story about their relationship to struggle, survival, and/or privilege in sixty seconds or less. This is their first act of media production. We try to limit this first act of "news-making" to sixty seconds because we condescend to the constraints of 21st-century media only insofar as we recognize that "media" is a part of "im-media-cy": our goal is to listen, respect, and share with everyone who comes to our circle.

"I am no-iden-tity—poet, elder, disability, and poverty scholar."

— JOYCE UMAMOTO

From the beginning of POOR Magazine's herstory, we have defined and produced media as a family, a circle, wherever that circle may be, to actively heal from the pain of silencing through recognition and voicing. In 1996, when we first began the revolution that is POOR, our circle was formed in a welfare office, the SSI line, and the food line where me and my mama and our fellow skolaz were seeking services and government crumbs.

"Ha ha ha, I am the Black Kripple, look at me, look at me, look at me . . . breaking down white picket fences, downing southern comfort." — LEROY MOORE

In 1997, when we began creating stories, art, and resources for volume two of POOR Magazine, the HELLTHCARE issue, our circle was created in county health clinics, county emergency rooms and shelters where me and my mama and sister sought poor-people hellthcare. This was hellthcare meted out by overworked, tired, and often angry hellthcare staff to us poor people, who, within the scarcity model of the western medical industrial complex, are seen as a burden on all systems because of our poverty. "Scarcity model" is a notion that comes from the welfareQUEENS' critiques of the U.S. model of welfare, which relates to poor people by asking, "How little can we give you?" instead of "What do you need to survive?" This can be contrasted with the models of welfare in Canada and Western Europe, which have been—until recently—cradle-to-grave welfare systems that are set up to actually support people by giving them free health-care, free childcare, and quality housing. The scarcity model is rooted in the original forms of welfare in the U.S., which gave welfare only to the "deserving poor": the white widows of war veterans. Even with the so-called deserving poor, welfare in the U.S. has always given people just enough to get by, just enough to keep people on their toes so they don't have a revolution. The scarcity model holds the root of the criminalization, marginalization, and shame of poverty that continue to oppress and harass poor people and families in amerikkka.

> *"S to the U to the P to the E to the R. Baaaaaaby mamaaaa . . .*
> *I'm Jewnbug, Ghetto Homemaker."* — JEWNBUG

In 1998, when we began bringing together skolaz for volume three, the WORK issue of POOR Magazine, we held the circle on street corners where people were selling street newspapers, unlicensed products, and their own day labor, alongside me and my mama selling art and products without a license, all in order to subsist in amerikkka.

In 1999, when we began work on volume four, the MOTHERS issue, the circle convened in childcare centers, laundromats, and family shelters.

And in 1999, when POOR received a small grant to be the first welfare-to-work training facility to teach journalism to parents transitioning off of welfare, we held our first circle (and classroom) inside of a small office.

> *"I am Bad News Bruce. They told me I was 'illiterate.' I believed it*
> *my whole life—now I'm a beat reporter for PNN."* — BRUCE ALLISON, 60

The newsroom is the core of all POOR's media production. In every session of newsroom, we try to hold the deepest pain, trauma, and violence of all of us who have always been shut out, exploited, criminalized, talked about, and talked for in corporate and so-called independent media channels.

> *"Soy Tiny, hija de Dee, mamá soltera de Tiburcio and la reina del welfare,*
> *incarcerated for crimes of poverty—that's being houseless, poor, and on*
> *welfare in this capitalist society."* — TINY AKA LISA GRAY-GARCIA

Once I clearly began to understand the colonization of our voices and how the covert and overt silencing has been perpetrated on our poor youth, adults, and elders in struggle, I realized we not only needed to redefine the space where media is launched, but how it is decided upon, assigned, and then transmitted, used, and shared.

> *"Yo Soy Teresa Molina, soy mamá de cinco hijos, líder de mi comunidad,*
> *y reportera de Prensa POBRE."* — TERESA MOLINA

The community newsroom is always formed in a circle, rooted in indigenous traditions of our ancestors: healing and true sharing is necessary; no one is given power over anyone else. We face inwards, eyes and bodies in collaboration, sharing respect and media equity in real time.

After the bio-news portion of newsroom, we open up the floor to community in struggle or in resistance who come to POOR's circle to get news coverage, launch direct action, get help, or just be heard. From mayoral candidates to sex workers; from criminalized youth facing gang injunctions to elders getting eviction notices; from migrant workers getting profiled by Po'Lice to indigenous elders launching resistance to the removal of our ancestors; from mamas who have lost their children to Po'Lice murder or the violence of poverty to visual and hip-hop artists needing promotion for their new album, our newsroom has held every flavor, shape, language, and dream of peoples in distress, revolution, or crisis.

"I am here because my son was shot by Oakland police two years ago."
— MAMA SCHOLAR, 54

We launch different kinds of media depending on what the community wants and needs. POOR uses media as a direct tool for survival, action, and response. We never make media for media's sake, but rather to save lives, demand justice, honor the never-honored, or get to some unseen, unheard truth. We enlist corporate media alongside independent, revolutionary media and social media if we need to reach the largest possible audience.

"I have been incarcerated for twenty-two years in San Quentin for a third strike of stealing a Coca-Cola. I just got released and I am here to begin to write my story, but I don't know how to write."
— PRISON INDUSTRIAL COMPLEX SCHOLAR

Decisions as to what is published in our online magazine, broadcast on PNN-Radio or PNN-TV, or shared with our revolutionary media partners are made together and by consensus, guided by the questions: "Is it a POOR Magazine story? Does it relate to the oppression, resistance, revolution, or healing of peoples in poverty, peoples in diaspora, peoples of color?" Once this is clear, we open the story up to questions, additions, tweaks, solutions, and possible actions. Then other issues are addressed: how do(es) the author(s) want to share? How will the story get manifested? Who will execute the different parts of the media? Who needs to read, hear, and watch the story?

"I am currently living in my car and have gotten harassed by the police every night for the last three weeks, no matter where I park." — OCTAVIO, 18

There are many stories shared in the community-newsroom circle that only reach the "audience" of our circle — the most sacred of our stories, which are rooted in our deepest cultural structures, or underground economic strategies of our criminalized lives.

"I am here because the SF Housing Authority told me they 'don't work with Indians,' and now I am homeless with my two sons." — ANONYMOUS

Johnny X is one of our founding members and lead poverty skolaz in residence. He deals with post-traumatic slave syndrome as well as the trauma of being houseless and criminalized in amerikkka, manifested as constant Po'Lice harassment when he is working in his underground economic micro-business as a recycler, twelve to eighteen hours per day.

Johnny has been labeled "illiterate" by jobs and schools countless times: he only reads and writes to third-grade level because he was pushed through grades in Amerikkklan public schools without support or recognition of his special—or even basic—needs. He became houseless with his mama at age nine, and because they didn't have an address, she couldn't even enroll him in school.

Johnny X came to newsroom for the first time in 2002 because he saw himself included, without his permission or knowledge, in an "exposé" in a Bay Area corporate newspaper on "homeless people" who "steal" out of recycling bins. The silencing was complete. Johnny X was exploited for his image, framed and reported on as a criminal through the point of view of corporate media, corporate recycling companies, corporate governments, and racist, classist homeowners and renters. His opinion or quotes were never sought, his image never requested, his hard, honest work never recognized or even seen as work. His concept of himself was ignored, as he was unable to answer back or debate their lies about him. All of this is solidly rooted in the lie of his so-called illiteracy.

We at POOR have seen this kind of abuse many times over the years. Johnny X is one of easily 100 skolaz who have come to POOR after this particular kind of missionary media violation: having their images stolen and lies told about them, without anyone ever asking any permission. It is a horrible, specific, deep kind of wrongness, and we've seen it over and over.

But at newsroom we saw Johnny X as an expert, a poverty and race scholar, a reporter and writer on the Po'Lice harassment that he and his fellow recyclers experience. His scholarship helped to launch an action against the media and anti-recycling legislation being put forth by the local government.

POOR has supported, recognized, and cared for his growth as a writer, radio broadcaster, and race and poverty expert through a multi-tiered process, which has included writer-facilitation support, education as a student and teacher at PeopleSkool, ongoing decolonizing, and love.

Eat Free / Stay Healthy, Excerpt from POOR Magazine Food Reviews

JOSEPH BOLDEN

REPRINTED WITH PERMISSION FROM POOR MAGAZINE

03 SEPTEMBER 2010

If you're the working poor, jobless, or homeless, being healthy is priceless! I have one page to do this on—so forgive the briefness. Good/bad free eats:

First stop: St. Vincent De Paul in Oakland serves 7 days, 11 a.m. to 1 p.m., except 1st Wednesday of each month. You get two napkins, one fork. My opinion? St. Paul is consistent—consistently bad! They make good pasta and meat meals sometimes, but mostly it's flat, tasteless fare. But the price is right. No lines because most of us are in line in banks, getting GA (General Assistance) checks, some spent unwisely.

Philadelphia Seventh Day Adventist Church, 2520 Bush St. (between Scott and Divisidero). Vegetarian with juice, homemade cornbread, and cookies. If you stay awake during the sermon, then you'll have as many servings as you want. For 50 cents, you can take a meal or two home. The food has variety, is healthy, and tastes as only home cookin' can. Monday through Thursday, 12 noon to 1:30. The lunch may begin late—don't sweat it, it's worth the wait.

Another healthy place is Martin De Porres (actually St. Martin—an obscure Black saint). 225 Potrero Ave. (near 16th St.). They serve hot oatmeal with raisins and brown sugar, along with cream, powdered or regular milk, different kinds of bread, and hot tea or broth. It goes down easy, sticks to the ribs, plus you'll get seconds, thirds, fourths, and fifths, but be warned! Being mostly liquid, it goes through you fast! Don't get hooked on brown sugar—it's healthier than regular sugar, though bad for teeth. I return to Martin's at 1:23, eat and get free vitamins. Though I am late, I get a short line, and a week's worth of C-B-A and multivitamins. In '94, '95, we used to automatically get two weeks' worth, then it was cut to a week. It's a mostly veggie meal with bits of turkey in it, and wheat bread. I ate the salad that comes with the meal and washed it down with water. I wait on line again. Because many people aren't in line, I get two extra bags of vitamins added to the one I have, which equals three weeks' worth of added health. Tuesday through Saturday, 12 noon to 3 p.m. (Now vitamins are Tuesday through Thursday, 12:20 to 1:30 p.m.) There's also bleach to clean needles, toothpaste, brushes, combs, condoms, and towels to borrow. It may have changed, so ask the regulars about it.

PoorNewsNetwork/PNN

"That's PNN—Not CNN—People . . ."

"All the News that NEVER Fits!"

"Published Weekly . . . Experienced Daily"

Two years after POOR Magazine was founded, we were limping along, unfunded, begging, borrowing, and stealing to keep alive the dream and revolution of poor-people-led media, by any means necessary. Me and mama were still selling on the street, fourteen to eighteen hours a day, bouncing in and out of evictions and houselessness, supplementing our non-income with food stamps and the tiny cash grant they would give to po' folks — government "cheese" crumbs.

After receiving a "welfare reform" threat of six months more aid from my welfare case worker in her office, I hijacked a Request for Proposals (RFP) from her cubicle wall, never intended to be seen by "people like me."

Eight months and sixty-five pages of extremely complicated bureaucracy-speak later, we received a tiny grant from the City and County of San Francisco to launch the first welfare-to-work training program for parents in poverty transitioning off of welfare. It wasn't near enough to stabilize our unstable economies, but it allowed me and mama to take a tentative break from selling on the street for at least a little while. I was able to create a revolutionary case-manager job for my mama and an administration position for poverty scholar and POOR Magazine founding member Uncle Joseph Bolden. With that tiny drop of water, POOR Magazine was able to GROW!

We rented a classroom for our new journalism/media-studies program, which would later become PeopleSkool and the Race, Poverty, and Media Justice Institute. We launched a formal sacred circle for community newsroom, began our KPFA/Pacifica broadcast of the PNN-Radio show, and launched the PoorNewsNetwork/PNN online news service.

The goal was to create the first and only (that we knew of) revolutionary poor peoples' online news service—dedicated to re-porting and supporting the news that NEVER gets heard in corporate or independent news channels. Students and graduate poverty skolaz from our media-studies program would produce content for revolutionary presses and newspapers like the *Bay View, El Tecolote*, the *STREET SHEET*, the *Detroit Voice*, and *Street Spirit*. They would even feed content to the local and still slightly "open" corporate op-ed column in the *San Francisco Examiner*. We would create radio content for Pacifica and other underground radio stations.

All of the content would be launched in our indigenous news-making circle, on the streets, in welfare offices, shelters, and schools. It would be led by all of our peoples, our scholarship and our stories. No one would tell us what is "real" media, silence our voices, criminalize our lens, or direct our editorial voice. We would produce truth-based media, and, in the process, we would reshape society's views on poverty, racism, disability, migration, criminalization, incarceration, gentrification, displacement, and indigenous resistance.

We dreamed of having a PNN correspondent in every poor community of color across Pachamama. To date, in addition to our Bay Area chapters, we have launched PNN Washington and PNN Texas, as well as a PNN Indigenous Peoples Media Correspondent in Colorado.

In 2009, when Tony Robles became the co-editor of POOR Magazine, he launched the "video" or broadcast arm of PNN. PNN-TV's function, similar to PNN-Radio, was to add a live-action aspect to all of our re-porting. Since the launch of our YouTube channel, we have produced over 100 short PNN reports on protests, marches, actions, and crises. From Indigenous Peoples Media Project to Voces de In/migrantes en Resistencia, we have reported on issues that often have no other coverage. Each PNN-TV report is led by the people who are impacted firsthand by poverty, racism, incarceration, and border fascism.

Due to our lack of resources to purchase computers with enough power to run video-editing software, we have not been able to teach video editing in PeopleSkool, but we have taught video shooting, production, and script-writing to support the leadership of poverty skolaz who decide the "lens" of the gaze: who or what gets filmed, who gets spoken to, and who gets heard.

EXCERPT | Shelter Beds Are NOT Housing: The Fair Shelter Act, A PNN report

MICHAEL GLYNN/POVERTY AND PRISON INDUSTRIAL COMPLEX SCHOLAR
REPRINTED WITH PERMISSION FROM POOR MAGAZINE
18 JULY 2011

Trying to get Government Assistance (welfare) wasn't what I had in mind while waiting to be released from prison. Sitting in that cell, I pictured myself setting tile, building homes, or maybe even washing dishes to get my life on track, make some money, and start being a part of my daughter's life. Yes, I thought that I would do most any job, so long as it wasn't illegal, to be there like a father should.

When the reality of my situation finally took hold after innumerable phone calls, résumés, and "yeah, right" looks when the part about prior felonies emerged in the conversation, I decided to try to temporarily get GA . . . just until I could find work. I still hadn't given up on hope that something would come my way, but the pressure was on.

I applied for food stamps and received them. Needed them, too! Every month left me a zero balance way before the end of the month, and I was unable to purchase basic hygiene items like toilet paper, deodorant, toothpaste and toothbrush, razors, soap...

I decided to apply for GA when I needed to buy some shoes. Already discouraged by my prospects, and expecting this to be another dead end, I found myself well prepared for the experience.

Last week, the San Francisco Board of Supervisors met to hear a proposal for the upcoming November election called the Fair Shelter Initiative which, if passed, would return General Assistance dollars to 500 San Franciscans without homes who are lucky enough to have been granted their claims for GA, now known as CAAP. This measure would return the funds redirected by the "care not cash" initiative to the homeless receiving benefits from CAAP.

In 2002, Measure "N," or the "care not cash" measure, took cash aid going to people without homes and gave it to shelters in San Francisco like the Tenderloin Housing Clinic (THC), run by Randy Shaw. THC gets the lion's share of the "care" funds for reserving beds in its shelters. However, according to the Fog City Journal, THC's reserved beds represent 40 percent of the available beds in the shelters, when the percent of houseless persons receiving CAAP funds is something like 8 percent. Meaning, over one-third of the total beds available for the homeless in our city are being reserved for 8 percent of the homeless.

During last week's meeting, one might expect that local poverty pimps and so-called affordable housing developers had some very smooth talking to present a case for the over $150K every month in withheld "care not cash" funds.

That money should be being spent by homeless people receiving aid.

I finally gave up trying to get GA, but I might try again because my need has only grown, three years and two stays in prison later. I just hope that if my claim is honored, that my money gets to me, and not to poverty pimps. I doubt they need it as badly as I do.

Indigenous Peoples' Media Project

It took many years for my poor, indigenous Taino/Afrikan/Roma/Irish mama to find her culture, stolen from her so many generations before by orphanages, displacement, poverty, racism, and the loss of all her peoples in diaspora, slavery, and poverty. My mama came from so many removed and hated peoples, it was hard to hold all of them. And she held all of that loss in one brown broken body. I tried to hold her beautiful tortured body with as much love and as carefully as I could, but it was never enough.

The first time my mama began to lay a trembling hand into her ancestral memory was the day she began to learn about the Yoruba tradition of her enslaved Afrikan ancestors, one part of the many pieces of our cultural herstory she had been displaced from. A Yoruba priest did a reading for her and found she was a child of Xango—a fierce spirit of thunder and lightning—which made complete sense to me. My mama breathed and wept everything fierce. From that moment on, her decolonization began — from all that was western and white, that she had appropriated to stay alive and (she thought) thrive as a poor womyn of color, unwanted and unloved by any blood relative. All that began to slip away, like poison gas seeping out of a recently opened enclosure.

POOR's Indigenous Peoples Media Project centers and supports media, art, and resistance produced by indigenous peoples across Pachamama (Mother Earth). We aim to center, foster, support, love, hold, and make deep space for the multitude of displaced, removed, and disaporic voices of revolutionary indigenous peoples, walking softly, fiercely, with spirit and in resistance.

Making Business Proposals with Ancestral Lands:
The Fight for Oak Flats
PHILLIP STANDING BEAR
PNN INDIGENOUS PEOPLES MEDIA PROJECT

"Paha Sapa, the heart of everything that is," at least that is what my people, the Lakota Sioux Nation, say about our homeland. The dark black rolling hills filled with the smell of pure oxygen, thanks to the pine trees, sticky with sweet-smelling sap, made into a syrup source by my peoples, and small clear creeks filled with minnows. Hot and green during the summer, and cold and snowy during the winter. The tall majestic pines are a testament to the Earth's fertile, dark, pungent soil, which I think of when thinking of the struggle of Oak Flats. The Lakota creeks were clean enough to drink from, the sky always blue and clear, even when a storm rolled through. The Paha Sapa changed any fearsome storm to a calming downpour, with the smells of the pines only amplified with the rain. Any snowstorm was welcomed with the thought of being surrounded by "Christmas Trees" as children. Paha Sapa, like any land as gracious as that, would be considered sacred land, but as we say here at Deecolonize Academy, nothing is left sacred.

I find the theft of land today still appalling. My name is Phillip Standing Bear, super baby daddy and young Lakota warrior, here to inform you of the atrocities of land theft. I can attest to the wrongful act of land theft through my own Lakota peoples' Paha Sapa, as well as the Black Hills of South Dakota. Just like Oak Flats, the Black Hills of First Nations Lakota peoples was stolen for the fact that gold resided in the depths of the land. Treaties were broken for the sake of profit. Even today, treaties continue to be violated for the sake of profits. The only way we get that land back is when it is destroyed and is no longer the place we once called home.

Oak Flats is a recreational park, and is used by the Apache and surrounding tribes as a sacred ceremonial site. This is where coming-of-age rituals were, and still are, performed. Now Oak Flats is in danger of being given to a foreign mining company, Resolution Copper. What happens next are three things. First, First Nations are losing more land, yet again, for the sake of profits. Second, rock climbing, camping, and fishing will no longer be able to occur, for the sake of profits. And third, you lose the natural beauty and wonder of such a sacred site, for the sake of profits. For those of you who believe you have a job coming your way, this is a foreign mining company, which means they will have their own workers at their own wages. Which means while you sit on the sidelines hoping to get a job, someone, not from here, will come along and get paid terrible wages for a job they likely don't even want to have. You therefore condone slavery on a deeper level without even realizing it.

Let's look into how treaties held between First Nations and the U.S. federal government were broken. Treaties were usually made to protect First Nations peoples, sacred sites, and religious freedoms. However, land ownership was not something we, as First Nations, understood. What we understood was that we, as people, NEVER owned the land around us. Rather, the land owns us. We are as much a part of this landscape as the rocks, plants, and animals we share the space with. So, with every treaty, there came a "business opportunity." Herein lies the problem. While promising our peoples better land, The U.S. federal government was making business proposals.

Every year, thousands of avid rock climbers, campers, and fishermen come to this region for its natural beauty, and even more First Nations people come here for their sacred ceremonies. There is no justice for Oak Flats, just another battle.

This is Phillip Standing Bear, young indigenous warrior, super baby daddy, and Indigenous Peoples Media Project correspondent from Deecolonize Academy, Homefulness, and POOR Magazine, signing out.

Sogorea Te Sacred Site Is Ours Collectively:
An Open Letter from Corrina Gould

CORRINA GOULD
SPECIAL TO PNN INDIGENOUS PEOPLES MEDIA PROJECT
REPRINTED WITH PERMISSION FROM POOR MAGAZINE
18 APRIL 2012

Dear Warriors, Supporters, and Friends of Sogorea Te,

I want to first start this letter by thanking each one of you for your support to protect and preserve Sogorea Te, a sacred site that has been in what is now Vallejo, CA, for over 3,500 years. During our occupation of the land from April through July of last year, you were all instrumental in putting aside your lives, giving of yourselves unselfishly, and participating in creating a living community that really allowed us to all not only protect a sacred site, but to also see what is possible for humans when they come together and rely on one another, centered around a basis of spirituality and the belief in one another. Each time someone walked onto that land and paid respects to the fire, it strengthened the community as a whole. The miracle was not in just protecting the site, but in protecting each other and allowing the space to include almost anyone that came with a good heart and good intentions.

Over the months that we lived together, we endured weather hardships, boredom, laughter, tears, celebrations and disappointments. We created bonds that we will have forever, sometimes with people we would have never imagined being in our lives before Sogorea Te. We were truly blessed by the ancestors, because we took a stand, and because we opened our hearts and allowed a healing to happen. No one and nothing can take away these gifts. Our lives have been transformed and we can never be the same, nor should we want to be. We were all a part of something more than history; we were a part of a miracle, a complete transformation. When that sacred fire that burned for 109 days finally went out in the physical sense, it continued to burn in each of us, individually. When we come together, our shared experience rekindles those flames and reminds us that we are human beings with a purpose.

Over the last few months, people have posted pictures on Facebook, have written things about Sogorea Te, and have generally tried to stir up people that hold this sacred land close to their hearts. We have tried to look into each thing as it has arisen, and want to be transparent with everyone that involved their time and lives in this sacred place. Some of the Committee went to Sogorea Te when the land was beginning to be transformed; some of us, including myself, only really saw it in October when we were able to end a Sacred Walk there. Let us not mince words — the sight of our beloved land was devastating. We knew when we crossed that gate on July 31 that, when we came back, Sogorea

Te would never look the same. But what we saw was nothing short of getting kicked in the gut. It literally took my breath away. We mourn what once was. We celebrated a victory, and looking at the land now makes the victory taste bitter in my mouth. Of all of the things that GVRD (Greater Vallejo Recreation District) wanted to do with the land, we only asked three things: that they not build bathrooms on the sacred site, not include a 15-car parking lot on the sacred site, and not grade a hill that there are burials/cremations in. These are for the most part what we won. They are not going to build a bathroom, the parking lot is going to be moved and only allow for two accessible parking places — but the grading happened. We knew that they were going to take out the invasive species of plants and tear down the mansion and, yes, even put in trails.

When I went there several weeks ago, what I saw was that the entire site had been molested. The creek is virtually exposed, all the trees have been cut down and, yes, the grading has occurred. We talked to tribal monitors and other tribal representatives, who appreciate the assistance that we gave in getting the "Cultural Easement," but they blatantly stated that they don't have to answer to anyone. What they did say while walking me around the site is that they did not find any cultural artifacts or remains and that the hill was "fill." As I walked along the area where the hill once stood, I looked for anything that would stop them from continuing to do the destruction, but couldn't find even a shell. What the Tribes told us was that they would preemptively use specialized canines trained to find ancient burials or hand-screen the area, but that didn't occur.

The fact is that there were many cremations and that the land had already been moved before and it was going to be impossible to find remnants, especially after they had already removed 5 feet of the hill. Frustrating was the fact that they didn't have any answers. When was the project going to be finished? "I don't know." Why did they take out native plants and still leave some of the invasive? "I don't know." Will the tribe make a statement or have a public meeting to let people that supported the tribe in obtaining a cultural easement know what is happening to the land? "No. We don't have to answer to anyone." The other fact is that a tribal sovereign government is still a government. It is also a fact that this same tribal government has allowed desecration before Sogorea Te and continues to make concessions to other developers at different burial sites.

POOR Press

People who are enmeshed in the "accepted" institutions of academia or other industries, once deemed "published writers," are then considered "experts" on poverty, racism, incarceration, immigration, art, and different forms of local and global oppression. They are then supported and heard, which feeds them into even more channels of access to future recognition and publishing.

Indy presses use the liberatory narrative of independence, implying access for all, or purporting openness and possibilities. And yet, to be a part of those "independent" presses you must be a part of the same academic channels of access. You must still speak with the same linguistic-domination fluency or know someone who knows someone who can make those inroads possible.

As lied-about, oppressed peoples not given any access to these industries or channels to preserve our voices, stories, histories, and art, we felt it was urgent to begin the book-publishing arm of POOR Magazine.

Sadly, when we sought some meager foundation funding for this project, we were asked by more than one philanthro-pimp, "What is the point of poor people being able to publish books? How would that solve any of their 'real' problems?"

We have been told many demeaning and deeply hurtful things like that by philanthro-pimps, but the rejections we received when requesting funds for POOR Press seemed to include extra vitriol. Consequently, since it was founded in 2003, it has never been a funded project.

POOR Press has published many deeply revolutionary art texts and anthologies on race, displacement, poverty, and migration, including the first version of this book, Poverty Scholarship, done without linguistic-liberator help and only edited by my revolutionary Mama Dee in 2003 while she was dealing with the illness that would take her on her spirit journey. POOR Press also published the powerful anthology Los Viajes, a bi-lingual book of stories of peoples crossing all the false borders across Pachamama.

To date, we have published over sixty-five books by poverty, disabled, indigenous, youth, and migrant skolaz on issues of incarceration, poverty, mental illness, Po'Lice brutality, recovery, addiction, indigenous resistance, migration, family separation, child abuse, spirituality, and houseless/landless revolutions. They have all been written by folks who have experienced these struggles firsthand and can determine, write, and reshape our own histories, herstories, and forms of self-determined revolution through words, art, and images in print.

POOR *press publications*

In 2003, we launched the Digital Resistance program, meant to resist the very real digital divide by teaching all of us poverty skolaz self-publishing skills and how to run design software. In this way, each scholar was directly involved in their own self-determined publishing, as well as gaining access to an inaccessible piece of technology.

From Illn N Chilln to the Krip Hop Nation: Silenced Voices of Disabled Peoples of Color Resist

LEROY MOORE

Being Black and physically disabled as a child in the white community of East Hartford, CT, in the late '70s and early '80s, I spent a lot of time alone, reading and writing. A group of Black disabled boys, including myself, started a letter-writing campaign about being Black and disabled. My poetic, journalistic writing/activism was born; but teachers didn't like my political writings or choice of poets.

When my mother and sister passed away in 1990, I moved to San Francisco. In the mid-'90s, open mic was hot in the San Francisco Bay Area. A group of us poets used to hit all the open mics on both sides of the Bay. On a Thursday night in 1997, I walked in the spotlight of Berkeley Rep Theater. When all the lights came up, a skinny young womyn (Tiny) approached me with an older woman (Dee, her mama). The friendship between myself and Tiny birthed the first online column dealing with race and disability, called Illn-N-Chillin.

With POOR, I was able to make another of my childhood dreams come true, and that was to be on the radio, at KPFA 94.1 FM. That led to my short but enjoyable times on the only Black radio station in the Bay Area, KPOO 89.1 FM in San Francisco. At the same time, my life-long subject, race and disability, expanded to my love of music. But where were musicians of color with disabilities in music, past and present, from blues to hip-hop?

Krip-Hop Nation was born during my radio days on KPFA 94.1 FM with POOR Magazine and with another radio collective that I was involved in at KPFA, Pushing Limits, a news/cultural radio magazine dealing with the disability community. I have started a column on POOR Magazine called Krip-Hop, and am working on a book about Krip-Hop Nation. Now, with Emmitt Thrower, a disabled ex-NYPD officer turned theater and film artist and poet, I am also making a short documentary on police brutality and profiling against people with disabilities.

The Deaf Want to Be Heard:
Fighting Criminalization and for Liberation in Nigeria
LEROY MOORE

Leroy Moore, a poverty and disability scholar at POOR *Magazine, interviews Julius Shemang, a disability activist based in Kaduna State, Nigeria. In 2006, he was the founder of* Kafanchan Times, *a newspaper that highlights disability activism in Nigeria, among many other topics. He was one of a group of disabled poverty scholars who organized the occupation of the Kaduna State Government House in protest of laws criminalizing disabled people working in the streets of Nigeria.*

Leroy Moore: Thank you, Julius Shemang, for agreeing to be interviewed. I want to go back in time. Can you give us brief historical roots of Nigeria, from the time of independence from the United Kingdom to now?

Julius Shemang: The history of Nigeria since independence in 1960 is tied to the fact that our leaders love to pay lip service. Every year, they read their budgets and earmark billions for the disability community. This money will never have an impact because they are misappropriating and diverting it into their private pockets. As a matter of fact, if they are truly committed to providing infrastructure and adequate facilities for our people, the issue of begging would be limited. But it is not so here. Taskforces are randomly sent out to harass and intimidate supposed beggars—many of whom are orphans, widows, without jobs, trying to eke out a living. And since the government has no plans or adequate programs to address their plight, they are found begging all over towns and cities. We work with political parties and vote during elections, but no post or status is accorded to us other than to "assist" oppressors. This ugly trend continues from independence on October 1, 1960, until today. Really, one should be worried, being marginalized and very much deprived in his father/motherland. We are trying, of course, and with a little support we can make huge inroads and impact, but the help is not always forthcoming.

LM: Now can you give us a window into everyday lives of Nigerians with disabilities, from children to mothers?

JS: Every day people with disabilities (PWDs) in Nigeria, from a little infant to an older adult, face challenges. Many are indigent, have no work, and don't know what the day will hold. Those who have work must still wake up to the reality that they can be sacked or suspended from their workplace! Sometimes, some people who are anti-disabled will frame an innocent person with disabilities (PWD), and that will lead to their dismissal, all on account of their disability and the absence of laws to protect them. There is huge competition for work, as even university graduates roam the streets looking for jobs for many years. The PWDs are the least-paid workers. They also enjoy little benefits, unlike our able-bodied counterparts. So many younger able-bodied people boss their disabled counterparts. Some are wicked—they have this negative mindset and think, "Thank God that I am not disabled!" and won't allow this person to get too close lest he or she "infect" me with disability! Many disabled parents struggle to feed their young, and to pay school fees and for accommodations, etc. It's not easy, as their take-home pay is small. Many of them also have aged dependent parents and relations to care for.

Those who are self-employed complain bitterly that able-bodied people do not patronize them because of the fear of catching disability, but we are able through our associations to organize many workshops and seminars to educate and create awareness that disability is not contagious. We also fight for our people's rights, but all these activities need funds. We are really struggling with funds, especially with economic recession staring us in the face. Therefore, we shall be appreciative and grateful for any meaningful support we can receive from any individuals, groups, corporate organizations, etc., both at home and abroad, to further empower us in our drive to create awareness and to empower our people.

LM: You told me that you became Deaf later in life, and also became active in the disability rights movement. What is the difference from when you first got active to now, in the disability rights movement in your city/country?

JS: Coming into the Deaf and disability world from the world of hearing was like being in the flames of hell. I came to see that everybody was not given equal recognition and opportunities, and that the disabled suffer more discrimination in society. I got upset at the way the able-bodied population viewed disability with charity rather than as a matter of rights. I began to think about ways of helping myself and other disabled people in the state and nation at large.

I went to *New Nigerian Newspaper* (*NNN*) headquarters here in Kaduna State, with the sole aim of seeking space in the paper where I could put pen to paper on issues of the disabled, so as to advocate and draw the attention of the government and society at large. A man I was introduced to, who I later learned was an editor of the paper, told me, "SPECIAL EDUCATION IS NOT JOURNALISM," and that since I studied special education, I should go to a Deaf school and look for a teaching job there. His comment didn't deter me. I told him that I had what it takes to write a story and that I should be given a chance to at least prove the ability in my disability.

He then directed me to see the news editor at the newsroom, and I did my first write-up in the paper, titled, "THE DEAF WANT TO BE HEARD," which discussed how the Deaf were being denied admission into higher education and to take courses of their choice, the lack of employment, and many other issues. Apart from NNN, I also got involved in writing and reporting both news and features/opinion articles in other media organizations, including television and radio. People began to rethink their assumptions about people living with disabilities.

From there, I took the initiative further by founding my own newspaper—Kafanchan Times—with help from some journalists who partnered with me. The paper was established in 2006 as a grassroots voice showcasing ability in disability, and seeking to bridge the gap between the disabled and the able-bodied.

LM: You are the fourth Nigerian with a disability I've had a chance to interview in the last five years, from musicians to activists. Tell us about organizations for people with disabilities in Nigeria, how they got established, and what they have been working on.

JS: There are different organizations OF and FOR people living with disabilities in Nigeria. Organizations OF people living with disabilities are those organizations that are formed by Nigerians living with disabilities. The Joint National Association of Persons with Disabilities (JONAPWD) is the mother, or umbrella body, of all Nigerians living with disabilities, with headquarters in Abuja, the Federal Capital Territory, and branches in each of the 36 states in Nigeria. JONAPWD is a coming together of the various clusters of the Deaf, the Blind, the Albinos, people with mental disabilities, the physically disabled, the lepers, and other categories, under one big umbrella, in order to fight as a united and common front. Other organizations of people living with disabilities also exist and are playing supportive roles.

On the other hand, organizations FOR people with disabilities are those organizations that are established by non-disabled people with a general focus on issues of people with disabilities. We have been working tirelessly on inclusive policies such as education, employment, the electoral system, economic empowerment, information, accessibility, participation, etc., as well as ongoing advocacy and campaigns to get the Nigerian government to sign and pass the National Disability Rights Bill into law, with an independent implementation commission in line with the United Nations Convention on the Rights of Persons with Disabilities, of which Nigeria is a signatory. Nigeria currently has a huge population of 180 million, out of which 25.5 million are people living with disabilities who deserve a better life. The government recently came up with a law banning street begging, especially in the marginalized north where the number of beggars is high. This law goes against the human dignity and rights of our members, and is in violation of the United Nations Convention on the Rights of Persons with Disabilities. This is something we have been working on, and it is ongoing.

LM: Beyond passing the Disability Rights Law, what do you want the government, the citizens of Nigeria, and the international disability/non-disability community to do?

JS: We want a proper Disability Empowerment and Vocational Training Center so people with disabilities can be self-sustaining, as many are jobless and wandering the streets of major cities, looking for food and sustenance. This means they will be trained, and that the government or donor agencies will help us fund the training, since most of them are from poor families who may not be able to pay. There is a piece of land given to the associations by previous administrations (Kaduna State Government). If we can get funds to develop it into a vocational training center and modern shopping complex, it will go a long way in bettering the lives of our people in the state. We also considered transportation and farming skills for our people. If we can have farms where we can produce food, there will be money and jobs.

To really assist us, we need help to conduct a population survey to know the actual numbers of disabled people in our country. If we have an accurate head count and file for each PWD, including those living in remote areas, our advocacy work will be easier. We need equipment and knowledgeable staff to carry out the head count, and to issue a certificate of disability to each member. We must identify special schools and disabled people's organizations so that administration will be easier.

This is where your organization and others can come in. We are even looking at the possibility of traveling, to study some disability-based organizations in order to learn best practices and obtain knowledge and information. Unfortunately, we rarely get sponsorship, as governments and people we look up to always disappoint. Anyway, we thank you so much for this interview. God bless you richly good.

Revolutionary Worker Scholar

TONY ROBLES

I grew up seeing them, workers. They were uncles and friends of uncles and, of course, my father. They were janitors or hospital porters or line cooks—mostly janitors. They worked and told me to stay in school, to study hard. They told me that they didn't want to see me grow up to be like them. I was going to be different. I was different. I looked at my uncles, checked out the way they talked, walked—exuding confidence and spirit—not in the university or academic sense, but in the real sense. They could kick ass, they could speak without pretense, and when necessary, they could cry.

They had a sense of who they were as men of color, young men who had seen men like themselves excluded from academia, had seen many young men and women with potential relegated to their "place" in society. They had fire in their bones; they didn't forget—couldn't forget—who they were as Filipino and Black people. They spoke with tongues stained with soy sauce, hot chili, fish sauce, roast pig, carabao dung—it was our ancestral struggle that accented the words they spoke, gave meaning to their sounds, their marginalized syllables formed from church claps, the thundering drum, the boiling pot of rice, and broken English spoken by their parents at the kitchen table.

They would tell me that there was nothing for free in this life, and if you wanted anything, you had to get off your ass to get it—you had to work for it. You don't want to swing a mop like me, they'd say—you don't want to clean toilets, do you?

So I went to school. I was a fairly good student—as my uncles would say, "An educated brown boy." I ended up with an office job in the financial district. My uncle would visit me and look at my desk by the window, strewn with half-written or crumpled-up poems that failed to inspire me or anybody else. "You an executive!" he'd exclaim. "I'm a customer-service rep," I'd reply. "I answer phones. Any fool can do this job." My uncle would beam and repeat, "You an executive." I'd give in. "Okay . . . I'm an executive," I'd say. "Let's get the hell outta here." Then we'd take the elevator down and go to the hamburger place across the street, where he'd treat me to a burger.

"Let me pay," I'd protest, befitting of the executive that I was, but he'd pay, pushing my wad of one-dollar bills back into my pocket. "Save your ghetto roll, you'll repay some other time." We'd sit and talk about the faces of our people, our elders, their voices. My uncle is a born storyteller. As he speaks, I see the workers around me—the migrant folks picking up our trays, sweeping floors, wiping tables. What stories do they hold in their hands? I listen to my uncle and hear his voice and the voice of all workers who want to free their stories but never get a chance.

I look at his face and taste his words—his laughter is still there, it rises like fire. The workers hear it. It is contagious. It takes us to another place for a moment—an area of pause. Soon we're all laughing, its taste is sweet.

The Revolutionary Worker Scholar column on POOR Magazine/Prensa POBRE came from my life and struggle as a worker surviving, being fired from, and often organizing through a lifetime of work and jobs in a capitalist society. The Revolutionary Worker Scholar column also came from listening to the stories of my fellow workers—the stories of those whose minds carried so many "could have"s and "could have been"s. Carrying those stories and dreams makes it possible for poets to write about what can be, and for students and the youth to learn their history and fight for a better world. The Revolutionary Worker Scholar column is the humor and poetry and laughter and struggle of the workers, carved into the hearts of poets with words that only their hands can create. Revolutionary Worker Scholar is a pause—with respect and love for those who make it happen—the workers.

Youth in Media

"I sleep in my car with my mama and I dream of sleeping on a bed." — RAY, 16

"I help my mama figure out how to fill out the medical forms so she can get treated for her diabetes. Without me helping she would die." — LENA, 12

As a child of a houseless, disabled mama, I spent most of my childhood feeling like no one EVER would, or should, know about my life or my mama's life.

We were in hiding most of the time: hiding from Po'Lice, from school, from people, from systems. We were in a perpetual state of terror that someone would find out our "secret" and criminalize, incarcerate, or separate our tiny family unit.

The pain of this fear and isolation almost killed me and mama, and it is what led us to launch the Youth in Media project at POOR Magazine.

Young people's voices, in tandem with adult and elder voices, have always been a part of POOR Magazine's revolution. Youth appeared in the first issue of POOR: Volume 1, HOMEFULNESS, speaking their specific perspectives on the pain, isolation, fear, and confusion of a child in poverty in the US and beyond.

That said, POOR Magazine has always had a specific critique of youth-only programming in non-profits. Youth-only programming is very western. It rejects the indigenous eldership and intergenerationalism of most cultures and communities in diaspora that are forced into positions of poverty in the US due to migration, racism, and/or globalization.

Our Youth in Media project is created to help young people not only understand their positions of poverty and oppression but to have empathy, love, understanding, and awareness of the struggles of their parents and ancestors. The project helps them help their families do the work that has to be done to stay alive in amerikkka, and to understand the roots of the oppression they face daily. Each young person in poverty who enrolls receives a Po' Youth Skolaship to PeopleSkool and a stipend for finishing their media and art projects.

The "sexiness" of our Youth in Media project was the basis of a seed grant to POOR Magazine in 2002, which was pulled a year later when it was no longer "sexy" in 2003 (see Chapter 6). We requested the grant using "youth-only" language with the sole purpose of supporting the project, but we had an internal organizational understanding that this would be a "hustle" so we could pay the rent. We would continue creating the revolutionary intergenerational media, art, and education that we have always made.

Youth in Media has always included education, consciousness, and art in order to liberate the colonized minds of young skolaz struggling through the US skkkool systems. This includes teaching on race, class, incarceration, the oppression of indigenous peoples and peoples of color historically, and the ways our voices can be used to self-determine our futures, honor our parents and ancestors, and facilitate change.

In 2007, we launched the Family Project, working with very young children and making POOR truly intergenerational. The young children in the Family Project saw the deep wrongness of the video games around them so, in 2008, we launched Team POOR, a revolutionary video game based on the conscious superheroes created by all the youth and mama skolaz at POOR Magazine. Team POOR is based on two characters from volumes three and four of POOR Magazine: El Mosquito, a multi-lingual, pan-racial superhero who is a panhandler by day and defender of justice/ protector of the oppressed by night; and Super Baby Mama, who is a mama, a poet, a fighter, and a superhero. We ran a series of workshops with young kids of color in poverty, who were living in shelters and SROs, who were houseless, who were often bilingual, and we designed the storyboard for Team POOR. Together, we brainstormed and worked with different scenarios that the children in the workshops had experienced.

For example, in one storyboard, a family was being evicted from their home. El Mosquito threw a giant web over the sheriff and his marshals, while Super Baby Mama scooped up the families being evicted, put them in a tree, and built them a treehouse to live in. Unfortunately, POOR hasn't been able to launch Team POOR as a video game because we don't have the resources. But it will be an accessible, transformative media channel for young listeners, watchers, and readers, always operating intergenerationally—and given the access that kids have to video games like Halo, it's one of the most revolutionary things we could do.

We have launched Youth in Media workshops in schools, group homes, juvenile halls, street corners, and shelters. Youth in Media generated three main education- and art-focused projects. The first of these was Poison on Our Plate, which facilitated the youth and adult skolaz in PeopleSkool to learn about what they were eating, breathing, and drinking. Additionally, the project helped launch Budget Genocide, focusing on the impact of budget cuts on poor youth of color and elders. Finally, The Drum was a series of one-act plays on the herstories of slavery, incarceration, indigenous removal, and resistance, created by all of the students and performed as a final project.

There are many powerful youth projects across the US and the world, but Youth in Media is one of the few, that I am aware of, that is intentionally intergenerational and multi-lingual, giving young folks the skills to fight the separateness and media-promoted cult of independence promoted and supported by a capitalist system.

Youth are active in all of our journalism: they are reporting, using equipment, holding the camera or the mic or the pen, formulating and asking questions. This is simply taken as a given at POOR. All of our Youth in Media work seeks to create youth leaders who work together with their aunties and uncles, tíos and tías, abuelas y grandmamas, mamaz and daddys to realize the colonization of their whole communities and use media to decolonize, rewrite, reclaim, and heal their communities, their ancestral knowledge, and their power.

In the first drawing, a man with a cane and a trench coat stands against a wall, panhandling, holding out a cup. In the second, a winged superhero launches off of the Bay Bridge. This is El Mosquito, panhandler by day, superhero by night. Original art by Eddie Camacho for the WORK issue of POOR *Magazine,* Vol 3.

EXCERPT | from "Poison on Our Plate"
YOUTH, POVERTY, ELDER, AND INDIGENOUS SKOLAZ
AT RYME AND PEOPLESKOOL
REPRINTED WITH PERMISSION FROM POOR MAGAZINE
26 JULY 2011

RYME is POOR's Revolutionary Youth Media Education for youth 12 to 19 years old.

The RYME program includes teaching on radio, video, and online journalism (blog) production, and classes on poetry, hip-hop, performance, art, music, and theater as powerful tools of media, organizing, and consciousness-building regarding poverty, racism, migration, police brutality, and liberation. All classes are taught bilingually and include lunch. Full scholarships and stipends are offered to young people in poverty.

The Following RYME Youth Scholar Reports were written by the youth skolaz for the Poison on Our Plate project after their extensive research (We-Search, as we call it at POOR Magazine) and interviews with Eric Mar, who proposed legislation to prevent San Francisco restaurants from including a toy in their meals.

On Air—Kamaria Shanndoah, 14: I am Kamaria Shanndoah and I am fourteen years old. Poison on Our Plate taught me about all the pollution and radiation in the San Francisco air. I learned that some of the chemicals in our air are sulfur dioxide, carbon monoxide, nitrogen oxides, and hydrocarbons. I also found out that the radiation in our air has increased in the past twenty years.

On Air—Ya'mil Chambers, 12: I am Ya'mil Chambers and as a twelve-year-old, I am concerned about coal combustion, which causes air pollution. Every day an average adult consumes a total of 3,000 gallons of polluted air. This represents that simple coal combustion causes health problems. This means that we don't care about what goes into our air. This also means that if we care about our lives, if we don't pull it together, many will succumb to health problems because of the pollution in our air.

On Food—Rashida Talibah Banks Reed, 12: At POOR Magazine, we did a project called Poison on Our Plate. We learned about how many calories are in a Whopper and how much sugar is in a Coca-Cola can. It's so much I can hardly say. It's too much for humans to consume.

Students March to City Hall for Mario Woods

KIMO UMU, DEECOLONIZE ACADEMY YOUTH SKOLA

This story started on December 2, 2015. A man named Mario Woods was killed at the age of 26. He was killed in a cold-blooded murder. They said that Woods had a weapon in his hand but, really, he did not. So that is why Deecolonize Academy went to the student march down in the Mission in San Francisco, a place that is ugly and beautiful at the same time. You can smell all the markets selling items and you can see the people in struggle all around.

There were three Deecolonize students who went — Kimo, Tyray and Tibu. There were about 80 people at the start of the march, ages 12 to 16. More high school students arrived, and there were about 300 students all together. Chants were said all around, like "No Justice, No peace, No racist police!"

The students walked from the 16th and Mission BART to City Hall to let the city know that it is wrong for black and brown people to get killed for reasons unknown most of the time. Deecolonize students were at the march because they were invited and they knew that it was not right that another innocent person was killed by another trigger-happy officer, or shall I say trigger-happy officers.

Kimo and Tibu went up to say a few words. They said the reason Decolonize was out there with the students was because they knew it was wrong, and they knew some day there will be no more police brutality.

We Began the Day Marching for MLK

TY'RAY TAYLOR, DEECOLONIZE ACADEMY YOUTH SKOLA

During the annual Martin Luther King Day march that draws thousands from around the Bay Area to San Francisco, Deecolonize Academy students Kimo Umu, Ty'Ray Taylor and Tibucio Gray-Garcia Robles locked arms the way Dr. King and his followers used to do.

My mom and I drove downtown and met up with our POOR Magazine and Deecolonize Academy family. We started the march for MLK at 11 a.m. There were thousands of people; it was very powerful.

After the march, we drove to the Van Ness movie theatre to see the movie "Selma" about the life and work of Dr. Martin Luther King, Jr. The Selma director, Ava Duvernay, was not nominated for the Oscar because she is an African American and she made a powerful movie about Martin Luther King, Jr., a Black leader.

Police terror has killed lots of Black and Brown young men, then and now. The police are killing young men left and right for no reason. The fight for civil rights still exists in our neighborhoods today. Lots of young people have been shot in their own neighborhoods for gang related reasons.

Martin Luther King, Jr.
MUH'QUEENA, DEECOLONIZE ACADEMY YOUTH SKOLA

Last Monday I went to the MLK march. After we marched, we went to go see the movie Selma. At the middle of the movie, they marched for voting rights. At the end of the movie, we did a die-in.

Civil rights did not change everything, because these problems are still going on. The police terror did not stop, because the police are still killing Black and Brown people for standing up for their civil rights.

What I thought about Selma was that it was nice that the people had more unity back then. But, at the same time, the movie was sad because my family lost relatives in real life, fighting for our rights. Ava Duvernay did not get an Oscar because white Amerikkka will not reward a director for making a movie about a peaceful Black martyr that Amerikkka murdered.

After the movie, POOR Magazine and the Deecolonize youth skolaz invited the audience to join them in a die-in. Only two people out of the whole crowd participated with POOR. It gave me the feeling that not too many people cared about the rights of Black people today, so the struggle continues.

Poetry Journalism

Poetry journalism is resistance journalism. Poetry journalism is the journalism of the people. Poetry journalism is as valid and legitimate as essays or narratives that are linear and colonizer-defined.

Poetry journalism tells a story, covers the five "w"s (who, what, where, when, and why), and hears the voices of the issue. Unlike straight colonizer-defined, linguistically dominated journalism, it sings with the pain, whispers alongside the resistance, and dreams with the revolution of the story. Poetry journalism is journalism led with the heart, the soul, the spirit of the peoples being journaled with.

Through images, metaphor, and the form of stanza, poetry journalism can be written, spoken, or sung.

For peoples of color rooted in our indigenous ritmos and souls, poetry journalism is the sound of our investigation, and the way that we tell our stories and the stories of our communities. Poetry journalism brings a flow to the pain and a beat to the struggle, lifting each part of the story off the linear path of essay and into our hearts.

Poetry journalism was birthed at POOR Magazine in 2001 by me and my sister A. Faye Hicks, Po' Poet Laureate of POOR Magazine. She began a series of pieces responding to the welfare- and shelter-system abuse that she and other poor womyn were going through. She wrote on her experiences trying to survive in a scarcity model economic system full of hate and criminalization of poor people, which was increasing with every new legislator and billion-dollar poverty-pimped corporate welfare contract to come to town. Her poetry journalism was both exposé and lyric.

With poetry journalism, we hope to debunk the myth of "literacy." Many poetry journalists have been told that they are illiterate or that they can't be considered journalists. We resist the idea that investigation and reporting must manifest in a linear essay format to be considered "real" journalism.

What Good Is a Security Job?:
Poetry Journalism on the Struggle of a Security Guard

BRYON HAFFORD/PNN
REPRINTED WITH PERMISSION FROM POOR MAGAZINE
03 JUNE 2011

What good is a
security job when
an unarmed guard is
getting such little pay
to risk their life

To protect a rich
man's plantation
with their life

And they can treat
you any way they
like and get away
with it while you're
there

On the plantation
with them working
for them guarding
their place of business
and them too

A Blue Butterfly

AL OSORIO
REPRINTED WITH PERMISSION FROM POOR MAGAZINE
23 APRIL 2013

A blue butterfly had alit upon the hallowed ground, its wings moving up and down as if a tiny engine idled within. It was unusual to see one in that part of San Francisco during the winter, and her friend remarked on it. Pausing in the task of stuffing lunch bags, the Mom turned to appreciate the beauty of her tiny visitor. Abruptly, her eyes welled up with tears as a familiar scent entered her nostrils; her lips trembled as she felt the presence of a beloved taken from her.

He strolls thru a lush field, exchanging pleasantries with those who had been there before, or who would be there at some point in the future. A musical mosaic of human history lies within each passing soul, and he draws it from them, blending ancestral memory into a melody, trapping the harmonics coursing through the astral plane and casting a symphony back to those voyagers sharing this realm of existence. It is his gift, music, increased to an infinite level.

He uses this gift when visiting, weaving a concerto into her dreams, hoping to pass his message, but with little success. She still suffers. Contemplating a gentle breeze ruffling a patch of wildflowers, he harkens back to his childhood, and thought to pass the message...in beauty.

Its sensitive wings detect vibrations which register as sound. A familiar voice. Her voice! The colors were overwhelming, an entire spectrum invisible to the human eye. He saw her as no mortal was capable of seeing her.

Nerve endings in its legs transmit emotional residue of his final moments to the brain he temporarily shares. A flash of psychic pain, tempered by her voice and proximity. Tiny antennae detect her familiar scent. It brings him security still, as it did when he was a baby. There is another scent, that of tears. Colors of love enfold him, and the tiny wings relay soft sounds. She is praying.

The Mom studied the butterfly tattoo. She had taught him how to ride a bike. He'd ride around the block, passing the house with that big grin, waving to let her know he was ok. Soon, the block wasn't big enough and he rode across town with the other boys. It was part of the journey, part of growing up. She had understood the message. The tattoo would always be there to remind her of this new stage of his journey. He was telling her he was ok. She would be, too.

The friend noticed the blue butterfly first, seeing it alight upon the hallowed ground. Catching the Mom's eye, she inclined her head towards it. The Mom finished filling the lunch bag and placed it with the others, smiling warmly. She gazed with love, and longing. The Mom knew it would be the butterfly's final visit. She whispered her son's name.

Voces de In/migrantes en Resistencia

Voces de In/migrantes en Resistencia is a series of journalism workshops with migrante parents in poverty. Like everything at POOR, it began with one of our family members, a migrante mama of four who had crossed three false borders to come here in pursuit of support for her family in Guatemala, only to be racialized in jobs and housing and silenced, lied about, and fetishized by media and education institutions.

Each Voces workshop included on-site childcare, meals, and stipends, as there was no way the mamaz could take part in the privileged work of media production without POOR supporting them, albeit meagerly, so they could take time from one of many jobs they were working just to survive here and support family on the other side of the false Amerikkklan borders.

This project launched many media resistance actions, including a migrante worker-based public education project called "Don't Run/No Corra" as well as many radio and video documents and journalistic reports.

Don't Run/No Corra: Una campaña educativa de emergencia
GUILLERMO GONZALEZ/VOCES DE IN/MIGRANTES EN RESISTENCIA
REPRINTED WITH PERMISSION FROM POOR MAGAZINE
26 MAY 2008

Este artículo es el comienzo de Don't Run/No Corra, una campaña educativa cuyos líderes son los del proyecto Voces De In/migrantes en Resistencia de la Prensa POBRE (POOR Magazine, en inglés) que están respondiendo a los incrementos drásticos del crimininalización de comunidades migrantes/inmigrantes locales y nacionales.

Mi familia y yo estamos en EEUU ahora, precisamente en el área de la Bahía, años después de nuestro arduo viaje desde El Salvador, para perseguir el supuesto Sueño Norteamericano. Tengo 25 años. Estoy en la escuela para ser maestro, y a la vez, trabajando con POOR Magazine como escritor del personal y maestro del proyecto Voces de Inmigrantes, que enseña periodismo y a organizarse a los obreros inmigrantes y monolingues de bajos ingresos.

En todas partes de mi vida trabajo para devolverle algo a mi comunidad. Mis maestros en la Universidad predican sobre cómo debo dar las gracias a este país por darme el permiso de estar aquí. Me dicen que este país es tan bueno conmigo por darme una visa estudiantil. Pero es difícil tener ese sentido de aprecio ahora por el hecho de la recién crecida de redadas de trabajadores pobres, estudiantes y familias por toda el área de la Bahía, que curiosamente empezaron antes de las marchas del Día Internacional Del Obrero, el 1ro de mayo, en honor de todos los trabajadores y en solidaridad con la lucha de los obreros inmigrantes.

"Estas redadas son un acto brutal de venganza y criminalización por el ICE hacia los inmigrantes por marchar el 1ro de mayo," dice Tiny, periodista y coeditora de POOR Magazine/PoorNewsNetwork, y autora de Criminal de la pobreza: Criándose sin Hogar en America.

Empezando con las redadas de una cadena de taquerías bien conocidas, desde San José a San Francisco, asustando a los padres en la escuela primaria Oakhurst en el Este de Oakland, culminando en una redada en la escuela secundaria de Berkeley, ésta semana pasada han causado que los inmigrantes vivan en terror, aún cuando muchas de estas ciudades son "ciudades santuario."

El asunto es que no estoy preocupado sobre lo que me va a pasar en cuanto se venza mi visa, porque sé lo que agencias como el ICE me pueden o no pueden hacer si alguna vez me enfrentan. Sé de mis derechos civiles y libertades aún no siendo ciudadano estadounidense. El problema es que yo no soy el objetivo de las agencias de inmigración, porque saben que nosotros aprendemos en la escuela sobre nuestros derechos; no, ellos despiadádamente perjudican a los trabajadores migrantes que no tienen defensa cognitiva en contra de sus enfrentamientos agresivos y tácticas hostiles.

Desde que empezaron estas redadas más y más, toda mi familia vive en temor que un día un agente los enfrentará y seguramente los deportará. ¿Después, que haremos? Mi familia, tanto como muchas familias inmigrantes, ni puede funcionar económicamente sin que todos juntos estemos trabajando para sobrevivir. Si mi papá o mi mamá son deportados, ¿quién traerá las ganancias hacia casa para apoyar a mis hermanos y a mí? ¿Quién nos dará de comer, dar un hogar, protegerá? ¿Para qué sirve mi visa estudiantil? La realidad que se asentaría es que mi hermano mayor y yo no dejaremos que destruyan a nuestra familia. Encontraríamos una manera de hacer suficiente dinero para mantener a nuestros hermanos, y hay que ser realistas, no es tan sencillo que un inmigrante sin educación pueda ponerse un traje, caminar hacia Wall St. y encontrar un trabajo. Estaríamos forzados a cometer crímenes para sostenernos, así perpetuando el ciclo y los estereotipos que perjudican a nuestra comunidad.

Para todo problema hay solución. En este caso es la educación. Como una comunidad tanto de inmigrantes y ciudadanos conscientes, es urgente que trabajemos juntos para informar a la comunidad inmigrante sobre sus derechos. El hecho es que cuando uno es enfrentado por un agente de inmigración, todo lo que uno debe proveerle al ICE es su nombre, nada más. Si el agente de ICE empieza a interrogarlo a uno sobre su dirección o domicilio, o su fuente de ingresos, o aún si preguntan por documentos de inmigración (si uno es documentado), todo lo que tiene que responder es que desea irse. Tenemos el derecho a declarar la quinta enmienda (the Fifth Amendment) a cualquier pregunta acerca de nuestro estatus legal en este país. La cosa más importante de recordarcuando enfrentado por un agente, es que uno no debe ponerse en pánico, y pase lo que pase, uno no debe correr. Ninguna agencia gubernamental puede entrar a una propiedad privada por la fuerza sin un permiso.

Estos son nuestros derechos como residentes en esta nación, tantos ciudadanos, e inmigrantes, y el gobierno no tiene derecho a infringir sobre estos derechos. Así es queel verdadero Sueño Americano es la realización de nuestros derechos del constituto.

ENGLISH TRANSLATION

My family and I are in the US now, the Bay Area, to be exact, years after our arduous journey from El Salvador, in pursuit of the so-called American Dream. I am twenty-five years old. I am in college to become a teacher while also working with POOR Magazine as a staff writer and teacher of the Voces de In/migrantes project.

In all parts of my life, I work to give back to my community. My teachers preach to me about how I should express my gratitude to this country for allowing me to be here. But the feeling of gratitude is difficult to have as I hear about the recent spate of raids on poor workers, students, and families all over the Bay Area.

"I think it is very strategic that all of these ICE raids happened right before and after the May 1st marches," said Cesar Cruz, teacher, activist, and author of *Revenge of the Illegal Alien*. I spoke with Cesar after I heard about the families who were afraid to pick up their children from an elementary school because they were warned by the school's principal that there were ICE trucks parked in front of Oakhurst elementary school in East Oakland.

Beginning with a raid on a well-known taqueria chain (El Balazo), to the scare given the parents at Oakhurst Elementary School, and culminating in a raid on Berkeley High School, this last week has caused immigrants to live in terror, even though many of these cities are so-called "sanctuary cities."

I am not worried about what happens to me after my visa expires because I know what agencies such as ICE can and cannot do, if they should ever confront me. I am aware of my civil rights and liberties, even though I am not a US citizen. The problem is, immigration agencies don't target students like me because they know that we learn about our rights at school. No, they ruthlessly target the migrant workers who have no cognitive defense against the aggressive confrontations and hostile tactics.

Ever since these immigration raids have been happening more and more, my entire family lives in fear that one day an agent will confront them and deport them. Then what will we do? My family, like many immigrant families, cannot function financially unless we are all working together to survive. If either my father or my mother gets deported, who will bring the money into the household to support my siblings and me? Who will feed us, shelter us, protect us? What good will my student visa be then? The reality that would set in is that my older brother and I would refuse to see our family be destroyed. We would find a way to make enough money to shelter and feed our siblings and, let's face it, it's not like any immigrant with no education can just put on a suit and go to Wall Street and get a job. We would be forced to turn to crime to make ends meet, thus perpetuating the ongoing cycle and stereotype that plagues our community. This happens all too often to families just like mine. Families that get dismantled because immigration takes one of our members away.

As a community of immigrants and conscious citizens alike, it is urgent that we all work to inform the immigrant community about their rights. When confronted by an immigration agent, the only thing that one must provide is a first name, nothing else. If the ICE agent starts interrogating about an address of residency or a source of income, or even if they ask for immigration papers, all one must say is that they wish to leave. We have the right to plead the fifth amendment to any questions regarding our legal status in this country. The most important thing to remember is that when confronted by an agent, one must not panic and, no matter what happens, one must not run. No government agency can forcefully enter private property without a warrant.

These are our rights as residents of this nation, citizens and immigrants alike. The government does not have the right to infringe on these rights. So perhaps the real American Dream lies in the realization of our constitutional rights.

Seize the Gaze: Photo Journalism and Media Resistance

Since Dorothea Lange, photo journalists have been using photography to "document" our lives in photographic essays filled with images of our terrible conditions, our dirty and disorganized homes, and our "dangerous" neighborhoods and barrios. These "essays" often win prestigious awards, get printed in corporate and/or independent media, or lead to the increased funding of the photographer through grants, endowments, and academic fellowships.

In the US, the subject matter of this photo journalism runs the gamut between houseless/landless adults and families, youth of color, im/migrant workers, or disabled peoples who are located in "the streets" or on rural vacant land, in trailer parks or food lines. In the Global South, it is often focused on children, families, and/or disabled elders in indigenous lands crying, sitting, or dying. Often, the direction of the photographer's "gaze" is from above looking down, or from below looking forward, to elicit the response from the human eye that these people are powerless and can't survive without us.

In all of these cases, extremely high-priced cameras are used to "document" our bodies, equipment that, if sold, could feed and/or house the entire village or community being documented.

In corporate broadcast media, "stock" images of poor people are used in tandem with slogans, messages, or music specially crafted to promote hate or "sympathy" in a politrickster's, government's, nonprofit industrial complex's, or corporation's racist, classist campaign. Often these are blatantly transparent hate campaigns to "rid" the world, the neighborhood, or the community of human beings who look "like that." Or they may be more subtle, with covert messages to "clean up" a neighborhood or a community, "clean up" being code for getting rid of a people.

When the empire wants to mess with another country, the mainstream media will front the campaign with a picture of a child on a dirt floor with a swollen belly, eating out of a bowl. American people buy the lie that the US military needs to intervene to "feed the children." Within the US, when a city wants to "clean the streets" of houseless people, corporate media is rife with images of someone pushing a shopping cart. Stock images of this type were rampant during the campaign for the sit/lie law in San Francisco, which made it illegal to hang out on the sidewalk. Similarly, when a city wants to impose gang injunctions or otherwise criminalize youth of color simply for gathering together in public spaces, TV news will broadcast images of groups of young people of color hanging out on a street corner.

In corporate broadcast media, stock images like these are always from afar, fetishizing and signifying particular marginalized groups of people, without showing their faces or their humanity. Sometimes they show us working (recycling, panhandling, mothering, or standing in endless lines to get government crumbs). In the case of young peoples of color, incarcerated peoples, or day laborers, we are shown walking from the rear or convening on a street corner. Of course, these are all natural activities, but in this context, we are posed for voyeuristic viewers as a "threat" to the community's collective security (read: white and/or middle-class peoples' notions of security).

One rarely knows anything about the camera person or photographer. Why do they matter? Because they are taking images of thousands of other peoples who are turned into "subjects" and art installations and photo essays that are seen all over the world, their poverty, their private spaces, their struggles laid bare for all to see. Yet I know nothing private or real or sad or happy about the photographer, his or her family or his or her life, neighborhood, or culture.

With few exceptions, the endowed, funded, or supported photographer does not share their money with the poor folks that he or she is documenting, even while building their portfolios on the images "captured."

Some photo journalists are probably screaming at this page right now in anger, saying, "I do this for free! I get no compensation for this work." Perhaps, but how did you afford to get to Bangledesh from Los Angeles, from San Francisco to Guatemala? How did you afford to buy that camera and how do you pay your rent and buy your food?

How about sending the money for the plane fare, or the cost of the camera equipment, to a group of peoples in their land of origin and letting them decide if it should be spent on camera equipment or medicine, food, or blankets? Or, in the case of some of our houseless peoples in struggle, maybe spent on a bottle of alcohol to get through one more day of struggle in amerikkka? After all, no one questions you when you buy drinks with friends at the bar in Egypt after a particularly hard day shooting images of us.

Oftentimes independent photographers survive on trust funds or some support from family, allowing them to take part in the exciting activity of art-making and image capturing with no real understanding of the deep struggle of the peoples they are depicting.

At POOR Magazine we incorporate a two-day Seize the Gaze seminar into each Poverty/Revolutionary Journalism program taught at PeopleSkool. This helps us poverty skolaz realize the constant battle of media colonization perpetuated on us so we can work to change it. At the same time, it helps people enmeshed in academia, art, and media to learn how to truly see their different forms of access and understand the revolutionary ways that they can share them with poverty skolaz rather than continue to perpetrate harm against us with their cameras, lenses, and tripods.

After we critique voyeuristic, violent models of photojournalism, we offer some teachings on how to "seize the gaze." For example, it's never okay to photograph a person sitting or sleeping on the street, or who falls into a stereotype of a houseless person, unless you first build a relationship with that person in which you not only ask if it's okay but also offer remuneration (50 to 70 percent of what you're going to get for that picture, whether it's cash, a line on your résumé, byline real estate, or something else). But mostly we request that you just don't take that picture at all: realize that you have no "right" to take that picture, and consider simply not taking it. If a person in struggle asks you to take their picture, take it and give it to them. If it's a child, a person of color, or another often-marginalized scholar, have a transparent discussion about equity.

In the Seize the Gaze seminar, poverty scholars work on healing from the abuse of being depicted in stock photos. The only pictures we want taken are pictures showing us in power, in resistance, in formation, together, in family, in community, in progress. This is especially crucial for indigenous peoples, who have had our pictures stolen forever.

The art-theory concept that nothing is sacred, that anything is available as the raw material of "art"—this is the case for mostly white, privileged people who don't even know what's sacred anymore. We are teaching sacred, self-developed rules of respect around image capture, and we are teaching each other the ways we've learned to heal from the abuse.

The Bridge: Writer Facilitation, Byline Real Estate, and Other Forms of Horizontal Media Production

We at POOR had developed our new genre of "I" journalism and revolutionary media advocacy, but there was one thing missing: the bridge to the other side, the dominant tongue that is linked to access, to control of the pen and the camera. Linguistic domination determines what media is read and listened to. How could our work be not only read but included, considered, so that our ideas might actually be implemented?

My ghetto mama scholar and I created one of the key pieces of the POOR Magazine linguistic resistance processes: writer facilitation/media facilitation, which is a practice of educational, class, and race equity sharing.

From the inception of POOR Magazine, we have implemented several innovative models of deep equity sharing between folks with different forms of privilege. Young folks enmeshed in akkkademia came to POOR

Magazine by the dozens to help. They always came with the best intentions of love, caring, and advocacy, but always based on an old-school charity model which is inherently, albeit unintentionally, hierarchical, with one person bringing their perceived "legitimate" knowledge to a space or person or community which is perceived as needy or underprivileged or voiceless.

All of our trainings for folks skilled in the dominant language and people enmeshed in akkkademia begin with teaching each person to rethink their own forms of race, class, educational, and/or organizational privilege. We begin with articulating the ways that young folks with privilege are given the space and time to think, dream, rest, and conceptualize; the ways this enables some folks to go through the complicated process of filling out multiple applications, taking tests, meeting deadlines, finding scholarships, getting reference letters, and on and on. These subtle and not-so-subtle nuances are what we as poverty skolaz cannot focus on, because we are caught up in the daily struggle to live, raise children, find budget crumbs, jump through endless bureaucratic hoops, and evade police and community profiling, criminalization, violence, houselessness, and hunger.

So the training for folks with privilege begins with developing a true understanding that this access is just that: access, not skill or innate knowledge, but access, linked to the race, class, and/or organizational privilege that the person received from their life, their parents' work and time and love, their class status, their skin color, their communities' love, and/or their homefulness.

Once understood, this becomes the basis for the next concept: people with privilege must own those places of privilege. This is not to make people feel shame, because guilt is a useless and passive feeling that only inspires eventual withdrawal, usually referred to as "burnout." Instead, our concept is to activate their revolutionary equity sharing through empathy, which we distinguish from useless pity, sympathy, or charity.

Once the importance of empathy and equity sharing is established, a new form of horizontal media production is launched: a media production that de-otherizes all of the producers and articulates the voices of the authors.

This horizontal media production begins with the establishment of a relationship between storyteller/reporter and facilitator (the person with access to dominant language). Unlike safe, clearly defined, voyeuristic journalism relationships, this relationship is one of reporter and supporter, friend and family member, and is based on the understanding of the class and race differences of the facilitator and the storyteller. This relationship doesn't end with the reporting of a specific story but rather launches ongoing involvement of the facilitator in the reportee's life, which could include housing advocacy, protest, resource acquisition, education, food, court visits, legal advocacy, systems navigational assistance, and, most of all, time.

The deepest and most complex layer of our horizontal media production involves the creation of a relationship between folks with race, class, and/or educational privilege enrolled in POOR's Race, Poverty, and Media Justice Institute and poverty skolaz who are currently caught in the middle of their struggles—in their addiction; struggling with psychological, mental, or physical disabilities; and/or hard at work in one or more forms of labor-intensive jobs or underground economic strategies, such as domestic work, service labor, day labor, panhandling, sex work, recycling, or workfare. In addition to all of these struggles, one of the most powerful ones that impacts the vast majority of the poverty, disability, migrant, and indigenous skolaz in residence at POOR Magazine is the destruction of linguistic domination. Over 95 percent begin by identifying as "illiterate" or have been told they can't write well, can't speak well, or can't read. Many have been slapped with horrible fascist slurs like "retard," "dummy," and/or "pendeja." Decolonizing from the shame of a lifetime of linguistic domination doesn't happen quickly or easily, and oftentimes the power of this covert brand of oppression and domination is impossible to penetrate.

The mechanics of the facilitation are fluid and flexible, and the specific kind of facilitation is dependent on the needs and the abilities of the poverty scholar. In one scenario, it could include a facilitator crafting a story using the first-person voice of the poverty scholar, or the facilitator might include her/his own voice. In the latter scenario, both people's relationship to the subject matter would be covered. Teaching on both sides like this, from a place of empathy, can be deep. Both people practice the notion that the revolution begins with "I," and both are held accountable to truth and inclusion. In other situations, the facilitator's voice and perspective are not as important, and the focus should remain on the poverty scholar talking about her/himself.

Both of these story-creation scenarios include the shared byline real estate of both the facilitator and the poverty scholar—or, in the ultimate act of love and equity sharing by the facilitator, the name of the facilitator would be completely absent from the byline.

All of these scenarios of media resistance, like scenarios of housing resistance, racial justice, and educational equity sharing, operate with the clear understanding that we must realize the inequities in the production process of media and publishing itself, and that therefore all of these stories, struggles, and acts of media resistance belong to the storyteller (the person in struggle, the poverty scholar) rather than to the facilitator who happens to hold the pen, the laptop, the digital recorder, and/or the camera.

In the case of poverty and race scholar, and POOR Magazine elder, Ken M., his form of writer facilitation included a conversation, a several-hours-long transcription process, and ultimately complex editing of a forty-five-page story on the struggle of dealing with poor-people housing. The facilitator, Jennifer Maria Harris, worked for many days with Ken to rewrite the forty-five-page piece into a 600-word story, which we were able to publish in both a corporate media outlet that had a 600-word limit and POOR Magazine's online magazine.

Outside Is Safer than Inside an SRO

KEN M., POVERTY SCHOLAR/PNN
REPRINTED WITH PERMISSION FROM POOR MAGAZINE
4 SEPTEMBER 2010

I have lived outside—on the steps of the Calvin Simmons Auditorium, underneath the Peter Voulkos statue at the Oakland Museum, on the campus of UC Berkeley, in church entries, on benches at the Lake Merritt BART station, in abandoned buildings in Oakland and Berkeley, at the Oakland Airport, and in the waiting room of Highland Hospital.

I have lived inside—in several apartments, my own house, rooms with friends, and an SRO (a residential hotel). I felt safer outside.

On July 1, 1997, the sun danced a soft polka on my tired face. After three and a half years on the streets of Oakland, my body would be sheltered. My supportive-housing applications had been approved and I would finally be able to get a room in an SRO.

Within weeks of my arrival, my personal property and artwork were stolen, phone messages were diverted, mail was lost or stolen, and the break-ins of my room began. I changed the locks, reported sleazy managers, registered complaints—until I reached my threshold of safety and basic security. When my newly changed locks were broken into, I called the police, who tried their best to intervene. Then I could stand it no longer. I moved out . . . side.

What is a residential hotel? It is referred to on the street as an SRO (Single Room Occupancy or Sleeping Room Only). Despite tenants like myself whose rent is partially subsidized, in its pure form, the SRO is not subject to rent control because of its hotel status. SROs welcome long-term tenants only when they are stuck with high vacancy rates in pre-gentrified neighborhoods.

SROs are known to poor folks as the last place before complete "outsided-ness." If you can scrape together the daily room rate, between $22 and $60, you can get a shower and actually have a pseudo-roof for a night. Of course, paying exorbitant daily, weekly, or monthly "temporary" rates prevents the hotel resident from ever being able to save enough for "first, last, and security deposit," the required move-in fees for an apartment. The resident who desires homefulness is locked into a desperate cycle of poverty.

People such as myself, caught in this cycle, who exist on a low wage, Social Security, or public assistance, frequently turn all but $10 or $20 of their daily income over to the landlords of these establishments, just to be housed.

This leaves no money for even the basic essentials such as toilet paper, soap, shampoo, the laundromat, telephone bills, or clothing, much less any luxury such as aspirin, a pizza slice, or a used blanket from the Goodwill retail outlet.

Residential hotels can be well-managed, good housing options for low-income tenants. Examples are hotels managed by Community Housing Partnership in San Francisco. We, as low-income writers and artists, would go further. We'd like to suggest collectively run housing with studios and work spaces for low-income artists, including sweat-equity purchase options. This kind of housing exists in Europe. For the time being, it is imperative that existing SROs be regulated, and housing codes enforced, without the risk of tenants losing what scarce shelter remains.

I have lived inside—in several apartments, my own house, rooms in friends' houses, and a residential hotel. I am outside once again.

Corporate Media Infiltration

Independent and corporate media—print, online, radio, and/or TV—is a very important tool for use in all organizing campaigns. Unfortunately, the corporate media is driven by corporate interests and therefore it is a throw of the dice whether grassroots campaigns, actions, rallies, or press conferences will get any corporate-media attention, especially when campaigns are focused on issues related to traditionally marginalized communities and/or struggles.

So how do grassroots nonprofit organizations penetrate the corporate media when resisting and struggling with issues of poverty, racism, homelessness, profiling, welfare de-form, displacement/gentrification, police brutality, disability, youth justice, border fascism, and other issues related to communities struggling with poverty, locally and globally? Through corporate media infiltration.

Corporate media infiltration is a strategy that any organization or group can learn and use immediately, a strategy that POOR Magazine has employed many times with great success in campaigns against corporate developers; mayors and city, county, federal, and state government bodies; school districts; large HMOs; globalized corporate agri-businesses; and more.

"All media is good media," someone once said about media in Hollywood for actors. We apply the same concept to POOR's media: we use art, action, aesthetics, image, and humor when we do corporate media infiltration, a process that takes the root of the idea of the oppression and turns it into spin, a press action, or event – making it a "hot" concept.

This form of infiltration begins with an independent media "bed." We create a bed, or sacred ground, of poor-people-led media on a given subject through an "I" journalism series of radio, video, and text pieces launched by the poverty scholar personally impacted by the issue. Once the "I" journalism series is released—that is, once the story has been told in the scholar's own voice—it is followed by a spin that takes the issue and boils it down to one simple idea. A press conference and action is planned, and a press release is created and distributed. This way, because the story was first told by the impacted scholar, before we ever connected to other media makers or institutions, it can never be fully mythologized by someone else.

POOR teaches on corporate media infiltration to other poor peoples trying to use media as a survival tool and to communities needing emergency help from as broad an audience as possible.

Jerrification

It was 1999 and Jerry Brown had just become mayor of Oakland, replete with a progressive glaze and vague promise of the consciousness he would bring. Within a few short weeks of his mayoral tenure, he was making slurs about poor people and housing (for example, saying that rent control is "slumification" of Oakland) and making gentriFUKing deals with devil-opers, corporate housing pimps, and gentrifying "artists," all quicker than you can say "Oakland!"

In the absence of a just cause for evictions ordinance, there was effectively no rent control in Oakland, and poor people of color and "funky" trust-fund white artists alike were being evicted right and left from downtown and West Oakland to make way for the dot-com boom and what soon became known as Jerry Brown's 10k plan: a multi-million-dollar plan to re-devil-op the entire downtown Oakland area to "change the face" of Oakland.

Many of the poorest members of POOR Magazine's family lived in pre-gentriFUKed West Oakland, including me and my mama. Many of the artists with race and/or class privilege who contributed to POOR's Fun-Ding auction of 1996 and 1997 also lived there. Just by their very being there, they made the neighborhood just cute enough to shuttle in the really rich, mostly white people who were eventually going to colonize the entire West Oakland corridor.

POOR Magazine's family of poverty skolaz began meeting to conceive a plan of direct action through art and media and corporate infiltration. We hatched one of our finest corporate-media-infiltration actions, a brilliant art/performance/theater/media event to expose and shame the deep hypocrisy of Jerry Brown (his image was everything to him), and to promote the first "just cause" legislation to ever hit an Oakland ballot. We called our event Jerrification. And, as usual, it was led and conceived by poverty skolaz and artists in struggle, and everyone played a part: the default gentrifier artists with trust funds and "funky" aesthetics living in West Oakland "lofts" facing immediate eviction; the very poor and houseless artists who were barely surviving on the edges of the default gentrifiers' access crumbs; the poor families of color being evicted; the working-class craftspeople, micro-business people, and underground economic strategists being increasingly swept out by Po'Lice raids; and the economic-justice organizers working in Oakland on the ordinance.

We planned a press conference, followed by a tent city of all of us who were evicted, on the Frank Ogawa Plaza (renamed Oscar Grant Plaza in 2011 by Occupy Oakland). The tent city members would wear name tags identifying themselves as one of the following: Working-Class Artist with No Trust Fund, Houseless Artist, or Default Gentrifier Artist with Trust Fund. We created tents from eviction notices and organized a massive multi-racial, multi-generational, cross-class group of people to sleep outside overnight.

Two weeks before the event, two of us who had been evicted from the West Oakland area wrote a story for PNN, the *Bayview*, and our KPFA radio show. We created the sexy Jerrification frame and put out a massive press release.

On the day of the event, we had a press conference on the steps of Oakland City Hall, but the mayor tried to co-opt our press conference by creating one of his own at the very same time inside City Hall. It took us a minute to regroup, but we were prepared: after all, we were media, too! We marched into City Hall, flashed our special ghetto press "passes," went up to the mayoral chambers, and proceeded to hijack the press conference with questions about rent control, slumification, public housing, and Brown's 10k ("k" for killing) plan. It was *incredible*; we were running after him. CNN, the *Oakland Tribune*, Channel 7, and Channel 4 all got us on the nightly news, and we got Jerry Brown to recant his evil words on corporate media. It was a truly beautiful moment in poor peoples' herstory.

Later that day, we had another press conference where we formally introduced people from the "just cause" movement, who later formed the organization of the same name. It is always odd to me that they have never mentioned us in their organizational herstory, but perhaps it isn't so good for the grant guidelines?

The press conference was followed by a powerful tent city that lasted until the next day, when the Po'Lice came with a warning for us to leave. None of us po' folks could risk arrest, and that was never the intent, and so we left the plaza.

Art Carts

In 1999, we had a similarly beautiful action/collaboration with the Coalition on Homelessness in San Francisco when Mayor Willie Brown decided he was going to "take all the carts" from houseless people and put people in jail for stealing shopping carts.

Once again, our response action was rooted in art and performance. My mama was ever the brilliant conceptualist, basing her work on what she had read about the situationists of France in the 1960s and Dada art theory. She was always trying to figure out how poor peoples of color like us could use these art-action ideas to our benefit. The concept is that if you added or changed something and then called it "art," it was art. The Coalition on Homelessness loved the idea and also was trying to fight the criminalization of houseless people under Willie Brown. Our plan was that they would paint and customize the carts as art and we would bring a small piece of colored cloth to Civic Center Plaza and put them on all of the carts. We would give each houseless person a manifesto about the meaning of their carts as art. This transformed each cart into a piece of art and an exercise in each person's First Amendment rights to free speech. Concurrently, we created a huge press circus with multiple corporate media outlets appearing at the location where this was going to happen.

Once again, we achieved our goals. The mayor was publicly shamed: he withdrew his threat, and forever after POOR Magazine was seen as a danger to corporate and civic devil-opment.

POOR Magazine's (Revolutionary) Media Advocacy

Earlier, I talked about the supposed advocacy of much mainstream and independent media that purports to be helping poor people by othering and fetishizing us. In resistance, not only do we make our own media, we also do some true, revolutionary, media advocacy. POOR's revolutionary media advocacy is survival media. It originates with how we can use multiple forms of media as tools to solve immediate and constant attacks on our bodies, our families, our homes, our children, our cultures, our barrios, and our lives.

How can we fight landlords evicting our families and elders; Po'Lice framing us and incarcerating us; US injustice systems stripping our civil rights; ICE deporting us; and corporations stealing more of our lands, languages, and power?

POOR's revolutionary media advocacy is our HELLTHCARE campaign, speaking back through radio, video, blogs, and other media on the ways we are *always* lied to, not treated, poisoned, and/or killed by different agents of the western medical industrial complex. Revolutionary media advocacy is acting as an advocate for our sisters and brothers who are denied treatment, going into the appointments and calling the supervisors and demanding treatment when our sisters and brothers get sent home with kidney stones and bladder infections because they don't speak English or don't know how to speak up to the godlike doctors and their systems.

Revolutionary media advocacy is me and fellow poverty and race scholar Marlon Crump (both jailhouse lawyers without degrees currently outside of jail) teaching other poor folks how to advocate for themselves through letters and calls and media. It's putting our bodies into courthouses as witnesses and writing letters of support for framed, stolen, and incarcerated peoples.

Revolutionary media advocacy happens in picket lines, courtrooms, doctors' and lawyers' offices, shelters, corporate and government meeting rooms; in response to poverty pimps, devil-opers, and others. Standing in front of marshals when they are trying to evict, in front of judges when they are trying to convict, employers when they are trying to wrongfully terminate, and CPS when they are trying to separate families.

One of POOR's revolutionary media advocacy projects is Courtwatch, which focuses on giving media support to parents abused by the one-sided system in which Child Protective Services, juvenile dependency court, social workers, court-appointed lawyers for mothers and children, and judges are all oddly in bed with each other.

Courtwatch was launched by my mama and other mamas' pain and trauma from firsthand experience with the corruption and injustice inherent in the Child Protective Services system, which, sadly, has very little to do with the protection of children. Instead, it has everything to do with the criminal injustice system, the Po'Lice, and capitalistic values of separation of families, racism, classism, and abusive systems.

Revolutionary media advocacy is speaking back, yelling, chanting, endless phone-calling, showing up, letter writing, singing, rhyming, beat-making, art-making, spinning, and never giving up until we are no longer evicted, profiled, incarcerated, separated, deported, or killed.

Revolutionary media advocacy is not necessarily "exciting," "beautiful," or "lyrical" like a Dorothea Lange picture or a Charles Dickens novel, because real, felt, and lived struggle isn't always beautiful or shocking. It's often just very sad, overwhelming, violent, and brutal to the communities and families impacted. Fighting through revolutionary media advocacy is survival. And sometimes triumph.

We the people, communities of color, workers, migrants, grandfathers and grandmothers, mamas, daddies, elders, babies, young folks, indigenous ancestors and aboriginal peoples who have spent time and love and sweat and tears and prayers caring for, working, dreaming and loving this community, this barrio, this street, this tree, this garden, this flower, for generations, centuries and time beyond Gregorian, missionary calendars, have been displaced by the forces of money, power, real estate speculation, corporate theft, corporate government, philanthro-PIMPING, redevelopment, criminalization, and gentrification and now only exist as a cultural memory, an "art-I-fact", a reference, a brush stroke, a photo, an exhibit, a dream to be studied, theorized, painted over, documented and/or forgotten and erased completely as though we were never here. GENTRIFUKATION TOURS "R" US exists to document the theft, reclaim & take back the stolen spaces, memories, images, pictures, lives and dreams. To tour and document the default colonizers and 21st Century Missionaries, the erased and colonized culture and cultural stealers, to re-insert ourselves in the stolen landmark and to reclaim what little of us might still be left …

— MANIFESTO FROM THE GENTRIFUKATION TOURS R US
ART IN ACTION PERFORMANCE PERFORMED IN SPACES
WE AS DISPLACED, POOR / UNHOUSED PEOPLE NO LONGER ARE

—4—

Art
and
Cultural
Work

Clarion Alley mural by POOR Magazine. Photo: POOR Magazine.
Right: Mural detail showing ancestors, including Mama Dee.

A Mural of Resistance

LAURE MCELROY
REPRINTED WITH PERMISSION FROM POOR MAGAZINE
04 OCTOBER 2010

I took the bus down to the used-to-be low-down parts of the Mission. I climbed over SROs, which have been almost pulverized beneath the tide of lofty boxes. I squeezed past the mocha-latte-sucking poetry mafia in their faux-thriftstore chairs, in the wasteland of the Valencia cafes. I passed all the places I used to know until I found POOR's powerful new mural of resistance, struggle and revolution on Clarion Alley. The first thing that returned to memory as I beheld it was my experience at the California State Summer School for the Arts (CSSSA). I was part of the writer's program; it was the only formal art training I had ever received

CSSSA was where I found counterculture. There were hippie kids, rastas, punks, gothics, metalheads, skaters, skins, surfers, emos, and even some hip-hoppers. At the time I thought it was the height of diversity, regardless of the fact that whatever the subcultural flavor, the majority of the kids were white.

When I came home, it wasn't long before I threw away my Swatch watch and started constructing what I thought of as my personal statement out of found, bought and cast-off clothes and handmade jewelry. I still think of CSSSA with great nostalgia because it was the place where I first began to question the mainstream values instilled in me as a child. Needless to say, that questioning began the way it does for so many disaffected white suburban kids (although I was neither white nor suburban): it began with aesthetics.

I have shed my black eyeliner and goth velvet for jump drives and a laptop. But this is not to say that I do not occasionally miss the satisfaction of crafting a "look" and being completely certain that it stands as my manifesto. I could never go back to that brand of shallowness, but I couldn't help remembering the relative simplicity of it as I thought about the POOR Magazine mural project in Clarion Alley.

The Clarion Alley Mural Project seems to have begun as a way for native, indigenous, and default-gentrifier artists who lived in the Mission in the late 20th century to simultaneously mourn, mark and resist the homogenizing effects of the full-scale gentrification of the Mission.

I have always assumed that an anti-gentrification stance is by definition pro-neighborhood, but the first Clarion Alley party I ever attended looked nothing like the neighborhood that hosted it.

I remember walking alone into a bunch of mostly white hipster kids. I remember hanging at the party for two hours, drinking exactly 4 beers, and never being spoken to, barely even looked at by anyone. Hardly the Mission I knew outside of the alley. Everyone seemed so . . . cliquish.

It was neo-hipster artsy default gentrifiers at their finest; everyone dressed in such very similar ways that it had me wondering if we were violating any gang-injunction regulations by gathering. Old sneakers, boots, tattoos and thrift store finery; it was art-school lite all over again.

I felt at that party just as Tiny and her Mama Dee felt for years living as poor artists in the Bay Area.

Tiny sees the POOR Magazine mural as penetrating the privilege divide using the access that local artist Caitlin Seana has to the alley.

"It was interesting to have Caitlin, the artist who got us into the alley and who in many ways represents the often-exclusive art world, show so much empathy and understanding about why it was crucial to have POOR in the alley. The alley is a space that, though hyped mostly by children of middle class privilege, still positions itself as at the heart of resistance to the gentrification of a traditionally working class/poor neighborhood. And because she, as a member of that privileged art school world, is the conduit, the mural would not have happened without her," said Tiny.

Mural space on Clarion is extremely hard to come by, due to the popularity of the venue; Caitlin was given space because she helps organize the mural-painting part of the Clarion Alley event.

"I wanted to make [my mural space] something bigger than just a personal statement," said Caitlin, who describes her murals as message boards and not just beautification. "I wanted to bring POOR Magazine to the wall to show people that there are roots in this city of dope people doing amazing things to affect change in original ways. Offering a mural was my way of supporting POOR and honoring the work that you all do," said Caitlin.

Clarion is located between Mission and Valencia, with 17th and 18th streets running parallel on either side. If one looks to the west while standing on the alley, one can see the Mission precinct cop shop squatting like a smooth, watchful concrete-and-tile gargoyle on the other side of Valencia. Our mural site rests in the body of the Community Thrift building, one of the district's most venerable old nonprofit thrift stores.

Oddly enough, directly facing the mural is a wonderful example of the kind of pseudo-"loft" condominium development that has spread like a bauhaus cancer throughout the Mission since the late 1990's, displacing thousands of working class and poor individuals and families from their homes, and even lower middle class default colonizer artsy white kids, as they are built.

The figures that dominate the mural are two of POOR's key mythic heroic characters, Superbabymama and El Mosquito. Superbabymama is our saint of the spoken truth. El Mosquito is our vengeful angel; his left hand crushes a Lennar truck as it wreaks havoc on the frightened houses. In keeping with POOR's practice of honoring the everyday poverty hero/heroine, these two ferocious sentinels are gatekeepers to the road that takes la gente out of the hells of oppressive anti-poverty laws, cruel urban profiteering, and murderous gentrification.

Our mural is not neat or pretty or polished. Our images are not idealized; they are obviously a reflection of our ongoing struggles with The Way Things Are as human rights like housing are being sacrificed to a wider margin of profit, in San Francisco and everywhere. Other murals on Clarion use text, but our text is crawling, swarming, kinetic, like a barrage of ideas that may not be comfortable but are ignored at the peril of the thinking person.

Radical art is only as radical as the message that gets through, and for me, attending that summer art program and willfully taking control of my personal aesthetic was my first step toward a rebellion, a dissatisfaction, which would eventually help shape my entire outlook, including my political stance.

But effective activism cannot be rooted in, say, colored hair and ripped clothes alone; a benefit to pay for an eviction trial must not stop at just one show, one reading, or one art sale to stop the only the warehouse-gallery where all the artkids go to look at each others' latest from being converted into a TIC (Tenancy in Common).

In a 2002 SF Bay Guardian article, Glen Hefland generated a new term to describe the mostly art school trained, mostly privileged white-dominated art scene of the Mission: he called it "the Mission school." To me this "school" represents colonization and thievery of land and housing.

The POOR Magazine mural is a piece of multi-layered public art that resides in the eye of the needle of the undeclared war of gentrification on poor people and peoples of color in the Mission, and it lives in a place that we kicked-out poor folks can't. And, by its residence there, it is not a cutesy, palatable snack of culture and real-ness, like a tour to the Natural History Museum or the zoo, but rather, a powerful form of resistance and an offensive attack on the rampant gentrification and displacement of that neighborhood through a very public form of art.

***

Poor and indigenous peoples have been creating art since the beginning of time. We make art to wear, to read, to walk, to communicate, to carry water, to cook, to keep our babies and bodies warm, to teach our children, to educate our communities, to bring our sacred ceremonies, and to care for and adorn our elders, ancestors, our mother earth, and ourselves.

The art of poor and indigenous peoples has been criminalized, fetishized, archived, stolen, silenced and disrespected since the beginning of colonization. Our skill and artistry have been marginalized to the concept of "low" art or low culture by the colonizer/stolenland class who have always viewed art and artists as a commodity to be bought and sold. An entire body of images, music, dance, and other cultural work ceased to be recognized as beautiful, sacred, precious, or private and instead was transformed into trinkets, souvenirs, strange, frightening, crazy, trash, noise, or ugly. Gaining the titles of outsider art, popular culture, folk art, craft, regional art, or fetish. Once our images were no longer deemed sacred, beautiful or real they could easily be stolen, desecrated, studied, archived, and/or discarded.[5]

Poverty skolaz Tiny, Muteado, and Carina hold a banner outside of the DeYoung Museum which reads "GentriFUKation Tours 'R' Us." The tour stopped at the DeYoung Museum to reclaim stolen indigenous artifacts of the Olmeca people.

Conversely, high art is not only considered sacred, beautiful, and valuable in the context of a white supremacist capitalist monetary system: it is another thing to be bought and hoarded, an asset, and ultimately an example of wealth to sell, own, and display. An entire capitalist industry was built around "high" art, with galleries, collectors, curators, overpriced art schools, and an entire body of akkkademik science. It encompasses some of the most violent forms of colonial perpetration: archaeology, anthropology, and the multibillion-dollar endowed warehouses of stolen indigenous art and sanctioned "high" art known as museums.

Art schools are filled with the children of the ruling classes, who were successfully disaffected by capitalist beliefs and the hoarding of stolen resources, so they now question what the point of life is, while they sip lattes and make angst-ridden art. The art industry plays a crucial role as a tool in post-colonial gentrification, displacement, and the dismantling of working class communities of color. Without the wite "alternative artists" or "urban pioneer artists" as they are ironically named, the violent wheel of gentrification wouldn't roll out so seamlessly in so many communities of color.

The Back-Story of His-Story

When European colonizers began their "illegal" migration across lands and seas, unleashing their genocidal tactics on the peoples of Africa, Turtle Island, and beyond, they also brought their perspective on art.

When they came to Turtle Island, land was spoken about as though it was empty, with only "savages" or heathens in the way of the kind settlers, benevolent missionaries and early devil-opers. The genocidal removal of indigenous peoples began. The art and ceremonial icons of indigenous peoples were stolen, discarded, and fetishized. The colonizers killed and displaced many nations of native peoples, eventually sticking us on barren land known as reservations and relegating our artwork to souvenirs to be purchased in settler towns. Our ancestors' sacred resting spaces, filled with the art we had laid to rest with them, were raided and destroyed or held hostage in their akkkademik warehouses, museums, and laboratories.

They are held in basements like the one at Bancroft Library at the "esteemed" University of California Berkeley, where the stolen remains of Ohlone ancestors—the First Nations peoples of the Bay Area—sit in hefty bags, boxes, and file cabinets, taken from desecrated graves by sanctioned gangsters known as archaeologists. (See Photo.) Or 7 of my people, the Taino who are the indigenous people of the Caribbean, which were only returned in 2003. They had been imprisoned in a box in the basement of the Smithsonian Institute since 1915 when a grave in Cuba was robbed by another group of colonizer thieves.

Similarly, the music, art, ceremony, dance, and aesthetic of Afrikan peoples in forced diaspora were criminalized, silenced, destroyed, or desecrated behind the genocide of slavery.

If you want to destroy a person's soul and spirit, remove him or her from all that is sacred to them. Included in the sacred is the art of indigenous peoples. For example, the language of the drum is an essential part of ceremony and celebration for all African peoples, but the slavemasters criminalized and destroyed it. To accomplish this they used coded language like "barbarian" and primitive, which fit into the narratives of the Missionaries who placed "God" on the side of the genocide of indigenous peoples.[6]

Ocama.... Ocama... Ocama. Pachamama.

Fast forward through 400 years of theft, betrayal, and genocide to the late 19th century and Mayor La Guardia of New York, who waged one of the largest-scale acts of gentriFUKation on thousands of immigrants in poverty.

Most of the residents of the so-named slums were very poor indigenous families in diaspora from Ireland, along with some African decsendent workers who had intermarried with Irish immigrants. Contrary to the stories of stolenland class media, legislators, and most of the big "charity" organizations, there were thousands of poverty heroes and heroines who managed to survive on almost nothing. They raised children and maintained their culture and beauty under the boot of the slumlords and brutal bosses who controlled the stolen property, commerce, and jobs.

Art-giving from the Irish immigrants was primarily centered, as it is in most indigenous communities, around spirit, prayer, and ceremony. The altar was central in almost every home. Altars held ornate, multi-colored handmade expressions of love and respect for the spirits, icons, and deities, which had been reborn as saints to make them acceptable to the Catholic missionaries who colonized Ireland but couldn't colonize the spirit away from the peoples' hearts, or their magic, their love, or their ancestors. The altars included drawings of ancestors and paintings of saints, hand-made candles and frames, found objects and flowers, hand-made prayer beads, complicated crosses and rosaries of every shape and size and color.

There was also powerful political art, such as the brilliant flyers about Tammany Hall and the other groups pushing for political power and civil rights for the community, in the face of so much hate. There was the art of the small businessman with his food cart. There was handmade clothing, shoes, quilts. There was puppetry and song. There was so much art and beauty and laughter and resistance in the "slums," like there always is in our ghettos and barrios and hoods, that is *never* considered art. Living, breathing, singing, speaking, dreaming—right inside and in resistance to serious pain, hate, poverty, and struggle.

When LaGuardia began his tenure as mayor, he launched a process that is straight from the capitalist mayor handbook in Amerikkka, still in use today. Using standard fascist anti-poor-people language, he began referring to immigrant neighborhoods in the Lower East Side as "slums," "dirty," and "crime-ridden". Supported by a corporate media campaign that blasted a daily report of the "filth" and pestilence to be found in the poor people communities, he claimed like crabs in a barrel because of the survival-of-the fittest-bootstraps-capitalism framework, were told how to think about the "dirty poor," there was little opposition to the all-out war he launched on the immigrants of New York's tenements. His process was emulated almost word for word by Rudy Giuliani in the 1990's who instituted the infamous Business Improvement Districts and broken window theory that enabled the dismantling of US cities' single adult welfare programs.[7]

Colorful chalk art by Maria Machetes and Ruyata Akio McGlothlin on the sidewalk of the gentrified zone of Valencia St reads "GENTRIFUKATION" in block letters. The chalk is outside of the Born 'n' Raised in Frisco art project in San Francisco. Since the early 1980's, the Mission District "art scene" in San Francisco is a classic example of default gentrification perpetrated by people who have no investment, ties, or roots in the communities they make art in (or on), with "projects" created by mostly white artists connected to academic/institutional support systems. It is a classic example of colonization through art-making.

In the decades since, all over the United States, from Oakland to LA, from New Orleans to New York, urban communities of color have faced displacement. The forces of displacement are interlinked with poverty and racism and, in many cases, art.

West Oakland, California, was famous in the 1940's and 50's as a thriving African-descendent community, whose residents had participated in the Great Migrations from the Jim Crow South to work in the well-paid shipyard and port jobs of Richmond and Oakland. Eventually the jobs dried up and left thousands unemployed. And in the 1970's, Oakland city politricksters made matters worse by collaborating with developers to force intentional blight on the last vestiges of a thriving community. They re-zoned residential and business areas to allow the release of a plethora of liquor licenses, enabling the free flow of cheap alcohol and poisonous food into an already-struggling neighborhood.

After the destruction of this thriving community of color, underground economic strategies became the only way to survive. Coupled with the CIA dropping crack cocaine in poor communities of color in the 1980's, the capitalist fix was in. (Stolen) property values "dropped" and the default gentrifiers — aka mostly white, privileged artists or "students" — descended on the neighborhood.

La Misión / The Mission

MUTEADO SILENCIO
REPRINTED WITH PERMISSION FROM
LOS VIAJES: A LITERARY ANTHOLOGY AND *POOR* MAGAZINE

La Mission es pa'que nuestra gente se quede y no se aleje
The Mission is for our people to stay and don't go away
See cause the new conquistadores are here, developers,
speculeros,
hipsters with pockets full of greens, can you dig
La Misión
Imposible sería no pelear o luchar por nuestros barrios,
comunidades que poco a poco están desapareciendo.
The Mission
It would be impossible not to fight and struggle for our
barrios, communities that little by little are disappearing.
La Misión/the Mission
Aquí estamos y no nos vamos
La Mission es más que una calle o una Avenida
es un libro de historia y cada calle es una página que relata
el pasado y el presente
The Mission is more than a street or an Avenue .
Is a book of history and each street is a page that narrates
its past and present
16th and Mission is our Gente plaza, I remember the
beautiful weekends I have spent chopping it up with some elders
"Oye hermano yo soy Cubano" as we bathe in the sun, an elder shouts out
As we break the law by sitting side by side
Guantanamera playing in an old boomBox
While my eyes wander as I contemplate la belleza Latina walking by,
the beautifulness of Latina woman
The scent from three blocks away of hotdogs wrap with bacon oh my god
I think am in heaven
No is just La Misión
Y sus perros calientes
La gente de diferentes países, colores, pintando lo que llamamos La Misión
The people from different walks of life, colors, Flavors paint what we call
The Mission
La Misión Sus calles, maltratadas, mal cuidadas, como nuestras
comunidades
The Mission your bruised streets, decayed, poorly taken care of,
like our communities
Aquí Estamos y no nos vamos
We are here to stay
Aquí Estamos y no nos vamos
We are here to stay
Like Sandra said we will be the last poor gente to get
gentrified
y no nos dejaremos

City after city across the US follows this pattern, using art and artists' desire for cheap rent to fuel the gentriFUKation process. In the 21st century this displacement looks like Business Improvement Districts (BID's) and Sit-Lie Laws which are meant to criminalize public space for anyone not seen as "desirable:" houseless people, recyclers, micro-business people, and artists selling their art to survive.

The Venice beach boardwalk was thriving with organic street life in the 1980's and early 90's. Then suddenly, almost overnight, speculators began trolling the neighborhoods like hungry wolves, their mouths and eyes dripping blood, mouthing oddly cryptic phrases like, "It's just a matter of time," and "these people will all be gone in a few years." pointing to young people of color using the local rec center. They drove their BMWs and Mercedes through our racially segregated neighborhood known as "Ghost-Town." The neighborhood was filled with poor families like me and my mama and my cholo-step-father who watched as they walked through our tiny apartment with potential "buyers."

The artists were many. Jack was a houseless watercolorist who painted as medicine. Like most street-based artists, Jack was called "crazy" by mental health professionals. Due to his refusal of "treatment"—aka institutionalization and drugs—he was denied any help to get housing or healthcare. Jack, like so many other houseless or vehicularly-housed street artists, was cited and arrested multiple times for the sole act of selling or displaying his art.

While the property values rose to insanely high levels, the profiling and harassment of youth of color, people of color, and houseless folks rose with them. Taggers and graffiti artists were suddenly accused of vandalism and trespassing, houseless people of soliciting, and the organic, accessible, un-criminalized market was gone forever. We as underground artists will always sell, somehow, but our art is never honored and protected like "high" art is. Rather our art, the art of the "outsider artist" in the public domain, is continually threatened with seizure and confiscation.

Incarcerated Art: The Po' Poets and welfare QUEENs of POOR Magazine go to the De Young Museum

"I'm sorry, there isn't enough food for *you people.*" The young woman stood, her face a chiseled rock of stillness, her black museum-approved pumps planted firmly in front of the cavernous wooden doors of the De Young Museum in San Francisco. The sepia-tinted pillars at the entrance to the Museum stood like daggers ripping into the fabric of early evening sky. Our small crew of Po' Poets and welfareQUEENs arrived to speak at an event in the museum. It was an art show about a neighborhood rooted in a poor community of color. A neighborhood documented, painted over, muralized by artists who claimed intentions of "helping" the poor people who lived there. Or maybe they just meant to paint the poor people who lived there with no other intention but to make "interesting" art to enhance their portfolios with the glaze of "diversity."

That night at the De Young was a celebration of the release of a brightly colored, glossy coffee table book on murals in San Francisco's Mission District. Funded by grants from philanthropists who have roots in the funding of eugenics and other studies used to colonize or dismantle indigenous and poor communities of color globally for hundreds of years.

"All these kids are in jail now." One of the featured mural artists, flown in from New York to present a series of slides about his years living and working on Clarion Alley, paused momentarily on the image of a young brown child, looking down the alley, his alley, his family's alley, an alley where he and his family no longer reside, due to intense real estate speculation and subsequent displacement. The artist's words, spoken in a disconnected monotone, shattered my heart into a thousand small shards.

Displacement is death, and gentrification is genocide. After we are displaced, our voices, our truths are permanently lost, only to be re-framed and re-told by our destroyers, the intentional and unintentional perpetrators of our removal.

After over 45 minutes of more slides of his work, his slideshow finally ended with an image of nine young boys of color, standing against a paint chipped fence on Clarion Alley, at which point he paused and added, "We finally got them to commit to helping with a mural for one summer, but they rarely showed up to paint." He ended with a short chuckle.

The Art Us Po' Folk Create Every Day in Amerikkka

"I work really hard to get it like that." Tommy R spoke to me slowly as he arranged and rearranged two shopping carts which he had tied together with tiny bits of aluminum wire in the middle of Peralta Street in West Oakland. He was careful to point out the many layers piled on the carts, containing over 75 bags of different media, color-coded. There were carefully stretched plastic bags for the large plastic bottles versus the smaller glass bottles, for the tall soda cans versus the shorter cans. Tommy R wasn't called an artist, he didn't call himself an artist, but his installation of found objects, color, and light was art. And it was, in my humble opinion, the best kind of art, art that was non-static, that moved and swayed in the breeze, captured the sun in the afternoon and the lights at the curb.

"I like to place the smaller pieces right here next to the curb," Herbie was creating an installation of his multi-sized drawings and sketches on pieces of found cardboard, the backs of thrown away pizza boxes, newspaper and shoe-

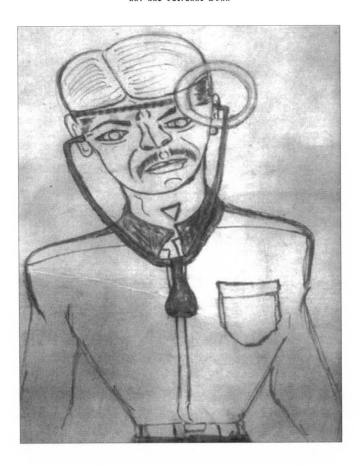

"The Doctor," a pencil drawing of a stern-looking doctor. By Herbie, an unhoused poverty scholar artist, who is also featured in HELLthcare Vol. 2 of POOR Magazine (Print Edition). One of Herbie's drawings on found cardboard (the back of a discarded pizza box).

boxes and other remnants of capitalism Herbie picked up as a houseless artist.

Herbie grew up in poverty in Pittsburgh in the 1940's, the son of a preacher. He was an artist since birth but po' folks artistic "leanings" or skills are never viewed as important, and so art school was never an option for Herbie. Instead he was sent to Chicago to learn to be a shoemaker.

In Chicago he found out the shoemaker apprentice opportunity was already taken. He ended up becoming a "boot-black" and later a bellman for some of the biggest hotels in Chicago. For twenty years he struggled to come up and out of poverty by working hard as hell, to no avail. In the 1980's he came to California with the dream of making and selling art. He launched a storefront shoe-shine business and pool hall until drastic rent increases caused his business to close, and him to become houseless.

Everyday, Herbie would create and install his "cheap art gallery" on the curbs, doorways, and sidewalks of San Francisco's Haight Street and North Beach districts. He was constantly harassed, cited, and arrested for the sole act of being Po', black and outside, selling his hand-drawn crayon masterpieces of art for anywhere from .30 to 3.00, while $300 "arty" shoes and $3,000-30,000 "fine" art pieces were bought and sold in the elitist art galleries that surrounded him.

EXCERPT | **The Real Truth: John T. Williams**
CAT CONDEFF, E. DUPLESSIS, PESHA, AND LOLA BEAN
FOR PNN WASHINGTON
REPRINTED WITH PERMISSION FROM POOR MAGAZINE
15 JUNE 2011

> *"I remember John T. Williams as he was, transforming ordinary to extraordinary. He was a creator, red sun in the Montana sky, moon rising up from the eastern horizon, the sound of crashing water, brought things to life that appeared dead, resurrection, sound of justice/a cloud of rain. He still rains down on us today and that's how we know he's still here/an eagle of art and justice. He carved the silence away from wood to set free stories."*

The pages of POOR Magazine were filled with the art of houseless, unrecognized artists, laid out beautifully, and intentionally in full bleed designed pages accompanied by poetry and art written and produced by poverty scholars. Many of these artists came from a powerful street-based organization called Hospitality House, which operates a drop-in art studio for houseless people such as Jane in Vain Winkelman, Larry Clark, Marco Paredes, Bob Burke, and Jorge Koyama.

When We Try to Be Viewed as Artists

"You are WHAT?" The welfare worker stopped typing in horror when she heard 18-year-old John's reply to her question: what kind of careers do you hope to pursue? Under his breath, with more humility than most people show in their lifetime, he repeated, "I am an artist. I would like to be a professional artist, or maybe... go to art school." He stopped talking completely as she overtook the conversation with a rant about how he needs to get real, he is lazy, he is on welfare, he has no support and no job skills and is lucky to get a job, much less become an "artist or whatever."

Within 24 hours John was employed at Walmart working 54 hours a week. John had worked dutifully for years of his young life, in a free art studio, while dealing with poverty and caring for his grandmother, to make a powerful and breath-taking body of paintings, sculpture, music and poetry. In a 15-minute evaluation he was told he was lazy.

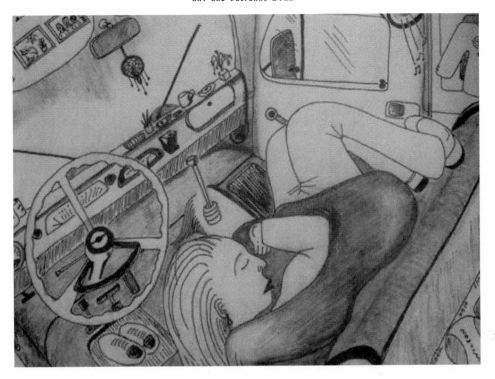

In Seattle, Washington, Cat, a houseless painter, and Lola Bean, artist/writer facilitator and poverty skolar, work in collaboration with other houseless artists in street-based workshops. In this piece of Cat's art, a woman is curled up in the front seat of a car, sleeping.

Incarcerated Art, Criminalized Art: Graffiti as Art, Tagging as Media

Since the earliest recorded herstory, graffiti has been a part of our world. Culture to culture, region to region, and era to era it changes design. But for indigenous and poor communities of color it is a form of storytelling, of marking, of remembering, of naming, of owning. This last purpose—owning—is one of the most problematic, because so many of the people who do the graffiti own very little of their communities because of displacement and colonization. In so many ways graffiti is resistance to capitalism, but the only way graffiti artists can "make" their art without risking jail time is if they get permission from the owners of the public spaces they do their art on.

Within the world of graffiti there are clear class and race lines distinctively drawn. While young people from the West Coast were taggin for their cliques in East Los Angeles, Wilmington, and Venice, and community murals were just starting to get hip, young people of color like Fab 5 Freddy from New York blasted onto the scene when hip hop started to get Hot!

Sadly this "hot-ness" marked the fetishization of poor people of color art by white hipster and punk artists like Debbie Harry of Blondie, who

An image of a board game called "Parlor Game" by Jane "in Vain" Winkelman and the Coalition on Homelessness. Colorful squares include a person pushing a shopping cart and words like "Lose again!" and "Get a ticket!"

included graffiti art in their concerts and multi-media performances. Famous "art-collectors" like Claudio Bruni began to take notice of graffiti as an "interesting" art form that might produce profit. This led to the "outsiding" of poor people of color artists like Jean Michel Basquiat, a houseless Haitian artist born in New York, by the subtly inside artists like Keith Haring, who was white and had gone to art school.

For poor people of color, the use of graffiti is often survival based, connected to our neighborhoods, our struggles, our ancestor-honoring, our life and death messaging. For wite hipster artists it is a trend, a cutting-edge medium. The one thing both communities share is the use of public space as an accessible canvas, a point of mass consumption. There have been more humble, conscious artists who are still privileged by education, race and/or class—artists like Barry Mcgee, RIGO, and Aaron Noble—but their forays into public art were still part of their portfolios, grant-funded and part of the gentriFUKation process of the communities they were trying to "help."

While these accepted artists were shuttled away to gallery shows, commissioned projects, and teaching gigs, the young, poor, and indigenous artists were still there. Our days were numbered: we had been encroached upon. We were suffering rent increases and removal in grand scale, and now our indigenous practice of marking and tagging was used against us as proof of kkkrimes committed in our newly po'liced neighborhoods.

How can one type of media be seen as ok when others are so clearly racialized, criminalized, and silenced? When a young person tags, he or she is speaking up in a public way through that tag. Yet when Clear Channel, a Republican, right-wing controlled public relations company slathers commercials for foreclosure perpetrators like Wells Fargo or Bank of Amerikkka on every bus shelter and billboard, we have no say about it. How is this corporate sponsored violence better? How is one group provided carte blanche access and one is criminalized? Billions of dollars—that's it. That's what buys public viewing access, and that's what criminalizes it.

Tourism as Colonization and Sacred Resistance

Aboriginal art is rooted in the understanding that spirit is in everything and everything is art. That to be alive is to see, feel, hear, touch, and smell art. It is humility to recognize our lives are art. Many aboriginal cultures and nations have struggled to maintain ownership of their art. But to survive in this post-colonial reality many cultures, from Hawai'i to the Congo, will sing, dance, and speak some of their most sacred traditions for the tourist industry. As many indigenous peoples fight for sovereignty, they fight for the right to own their own tourist industry and the profits from their own art.

Untitled
AMELIA NIUMEITOLU

I was born in Tonga with the rooted connections to Samoa, Fiji, Aotearoa, Chuuk and Oceania. Art is not separate or outside of who I am, it is in my blood and pieces of daily life. the first artist in my life was my grandmother, Vai. Maybe it was the way she climbed trees to make me a fresh kahoa (lei, garland necklace), her gardening and having my little fingers touch our earth, helping or watching her cook hot meals for our large family, heal neighbors with indigenous plants and gracious prayers, or just having memories in which I always smiled and believed I was loved.

I am a messenger, a storyteller. I am grateful for the sacrifice and ex-amples of my ancestors, grandparents, parents Tangata 'o Lakepa and Litia, my siblings, Fui, Loa, David, Moana and Lavu. I am thankful for the shoulders I stand on from the Indigenous nations and tribes here to the Black/African American from slavery to civil rights. I stand because Latinos and Asian Americans created movements for many generations.

Tof'ia: Heritage was taken on a quick visit to the village Veitongo in the country, Tonga.

This little boy stood in front of me while I was taking photos of family members and neighbors playing bingo in an impoverished setting. There are women on the side weaving traditional cultural dressing from plastic to sell. The can of corned beef on the left represents the colonization of Tonga and Oceania and the lingering impacts on our once-independent now dependent communities, our bodies struggling with heart disease, diabetes, cancer, and mental health issues.

Our dependence on convenience and bartering or trading of indigenous forms of sustainability like gardening, fishing, diving, and the physical and spiritual connections to what we eat. In the midst of what we say in pride to be Tongan or from Tonga or Oceania this little boy is alive, here, in a type of poverty different from that of the United States, Australia, and New Zealand.

The motto of Tonga: "Ko e Otua mo Tonga ko hoku tofi a." "God and Tonga are my Inheritance."

The Art of Homelessness: Me and Mama Dee

My mama's art came from the deepest part of her broken soul. Like art for most people, it was a deep form of healing. For her healing was laughing, so for us art was filled with laughter. Our art was one gigantic ruse on Eurocentric colonizer culture and its bullshit, its mythologies, its hypocrisies, and its ongoing destruction. In retrospect, I realize that my mama was so completely broken off, hated, and distanced from everything that would be considered "normal" that she was pure innovation. And in so many ways she inspired and raised me that same way: to truly understand that the entire story we are sold n told is bullshit. What art is, and who is considered an "artist," is one of the biggest lies of all.

My mother was a conceptual genius and I her willing side-kick. In Venice Beach, we set up huge installations and staged interactive theatre pieces, always including music. It was a hustle, it was comedy, it was tragedy, and above all it was Hollywood! My mama was a brilliant and tortured textile artist. She would begin with old clothing and re-make it into a story, a costume, a walking stick, an allegory. I realize now as I delve into our lost cultures that she was making her Traje, as they say in Danza. Each one had a powerful animal spirit, a series of colors and attachments that represented pieces of her lost story, her communities, our neighborhood, our lives. With no institutional learning she would create these Trajes out of her head. And for everything she would create, I was the model.

TOP TO BOTTOM, LEFT TO RIGHT:

A group of young people in Oakland stand, leaning on bikes with intricate, colorfully decorated wheels. This is the Scraper Bike movement, sculptural art forms of resistance from young Black and Brown artists in the hood.

A portrait of Brother Malcolm, aka Malcolm Samuel, a sidewalk scholar, former Black Panther, union worker, father, people's activist, poet, tailor, and outspoken speaker. He passed away on July 29th, 2005, from complications of diabetes – but these complications came by the hands of police and the non-existent medical care in prison and in so-called "vocational hospital."

A man plays the drums on a dozen 5-gallon buckets, pans, water jugs, and other instruments. This is Larry Hunt, "Bucketman," who was criminalized for bringing ritmos to the streets of San Francisco.

Based in the Democratic Republic of the Congo, Staff Benda Bilili is an orchestra of six musicians with polio and two street kids they fostered years ago. Their unique style lies somewhere between James Brown and Buena Vista Social Club. Their lyrics are like advice to all the people who live in the streets like them. They are like the godfathers of all the street kids and very respected personalities of the ghetto. They're married, have kids, and apart from music they're gifted electricians, sewers, and hairdressers. (Caption excerpted from "Godfathers of Street Kids" by Leroy Moore.)

Eventually, we migrated to the Bay Area. My mama finally found a way to go "to art school" without paying. The booshie private school where she learned some complicated cloth-dying and paper-making from plants and weeds straight kicked us out, but with hushed Berkeley tones of hippie hate and furtive glances of gray-haired instructors with fake smiles pasted to their makeup-free faces.

The state school was easier. We went to San Francisco State University's short-lived "interdisciplinary art program" which included some liberatory conceptualists like Leonard Hunter. My mama and I learned about the her-story of conceptual art, "post-modernism," and the stories of art school-sanctioned artists like Marcel Duchamp and Dadaism from the 1920's. These were the booshie disaffected art school students of their day. They realized their privilege and the violence of it and the uselessness of the art industry and then created cutting-edge work like art out of toilet seats and other such "risky" ventures. Eventually they would slip further into akkkademia, become boringly complacent or dangerously depressed, and do themselves in with drugs and alcohol. But the whole time they were allegedly "pushing boundaries" by questioning, always questioning: "What is Art?" Of course, while questioning, they were making money, getting publishing access and art industry hook-ups on the questioning itself.

For me and my mama, this time of art practice and learning was also a time of deep, mind-numbing struggle. We struggled with houselessness, poverty, hunger, eviction, no heat, murderous landlords, kkkourts, no law-yers, incarceration, profiling, constant car break-downs, car tows and cita-tions for sleeping in our car, no hellthcare, tooth pain, no dental care, and all the other experiences of poor families in Amerikkka. When we could, we lived in squatted storefronts and created complicated installations about houselessness. When we were evicted, which we always were, we lived in motels and, in the worst moments, on park benches, in doorways, shelter beds and the backseat of our car, if we had one. And through all of this was devastating emotional realness: not theorized about, conceptualized about, or akademikly lectured about, but deeply felt.

It was also in this time that we made some of the most genius work we had ever done:

My mama, a severely abused, neglected, and unwanted child was at once re-telling her story and the story of so many other unprotected chil-dren of color barely surviving the Amerikkklan nightmare.

How we kept up making art was somewhat of a miracle. We were in so much psychic, physical, and emotional pain and yet there was so much irony and humor and sarcasm in my mama's constant critique and our work together that I know it also kept us alive. For her it was constant and real-time processing of her pain, therapy through art, healing through imagination. What I didn't know at the time was that we were in fact becoming the "outsider" artists we always learned about. We were never invited into gallery shows or panels. We were never offered a grant or fellowship. In fact, we were never offered any kind of support at all for what we were doing. Instead, we found out later that one of the teachers of this time, believing our complete insanity to be true, had made a video about a mentally ill mother and daughter duo, based on us. This person is a consistent winner of NEA endowments and akademik fellowships to this day!

Ultimately the wite deep structure (as they say in Black Psychology) devoid of spirit, the sacred or soul which was the backbone of this art "world" misunderstood, marginalized, fetishized and/or rejected us. For us, like other "outsider" artists, this experience mirrored other colonizing experiences we had had throughout our entire lives, experiences that had destroyed, rejected and misunderstood our cultures, our spirits, and most of all our art.

***

The colonizer has locked in the definition of art, art-making, and aesthetic. So if that's not the real definition of art, what is? It is my humble belief that art is the handmade-by-mama dress of a little girl in the Philippines and a quilt by a grandmother in Arkansas, and a puppet show by a poor Roma immigrant in New York, and a hand-made rosary on an altar in Spanish Harlem, and the altar itself, and a complex Mayan headdress made to accompany the traje of a danzante, and an African icon for the Orisha Xango or Yemaya, and the ritmo of the drum used in the ceremony to honor these powerful Orishas from so many Africans in diaspora across Pachamama.

As we truly move to decolonize from colonial institutions, let's lift our minds completely out of their definitions of us as artists. I hope we can follow the roots of our ancestors and make art only for spiritual, cultural, revolutionary purposes, for healing/inspiring/teaching our families and communities.

None of the galleries should exist. No philanthro-pimp should approve of our "projects." No one should even take pictures of our multiple, beautiful art forms. None of them should ever be posted on Face-crak, or become a photographic essay for an akkkademik thesis. Art should only feed and be fed by the people, on the street, by the children in our homes and our communities, by each of us for Creator, ancestors, and Pachamama. Community Reparations should be paid for destroyed and gentriFUKed communities to create their sacred art and spiritual texts to bring their healing and cultures back. The reparators should in no way dictate what happens to the art, what it looks like, or who it's for.

As we walk this walk at POOR Magazine we have created sacred texts of art and love. Things that we and we alone define from our spiritual values as landless, indigenous peoples as sacred. Our Declaration of Interdependence and our Manifesto for Change are two sacred texts which do not exist as a pdf, jpeg, or a blog. You can't google them and find the original pieces. They are only mentioned and spoken about by people who have seen them. Even in this book their partial images will only be excerpted. These are our indigenous sacred paintings: our cave paintings, if you will. They are not meant for mass, disaffected use and dis-use. We share them only with other revolutionary landless peoples' movements who respect and honor the same values we hold and who understand that to truly decolonize our minds and hearts we must move off all of these colonizer-dominated institutional frames back to that which comes from our hearts and souls.

The art of poor and indigenous peoples will continue to be made with or without the sanctions, approval, critique or involvement from the stolen-land class. The challenge is to make the art without their unwanted documentation, fetishization, pimping, and abusing.

We are not silent. We haven't stopped dancing, honoring, creating, or story-telling. But we have pieces to pick up under the feet of the oppressors, images and songs and dreams.

A storefront with a "Closed" sign in the door. Handmade signs fill the windows. In "Fear of the market place," people had to choose a product and throw money in through a small crack in the window with a note indicating what they wanted to purchase, never knowing when or where—if ever—they would actually get what they requested.

Tiny stands in a brown leather jacket in front of a squatted storefront reclaimed by her and Mama Dee. The hand-painted sign above the door reads: "K'ahtic: store as performance." Part of the "Things people said about us" installation.

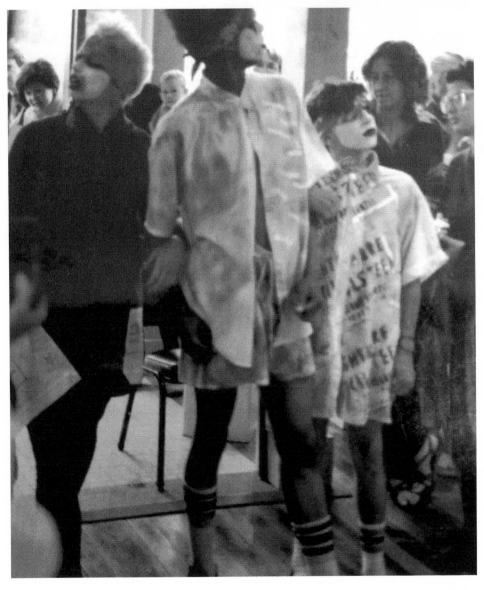

"Minstrel Clothes: a performance and fashion show by Mama Dee & Tiny." Three Black and Brown people pose arm in arm, in whiteface, as an audience looks on.

No matter how many times you study me it doesn't get me a home

— TINY

5

Poor People-Led Education, We-Search, and Information vs. Institution-Led Akkkademia, Research, and Destruction

Lowrider Lecturer

Dedicated to my tio Jose Cuellar aka Dr Loco, a poverty skola / akademik.

Angel Baby, my Angel Baby
Oooooh, I love you, oooh I do
No one could love you like I do.

The lowrider lecturer presents his thesis on
the back seat of a Chevy impala
the words sail thru the sky and out the narrow institutional skoo window
refusing to be caught by the mandate of white supremacist TESTS-
the story that only some people can b teachers while others are set for arrest
The Cholo Docta has letters behind his name that sway and sashay
to the sounds of War and Frankie Valli
When i hear the Cholo Docta my corazón skips a beat cuz he teaches that
the knowledge is within us — our corazones — our almaz — pro amor —
our hands — our feet — our work — our struggle —
La vida Loca and the institution can meet
The Cholo Docta brings medicine to the minds of all of us caught in the
trauma of colonization and gregorian time- to my boricua ghetto fabulous
mama who was told she was nothing- and could be nothing and no matter
what refused to believe their pinche lies
the Cholo Docta is yo mama-your uncle, yo abuela - your street corner
preacher, your gardener - your dishwasher and lives in your own mind
the lowrider lecturer delivers lecturez in poesía and música and prayer and
dreams
The lowrider lecturer is busy — he and she are mixing their trajectories and
developing their newest canons while they wash your dishes, mow your lawn
and make your burrito with beans —
they are having their think tanks and their test prep sessions in front of the
home depot and if u want to pass the test called life you better listen carefully
to their lecturez cuz they don't have time to repeat them or say them twice
between holding down three and four jobs care-giving for your babies,
struggling with false borders and fake notions of who is a skola and who is a
teacher for life

Son of a Janitor

TONY ROBLES
REPRINTED WITH PERMISSION FROM *FILIPINO BUILDING
MAINTENANCE COMPANY* (POOR PRESS)

The house of a janitor is supposed to be clean. One would assume this to be true because the janitor performs his duties with the sacred mop, broom, and toilet brush. My father was a janitor for some 20-odd years at the San Francisco Opera House. It would be 10 years before he'd realize his dream and start the Filipino Building Maintenance Company and go into business on his own.

At the dinner table he'd ask me questions such as, "What did you learn in school today?" I've always been somewhat of a bad listener. "Nothing," I'd reply—I always replied "nothing." Not that I was indifferent to school— even at a very young age. Yes, I was very aware of the things they were doing to me in school and after the bell rang I'd let it fall from my mind like some brown, withered old leaf falling off a tree—destined to be stepped on by some kid on their way home. My father always told me if I didn't do well in school, I'd end up cleaning toilets all my life. My father didn't graduate from high school and I guess he carried that with him. Somehow he felt that the high school diploma was a key—some kind of rocket fuel which would kick start you into the realm of possibilities.

"Do you know how to clean?" Dad would, on occasion, talk shop with me—an 11- or 12-year-old kid with no work experience. "Yeah, I know how to clean," I'd reply. Ok, he'd say, how do you remove chewing gum from a carpet? I was supposed to use logic and deduction in finding the correct answer. "I would take a pair of scissors and cut the gum off..." At this point my father would belch or fart, or perform both simultaneously. Shaking his head he'd say, "It's very apparent and clearly evident that you don't know anything about cleaning. The way to remove gum from a carpet is to take an ice cube and place it on the gum. Wait 'til it hardens, then remove it with a putty knife." I never asked him what to do if you didn't have an ice cube—perhaps I should have.

The one thing I was fairly proficient at was cleaning the toilet. It was one of a couple of chores assigned to me. The other chores were drying the dishes and vacuuming. My father didn't clean at home—he left that duty to my stepmom and I. Why would he want to bring his business home? I remember once during the Christmas season my father worked during the showing of the *Nutcracker*. This meant lots of kids. Dad not only had to mop floors and empty trashcans, but he had to get on his hands and knees and pick hundreds, perhaps thousands of sunflower seed shells. He came home exhausted, complaining that those kids made him "sweat his ass off" that day. At home, my father took to gardening, which proved therapeutic. He would take a spray bottle and sprinkle water on his plants—large and unique cacti, whose spines climbed the walls.

My father continued after me about things over the years. I can't blame him really. I wasn't particularly talented but I managed to get out of high school and out of college. The getting out was the most rewarding part. When we eat dinner these days, he doesn't ask me about what I learned in school, which is good because I remember nothing. But the one thing I do remember was cleaning those toilets. And believe me, it's helped me a lot more.

Skoolin' Teachin' Learnin' Speakin' vs. the Akkkademik Hustle

"One should pay attention to even the smallest crawling creature for these too have a valuable lesson to teach us." — BLACK ELK

Education, like art and media, is everywhere. It is in the wind, it is in the whispers, scolds, stories, love, advice, and songs of all mamaz and daddies and grandmothers and grandfathers, plants, animals, Mother Earth and Father Sky. It is in the multi-voiced spirits of our ancestors. It is in our hearts, it is in our rage, it is in our prayers, and it is in our dreams.

Lived education is hard. Lessons, tests, and reports given by our families, communities, ancestors, and elders are difficult and confusing. They are subtle and much more complicated than anything you could learn in a textbook.

Education from our peoples doesn't come when you are "ready," when you enroll in a program or pay tuition. People-grown teaching, information-giving, learnin' is painful, beautiful, and time-consuming.

But according to the airtight lie of institutional-led education, aka akkkademia, there is no education except the one that they constructed. That education isn't legitimate or important unless it is applied for, paid for, and changed for. Education has no value unless they say it has value, unless it is crafted and "accredited" by them. This is institutional domination at its finest.

Akkkademia: one of the biggest gangsters with the best hustle in town. A hustle so grand that you will cross multiple false borders, risk the lives of yourself and your family, sell beloved belongings, work at back-breaking capitalist plantation jobs for decades, endure racism, hate, oppression, and sickness, disable your body, and risk housing stability with bankgangster mortgages just to pay for it.

How did the idea that people should hoard money "just to pay for college" become a mandate for wite upper- and middle-class culture, a goal for working-class communities of color, and a dream for very poor and indigenous peoples in the Global South? Bonds are put aside, CD's are launched. People are told not to have children, or are fraught with guilt, anxiety, and feelings of failure if they don't have money for their children's "college" funds.

People go into massive and dangerous debt just to pay for kkkollege. They're told that this institutional college debt is "good debt."

"Hello Ms. Garcia, we are calling from the Canan Corp. We are calling about Dee Garcia's unpaid student loan."

"My mother passed away last year."

"Well, I'm sorry, but that's not an adequate reason to not pay her bill."

My own mama was sold and told—as so many are—that akkkademia was "the way out" of her extremely difficult life of racism, poverty, and oppression. After a life of torture and abuse in foster homes and orphanages, my mama was sent to California to finally reunite with her over-stressed, indentured servant (live-in domestic worker) mama. She was enrolled in high school, and began trying to re-invent herself as a wite girl.

One of the ingredients to the re-invention was to aspire to go to college after graduation. She tried everything to get into college, including scholarship applications, multiple college applications, and tests on top of more tests. But my mama never had a parent, or anyone for that matter, who cared for and protected her, or helped her navigate the complex system of akkkademik acceptance, homework, or even consistent attendance in school. And so, like so many young poor peoples of color in amerikkka, she didn't pass the SAT, didn't properly complete the applications, never could get ahold of her transcripts, and barely graduated from high school.

But being my ghetto-fabulous-never-giving-up mama she never let go of her dream of getting "the paper" and "getting out" of poverty. She spent 12 years on and off attending community colleges and eventually a state college. She went through multiple drop-outs and push-outs by college counselors and supervisors, ending up in a social work graduate school that suspended her and threatened her with "insubordination" and told her she was "unsupervisable" for holding a "client's" hand in a lockdown mental hospital. After all that, she finally got her Master's Degree in Social Work. Of course, she eventually rejected most of what she was taught as being full of wite-male-Eurocentric science that had nothing to do with making revolutionary change or healing broken indigenous peoples like her and me.

"I crossed three borders, risking my life, so my children could get an education."
— DELORES, MIGRANTE WARRIOR MAMA OF FOUR CHILDREN FROM EL SALVADOR

One of the most tragic aspects of the Akkkademik hustle is the myth of a "good" education for millions of migrant peoples who cross murderous borders into the US and Western Europe.

The lands and economies of indigenous peoples have been stolen, mined, and destroyed by trade agreements, unjust treaties, imperial agendas, and the military industrial complex. These communities were sold on institutional knowledge through the process of colonization, which always enlisted "teachers," missionaries, and social workers to perpetrate colonial agendas. Education is the user-friendly path undergirding colonial theft and genocide that continues today.

As the myth of wite-people-owned educational betterment rose, more and more people sought the tiny crumb of akkkademia for their children and grandchildren. This has resulted in millions of people dying and risking death through separation from their powerful indigenous forms of education, lands, and relationships.

The same kkkorporate interests that were luring us away from our lands and cultures of origin were colonizing, stealing, mining, poisoning, and thieving those lands. What a brilliant heist.

 Questioning akkkademia is a complicated and sorrowful process. My intent is not to hurt or disrespect anyone, their family, or their ancestors' struggle to achieve something from akkkademia. Rather, I want to begin to help us all detangle and un-confuse our minds from this idea that institutional education, designed by the people who have stolen so much from all of us, is the only way to learn, advance, and "succeed."

The People who "Built" Amerikkka?

From Leland Stanford to Harvard University to the University of California Regents, universities and colleges across the US were founded or funded by wite-supremacists whose interests were the "protection" of their own witeness—or what they called the Aryan race. Some of the earliest examples were in the funding of fellowships and endowments dedicated to eugenics.

These fellowships and endowments set up the framework for the genocidal assimilation campaigns which were perpetrated on indigenous peoples in the US, Australia, and Canada. Thousands of dollars were spent and entire university departments of science, archaeology, anthropology, and medicine were launched to prove that wite people were inherently smarter, faster, stronger, and more skilled than peoples of color.

These institutions measured the different races' brain sizes, stole ancestors' bones from sacred sites, and launched allegedly scientific genome "studies" to prove that race-mixing would increase the intelligence of peoples of color. These endless investigations into wite-ness were necessary to excuse and explain the theft of Indian children from their families, forced abortions and sterilizations, and the atrocities of medical experimentation on peoples of color.[8]

How Did It Get That Way? The Herstory of Akkkademic Colonization

The first image showed a tall wite missionary woman standing in front of a small wooden-frame building, looking down, smiling at a Filipino man dressed in the regalia of his peoples. The image was classic colonizer lens. The frame was broad and high and the man, who could have been an elder, a warrior, or medicine-giver, seemed tiny, almost insignificant, and nude, in relation to the bright-wite covered-up savior lady.

In the next image people with starched collars stood like small wite wardens incarcerating the necks of the brown warriors, chiefs, story-tellers, teachers, and hunters.

The fix was in. From one *National Geographic*-esque picture to another, the US missionaries sealed the deal of colonial take-over of the Philippines with their offer to bring "education" to the people. *Their* education, defined and prescribed by the colonizers. An education that ultimately benefited the colonizers' agenda of theft and genocide, but appeared to benefit the indigenous peoples. What a beautiful scam. The people they came there to steal land and spirit from were now beholden to them.

The colonizers brought the "savages" into their trap with the promise of education that had no space for the deep and powerful, layered and complicated knowledge the indigenous peoples already held.

The people in starched collars gave no credit to the powerful scholarship about what food to eat to stay alive, what plants make medicine, how to love mother earth, how to be humble and fierce and listen to your elders and take care of your children, what the ancestors say, what prayers to bring to the land and the people, who is a teacher and a student, and who has knowledge.

The images were part of a Filipino history exhibit at the San Francisco Library. The promoters were philanthro-pimped foundations, government agencies like the consulate, and tourism promoters like Philippine Airlines. The exhibit included images taken in the Philippines in the early 1900's to present-day San Francisco. It did not include images of the International Hotel struggle waged by low-income Filipino and Chinese elders, poets, and revolutionaries like Al Robles and Bill Sorro in collaboration with activists and tenant advocates. They refused to be quietly evicted by a devil-oper so a parking lot could be built and more rich people could work in Downtown San Francisco at the expense of over 220 elder residents in poverty.

The photos from the exhibit were just one example. Worldwide, under the guise of "research," well-documented atrocities were perpetrated on indigenous peoples of the world.

In the early nineteenth century, the South African Khoisan woman Saartjie Baartmen was put on display throughout Europe to be fetishized for her indigenous physique. She was studied by European "naturalists" and depicted by scientific painters. After she died, she was publicly dissected. Her sexual organs and brain were pickled by Napoleon's surgeon and put on display in a Paris museum, along with her skeleton.

A man named Ishi, indigenous to lands in what is now California that were desecrated by mining, was a live research subject of anthropologists at UC Berkeley from 1911 until 1916. After his death, his body was dissected and his brain was preserved in akkkademik laboratories in the Smithsonian Institution. His stolen brain remained there until August 10, 2000, when his descendants of the Redding Rancheria and Pit River tribes received the brain.

A pygmy named Ota Benga (or "Bi," which means "friend" in Benga's language), born in 1881 in central Africa, was bought to the US as a chattel slave by a French slaveholder. He was displayed as an "emblematic savage" at the 1904 St. Louis World's Fair in an anthropology exhibit that aimed to be "exhaustively scientific" in its demonstration of the stages of human evolution. The exhibit's creator, W.J. McGee, required "darkest blacks" to be set off against "dominant whites." Ota was later "displayed" at the Louisiana Purchase exposition, and eventually locked in a monkey house in a zoo.

Ongoing Akkkademik Desecration

All of this akkkademik-supported genocide is brought current with the sacred site desecrations that continue today across the US and beyond. In California alone there are hundreds of sacred shellmounds desecrated, rolled over, poisoned, and built upon by the un-holy alliance of archaeologists and anthropologists who team up with multi-million dollar re-devil-opers.

The Emeryville Shellmound in the Bay Area was a sacred site that held the remains of Ohlone ancestors from over 3500 years ago. In the 1900s it began to be desecrated with poisonous landfills and by akkkademik archaeologists who embarked on a huge excavation, stealing and warehousing sacred Ohlone tools, ancestors' bones and other "specimens" under the guise of archaeological study. Eventually they were to determine that this was one of the oldest settlements in California. From this "discovery" they began recording information that, of course, all of the Ohlone leaders already knew. In all of this documenting, studying, and theft, it is ironic that the Ohlone Nation has still not received federal recognition.

After allowing a huge industrial site to operate, government officials approved a massive shopping center to be built on top of the sacred site. Where the shellmounds had been the devil-opers left only a plaque, an artistically rendered Ohlone bowl, and two streets in the shopping mall named Shellmound Street and Ohlone Way. Dutifully, Ohlone leaders like Corrina Gould and WichahLuta Candelaria and Wounded Knee Deocampo come out on the capitalist holiday of Black Friday every year to protest the desecration while Ikea shoppers whiz by in their Priuses.

In a controversial example of resistance, one Ohlone woman, Rosemary Cambra, was protesting in the '80s when another set of arrogant archae-ologists were desecrating the site and stealing remains with the impunity of wite akkkademia. She took a shovel and hit one of the archaeologists on the back. As a woman of color in Amerikkka she was convicted and her poor body of color lost everything, while the archaeologist continued to desecrate.

Colonial Education

Ngugi wa Thiong'o, a Kenyan writer of Gikuyu descent, began his work writing in the colonizer's language aka English before turning to work almost entirely in his native Gikuyu. Ngugi's last work in English, *Decolonising the Mind*, explains that the English language in Africa has been like a "cultural bomb" that has damaged and desecrated indigenous traditions and memories. The colonizer's language is a way to perpetuate a subtle form of colonialism.[9]

He wrote that colonial education "annihilate(s) a people's belief in their names, in their languages, in their environment, in their heritage of struggle, in their unity, in their capacities and ultimately in themselves. It makes them see their past as one wasteland of non-achievement and it makes them want to distance themselves from that wasteland. It makes them want to identify with that which is furthest removed from themselves."

Not only does colonial education eventually create a sense of wanting to disassociate with native heritage, but it affects the individual and the sense of self-confidence. Thiong'o believes that "education, far from giving people the confidence in their ability and capacities to overcome obstacles or to become masters of the laws governing external nature as human beings tends to make them feel their inadequacies and their ability to do anything about the condition of their lives."

Often, the implementation of a new, allegedly "better," richer, cleaner, and ultimately whiter education system leaves the indigenous, now-colonized peoples with a lack of identity and a limited sense of their past. The indigenous herstories, practices, values and customs slowly slip away.

The Amerikkklan "Dream" and the Myth of Success

So once you have accepted and sacrificed for all of the pieces of the ak-kkademik myth, and then manage to make it through the eye of the needle into the polished (by low-wage workers) halls of academia, into the "paying job" that you are theoretically guaranteed when you graduate, begin to hoard blud-stained dollaz so you can purchase a stolen piece of land through bank gangsters and settle into the cult of independence, you have now begun to be one of the oppressors, thriving because of the pain of someone else's survival.

But capitalism survives on the "I Got Mines" philosophy, and akkka-demia is billed as one of the channels to "Get Yours." So killing yourself, leaving yourself, hating your soul and the spirit, language, and culture of your people is necessary: hey, I got a chance to Get Mines.

To deconstruct and challenge academia is to decolonize our minds, to realize that as indigenous peoples, poor peoples, as peoples in diaspora, as peoples of color we hold enough information in our hearts and minds and spirits already to teach our children, grow our food, take back our land, learn back our original languages, and rediscover our own spirits.

From Haiti to Hayward: The Myth of the Orphan and Education

The herstory of oppression of children and youth begins with the racist, classist herstory of the orphan (see Chapter 8). For hundreds of years from the Americas to Australia, missionaries targeted native children as a key element of their assault on indigenous cultures and languages.

In Australia, Canada, and the US, children were stolen from their families to enable forced skkkooling—which meant abuse, rape, harassment, and cultural genocide—through the "boarding school" system. In what is now Canada alone, there were over 50,000 indigenous children stolen, murdered, and disappeared–seized and stolen from their families and forced into these so-called "schools," where they were not only disappeared, but raped, murdered, and trafficked into sex slavery by the missionary priests.

To write about these atrocities, which took place under the guise of institutional education, is to pray and cry and scream in pain off the page. So I want to take a moment of textual silence to hold these millions of children in our hearts and hands.

The blurred lines between kolonizer, killer, caregiver, and educator has always been present in the child-stealing/fostering/adoption industry (see Chapter 7). In the days of the trans-Atlantic slave trade, a portion of the money made from that murderous project was used to build and fund the early orphanages in Liverpool, England. These homes were filled with impoverished children of Irish descent, whose parents were sold on a chance at hegemony, through formal education meted out to them as a form of charity.

I recently heard the tale of a missionary group who set up shop in a small village in Nicaragua. They spent several thousand dollars and a huge amount of local resources building a state-of-the-art school. After the group built it and tried to get students to enroll, no one in the community could afford the tuition. So with the mystical gift of institutional education as their carrot and rationale, the missionaries offered free tuition to the local families if they would send their children to come and live at the school. The local families agreed, seeing this as a good deal. Suddenly, this town had hundreds of children which this group billed to the outside world as "orphans." They were seen as providing benevolent care, board, and education.

Akkademia Exists Because of Poverty Scholarship

Akkkademia has been built on collecting facts to support the domination of poor peoples, to keep us in our oppressed space. As far as the ruling class is concerned, the stories, traditions, cultures, art, and problems of indigenous communities, people of color, and communities in poverty only exist in the so-called "canons" of academia if they have been exploited as products or subjects for research, thesis projects, and lectures. In fact, the act of naming, studying, and researching our issues; writing about our problems; calculating our poverty and lack of access into their industries, jobs, and schools; and fetishizing our cultures is what fills the hallowed halls of academic study.

Corporate-owned, Eurocentric education policies and mandates were one of the original causes of the Oaxacan teachers' strike in 2006. The strike eventually resulted in a large-scale attack by the Mexican government on the rights of the pueblo and a powerful poor-and working-class-led resistance to corporate media and corporate education. The teachers, who were conscious and "community-focused," with values rooted in indigenous ways, were striking for better pay and basic needs, and against the implementation of a scripted curriculum that washed pre-Columbian indigenous peoples' history out of the required texts given to elementary and secondary grades. An almost identical version of this same scripted curriculum was pushed on US elementary students with the implementation of No Child Left Behind (Alive). It included a demand that parents must agree to have their children's information released to military recruiters in order to receive an education.

And what is equally ironic is there is very limited access for our children to enter into their kkkolleges, universities, and subsequent jobs. From the rise in tuitions, to the growing racism, classism, criminalization, po'lice brutality, and budget genocide in our K-12 education systems. From our high school programs which have more po'lice presence than well-paid or experienced teachers, to scripted curriculums with no more social studies, writing programs, history, or PE, who would want to go to school? But if you skip school you are summarily put in jail or swallowed up into underground economic strategies.

What academia doesn't understand is they don't exist without us. Or maybe they very clearly understand this and that is why they keep us far away from genuine resource-sharing. What if academics were barred from launching studies about our issues, what if critical theorists no longer had our "trends" and "problems" to mull over? What if anthropologists no longer had our art and culture to steal and deconstruct, what if the investigating, researching, and quantifying were replaced with engagement, inclusion, and sharing?

There are many examples of "benevolent" akkkademic theft:

A $75,000 grant to Stanford University, to study the impact of increased drop-out rates of poor black and brown high school students.

How about giving the $75,000 to the leeched budgets of schools whose programs have been destroyed by budget genocide, to the neighborhoods whose recreation programs are no longer there, to create jobs for the families who are constantly struggling to care for their young people, to jobs for the youth who are personally experiencing the set-up?

$500,000 to fund a center to study poverty

What about $500,000 to pay rent for a year for several families in poverty facing eviction or foreclosure, or medicine for poor elders and children?

Billions of dollars to create endowments and build museums to hold stolen art, culture, ancestors.

What about giving the stolen art, information, money, and resources to the indigenous peoples from whom it was stolen?

Ultimately, these industries and institutions were created so that wealthy white people can not only control thinking and action in order to keep their accumulated wealth in place, but also so they have something to do: jobs, parties, goals, activism, and interesting "problems" to write about, think about, work on, and "solve," while little bits of our stolen resources are meted out and thrown back at us.

Organic Intelligence: José Carlos Mariátegui

VINIA R CASTRO / MAYAN, GHETTO SKOLA
REPRINTED WITH PERMISSION FROM *DECOLONIZER'S GUIDE TO A HUMBLE REVOLUTION*, POOR PRESS

"We do not want, certainly, that socialism in Latin America be carbon copy. It must be a heroic creation. We must inspire our own reality, our own language, an Indian American socialism." —JC MARIÁTEGUI

Jose Carlos Mariátegui was born in 1894 into a poor family headed by a single mother in Perú. He was considered an influential thinker in Latin America who influenced Ché Guevara and others. At a young age he suffered an accident which left him disabled and caused excessive health problems for the rest of his life. He began to work at the age of 14 to help support his family and pay for his medical bills. He did not receive a "proper" education as defined by the system; he did not finish secondary school and did not attend college, but rather focused his energies in learning through his own means from his community and elders who taught him about social struggles throughout Latin America and Perú.

His work at a newspaper publisher led him to learn about media and writing. He mingled with left-leaning thinkers and developed an affinity for political thought. A pragmatic thinker, he used very simple wording to express complex political ideas, a first for many intellectuals, which made his writings very accessible. In 1920, he was deported to Europe by the Peruvian government because of his broad appeal. In Europe, he deepened his socialist and left-leaning ideals.

It was here where Mariátegui moved away from other "intellectuals" and political theorists. He did not believe that there is a specific mold or method to create social, political, and economic change. He believed that each community needs to define itself and make change for themselves through their own means. Mariátegui was significantly influenced by Quechua Indigenous thought, and he named his newspaper *Amauta* ("teacher" in Quechua). His theory was not confined to a school or dogma but rather in conversations with his communities because the reality is that not all people in Latin America had the privilege of an education because of poverty or disability. He was the living example of not having that privilege and still was capable of becoming one the most influential thinkers still relevant to Latin America to this day.

Zapatista Autonomous Education

Education is crucial to the struggle of the indigenous Zapatista Army of National Liberation (EZLN, in its Spanish initials) in Chiapas, Mexico. Rather than relying on poor-quality government-provided education, they have created their own education system. Their autonomous schools are rooted in their own language and culture and include education about their own history and how to care for their land.

These schools are free and open to all ages and all people. There is no competition; learning is a shared, collective experience. The schools are staffed by volunteer "education promoters," who earn no wage but are usually given food and shelter by the community. In these intergenerational schools, even young children are viewed as having knowledge to share.

Education is based on the needs of the community.

"All this is undertaken despite seemingly overwhelming odds: grinding poverty, no resources or equipment, and increasingly, direct attacks conducted with total impunity aimed at breaking the will to resist and thereby destroy the entire movement," writes Jessica Davies in a profile of the Zapatistas' education system for upsidedownworld.org.[10]

The People's Schools vs. Factory Schools

"The choice is oppression or liberation." —RGB STREET SCHOLAR

The schools of the people are many. They exist in our own homes, at our kitchen tables, in the donut shops, lavenderías, prayer circles, diners, barber shops, park benches, public buses, subways and cabs, parks, basketball courts, karate and kung fu studios, fútbol fields, boxing rings, shelter beds, out of our elders' and mentors' mouths, and many digital streets often un-traveled and rarely google-found.

Our Peoples Teachers, rarely seen as teachers, are living and speaking and teaching as mamaz and daddys and uncles and aunties and grandmothers and grandfathers and friends.

But sadly, so many of our most powerful Peoples Teachers are lost, their lessons silenced from classrooms and students by plantation prisons, plantation skools, plantation jobs, and plantation housing, all created as age-separated, language-stolen, scholarship-humiliated spaces. Our youth skolaz languish in childcare centers away from us. Our elders waste away their deep and long-studied-for skolarship in elder ghettos known as "old peoples' homes." And so many of our students and teachers are criminalized and incarcerated by Jim Crow laws, ugly laws, racist and anti-poor people laws, enforced by occupying armies known as po'lice.

All of this has made our organic forms of teaching like talk-story, story-tellers, and herstory-making rare, replaced by the beginning of corporate story-selling. Our youth are no longer working to feed their families and caring for their elders and siblings, practicing eldership, learning math through gardening, patience, love and spirit through sweeping. Instead they are learning and practicing through what they see and hear on television, in video games, and on the internet or their phones. The disembodiment comes early, introduced through the over-work and over-stress of our indigenous parents in corporate-defined labor where the perfect worker is the mobile worker, who has no ties, no connections, and no responsibilities. This perfect worker must be away from their children, working for someone else's capitalist agenda, watching someone else's child.

Our children become fodder for a giant plantation/factory skool where they are encouraged to fall through the (always-there) cracks and become part of the prison industrial complex, full of useless "lessons" learned through corporate ad campaigns full of fetishizing images, teaching everything you should never be taught about sex, relationships, love, selfishness, and angst. When we aren't in the institutions of higher learning, we are encouraged to waste hours of our time in the digital streets, in front of computers, televisions, game equipment, and phones.

A group of children at a school run by the Zapatista Army of National Liberation (EZLN) in Chiapas, Mexico stand in a group together, many with one hand in the air and their faces partially masked. This photo is from a Zapatista press release.

163

Long ago, without being exactly sure when or how, we were collectively sold away from our community teachers by the lie of advancement: everything will make us faster, prettier, healthier, cuter, handsomer, and above all richer. Even the way we learn is sold to us through its expediency. How fast we can get the papers enabling us to do things that in all ancient cultures would take decades to accomplish. Medicine in all indigenous cultures is an art as well as a science. It is love and care-giving, it is thought and a felt-sense and just because you do real well on math or science tests does not grant you the access to it. You must become part of a culture, ask permission and then still, if granted and trusted, spend years in mentorship with an elder who has practiced this same art.

It is why we have scientists, doctors, dentists, and nurses only willing to doctor, teach, investigate, and think for money. It is why we have scientists that "experiment" in eugenics and create seeds that steal from indigenous peoples and poison children and destroy Pachamama. Teach law students to convict innocent people and facilitate the stealing of homes and lives. The unholy relationships between Monsanto & akkkademia, Bill Gates and public skkkools and Coca Cola and high school campuses are all logical within a system that steals, rapes, and exploits, rather than feeds, protects, and cares for.

But our Peoples Teachers are everywhere. They are created in the tradition of the Zapatistas, PeopleSkool/Escuela de la gente @ POOR Magazine, University of the Poor with the Kensington Welfare Rights Union, Ron Casanova, the 50/50 Crew, Willie Baptist and the work of the Poverty Initiative, Vandana Shiva and Navdanya, The Living Tongues Institute, Manzil,[11] Blackademiks & the RBG Street Scholar, home-schools with mothers and fathers everywhere, sitting on corners with elders, in sweat lodges, drum circles, and in prayer with elders and Pachamama.

Escuela de la gente/PeopleSkool

We as landless, poor, street-skooled, hard-knock-edumakated, indigenous liberators and poverty skolaz launched the PeopleSkool/Escuela de la gente in the General Assistance (welfare) office and in shelters, in the doorways and in community rooms inside of plantation (project) housing in San Francisco and Oakland. From society's point of view we were the "homeless" people, the illiterate, mentally challenged, deaf and dumb, retards, learning disabled, and/or crazy. We were the clients, the target population, the great underserved. But we knew that we were the teachers, the writers, the media-makers, the lecturers, the experts, and the scholars. *We* should be heading up "institutes" on poverty, racism, incarceration.

Our challenge as educators was similar to our challenge as media-producers: was the teaching by lived skolaz "legitimate"? Could a learning institute that overtly named un-formally educated peoples with advanced degrees from the skool of hard knocks actually be considered a skool?

We poverty skolaz used the "legitimacy" of our paper magazine and my ability as a word hustler to set up PeopleSkool as a "welfare-to-work" program for poverty skolaz (see Chapter 3). This gave us the boost to get an office large enough to hold our indigenous news-making circles, Community Newsroom, and class space for our first incarnation of PeopleSkool. Many times we tried to attain "accreditation" from the Western Association of Schools and Colleges, and at one point we got really close. But the powers that be were not in our favor.

For the two years we had a "skool" that taught radio and online and video journalism to mamaz and daddys in poverty who were allegedly transitioning off of the man's tiny crum into the bright world of "work." Under the overseer's watchful eye, we kicked so much political, spiritual, and power-FUL ass that we began to be taken very seriously as a threat. At the end of the two years, they were so shaken by our ability to facilitate the skolaship of so many intentionally silenced poverty skolaz that they pulled ALL of their funding in a horrible Salem Witch Trial sort of "Inquisition." Their excuse was that we were unwilling to abide by the overseer's demands for "reporting." In other words, that we didn't kick out people who didn't show up on time, every time, for class. Lateness, sickness, and crisis are privileges not granted to poor people depending on the plantation for crums.

Of course we didn't go away. In and out of our own houselessness and organizational and personal poverty, we continued skooling together with poverty skolaz By Any Means Necessary.

We are VERY clear that we are not teaching on top of the skills people already have, but rather facilitating their existent deep scholarship through the confusing world of the witemanology and linguistic domination that is used on so many peoples of color and indigenous peoples to keep us silent and submissive.

What we do teach each other is that we are poverty skolaz. That we are not defined by our need for housing, for clothes, for food, for a job, for childcare, counseling, or a crum. That we have much to teach, speak about, and preach about. That we hold skolarship that no one can take away from us, and that we need to take it back.

We focus on sharing multiple forms of media and storytelling as that is a tool for us to be heard. To use the witeman-created tools and words for our survival and as a resistance tool against them. And to heal ourselves from so many lies and myths. But we also teach our own herstories and histories, we teach back our stolen cultures and spirits and languages and problem-solving. We teach each other how to love and care for each other, decolonized and without the kolonizer in our lives. This is the hardest of all because we are all still on the tit of the "man."

THE PHOENIX

WRITING TO REGENERATE COMMUNITY

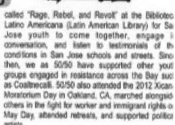

5050 CREW

Winter 2012

OUR VISION

We envision a world where communities are self-determined, where many worlds and cultures flourish, and where we look after the well being of ALL forms of life. A world where our lives are liberated from oppression and domination and where the people we love do not have to die in order to live.

The world we envision is created by nurturing our relationships and our commons. This means we build community and keep it alive through our lands, the wisdom and culture of our elder generations, and sharing our knowledge using our languages and voices.

It is created through trust, respect, and caring which will heal, nurture, and strengthen our spirits and our work. And also created by walking with our struggles together ready to fight while using the power of our dignity to create change.

Our role as 50/50 crew is to engage with youth and families in the South Bay to reclaim commons and build spaces of cultural practice, learning and action. We engage some of this work through workshops, talking circles, encounters, learning to be well, and political action. We believe that our humble contributions will help manifest the world we envision.

We came together as 50/50 Crew because we saw a need for change in our community. Each one of us has a purpose and a desire to transform our dreams/vision into a reality. We can no longer wait for change to come. We have to resist and fight to create change now. It is not only the duty of 50/50 to work towards the world that we envision, but it is a vision that wish to share with future generations.

50 / 50

We came together as a collective in the summer of 2010 when a group of young people came together due to their frustrations with youth non-profit programs, and college organizations in San Jose, California. The collective wanted to help build a space where youth could come together, learn from each other, and take action towards injustice in society. At the same time, we envisioned a group where power and duties would be shared equally across all members, or as we said, "50/50". As a collective, we started to create and facilitate workshops at youth centers and local high schools to get other young people involved. At this point, people started calling us "50/50 Crew." In the Spring of 2011, 50/50 started to do "Know your Rights" workshops at Gardner community center and supporting youth in their actions to keep the community center open. 50/50 kept facilitating various workshops across San Jose including a movie showing of the Hollywood drama "Panther," which is a film about the rise and history of the political Black Panther Party for Self-Defense. In the summer of 2012, 50/50 held a political kick back

called "Rage, Rebel, and Revolt" at the Biblioteca Latino Americana (Latin American Library) for San Jose youth to come together, engage in conversation, and listen to testimonials of the conditions in San Jose schools and streets. Since then, we as 50/50 have supported other youth groups engaged in resistance across the Bay such as Coatnecalli. 50/50 also attended the 2012 Xican Moratorium Day in Oakland, CA, marched alongside others in the fight for worker and immigrant rights on May Day, attended retreats, and supported political artists.

Across the Bay and the world, through our actions we have been spreading the message that "We Are Not Criminals, We Are Youth In Resistance". Our current action is the creation of this newsletter to document our experiences, stories, struggles, and to let our voices be heard. We hope to spread our stories about the neglect, abuse, and criminalization of youth that takes place in city streets, schools, and oppressive institutions across the Bay so we can mobilize everyone to get involved in the fight for a dignified and respectful life for all.

THE WORD

An East San Jose High School Practicing Prison Politics

I pulled into the parking lot at Andrew Hill High School as the bell rang for class to end. I noticed a regular commotion of students walking to and from class but there did seem to be an intensity different from other days. I stood around to make sure everything was cool. Sure enough, the bell rang for class to start and all students went to class. It seemed that nothing was going on, and I went about my business. A few days later, a student of mine informed me that he got cited by campus police for what supposedly went on during that passing period. The student received a citation for conspiring to start a fight, even though no actual fight occurred (there was a stare down but the student explained he did not want to get in trouble so there was no fight). The student asked that I go with him to speak with the assistant principal at the school about the whole situation as my voice as a staff member may offer some validity to his statement that there was no fight. The student explained the situation to the assistant principal who explained to him that the only way they could void his citation was if he ratted out anyone that brought drugs or weapons to campus. The staff

member said "you have to do something for us if you want us to do something for you." Essentially, the staff member was bargaining the student's induction into the justice system. The student did not want to get into any problems with his peers so he just took the citation.

This story shows what undoubtedly happens often at our schools. Administrators have the power to apply solutions that would create a more united student body, but they don't. Instead they create solutions like suspensions, snitching, and citations, which result in more divisions and feed into the criminalization of youth. At the end of the day, these administrators only find out what happened and what led up to the fight rather than working to actually resolve and prevent a future incident not only in the school but in the community. They abuse their power because they try to manipulate students to snitch against their own peers and punish them for not cooperating in reproducing more divisions. Ultimately this process neglects the reasons why students might engage in a stare down or see violence as solution. What is even worse is that we trust these adults with the well being of our youngsters but their priority is not the true well being of the youth, but rather exercising a quick fix to a problem through manipulation, punishment, and criminal citation.

The cover page from The Phoenix, *a publication of the 50/50 Crew. The logo of the paper is a line drawing of a phoenix rising out of flames.*

We teach each other how to heal through art and writing and liberation from the deadly pain of so many years of current and ancestral destruction of our souls, spirits, peoples, and cultures.

We also teach each other to be teachers and begin to realize that we have so much already in us to teach. The first thing I have to do is help people recognize that our teaching tools aren't rooted in formal education mandates of what makes a teacher.

In 2006, me and my sister JewnBug launched the Family Project at POOR Magazine to provide arts and social justice-based curriculum to all the children of the mama and daddy skolaz who came to Peopleskool. We run a multi-generational classroom which teaches through practice indigenous notions of eldership, social and racial justice, ancestor honoring, and family togetherness which are never taught in factory skools. In 2013, we expanded into a K-12 liberation skool at Homefulness called Deecolonize Academy.

The children's curriculum includes the same decolonizing lessons we teach/share with our mamaz and papaz: that there is no shame in houselessness, poverty, eviction, and displacement, but rather there should be shame among the people that perpetrate it. We honor and reacquaint young people with their own natural instinct to care for and love their communities and their families. Older children take on leadership roles as Youth Elders, acting as co-teachers in the classroom setting.

We teach classes like Revolutionary Construction, which began with each child writing, drawing, and talking about their own family's stories of eviction and houselessness. Then they attended and reported on actions in support of families suffering the massive gentrification impacting poor families of color in San Francisco. They interviewed legislators proposing legislation to protect children in eviction proceedings in San Francisco. The class culminated with them learning about the vision of Homefulness and then building a scale model which included all of their own beautiful ideas and perspectives, including The Michael Jackson Memorial Sweat Lodge.

Since our inception us poverty skolaz have taught hundreds of classes: Criminalization of Poverty, Philanthro-Pimping #101, Racial Profiling, Fighting Ellis Act Evictions, Learning Back our Indigenous Roots, Indigenous Removal, Border Fascism, CPS, Mestizaje Culture, Healing from Plantation Diseases, and the United Nations Declaration on the Rights of Indigenous Peoples.

Before each semester of PeopleSkool begins I take all of us poverty, migrante, indigenous, race, elder, youth and disability skolaz through a 4- to 6-week teacher prep where we create a curriculum based on our own experiences. Then we write, produce, and direct 6-8 Theatre of the POOR presentations, focused around one central theme that each skolar sprouts into their own individual theatre learning presentation.

Mentees in PeopleSkool

"Non-profit, don't get no profit, Nine to five ain't got no time." —LEROY MOORE

We do teach people who have gone through the man's skool to begin to un-learn the lies they were taught and re-learn the knowledge of the people. These students are considered "mentees"[12] who are well-versed, success-fully propagandized, bred and/or raised on witemanology. These are usually the peoples with skin and/or class privilege who have parents or family who operate within the plantation system and benefit by its oppression. They may have access to trust funds or support that comes—even if indirectly—to them. They are young folks who have been raised on the desire of becom-ing the land-stealers and money hoarders, because that is the only model offered to people to thrive in this Amerikkklan system. They have been taught that the goal to accomplish in life is your own singular, self-centered happiness or success. They have been taught the cult of independence.

We teach people of all colors with class privilege who are coming to us as mentees that they have the privilege of an organized life. Of some-one who has watched over you and taken care of you, fed you and clothed you and done the subtle things never spoken about to ensure that you are focused and relaxed in skool. That you aren't worried about the three thousand things that work to confuse, undermine, and terrify poor children and poor families every day.

To be clear, if you are a person with race, class and/or educational privilege, you don't become a poverty skola just because you go through a semester or even several years of PeopleSkool. Poverty Skolaship, just like race, disability, indigenous, im/migrant, or elder skolaship, only comes from experiencing ableism, poverty, racism, migration, border fascism, etc.

We don't give you a piece of paper "accredited" by a formal institution, or sanctioned by supervisor, with a series of letters and periods on it (MD, Phd, MA AA, BA). What you do with us doesn't necessarily lead to a job, and the work here is not considered an "internship." You are instead considered a "mentee," or simply a student with much to learn.

But to "graduate" from PeopleSkool with a GD or GS (Good Daughter or Good Son honor), you need to become just that: a good daughter or son, demonstrating your ability to care, respect and love your blood family and extended family, respect and honor and take care of your spirit, your ancestors, and your community with humility. To practice reparations and empathy as a Community Reparator, because your family and/or ancestors benefit from race and class privilege or you continue to right now. To share the linguistic-domination skills and hyper-technological multi-media skills you were blessed enough to learn, practice, and fine-tune. The skills came

Children of many ages listen to two children who are standing at a mic performing. JewnBug, sitting with the kids, is leading the Family Project at POOR Magazine, providing arts and social justice-based curriculum to all the children of the mama and daddy skolaz at Peopleskool.

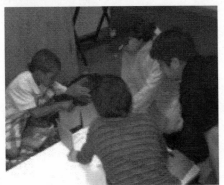

BOTTOM LEFT TO RIGHT: *Four children are gathered around a box of supplies, with older kids helping a younger kid. Youth elders lead children's curriculum at PeopleSkool. A child is learning music at PeopleSkool, focusing on playing a small guitar while sitting on a man's lap.*

to you because your family helped you though life, providing food, secure shelter, healthcare, clothes on your back and shoes on your feet. They may have provided love and time with your homework and skool navigation so you could fill out endless applications and jump through akkkademik hoops. You could sit relaxedly in classes "learning," not worrying about where your next meal would come from and if you were going to have a safe home that night.

A mentee can practice reparations as a media facilitator, practicing co-authorship, non-voyeuristic media advocacy. Reparations can mean sharing your resources and time and clear organizational skills. If you have a law degree, or just the strength to make calls and fight with systems, you can be a revolutionary legal advocate or revolutionary care-giver. Or an artist who actively resists gentriFUKation by making space for poor artists' work. Or a revolutionary doctor or nurse or dentist who dedicates 50-100 percent of your practice to caring for people for free, not paid by any NGO or NPIC or any harmful or allegedly-good body, but just in the community or behind

Original art for POOR Magazine/Decolonewz by Poverty Skola/ Poet. Revolutionary Artist and Media producer Jose VIllareal—hand—drawn while he was incarcerated in the SHU -Secured Housing Unit aka Solitary Confinement at Pelican Bay Plantation (Prison) Jose VIllareal (who was recently released) can be heard weekly on PNN-KEXU 96.1fm radio (www.poormagazine/org/radio) and is also the founder of Aztlan Press. Right: "POWER" by Anthony Sul (Ohlone), another cover image for Decolonewz.

graphic by: Anthony Sul

To submit a story , poem, photograph or art or
become a community reporter for Decolonewz,
please come to Community Newzroom which
meets on the 1st Tuesday of every month at
POOR Magazine at Homefulness-
8032 BlackArthur (MacArthur Bl)
Deep East Ohlone Land (Deep East Oakland)
in the back house Free healthy meal,
child care and translation provided.

Thanks to Diallo McLinn and Tiny
for layout and design of this second issue.

171

plantation walls. Or an activist who moves with humility and does not per-petrate more "well-intentioned" activation. Or a social worker who actually listens to his or her clients and makes sure that he or she leads with, stands with, and works alongside poverty skolaz without the Eurocentric notions of boundaries and separation and criminalization.

The Angst Factor

One of Mama Dee's most important sets of "required readings" are a series of films taught at PeopleSkool: *Real Women Have Curves, Daughter of Danang,* and *Rabbit-Proof Fence.* In *Real Women Have Curves,* the young Xicana daughter of a Mexican family living in Los Angeles is lured away from her mama's very hard education, her father's love, and her sister's indigenous micro-business. She is lured by the simplicity of "I" away from the compli-cation of "we," lured to the institutional "safety" of legitimacy and success, away from the messiness and confusion of community herstory, relation-ships, family, work, time, and love.

For this young woman, the luring began in busing her to the almost-all-wite Beverly Hills High School, where she was taught by an already-in-the-system Xicano teacher. She was hit with wite-peer pressure (like my Mama Dee was) that fueled her desire go to an akkkademik institution as far away from her family as possible. And she fine-tuned an "angst" and disrespect of her elders as their sometimes patriarchal or straightforward lessons appeared too "simplistic" in contrast to the complicated other-ness of the institution. The angst, disrespect, and disgust of all things indigenous to your family and community is necessary so that when the "gift" of ac-cess to their education is meted out through scholarships, it is begged for, dreamed of, sacrificed for. In the end, this means being lost to your own communities' love, vision, and understanding forever.

When we teach mentees to unlearn their multiple kolonized lessons as students at PeopleSkool, it begins with un-learning the lie of angst and educational productivity. It means unlearning the idea that if you create enough papers on enough subjects having nothing to do with you or your family, you achieve this "grade" of excellence. Unlearning the lie that the further the subjects and the projects are from you and yours, the more important "the work" is.

This angst and subsequent separating of children from their families and communities enables the other crucial lesson of akkkademia: the les-son of individualism, individuation, selfishness, self-centered actions. This produces the perfect capitalist consumer with all the elements of a future gentrifier and Ikea shopper. It produces people who become complicit in

A row of young white "mentees" watch and listen to two poverty skolaz performing in PeopleSkool.

age-separatism, ghettoizing their own elders in homes and children in age-separated schools and child-care institutions.

The Empathy Exercise/Crisis Dialogue

All lessons in PeopleSkool begin with what we call the empathy exercise/crisis dialogue. It serves several purposes. The first is to show that all people, wherever they are from, have experienced crisis. This enables the beginning of empathy in privileged people. It begins to dismantle the labels put on us poverty skolaz, which intentionally silence Peoples Teachers, turning them into clients in need of saviors and sympathy.

The second is it begins to unravel the deep shame that all us po' folks walk with, which tells us that we should be ashamed for our poverty, disability, incarceration, and oppression. It tells us that instead of being proud of the struggle we have survived, we should be embarrassed, that we have accomplished nothing if we have no alphabet behind our name. This shame fuels hegemony and is a crucial aspect of the hustle of akkkademia and capitalism because it has the effect of making indigenous peoples hate what they came from and desire what the perpetrators have.

The third is to clearly establish who holds poverty skolaship. What it is and how it is legitimate and necessary in the production of media, research, and activism on poverty. And how that poverty skolaship leads to our motto: *the revolution begins with I and then becomes WE.* This dictates the perspective of ALL of our truth-based media and revolutionary advocacy.

PeopleSkool vs. Institutional Knowledge

PeopleSkools's teaching helps people begin to unravel the lie of institutional knowledge production and domination. First and foremost, this unraveling happens by challenging who the teacher can be, what learning itself can be, and who it is for. Secondly, it happens by rooting the knowledge production, creation, and benefit in the community and family. Throughout the institutional learning experience an immense amount of time is spent, emotional equity is lost, and hoops are jumped through for the sake of the teacher, the counselor, or just the requirements themselves, which seem to take on an odd life of their own. Studies and tests and exams and presentations under the guise of learning. And yet who does it benefit? How much pesticide-free, GMO-free food could be grown in the pursuit of a good grade on an exam on agriculture? How much social justice could be attained in the study of social justice? How many indigenous languages could be decolonized from colonizer languages in the study of linguistics?

It is true that through the push-back by peoples of color and indigenous peoples in the '60s and '70s, through movements like the Third World Majority at San Francisco State University, University of California Berkeley, and other movements across the country there are now powerful ethnic studies programs in universities that provide students with exposure to mentors and thinkers that challenge wite supremacy and the dominant paradigm. They give students access to Black Studies, La Raza Studies, Native American Studies, and the like. These programs are often fighting for their lives within the different institutions, but they do a lot to help the beginning of the decolonization of students of color and wite students.

Anthropology, Ethnography, Psychology: The Study About Us Without Us

City and community colleges and adult schools are beautiful resistance movements for students in poverty. Schools like City College of San Francisco and Laney College in Oakland saved this poverty skola's life, not because of the classes, but because of the community-based support networks that were allowed to thrive on these working-class peoples' campuses: groups for houseless vets, single mamaz and daddys, gender- and culture-based organizing and self-actualization. And it's no wonder that the corporations are trying to kill them now, because there is money to be made selling poor and working-class peoples on "skool" and career options rather than truly enabling peoples to learn, think and grow without a capitalistic agenda.

Deconstructing Our Struggle While Our Communities are Dismantled and Left in Rubble

But the reality is that most of the work that is done within academia is done by researching, photographing, or studying poor peoples, indigenous peoples, and their sacred communities. It's often done to the detriment of the communities being studied or photographed. So the student not only acts in an exploitive manner to the peoples they are endlessly studying or stealing from, but also, their work never benefits the their own families or communities or ancestors.

And then you have people of color in akkkademia taking part in the "industry" of knowledge. The grant pimps, the fellowship pimps, the plantation pimps, perpetrating for the sole act of holding up the institution and never actually taking part in the resistance of their indigenous communities. There is a fine line that must be spoken about here where the peoples of color professors and fellows and akkkademiks need to do the jobs to get paid, to support their families, to be good daughters and sons. But then somehow they make the leap into pure emptyakkkademia, no longer in touch with their fellow indigenous survivors of false borders and plantation walls and anthro-wrongology and psychology.[13]

Who does the picture-taking and story-making and who gives the tests?

Within the "walls" of the PeopleSkool we resist this trend with The PeoplesTest and Community GiveBack.

The Peoples Test

Please write/tell a story, write a song, dance, orcreate a chant that is respectful and inclusive of your elders and ancestors' knowledge, makes your mama, father, tíos y/o tías smile, entertains and teaches your sisters and brothers and community's children.

> *You will have full access to all of the crucial tools needed for this project:*
>
> - *Drum*
> - *Two drums*
> - *Other drums and sound makers*
> - *Your body*
> - *The knowledge and teaching and love gifted to you by your families, elders, and communities*

I created The Peoples Test as a way to redirect the time, knowledge, energy, and spirit used to create a thesis, complete the final exams, pass the quizzes, and labor over dissertations required by formal institutions of learning back into the families, communities and ancestors upon whose shoulders the students are standing. We use the Peoples Test when we are invited into academia to present our poverty skolaship as a challenge to the minds of the propagandized as part of a Theatre of the POOR/Race, Poverty and Media Justice Institute.

Community Give-Back Contract

When Mentees enroll in PeopleSkool we explain to them that, unlike institutes of formal learning, we don't practice voyeuristic learning, masturbatory thinking, or exploitative studying. Mentees, like our family of poverty skolaz, are now family of POOR Magazine, and they are forever in our hearts and minds, and our lives are forever entwined. Just because they graduate from PeopleSkool doesn't mean our relationship is suddenly over and our commitments to each other are over. To be good family members to their POOR Magazine family we ask, among other things, that their work no longer perpetrate voyeuristic, fakely objective media or hierarchal institutional service provision. That they carry our poverty skolarship curriculum into the akkkademik channels they have access to and that they understand their roles in society as care-givers, facilitators, community reparators, and co-authors. And similarly, after they receive our decolonizing education about their families and communities, the give-back contract needs to articulate their commitments of eldership, love, and angst-free caregiving to their own families, with "extra credit" given for mentees who commit to moving home with their families.

One of the most power-FUL and difficult lessons each mentee learns is how to decolonize their minds from the neverending and hard-to shake lessons of capitalist separation, angst, hate, and disrespect. Their own complicit acceptance of these values enables the many destructive processes of the capitalist machine, including gentriFUKation, ghettoization, criminalization, racism, and poverty.

So, one of the most powerful ways that they can demonstrate the PeopleSkool-attained knowledge is by learning to love their own families again. The second and not-as-easy job is to help their own elders unlearn their deep colonization that is perhaps as strong as, if not stronger than, their own. This requires an ongoing process of community and family connectedness, love, involvement, and presence.

Tha' Gee-E-40-Dee

DR. G.S. POTTER

In Seattle, the King County Jail gives out more GED's through their educational program than the community college system does through theirs. In Seattle, over 80 percent of the incarcerated population is people of color, even though we represent only 8-9 percent of the general population. Having grown up in a family of multiple colors and cultures that bobbed between working and under class status, I don't have to read a book to tell me that intelligence has nothing to do with educational achievement and even less to do with whether or not the racist system has put you behind bars.

At the time I was teaching in the King County Jail, I was also teaching a subsection of a critical history of education class at the University of Washington. I often discussed the same topics with my students in the jail that I did with those in the towers. The skolaz would've wiped the floor with the scholars any day on any topic, but they didn't have the papers to prove it.

One of the reasons is because most forms of standardized testing are racist and classist. Most teachers gravitate towards strange methods that try to force students to ignore that fact and blame themselves for failure. This never made sense to me. I try to be honest with my students. And they make that very easy.

At the jail, the teachers had sample GED tests to use to work with students. One of the sample tests required students to read a jack frost poem and answer questions about it. One of the questions asked the students to describe the character of the man in the poem based on his actions. The action described was that the man bought an expensive piece of jewelry for his wife. The options were something like: a. Thoughtful. B. Thrifty. C. Selfish. D. Hardworking. The answer key indicated that the man was thoughtful. But every single student in my class answered "hardworking."

They were upset and argued that the book was wrong. And I would argue that they were absolutely correct. If you come from a white middle-class or upper-class background and know about cultural references like figgie pudding and gravy boats then perhaps the gift of jewelry would be nothing more than a thoughtful gesture. To my students, jewelry was a luxury. Many of them expressed wanting to give diamonds to their girlfriends and babies and mamas. But that to do so, they'd have to find 3 more jobs. So the guy that bought his wife some jewelry for the holidays must have been hardworking.

Again, I would argue that they were absolutely right.

The GED scoring machine would have marked them wrong. But then again, it's scoring a racist test. As a PhD candidate in Education Reform policy, I have spent years studying the methods used to keep people of color and the people in poverty from educational achievement papers, such as GED's and high school degrees. It's no secret that testing, among other things, has been used as a gate-keeping tool long before the Prussian system was adopted in the US in the late 1800s. The secret is, however, being honest with our students about that.

So I told them they were right. The test was classist. And their answers made perfect sense. But I also had to figure out a way for them to know that the test was set up to trick them, but also give them the strategies they needed to trick the system back.

In my opinion, jack frost had nothing on E-40 when it came to rhymes. And my students in the jail could run circles around my students in the towers when it came to poetry and hip hop. So I knew understanding the mechanics of poetry wasn't the problem. It was understanding the racist and classist references used in the GED test.

Once that was removed, we could really get into developing and understanding poetic content, structure, style and meaning. I created a GED test that used similar questions as the ones on the actual test, but I used E-40 lyrics and questions. Sometimes Tupac came in. I'd let my students pick who they wanted to decipher as time passed. Then we translated those concepts to the concepts on the GED test, openly admitting the whole time that we needed to LOOK for the racist and classist tricks so we wouldn't get caught by them.

"Happy To Be Here"
(E-40 feat. D.D. Artis)

[female singer - repeat in background]
I'm just happy to be here!   (1)

[E-40 over singer]

2 Feet stickin through my shoes, skid marks in my drawers (2)
Garage sales and flea markets, we never shopped at malls
No dental plan, no medikit - we poor like rain
Colored folks think that castor oil cures everything   (5)
Pork chops and chicken, we like our food fried
Hypertension, Prenavil pills and hydro-chlorizide
Some of my family still living, some of my family died
Health complications, natural causes and homicide
Just tryin to survive, nothin to lose but plenty to gain
Started hustlin, flea flickin and servin that candy cane
Put all my cars in my lady name, as a true hustler should
She had a 9 to 5, worked at Planned Parenthood
While I was in the hood, up to no good

with a hoodie over my head, tryin to outslick the feds
Or should I say cops, at this point in time I only had rocks
Went from a little a jelly jar up to a soup pot
The fast quarter my negro, don't want the slow nickel
I done seen yola the same color as peanut brittle
I done seen hella people relapse   (26)
I done seen my homey grandparents go back to crack
How sick is dat? Beggin my loved ones to send some pictures (28)
Pray for me over the phone and read me some scriptures

Which of the following describes the overall tone of
"Happy to be Here?"
a. anger
b. excitement
c. gratitude
d. hopelessness
e. frustration

In lines 26-28. How would you say E-40 feels about his homey's
grandparents going back on crack?

a. he is sickened by their inability to get sober
b. he blames them for his friend's struggle
c. he is shocked by the images of victimization he has witnessed
d. he is saddened that the elders in his community suffer from
   chronic substance abuse
e. he is scared that his family members will also relapse

Hard Lessons: The Education We ALL b Learning ALL the Time

*"Knowledge was inherent in all things. The world was a library and its books were
the stones, leaves, grass, brooks and the birds and animals that shared, alike with
us, the storms and blessings of the earth. We learn to do what only the student of
nature ever learns, and that is to feel beauty."*
—CHIEF LUTHER STANDING BEAR (1868–1939), OGLALA SIOUX

Hard lessons are the deep scholarship and theory we all have in our
barrios, streets, homes, shelters, gardens, prayers, songs—outside the
colonizer-launched institutions.

These are lessons that can be given, screamed, handed from yo
mamaz, daddys, abuelos, abuelas, aunties, uncles, children, friends, spiritual guides, mama earth, and ancestors. Here are some of those lessons,
as written by poverty skolaz:

Ingrid de Leon

I am Ingrid De Leon
Mother of four beautiful children
Daughter of Natividad and someone who in life was
David De Leon, a man that loved 48 years and left us
a 26 of November.

My parents have been a great example to follow, humble workers.
Poor but with honor.
I was only able to be with my father for a short time, I was only 10 years old, but I remember it very well.
Every night he went to my uncle's house, who is no longer with us either, when the darkness of the night covered all the land the dogs would bark loudly and then calmness. I could hear the steps saying "plash plash" as he got closer to our home in those nights that appeared deaf because of the silence.

He was always a strong man. My father always liked things done exactly right, he taught us to work fast and also taught us to leave things where they belong so when we need them again we won't be like chickens looking for their nest.

He also taught us to not grab anything that was not ours. He used to say, "If you have one cent extra you give it back."

Chanelle De Lovely

When I was young I wanted nothing more than to be a middle-class person. I hated my family and myself and people like us. I went to university with the plan that it was going to change me forever and I'd never be like my poor family again. No one would know where I came from because I'd learn to talk and think like middle-class people and I'd get to do all the things middle-class people do. Like be an asshole to cashiers and waitresses and sex workers.

I got scholarships and moved away and after four years of university, I realized it hadn't worked. I couldn't change enough to fit in with the bougie kids, but I had changed enough that my family didn't understand what the fuck I was talking about or doing (like grad school). The day I realized this, I pounded my desk in a fit of rage and tears, cursing myself and them and everyone at the same time. What the fuck had I done?

Ever since that day, I've been trying to unlearn all the messages I got that I was stupid and worthless for having been poor. Here are a few things I learned about academic "scholarship" from finally turning back to poor and working-class people and looking at them with respect.

1. Academia is so full of shit it runs through the hallways. 97 percent of academics know absolutely fuck all and the other 3 percent with lived experience scraped their way in and struggle to make space for their voices and ours. The 97 percent try to fool us into believing that lived experience is "subjective" and that being the *least educated person in the room* is "objectivity" and that these "objective" people are experts and experts should have all the power and privilege. How insulting. They can go fuck themselves.

2. Academia teaches you individualism and competitiveness, values that hurt us and our communities. Why, for example, can't your academic paper be written by more than one person? By you and your grandma? Why can't it be written by your community — or sung or performed? This is a world where feelings and experience can never be considered "evidence" and taken seriously, let alone hunches, visions, intuitions, lore, stories, poetry, art, or premonitions.

Leah Lakshmi Piepzna-Samarasinha

Shit or get off the pot.
There ain't no such thing as a free lunch.
You got one ticket to ride, so don't blow it.
And we're all going to die anyway, so you might as well go out like a
fucking meteor.

Those four phrases, along with *jeeeeeesus, mary and joseph*, were the ones I heard coming out of my mother's mouth my whole life (except my mama never said the f word). Can you tell my mama is a working-class-raised white lady from a rust belt town who grew up Irish/Polish Catholic and is a trauma survivor? I bet you can. ;)

My mama taught me to hustle. To always have a little money saved someplace that my husband didn't know about. To always have a couple of backup hustles in case I lost my regular job. To not trust social services. That the world is not just about me, so you think about how much space you take up, and you ask other people how they're doing, and you listen. That you either tip your waitress 20 percent or you don't go out to eat. You also stack your plates and bus your own table. That everybody was going to think I was shoplifting in stores, and how you held things up real high and never put them near your pockets for a minute until security relaxed. Two pairs of factory-outlet shoes a year are just fine, and you don't call long-distance, ever. Maybe ten minutes a couple times a year is okay. My mama had learned how to class-pass so she could sound bougie on the phone to the electric company and other places where appropriate, but she also understood and believed in the power of screeching, cussing out, venting, ranting, and going off.

Sometimes that shit was great, sometimes it was fucked-up and racist. My mama was a scared, white working-class lady in the racist-ass state of Massachusetts. But as her grown-up, mixed-race, mixed-class daughter, I live and heal from bringing my loud ass to sitting around a kitchen table or on a line or in a public bathroom with poor and working-class-raised femmes of color and white femmes. I bring my shit or get off the pot to discussions that have gotten kinda drawn-out and low-energy, where I go, okay, what exactly are we gonna do? And I know we're all gonna die and there's no telling how long this body is gonna last, so I might as well talk fast, wear bright colors, not fuck around or half step, so one day, when it's time for me to be an ancestor, I can go out like a fucking meteor.

Mesha Irizarry

* Listen to your Ancestors.
  Turn off the secular chatter in your brain, and their voices will come through loud and clear every day, and visit your dreams every night. They watch us constantly, and have our back.

* Turn off the ego and protect the village.
  There is no "I" without "us."
  The village is the leader, not me.

* My child Idriss Stelley taught me more than I could ever teach him. He taught me how to love, resilience, and revolution.

* Keep your friend close, and your enemy closer. Security culture has it that it is safer watching someone watching us, and feed them what we want to be reported to the poverty pimps, than kick them to the curb and be sent someone better trained at deception.

* Everyone is redeemable. If someone ran astray, and come back, embrace her or him again, as many times as it occurs.

* DO NOT CALL THE PO'LICE for petty shit. Sweat the small stuff through family council, only call the Po'Lice when a violent crime is in progress and getting in the middle would endanger your loved ones or get you killed.

Michael James

When I was growing up in the Western Addition back in the day when Rexall Drugs and liquor stores occupied the busy corner of Fillmore and McAllister, the men with the cleanest suits that I knew were *pimps* and *hustlers.*

And when we watched TV or read the newspapers, there would be pictures all of these well-dressed men (usually white men)—politicians, salesmen, and corporate front men, all talking with that assuredness, that smoothness, that twinkle in their eye. My mother, who always watched the news, would scoff at them: *"Hmph. Nothing but hustlers."* Many of us grew up learning to be *suspicious of men in beautiful suits.*

So-called *street sense* is not about understanding the rules of the street—it's about understanding that the *world is just a larger version of the street,* and the pimp game is operating from top to bottom. At the bottom it's more visible, more transparent. At the top, it's more disguised, more sophisticated, harder to penetrate. But in reality it's more dishonest, more raw, and more violent.

But what is also true in the street is that there is beauty, talent, brilliance, profound love, ingenuity, and a hunger for democracy. All of this is also visible and out in the open, because we have to live so much of our lives in the street. It is often our living room and our sanctuary.

Many people believe that if you are working-class or poor, you are not capable of reflection or any kind of critical thinking, because you are completely preoccupied with the grind of daily life. But when I was growing up back in the day (1953-1967), neighborhood people—most of whom had no college education—were constantly talking about deep things: nonviolence, civil rights, God and love, business and hustling, elections and Jim Crow. Even the wineheads on the corner were deep (at times they were the deepest). Not only did my parents and aunts and uncles—most of whom came up in theterrorist Southern States—have *consciousness,* they had a deep and complicated consciousness.

To be able to organize and provide for families with very little money, to be able to negotiate different job situations, sometimes all at the same time, to be able to establish a safe spiritual and psychological space for everyone—*these are practices that working and poor people put into effect every day.* The fact that we do it under the harshest circumstances indicates integrity, intelligence, resilience, and wisdom—qualities not generally characteristic of the privileged middle and upper classes.

Uncle Al Robles-Poet, Poverty Skola, Organizer, Ancestor member of the POOR Magazine family council (Board) and co-founder of the Manilatown Heritage Center. The Manilatown Heritage Center was launched after a herstoric 30 year long, landless peoples resistance to a devil-oper fueled eviction from the International Hotel in the Manilatown district of San Francisco. The beautiful resistance was led by Uncle Al, Uncle Bill Sorro and hundreds of very low-income Filipino and Chinese disabled elders supported by hundreds of community organizers refusing to be intimidated, silenced or dismantled by krapitalist, wealth-hoarding, land-stealers. Art by Carina Lomeli.

Hanging on to the carabao's tail — a poem of unity
AL ROBLES

*I have lived in the Manilatowns, Chinatowns and J-towns of America, in the ghettos
of bop city dreams, and soulsville loneliness & Fillmore Street blues crying the blues of
Big Mama Thornton—Bop City—listening to "All the things you are." I knew every
black, brown, yellow, red face.*

Sometimes my heart is Japanese
Sometimes my heart is Chinese
Sometimes my heart is Japanese
And Chinese at the same time
Sometimes my mind is Japanese
Sometimes my mind is Chinese
Sometimes my mind is Japanese
And Chinese at the same time
Sometimes my belly is Japanese
Sometimes my belly is Chinese
Sometimes my belly is Japanese
And Chinese at the same time
Sometimes my heart is hopi
Sometimes my heart is Navajo
Sometimes my heart is hopi
And Navajo at the same time
Sometimes my heart is black
Sometimes my heart is brown
Sometimes my heart is black
And brown at the same time
Sometimes my belly is black
Sometimes my belly is brown
Sometimes my belly is black
And brown at the same time
Sometimes my belly is Navajo
Sometimes my belly is hopi
Sometimes my belly is hopi
And Navajo at the same time
Sometimes my belly embraces all things
Swallowing black, brown, yellow, red
Belching up poems
Sometimes I am a water buffalo—
My tail wind-snapping
In the four corners of the world

Transportation Gentrifukation:
How a new Rapid Transit project (BRT)
is used to displace East Oakland

AN INTER-GENERATIONAL WeSearch PROJECT OF DEECOLONIZE ACADEMY

Editors Note: Youth and Family Skolaz at POOR Magazine submitted 14 FOIA's (Freedom Of Information Act) requests to 14 departments in the City-only to receive a series of messages from two of the departments saying "We have no documents". The WeSearch team created their own reports based on their own experiences and observations in their neighborhood and presented a demand to the City of Oakland and the Transit agency that these agencies support Oakland residents with the money they received from the "BRT" (Bus Rapid Transit) project as reparations for the millions of dollars they are receiving to displace low-income, working class communities of color out of Oakland.

The BRT
ZION

My sweet home is becoming a jungle of hell.

My home is fading away slowly, so slow people don't recognize it. Looking at homeless sisters and brothers on International Boulevard makes me think how they would feel with less sidewalks to rest on.

82nd street and International Boulevard; one side has clean, beautiful buildings. They use "power washing" to clean germs and sometimes to spray on homeless people to make them leave their neighborhoods There are dangerous chemicals in the "power-washing"

Investigating Bus Rapid Transit
AMIR CORNISH

The construction worker was wearing an orange and a bright yellow suit vest. When I saw the water sprayed on the payment where houseless folks were sitting it splashed like a water park pool party and hurt my heart. I was on the corner of International and 82nd Boulevard in Deep East Oakland, it was a construction site for Bus Rapid Transit and to create it they are slicing the streets in half in East Oakland.

My Oakland Home-Stolen
ZIAIR HUGHES

My home is being taken from me. They say Oakland is a beautiful place but why are our people on the boulevard streets?.

The police sprayed toxic water on the homeless people on International Boulevard. There is a store where the homeless people stay, it's like the world war 1. the police blocked off three lanes to build the B.R.T. (Bus Rapid Transit)

What is B.R.T? BRT is a government bus company, November the 7th we decided to go to the Oakland City council to deliver our FOIA's (Freedom of Information act) requests it was almost the end of class.We showed up at the Mayor's office.A lady that works at the Mayor's office asked," why are you here?" She was refusing to let us see the Mayor. We told her why we were there, to deliver our FOIA they made an excuse. so we would leave, so we gave them our FOIA, then 2 weeks after they said there were no documents.

Conclusion

As of the publishing of this youth and family WeSearch report The City of Oakland denied that they had any documents to all 14 of our FOIA requests even though ALL of the websites and Public Relations material state clearly that the City of Oakland is a funder to the billion dollar rail-line called the BRT.

In finality, the point we are making is the expansion of this transportation agency is directly leading to gentrification. We are seeing this happen in our neighborhood but it has happened before. 10 years ago in San Francisco, the T third street rail line otherwise known as the T-Line was opened, kicking out many people who lived on the intended route.

Oakland, following their example, is now mowing through our neighborhoods powerwashing houseless people and evicting housed people, many of whom have lived here their entire lives. This is just another excuse for the City of Oakland to kick out the actual residents of Oakland to make way for new, higher paying citizens.

I'm your patient, consumer client

*service resistant, difficult
and non-compliant*

whatever acronym

u can write it down in my PHAT file

I'm all those things u call me

*Every time u try to Case Mangle,
Anti-Social work & Non-profit off*

my broken poverty

— TINY

6

Liberating the Poor Body of Color from HELLthcare, Poverty Pimps, and Social Work

HELLthcare into Healing

The Pimp-Ho Philanthropy Stroll and Other Lies of Charity: Poverty Skolaz, Poverty Pimps, Philanthropy Pimps, and Community Reparations

Care-giving, comforting, talking, and being with used to be an integral part of healing. Doctoring, mending, and curing were all part of a whole process practiced by the person or persons who did the healing for a village or community. The process included all ills, mental and physical, spiritual and practical. Things we would associate with a trip to a psychologist such as depression and anxiety over a love lost or a family member's transition, a job lost or a cheating partner, would be as likely to be presented to the town healer as a fever or a broken leg.

The healing included rituals, ceremonies, prayers, chants, smoke, tea, oils, touch, the laying on of hands, and instructions. It is why in every indigenous community there are specific songs, chants, and dances that are prescribed and practiced in addition to a tincture, ointment, tea, salve, or syrup that address a multitude of problems as an integral part of any cure. And the birth of children or the transitioning of a family member or community elder is a many-part process of ceremony and ritual.

In the long, genocidal road to the capitalistic practice of incorporating everything, we began to corporatize care-giving. In addition to fixing wounds and healing our sick, basic things like caring enough for our children to make sure they aren't molested or abused; caring enough for our elders to make sure they aren't alone, un-washed, and hungry; caring for and loving our disabled skolaz in the ways they need; and talking to each other became industries and projects.

Mental, physical, and spiritual health were and are still enmeshed in most cultures, with a clear understanding (as they say in Chinese medicine) that these worlds are all integrated. Your heart's physical health can't thrive without your mental health, diet, and exercise in line, which is why in most Chinese communities no day begins without a city-wide exercise hour.

In the capitalizing of care, taking a pill, replacing an organ, and cutting into our bodies became the answers to all of our illnesses. All of our pain, sorrow, fear, and isolation became "fixable" through an industry that charged us for care, advice, and skills, as part of the corporatization of healing.

As part of the colonization of our human-ness, our care, our cures, and our medicine were colonized by Wite-science. Drastic, violent, and brutal experimentation on poor bodies and poor bodies of color "proved" that the only cure to our ills was this inhuman, disconnected, and monetary medicine, which birthed the medical industrial complex, Big Pharma, and subsequently the therapy industrial complex.

Wite-science could be shuttled in as the answer, the brilliant cure-all in all post-colonial societies across Pachamama as they other-ized the indigenous healers as witches and savages, as crazy and dangerous.

And then once our communities' healers were disregarded, society at large had no other options for healing but products. Wite doctors owned the right to cure, and subsequently, as they would say, "cornered the market." This brought on the rationing of care—"good medical care" versus poor people health care, based on a monetary system of access.

Similarly, they locked in their perspectives on healing, care-giving, loving, and sharing. As the Euro-centric therapy industrial complex took off, they began to further their agendas into parenting, elder-ship, skooling, and on and on.

In its brutal reign of terror under the guise of "research" Wite-Science perpetrated a multitude of medical apartheid[14] practices on indigenous women, children, and communities. The witeman science perspective viewed the human body as a specimen, separate from spirit, from ancestors, from land, from community, from soul, from love. A barrage of experiments were done to our poor bodies of color to "see" how their wite-science would work. My own mother's thyroid gland was subjected to high doses of radiation when she was a young child living unprotected in an orphanage, to see if it would withstand the radiation. Of course, due to these "harmless experiments," my poor mama ended up with thyroid cancer later in life.

The people that "get" to be in the wite-science healing industries are there because they have paper from the most exclusive institutions of higher learning. Every human who goes through medical skool in the US goes through a process that encourages them to lose their human-ness. After being subjected to labor-intensive, round-the-clock shifts working with poor and houseless peoples in a system that names poor peoples as not deserving of care, they learn to disrespect poor life. They learn to hate us poor peoples, to dread us, to disrespect us, and to criminalize us.

My mama said that my own kolonizer father used to be a prolific poet who had a heart, but as he was becoming a doctor he was physically sickened by the mandatory autopsy process. He didn't want to participate in it, but he was forced to, and afterwards, according to her, he was never the same.

Conversely, to become a healer in our multitude of indigenous cultures, where healers are chosen, mentored, and blessed through spiritual traditions and permisos, eldership and ancestor relationships, one has to go through a life-long process of learning, mentoring, and prayer. And to even be considered as a person to practice care-giving, doctoring, and medicine-giving, a person must possess the traits of patience, kindness, and sharing.

Back Orginal Cover Art of POOR Magazine Volume #4 MOTHERS by Eddie Camacho & Tiny

EXCERPT | **The Nature of MAMA:**
An Interview with Dr. Wade Nobles
DEE GRAY
REPRINTED WITH PERMISSION FROM POOR MAGAZINE
24 SEPTEMBER 2010

Dee: What is your current position at San Francisco State?

Wade Nobles: Full-tenured professor in Black Studies Department.

D: Can you speak on the psychological notion of individuation and how it affects people, especially African-American people?

WN: As I recall, this notion of individuation had to do with people's need or capacity to find something unique about themselves that separates them from other people. So it's a kinship to this notion of individuality, but it's seen more as a process wherein people strive to heighten – and the belief is that they benefit from - having this sense of individuation.

I don't recall any of the theorists who talked about it, but I believe that it's grounded in the philosophy that comes out of the Euro-Western tradition and to that extent it may not be applicable to all people who are not Western or who are not European people.

D: At one point you said something to the effect of: black folks do not believe in individuation.

WN: Look at the way African people live, the way they conceive of themselves, it's all rooted in their own cultural deep structure. And African people, particularly African-American people, have been an oppressed people, and as an oppressed people have never been given full license to embrace or to adopt Western standards. Consequently, we've simply retained our old African, even though it's unconscious, we've retained our old African belief systems and philosophical orientations. And those as I understand them are antithetical to this notion that what is most valuable about you is what makes you unique and distinct from everybody else.

D: Why do you think, though, that white psychologists and teachers of psychology promote this idea of individuation?

WN: I believe that it's more political than scientific or psychological. In societies that thrive on the basis of exploiting people, then you have to have people believe that they are separate from each other so that when they see the exploitation of someone else or some other group, they are satisfied that it is not happening to them so they don't have to do anything about it. If you keep a society full of individuals, you can exploit the whole population individually, and each individual believes that it's happening to the other guy and not happening to me.

D: Would you say this concept promotes capitalism?

WN: I think that capitalism and much of the constructs in Western psychology emerge out of the same philosophical grounding, and that philosophical grounding is based upon the idea of separateness, distinctness, domination, fear, and exploitation. So, capitalism is just the economic system that parallels individuation as a psychological system. So it's not that it promotes it, it certainly does reinforce it and allows for it to exist, because individuation would never challenge some of the precepts of capitalism. Capitalism says I've maximized my profits, minimized my loss; in order to do that, I have to exploit others. I won't exploit others if I believe that others are the same. So if I believe in individuation, then I certainly have a free license to exploit others.

D: Does psychology that promotes individuation cause a problem for African-Americans or other people when they're caught in the mental health system?

WN: Absolutely, a great deal of the psychological problems that African people and people of color experience are associated with their oppression and their exploitation—so if their psychological trauma is associated with exploitation and oppression and you have them believing in individuation then they never challenge the oppression or the exploitation. They think their problems are intrinsic. They think something that happened in their individual family systems are the cause of their psychological problems, as opposed to being systematic, which is: problems are caused by the nature of the society, not the nature of your mother.

D: The nature of mama! Yes, I like that.

Tiny: Can you speak to the fact that Western or Euro-centric psychology critiques and pathologizes the multigenerational family house where you have adult children living with the mother or the father?

WN: Well, you see, it becomes problematic in the therapist's eyes because to them the problem with the client is they're not being independent of that web of influences that are the multigenerational family, so they cast it as a negative environment, because you're not independent, you don't have volition, your own self-volition as opposed to viewing it with the notion of collectivism in the African family that is complementary and not oppositional.

D: But the psychologists who believe in individuation would say...

WN: You've got to break free from your family, you've got to break free from the influence of your grandmamma, from the influence of your uncle; you have no independent agency because in their minds you are submitting to the thinking or the feelings or the ideas of these other individuals, [and] you are just as independent as them, so why do you let them influence you? So they have you fighting with your kinfolk for the independence as opposed to fighting with a system that is dominating and exploiting human beings and human life.

T: We were taught by Pamela George at one point about the notion of transubstantiation, and she gave the illustration of [senator and sociologist Daniel Moynihan] in the sixties. Could you describe what the notion of transubstantiation is?

WN: The idea of transubstantiation is that in looking at the surface behaviors of a people, you can draw conclusions about the meaning and values of behaviors, but the meaning and the value comes from the deep structure of a people's culture and values. And so you have African people behaving in a certain way, based upon the African deep structure, but you have a person like Daniel Moynihan looking at that behavior and trying to interpret it from his own European culture deep structure. He draws the wrong conclusions. And so in the black family at the time that Daniel Moynihan was examining it, there [were] women without husbands raising children, which he deemed a broken home. [He said] that the broken home would cause negative things to occur in the development of children. The mistake he was making was the installations of values in the development of children is not tied to the mother-father linkage, it is tied to a system of eldership. And you have older brothers, older cousins, older uncles, older aunts, older mama, grandmamma, big mama, great mama, almost in this hierarchy of eldership, and all of those layers are what improve the development of children. So if you take one piece i.e., the father, it is not as devastating as it would be in the European family.

T: You mean the nuclear family?

WN: Yes, the nuclear family. Moynihan made a transubstantive error because he was judging the black family based upon the value system of the European culture.

D: What do you mean by eldership, can you be a little more specific?

WN: Eldership says that everyone older than you is responsible for your well-being and welfare. So it makes no difference whether it's your sixteen-year-old cousin and you're nine years old, that person is responsible for looking out for you. And then there's somebody above her and someone above that person, so there's a hierarchy of age grades, and everyone that is younger than me I'm responsible for looking out for, and they have to be obedient to me, and everyone that's older then me looks out for me and I have to be obedient to them. So I'm a 60-year-old man; if I see a 70-year-old in my family, I give deference to that 70-year-old, because they are my elder.

T: So that would be the actual construction of the village that is always talked about.

WN: That's how the village operates.

D: And why do you have to be obedient?

WN: Obedience is... be careful with the transubstantive mirror, because obedience is not the individual being somebody who is ruling you, obedience is listening to somebody who is guiding you. So the reason why you're obedient is because you're getting guidance from this person to become a better person.

Everyone in the village is responsible for guiding, for directing, and for making sure that the next generation advances to the next higher level, the person of good character. The goal here is not obedience that you will obey someone; the goal here is for your good character to evolve. Well, how do I as an elder help other people evolve their good character? I give them challenges, I give them assignments, I evaluate them, I give them feedback on what is good and bad about the decisions they're making, the choices they make, etc.

HELLthcare

TINY AKA LISA GRAY-GARCIA
REPRINTED WITH PERMISSION FROM POOR MAGAZINE
PRINT EDITION VOL. 2, HELLTHCARE, 1997

Give me an H give me an E give me an LLTH that's hellthcare!
Get hit by a car, thrown into a door, Slip on the FLOOR, any flesh torn
ponder dying
or start lying if you are poor

> Some people are blessed
> to not be stressed
> by the price of a suture,
> the cost of a cast
> the dollar amount of
> bed-rest

> But that's just typical —
> cuz we in a society
> where it's a privilege to be health-y
> and everything
> is about
> mon-ey

Once peoples had been colonized away from their indigenous communities, resources, land, and organic healing practices, and wite-science was clearly in place as the "only" legitimate cure for ill health, health was directly linked to a person's ability to work. If you were too sick to work, very possibly because you had been "worked to death" in the brutal, non-unionized slave work rampant in most industries in the 19th and 20th centuries, and you were no longer able to afford to pay for a doctor, you were simply left to die. Your meager options were Catholic "charity" hospitals and the minimal care available through the early settlement workers (social workers). All of these "charity" hospitals were outgrowths of the almshouses or poorhouses which were in place to "help" (read, corral and incarcerate) as many poor people as they could get.

But the reality is that most people just lived with open wounds, drastic scars, missing limbs due to routine amputations, abcesses and rotting teeth, with their untreated, wounded bodies which could no longer "produce" or function as laborers in a capitalist society. They would often take to the streets to beg for money, at which point they would be incarcerated under anti-poor-people laws like the Ugly Laws, which criminalized anyone who was "maimed or unsightly" in public.

When Medicaid was created in the 1960's, it mandated the care of poor people. But from its inception it was written to only include some poor people, naming families, children, and disabled among the few lucky enough to receive care. Meanwhile revolutionaries like the Black Panthers were providing community clinics without any government support, as they knew our bodies of color were not being cared for.

Medicaid or Medi-cal care has always been substandard, scarce and downright abusive in many cases. Countless times me and my mama sat in county clinics waiting for hours to get seen, even if our illness was an emergency. When my mama was diagnosed with congestive heart failure, she was told by a cardiologist that her "coverage" (Medi-cal), would not pay for the treatments that would save her life. My mama was never offered any treatment except the nine-pill Big Pharma cocktail for this illness, which eventually took her on her spirit journey. Her poor life was not worth saving. But if you have private insurance, you are offered a multitude of other treatments, including an extensive program of cardio-rehabilitation to increase the strength of the body, which extends the lives of middle-class and rich people.

There is an epidemic of hospital "throw-aways" where disabled, elder houseless people are literally wheeled out of hospitals and "dumped" into the streets, wearing nothing but a hospital gown or their underwear. A. Faye Hicks, residing houselessly in San Francisco, was discharged not once, twice, but three times with pneumonia into the streets. She would have died on the street but for the advocacy of POOR Magazine family to get her into a care facility.

And racism is always lingering nearby, with countless examples of racist medical staff refusing to care for, listen to, or even treat poor peoples of color. Many times my Mama Dee was accused of being too loud (read: too ghetto, too brown, too poor) and ejected from the hospital waiting room. Or there are cases like Vern Trayersie, a blind Lakota native brother in South Dakota, whose body was carved into while in surgery so that his stomach now bears the letters KKK.

EXCERPT | **Dumping the Disabled**

LEROY MOORE

26 JUNE 2007

In the 1990s Californians witnessed a campaign for force treatment policy toward people with mental health disabilities. And this type of treatment still exists today. For example, a paraplegic homeless man was recently dumped on the street by a Hollywood Presbyterian Medical Center van. This is not the first time this hospital has dumped people who are homeless onto the streets. According to the *LA Times*, this practice occurred in 2005 by the same hospital. A disabled San Francisco journalist, Laure McElroy, just wrote an article for the *San Francisco Bay View* newspaper about how an African American woman was forced to leave the Potrero Health Clinic with no adequate reason while suffering severe health problems due to a high-risk pregnancy. So what happened to the word "public" in public health?

When I was a teenager I saw New York police officers placing elderly and homeless people with mental health disabilities on Greyhound buses with a one-way ticket across this country. And when I moved to San Francisco, I witnessed former Mayor Frank Jordan's Matrix Program that cited people who were homeless on petty charges and had vans that circled downtown San Francisco letting people back onto our streets because of a lack of space in nearby shelters.

EXCERPT | **Medical Apartheid**

LAURE MCELROY, WELFAREQUEEN

> The rich stay healthy,
> the sick stay poor
>
> Out of the coma, into the fire
> Fuck all the Ritalin, stress got me wired
> High blood pressure and I'm hyper-tense
> Medical apartheid, Black body worth-less
> Head is filled with disease
> Arthritis bite into my knees
> As I crawl to the local
> Free clinic
> And guess what? Nobody
> Works in it
> ANYMORE
> Nothin' FOR ya
> In the budget
> Of California
> In San Francisco
> Or Michigan
> To pay the doctors
> To come in again
> ... Medical apartheid,
> ... me-me-medical apartheid

The deadly experimenting and researching continues today. The perpetrators are Big Pharma and the test subjects are houseless, poor, and/or migrant peoples.

Every year when the flu shot is brought out with a huge multi-billion dollar ad campaign, they mandate the shot on houseless people in the countless plantation shelters across the country. If a houseless elder refuses it they are often terminated from staying at the shelter, so they take it even if they know it is risky for them to do so. And then some die suddenly after it is administered. There is never an autopsy required or investigation called for.

A. Faye Hicks and Alfred P, two poverty skola We-searchers at POOR Magazine, reported on five such cases in shelters in San Francisco and New York. People were afraid to talk for fear of losing their beds, so they never would testify publicly.

Borders Kill Babies: The Karla Story

POOR MAGAZINE FAMILY WITH RO SEIDELMAN
REPRINTED WITH PERMISSION FROM POOR MAGAZINE
07 DECEMBER 2011

"Sometimes I feel like,
Poor people, when they get ill,
We're destined to die."

Muteado's words—as family awaits more information, more ca$h, a miracle, to get cancer treatment for his 23-year-old niece Karla—reflect the broken US medical system. It's leaving undocumented folks without the right papers/papeles, poor folks without the right ca$h, the land full of folks without access to decent medical care, without the right to survive preventable diseases.

POOR Magazine is holding an emergency press conference at Highland Hospital on Friday to address this scary and heartbreaking injustice affecting mamas and babies.

In New Jersey, a five-year-old girl who desperately needs a bone marrow transplant is being sentenced to death, because the US State Department denied a visa for her 7-year old sister in El Salvador who is her only bone marrow match.

Our POOR Magazine sister Karla, single mama to a 3-year old in East Oakland, said, "I want to stay alive for my son, he has no one to take care

POOR family member 23-year-old Karla in a gown, sitting on a hospital bed, during her struggle with the U.S. medical system.

of him." She's currently a patient at Highland Hospital, facing death in the ward, because she needs a bone marrow transplant to survive. But due to her immigration status, she cannot qualify for the support subsidies available for bone cancer.

***

"They told me nothing was wrong and sent me home," said Ingrid DeLeon, migrant and poverty skola reportera at POOR Magazine.

Healthcare for poor peoples, migrants, and working poor families is never mentioned when large corporate hellthcare plans like ObamaCare, which are intentionally directed at "the middle class," are discussed. But us po' folks talk about them to each other all the time, broken, sick, discouraged, and unsure where to go or what to do to feel better, get healed, or just not die.

In one week alone one of our migrante mamas at Prensa POBRE was experiencing severe pain, had a swollen stomach and intermittent fever. "It's only stress," they said to her on one of several visits she made to the emergency room and her county clinic about her increasing pain. She would have died of a kidney infection but for the revolutionary legal advocate intervention of POOR Magazine family who made phone calls to the clinic, demanding to speak to her doctor. Suddenly the doctor began to "discover" what was wrong and she finally received treatment.

In the very same week another working poor mama was being continually mistreated, told that her heart palpitations, dizziness, and weakness were "just stress." Again the intervention began, and the expensive tests and specialist referrals were suddenly ordered and it was found that she had a very serious form of thyroid disease.

Healthcare becomes hellthcare at the county-run poor-peoples clinics that accept medi-hell but threaten parents like me with a CPS call if I don't succumb to the Big Pharma bank-rolled battery of vaccines on my infant son. Or when I wasn't covered by insurance at all and had to convince the emergency rooms that I was really in an emergency when I was in the throes of a life-threatening asthma attack. Or my endless struggles and poverty crimes to attain dental care because us poor folks just don't deserve to have our teeth.[15] Or when POOR Magazine co-editor Tony Robles showed up at a doctor's office and he was lucky to get out alive, finding medical licenses long ago expired, paper medical files on the floor, dirt-stained medical implements, and an attitude of anger and disrespect from the doctor himself. When Tony tried to complain to the county referral system, they told him that was the only doctor that was available in his zip code.

Why Capitalism Needed the Euro-centric Therapy Complex

Not too long beyond the advent of wite-science and its inhuman theories about our human bodies, the therapy industrial complex was launched by MD's who were considered qualified because of their wite-science medical training to "deal" with our "minds" with cold, inhuman theories about our mental health.

Therapy promoted wite-science ideas of normalcy and pathology, sanity and mental health, which incidentally supported the concepts of separation, individualism, and capitalism as well as disturbing patriarchal ideas that placed the blame for incest on mothers.

Co-dependent, Personality disorder, paranoid, schizophrenic, agoraphobic... All of these "diagnoses" are based on a norm of sanity that is created by the dominant kolonizer class. What is co-dependence if you believe in interdependence? What is individuation if you believe in intergenerational family units? What is paranoia if your poor body of color has been under attack? What is schizophrenia if you channel the voices of ancestors and spirits like so many of our curanderas and medicine men and women do? And what is agoraphobia in cultures where people are NEVER alone like they insist we be in capitalism?

In order to incorporate every act of caring for one another, capitalism needed to sell people on the lie of advancement and the cult of independence. The lie that to live a full and real life we all must live "independently"—independent of our elders, our parents, our community members, our neighbors.

In Eurocentric therapy modalities, separate-ness from our parents, elders, and communities is not only rationalized, it is required to achieve their definitions of normalcy and sanity. The intergenerational family unit, the involved and integrated elder, and the community as collective caregiver and protector is criminalized.

From the earliest lessons we are skooled on "away-ness" from our mothers, fathers, and caregivers. The nuclear family unit is set up in separate newly rented apartments, constantly receiving messages to buy more and work more, which is equated with success and sanity. So we the workers/consumers are constantly purchasing IKEA furniture and utilities, believing this is necessary to "keep the ekkkonomy going."

The nuclear family unit is arguably completely insane. No other cultures exist where people are so alone as they are here. That aloneness itself is valued and taught as a barometer of sanity.

Little Noah

DEE GRAY

REPRINTED WITH PERMISSION FROM POOR MAGAZINE
17 AUGUST 2000

Cosmo is a member of the Media in Action group "POOR Parents Speak," a project of POOR Magazine. Dee is the co-editor of POOR Magazine and founder of the parents' advocacy group COURTWATCH.

"*Remember when life was young, little Suzy had so much fun, hoppin and boppin to the crocodile rock.*"

Little Noah's tiny diapered hips, emitting the light scent of powder and baby-ness, swayed to the Oldies music as he held on to my legs. It was near bedtime and I was dancing my son, Noah, to bed after his night-time bath and gourmet meal of Gerbers© chicken and rice. Suddenly, two large black boots lumbered toward us, shaking the earth as they came closer. A cold steel badge was pushed in my face.

"Police. Hand me the child, we're taking him in to custody."

"What are you doing?" I screamed. "Why are you taking my baby?" "What's going on here?" my wife shrieked.

"We're taking your child because you are unfit parents. You are being charged with neglect and emotional abuse, Mr. Franklin. I am a worker from Child Protective Services." She handed me her card, grabbed Noah and walked out of the room with the police. The last sound I heard was Noah's screams.

I stood there motionless as my wife started crying. I looked over at my father who was standing on the other side of the room. It all came together. I am poor, I wasn't very good at holding down a job, I was living with my father, it was not a good situation. We did not get along. He wanted me out of his house.

That was three weeks ago. Noah was permanently removed from my care. The reasons were fuzzy: it was never determined what my wife or I really did wrong. They said we swore in front of the child, that I swung him around too fast, that maybe there was drug abuse (there was not). But the real reason was my wife and I were poor and my father was not. We didn't have a chance in the court. Our extreme love and meticulous care of our very healthy seven-month-old was never considered, and when the court hearing convened, we watched them terminate our parental guardianship.

The decision to take our baby was part of an ever-increasing trend to terminate the rights of parents solely based on the income, financial stability, or joblessness of the parent. The implications are terrifying. Case in point: in New York, Mayor Giuliani said last week that if you aren't working you won't be allowed to get shelter and if you don't have shelter in New York, you automatically have your children put in foster care.

In California a father was arrested for yelling at his 14-year-old daughter when she refused to go to school.

In Wisconsin they are deciding whether or not to incarcerate mothers who are on crack so they can control the conditions of the fetus.

Will orphan trains for poor children be next, or baby factories run by the state only allowing certain people to actually "raise children"? The frightening thing is that many people would agree with these civil rights abuses because they are theoretically done "in the best interests of the child."

Unfortunately the public is unaware how increasingly arbitrary the basis of "abuse" determined by Child Protective Services has become, and how equally impossible it is to meet their requirements for reunification. It reminds me of the ancient fairytale of Rumplestiltskin who threatened to take the first-born child of the princess unless she spun a roomful of straw into gold.

Two weeks later I was able to visit my little Noah. He was hoarse from crying for days on end. His body now reeked of adult male sweat (his foster father's). His bright blue eyes were blood shot. He will eventually go to his grandfather's house and I will not see him again. He is my son and I loved him, cared for him and danced with him.

"Remember when life was young, little Suzy had so much fun..."

***

The notion of the village is criminalized by the Child Protective Services and Adult protective services industries. Many of our elders will relate how, in their day, if an elder in the community (read: village) witnessed any hint of inappropriate behavior by another adult, they would step in and intervene, or in my abuelita's beautiful words, "take a frying pan to the pinche cabrón who messed with anyone's baby, punto final."

In the same way, if my abuelita witnessed one of the local young people out late at night without a chaperone, she would take the back of her hand to the back of their heads, yelling at them the whole time until they were shamed enough to stop what they shouldn't have been doing and "go home where they belonged."

Now in our "advanced" society no one is allowed to practice our natural instincts of care-giving, eldership and protection. In the example of mi abuelita, my grandmother would get not only put in jail for attempted murder and aggravated assault with a deadly weapon (against the pedophile), but she would be criminalized and at risk of losing the custody of her own grandchildren for not calling CPS. In the second case she would have CPS called on her for "abuse" of a minor.

CPS is one of the arms of the many-headed snakkke known as the system. When my own revolutionary, indigenous, heart-always-open mama tried to enter the anti-social work world as a way to share healing and continue to process her own trauma, she was consistently nicked by the state and their agents for practicing love and true care-giving.

As a social work intern, my mama worked in one of the largest institutional therapy prison plantations in the country. Prior to resistance movements in the 1970s led by mental health industry survivors, this prison was host to forced shock treatment, shackles, and the massive discarding and institutionalizing of people. While she was there, my mama walked and worked in the dictated, boundary-laden,[16] institutionally-sanctioned ways that one was forced to work with imprisoned folks. Then one day, she crossed those plantation borders: she touched the hand of a developmentally disabled man whose family had thrown him in the institution because he "talked funny" and had trouble reading when he was 9 years old. He was 49 when my mama met him. She was immediately sanctioned and pulled from the institution and told for the first of 16 times throughout her institutional learning experience that she was un-supervisable and therefore not "student" or "therapist" material.

Pauper Laws, Welfare Codes, and the Helping Industry

Pauper Law circa: 1904: *Every county must relieve its own poor. Sheriffs, coroners, constables, and justices of the peace shall give information to their respective county courts of the poor; and the county court has the duty of providing for such persons. If satisfied that the applicants are paupers the county court shall order their commitment to the poorhouse, there to remain until discharged by an order of the court. County courts have the power to establish poorhouses, and when completed the court shall let them out annually to the lowest responsible bidder under bond for the faithful care of the inmates. In counties without poorhouses, the court may let the care of the poor to the lowest responsible bidder. The county is not liable for the support of any pauper who refuses to accept county aid in the manner provided above. The county court may cause the employment of each able-bodied pauper on work for the county.*

In the midst of the Depression in 1935, the U.S. had so many poor people and unemployed workers that 60% of the population was registered communists. To salvage the struggling capitalist system President Franklin Delano Roosevelt introduced the neo-socialist concept of the New Deal, which included limited services for poor folks and unemployed workers. It was established within a scarcity model that wasn't meant to help everyone, but rather set up as a white supremacist, Christian notion of deserving versus undeserving poor.

Welfare was one of the programs put into effect with the New Deal. It specifically stated that the deserving recipients were white widows of war veterans; women of color or women who were divorced or had their children without being married were not eligible. These racist, classist, patriarchal laws led to the welfare legislation we now have on the books.

In the 1960s senator and sociologist Daniel Moynihan went into the projects in Harlem to "study" welfare recipients with the goal of "improving" the welfare codes. What he "found" was single-mother-headed households, led by strong African-descendent mothers, grandmothers, and aunties with strong kinship groups of uncles, brothers, grandfathers, and cousins. From his white-middle-class perspective these households were pathological. Because he held power as a white male politrickster, his perspective was not only valued: it set the welfare code that we all suffer under today.

The scarcity model of welfare means that services are given within a punitive system that is set up to "discourage" the recipients from receiving services or aid. Sometimes I refer to this as the Non-Profit Industrial Complex (NPIC), or poverty pimpology. I also call it the poverty industry or helping industry.

Money is made in the poverty industry by separating people from their families and bringing in service providers, police, social workers, and other agents of the state to provide acts of care. Communities that historically practice eldership and interdependence are sold the myth of independence so that we can become products of profit for the NPIC.

Elders, children, and peoples living with disabilities are warehoused, and the state and private NPIC corporations trade human beings for several thousand dollars a month, while the pieces of the families struggle to stay alive, without our elders' knowledge, our children's laughter, our peoples' voices.

Once the system has successfully separated children and elders from families and community networks of support, they set up impossible rules. Make a mistake within these punitive systems and you are thrown out, evicted, and lucky to end up in a shelter bed. If you're not lucky, you end up in the new form of US public housing: jail.

The Journey Out from Under the Poverty Industry

"The Great Lie is that this is civilization. It's not civilized. It has literally been the most blood-thirsty brutalizing system ever imposed upon this planet. This is not civilization, this is the Great Lie. Or if it does represent civilization, and that is truly what civilization is, then the Great Lie is that civilization is good for us." —JOHN TRUDELL

Mama used to say wite culture isn't good for anyone, even wite people. As the melanin-challenged daughter of a strong Black Indian mama, who blended in with the dominant wite culture, I was "accepted" as one of them. For years I aspired to be nothing more than a popular wite gurl, as far away as I could be from my poor, different-looking, wild and crazy (all names my colonizer father and other people called her) mama of color and our crazy poor people life.

Sadly, my mama was complicit in this without even knowing it. Due to her poverty and her own colonization, she sent me to the man's factory skools, which together with corporate media taught me the lessons of separation, angst, individuation, and away-ation. It made me ashamed of my ghetto-fabulous mama and our unending poverty and taught me to be disrespectful to her wonderful, indigenous self.

My "skkkool" spanned 18 hours a day. At factory skool there was a constant onslaught of lessons about independence, self-hood, productivity, careers, money-getting, and "success," which always included more institutional skool. When factory skool ended I would trot back home to any of our tiny, isolated studio apartments, where I would lock the door and sit in front of the TV, taking in an endless stream of mythological capitalist characters who made up Amerikkklan television. The fix was in: I was successfully sold on everything that had nothing to do with who I was and who my people were.

My mama took me out of factory skool when I was in 6th grade, because I—like many of my brothers and sisters in poverty across Mother Earth—needed to work to help keep my family alive, and there really was no time for the hours of upon hours of skool. But it was too late. I spent the rest of my youth wishing to be part of that away-nation: to spend hours away from the person who gave me life, who dreamed revolution with every breath and who taught me EVERYthing I know.

Tha' Poor Peoples Plate: Race, Poverty, GMOs & Our Food

TINY AKA LISA GRAY-GARCIA
REPRINTED FROM POOR MAGAZINE
30 MAY 2013

The Poor Peoples Plate is rooted in capitalist hate for the three job working-mamazcaught in the welfare state...

"Here is your WIC voucher, these are the "approved" dairy products, cereal and dry goods you can buy," When my son was born and my mama got diagnosed with a fatal heart condition, I was thrown into another bout of severe poverty and houselessness, which meant I qualified for a program used by all poor and working poor parents known as WIC. I was hungry and my son and very ill mama was hungry too, so when they showed me the array of what I now know were non-organic, hormone and antibiotic-filled-milk and GMO-infused pasta and other dried food options, I felt blessed and eagerly signed up.

It wasn't until two years later due to my ghetto fabulous po' mamaz revolutionary fight for her own life that I began to understand that the very foods we were "getting" for such a "deal" were actually killing all of us.

As the corporate domination of our food, land, air and water continues and the resistance heats up to the monster known as Monsanto gets stronger it must be said that in the US its us Po' Folks of all cultures and ages that are getting the worst of it. Some obvious, most not. And no-one is really speaking for us.

> *Genetically Modified Organisms-Organisms, how U gonna'tell me it's a mechanism for betterlivin'?When ignorance in silence. . . . is how they keep us . . . but in reality, its violence . . . that's how they feed us.*
> —EXCERPT FROM 'CHECK Y' FOOD' BY VIVIAN FLAHERTY / PO' POETS PROJECT

The Po' Poets Project of POOR Magazine were invited to attend the Sacramento rally to Shut Down Monsanto organized by Stevan Payan and Occupy Sacramento. It was a challenge for us Po' Folks to go 100 miles out of town to attend a rally, as over-worked and never paid poor folks in resistance attending rallies in and of itself is a challenge, because it means we are spending gas money we don't have, losing work hours we need to pay rent, caring for children along the way, leaving sick elders or holding our own sick bodies into revolution, but this is the ongoing struggle of a poor people-led revolution like we do at POOR Magazine. When we arrived at the huge and power-FULrally, we felt blessed to be there but sad to see that we didn't see a lot of folks who looked like us. It seemed pretty clear to all of us, that, with the exception of our indigenous brothers like Stevan Payan, Greg Iron and a few others, this fight was being led and fought by mostly middle-class white folks. Sadly, this didn't surprise us – it only confirmed what we already knew. We are the ones who are consuming most of the GMO-filled food and yet we aren't the ones on the front-line of this fight.

From the morning to the evening, our poor bodies of color are being destroyed by killer foods and none of us have the time, the resources, the energy or the money to deal with this reality because we are too busy working multiple low-wage jobs to survive, fighting illegal evictions, fighting and working for government crumbs like food stamp and tiny welfare stipends that require us to work for below minimum wage, evading endless po'lice brutality, profiling and incarceration or just struggling with the multiple wounds of racism, classism and criminalization impacting our bodies and minds since chattel slavery, Jim Crow, colonization, and the endless lie of these false borders and our forced migration across them just to survive.

As most GMO-organizers know our breakfast is owned by Monsanto, from fruit loops to Total, from Quaker Oatmeal to Shredded Wheat, all of the things many of us wake up and feed our children, thinking we are doing right by them, because we are giving them a "healthy breakfast" those of us in struggle parents who can even manage to do that, are poisoning our children with GMO-filled wheat, soy, or corn.

As we prepare lunches with the "healthy lunch meat" like turkey or ham, the fix is in, willingly putting substances in our bodies deemed "unsafe for human consumption" by leading doctors in a recent study that never made its way to corporate media.

From Betty Crocker to Frito Lay- from Nature Valley to Nabisco, Power Bars and PregoPasta Sauce, all Monsanto-owned companies-its mind-numbing to figure out what foods, fruits and vegetables aren't made with genetically modified organisms which have proven to cause bizarre pubic hair loss in a controlled study silently released a few weeks ago and in rats for them to grow their livers outside their bodies

And even when we feed our bodies our indigenous' cuisines, we find insanely high rates of sodium, saturated fat, sugars and chemicals have snuck their way into our pre-colonial diets in the canned coconut milk filled with high fructose corn syrup, tortillas, rice, plantains, bananas, bread made with GMO'ed corn, wheat, soy and rice, refried beans pumped up with hydrogenated something or other, and large agri-businesschicken, pork and beef injected with sodium anti-biotics and preservatives. You only have to look at our post-colonial, in poverty, in struggle bodies to see the way these chemicals have destroyed our warriors, silenced our elders and placed our parents on endless Big Pharmaprescriptions many of us can barely afford.

My Afrikan-Taino Indian mama who was an orphan so she didn't even have access to her indigenous cultures recipes filled with healthy arroz con frijoles ate what I affectionately call poor peoples food her whole life, a steady diet of high sodium, fat-filled colonized and processed culture derivative food, refried beans from a can, chili from a can, and top ramen spiced with chilis, peppers and salt, and as much other starch and cheap meat as we could stretch the food stamps to buy with a lot of pan dulce, donuts and coffee thrown in to deal with her ongoing deep depression from her always in struggle life, leaving her over-weight and unable to fight the multiple diseases her poor body of color was constantly attacked by. When she finally made it off welfare into a full-time job, I was the classic latch-key kid, coming home to frozen food or a warm and hormone and fat-filled fast food meal from Burger King, Mickey D' or KFC.

When we became houseless (due to my mama's being laid off and then becoming disabled) when I was 11 our food went further down hill, chef Boyardee in a can from 7-11, Spam and Campbells soup and cheap White or Wheat Bread from the corners to, bascially whatever we could get and make with the killer, cancer causing micro-wave was that nights meal.

It was all about survival and poverty. There was No Way we could pre-pare fresh vegetables, fruits, salads or even beans and rice. If someone had told us to "change our diet" or only buy fresh foods we couldn't have, it was all we could do just to get through the night without freezing to death.

We graduated from the car to a shelter where we were happy to receive whatever they served us, most of the time, GMO-cereal in the morning, killer lunch-meat on white bread for lunch and a fat-filled, warm gravy over an undiscernable meat for dinner.

When I turned 18 I graduated to jail food, (being incarcerated for the crime of sleeping in our car in Amerikkka) which included food that didn't even look like food. Bread so white it almost wasn't there, filled with meat so green it looked like lettuce. Again, I ate it until I was sick cause it was all I had access to and suffice it to say, nutrition wasn't the first thing on my mind.

My families story is but one of billions of poor peoples around the world, unseen stories of survival, struggle and in the US eventual death from diabetes, heart disease or high blood pressure to name a few all in large part due to what we are eating. As indigenous, landless peoples living in shelters, plantation prisons, public housing units, over-crowded, substandard housing units with no land surrounding them, and so many years of colonial theft of our land and resources, corporate defined, under-paid labor taking us away from the organic work of caring and teaching our own children and our gardens, and racist laws constantly incarcerating our young peoples, corporate media selling us and our young peoples on the lie of advancement and convenience, healthy eating seems almost impossible.

And yet the whole process of coming at our poor peoples communities with demands to "eat better" or an endless stream of critiques and accusations about "our bad food choices" isn't helping, instead its just more racist classist hate against the poor, while the hypocracy of Michele Obama touting healthy food choices when her husband pushes the Monsanto Protection Act and most of his administration and a supreme court judge (Clarence Thomas) are former (and current) employees of Monsanto.

Rather my challenge to conscious food justice peoples is the same one I have to housing justice folks stemming from a frame of what I call Community Reparations. Work with the stolen resources you might have access to to make community gardens accessible to us, donate healthy un-GMO-ed food to food banks and shelters, schools and community centers, even if it means purchasing them out of your own pocket. Look at the model of Planting Justice who creates living wage jobs in permaculture for plantation incarcerated folks and then the model of Phat Beets in Oakland and Urban Tilt in Richmond who truly work inside communities of color to build, support and maintain community gardens and make fresh, garden grown vegetables accessible to poor folks. Buy free shopping gift cards for poor communities of color from markets who sell healthy,non-GMO-ed food like Rainbow and Berkeley Bowl (instead of Foods Co and Slave-Way) and if you work at collectives like Rainbow — offer free groceries to shelters, group homes, and grassroots, non-profit organizations on a monthly basis, not just when we sponsor an event, so we can feed our communities, members and families fresh food all the time.

At POOR Magazine we have been teaching folks wit race and class privilege to become revolutionary donors and support us, stand in solidarity with us as poor and indigenous peoples to launch our own landless peoples movement to reclaim Mama Earth from the capitalist lie of real estate snakkkeing and speculation with a project we call Homefulness

From this cross-class solidarity work and support, not savior dictation, we have been able to launch the Pachamama Garden community garden and take our poor bodies of color off of this killer capitalist grid. Each week we share healthy, non-GMOed, non-nitrite having meat purchased thanks to the support of the revolutionary donors, with the East Oakland community, this is an act of revolution in a community where so many of our poor mamaz and daddys, elders and young peoples dwell and have ready access to a lot of GMO-ed fast food, chips, sodas and liquor in corner sto's.

We also launched Healing tha (Neighbor) Hood series last year where we teach our young folks, mamaz and daddys how to decolonize their diets back to their own indigenous roots and strategize their bodies out of this food genocide available at every street corner, Walmart and Supermarket in Amerikkka and we are currently working on a poor peoples healthy cook-book co-written by our youth and mama skolaz at POOR. Because for us Po' folks its all about decolonizing, strategy and inter-dependence.

"In the end of the day its another way to kill us," Gerry, 67, said. After the Monsanto rally my family and I went to a trailer park way out in West Sacramento where the only store for miles was a Food 4 Less- we drove into the park to take some food and cash to one of our multi-generational, indigenous families in deep poverty gentriFUKed out of San Francisco due to real estate speculation, whose tenuous hold on stability was destroyed by the move and was now living in a broke-down trailer with hardly any of the family working and most of the people in some state of crisis. I told elder grandmamma Gerry and her adult granddaughter Felicia about the rally and Monsanto's theft of our food system. Gerry's tired eyes registered shock and fear and yet resignation, "its genocide cause they know we just don't have the energy to deal with yet another thing against us."

So start counting yo'change, cause a Poor Peoples Plate is on its way to a poor peoples neighborhood near you, and if you have .99 you can have some too!

Check Y' Food

VIVIAN FLAHERTY
REPRINTED WITH PERMISSION FROM PO' POETS PROJECT/
POOR MAGAZINE

Genetically Modified Organisms-Organisms, how U gonna' tell me it's a mechanism for better livin'? When ignorance in silence . . . is how they keep us . . . but in reality, it's violence . . . that's how they feed us.

Been sold out . . . that's what it's all about, left out . . . of the equation, conversation while the biggety-box food corporation up in this capitalistic nation . . . founded on genocide . . . we're eatin' pesticide . . . with lies in disguise while every single one of us dies . . .

The assumption through mass consumption of the mass production, artificially flavored thru' subliminal seduction for your self destruction thru' the advertiser-mesmerizer-hypnotizer . . . now y' pickin' up prescriptions every week up there in Kaiser . . .

> Check y' food, before y' wrecked fa' good
> Y' betta' check y' food, before y' wrecked fa' good
> Betta' check y' food, before y' wrecked fa' good
> Y' betta'...y' betta' betta' betta'...read the label

It's a set-up from the get-up-superlastic-bubbleplastic-melamine-fructose-corn-syrup-froggy genes...lizard gizzard-potassium-sodium citrate...Monsanto-formulated soy protein isolate...

See that little bitta' water...you see at the top of ya' botta'-r' grinded buggies in your ketchup-coagulated-infiltrated-inseminated-n' you just ate it
Cuz' the muthafucka' homicidal corporations made it!

Yeah...So...Now...Check-check-check y' food
Well...Check-check-check y' food
Y' betta' check y' food, before y' wrecked fa' good
Y' gotta'...y' gotta' gotta' gotta'....read the label

Diabetes...Type 2...that's you...now whatcha' gonna' do???
Blood pressure up high in the sky, cataracts in y' eye
While the medical-industrial-complex makes a killin'
On our community-intention-ally...that's why we illin'...now

So, check y' food, before y' wrecked fa' good
Y' shoulda' checked y' food, before y' wrecked fa' good
Checked y' food, before y' wrecked fa' good
Y' gotta'...y' gotta' gotta' gotta'....read the label

GMO's gotsda' go y' know
GMO's gotsda' go y' know
GMO's gotsda' go y' know
GMO's gotsda' go y' know

Healing the Whole Poor People Body

From the colonized, chemical-filled food we eat that makes our natural bodies sick and diseases our organs, to the poisoned water, soil, and air we breathe, to the ways our hearts and minds are essentially confused out of our original value systems, we are incessantly confused by the Great Lie of Advancement.

Whether it is post-traumatic slave syndrome as laid out by Joy DeGruy or the concept of historical trauma as discussed by many indigenous healers, there are many ways our worldview as indigenous peoples in diaspora, migration, or remission are left so that we can carry out the ways of the colonizer. We do this without his even needing to whip us or cut off our tongues or hands. We are collectively confused, and we have much healing to do.

"In Western medicine, the body goes to the hospital, the mind to the psychiatrist, and the spirit to church. In curanderismo, the healing takes place under one roof." So says Elena Avila, a psychiatric nurse and professional curandera who has for more than twenty-five years effectively combined the best of traditional Western medicine with the ancient health system of curanderismo.

Rather than the bible of wite-psychiatry known as the DSM (Deadly Science Menu), we learn from Curanderismo about Susto. Susto is a spiritual illness that is caused when a person experiences a sudden shock or a traumatic event in their life. This is also known as "Fright," "Soul Loss," or "Loss Of The Shadow." When a person has susto it's believed that their soul leaves the psychical body, unable to find its way back. Many things can cause soul loss. The symptoms range from irritability to heart palpitations. If you took this list of symptoms to a western medical doctor he would most likely diagnose this as depression and prescribe some kind of anti-depressant pharmaceutical. In curanderismo it's treated with herbal tea or ritual cleansings to restore the balance in the body and allow the soul to return.

Western medicine will diagnose according to "symptoms." A curandera will take into account the person, their experiences, their mode of thinking, their fears, their patterns of living, and the event that they feel led them to her. From all this information the curandera will know how to deal with that person's particular type of susto.

For all us poverty skolaz, susto could describe most of our lives, surviving so many crises, acts of violence, criminalization, isolation, removal, and genocide. And yet in this capitalist, so-called modern society, where survival is a full-time job, our souls, bodies and spirits are never given a chance to heal. Rather we are thrown into the next impossible situation, alone, maybe with the addition of a Big Pharma medikkkation or one of the colonizer's poisons always accessible.

When my Afrikan/Boriken mama and I began to learn about our own lost cultures we began to heal. We started to un-pack the Great Lie of Civilization, and we knew that we didn't belong in it. I began to heal from the deadly diagnoses perpetrated onto our family by wite-science. I began to rewrite the lie of co-dependence into interdependence, love, and caring. I was no longer embarrassed by the indigenous caring I did as an adult daughter of my mama, I was blessed to be able to take care of our family and fulfill my role of good daughter, a role written into my ancestral memory for thousands of years.

My mama began to voraciously study Black Psychology, indigenous healing, and the many stories of peoples in struggle and diaspora. There was so much to unlearn and seemingly so little time. My mama and me got it now, and we were able to launch the powerful poor people-led, indigenous people-led movement of POOR Magazine.

But a lifetime of crisis, fear, and susto doesn't disappear in a day or month or even several years. My mama, like so many of our poor, landless,

Indian, and Afrikan peoples in struggle was permanently harmed in ways I could never begin to touch. Ways that make me hold her beautiful, terrified heart in my hands for the rest of my life, hoping I can still somehow heal it.

The trauma of our folks who seek substances or violence is real. Decolonization and healing and loving is lifelong. The pain we perpetrate on our children, our elders, our communities is real too. Then that pain begets more pain and more and then we no longer remember where the original pain came from.

If we have any post-colonized spirit left in us, it might be buried under colonized religions, colonizer's poisons, or colonizer dreams. It is important to approach us and our revolution with love and humility. To not perpetrate the continued industrialization of our care, our liberation, our revolution. We don't need a savior, a pimp or an institution: we must build our own poor-peoples-led revolution.

EXCERPT | The UnderGround SRO Railroad and Other Acts of Dismantling the Plantation

TINY AKA LISA GRAY-GARCIA, DAUGHTER OF DEE AND MAMA OF TIBURCIO.
REPRINTED FROM POOR MAGAZINE
30 JANUARY 2013

Dog Betty's eyes watched the cooking show on TV, quivering each time the tall wite lady with the strange voice dropped a pat of butter into the sizzling pan. As Betty's eyes darted back and forth across the screen, her large regal spine bunched up against the motel bed frame inching further and further into the off-white walls. Betty was a service dog. She and her elder, disabled Afrikan descendent companion, Kathy Galves were houseless. They were covered in bed bug bites. They had been foreclosed on from their San Francisco home of 40 years and were running out of money to even pay for a motel room.

When I saw Dog Betty I knew there was something odd about her. I was convinced there was a revolutionary ancestor, albeit disgruntled, trapped in her large yellow-furred body. She would growl at everyone and each time a motel slumlord would illegally evict or forcibly move Ms. Galves, Betty would have a bowel movement on their parking lot asphalt or lobby floor to express her disgust. Betty was an Australian dingo dog, a pure-breed, and all in all was not ok with this whole situation.

Ms. Galves came to our family at POOR Magazine in the way that most folks do, through family, friends, or street-based referrals, in a position of fear and desperation. She was already foreclosed out of her family home, by the bank gangsters known as Wells Fargo. She was spending her meager social security check and pension and pawning all of her worldly goods to pay for nightly motel rates that would often soar up to $130.00 per night.

Ultimately we needed to come up with an emergency plan. Ms. Galves, like so many folks in poverty, was caught in a vortex of almosts. Her income was $50.00 too much to qualify for the most dire city-based support services, and yet nowhere near enough to pay rent on a gentriFUK-inflated apartment. Her age, disability, and service dog made her an "unattractive" prospect for a subjective roommate/shared housing situation and her seriously ill health and disability required her close proximity to her multiple doctors and therefore prevented us from moving her completely out of San Francisco.

And so the Underground SRO (Single Room Occupancy Hotel) Railroad was launched. As a family of poverty skolaz, un-hinged from the intense constraints of most of the Plantation-esque Non-Profit organizations, we looked to each other to provide whatever we could from our houseless and almost-housed lives of subsistence. We could always, worse case scenario, open our one rooms up to each other.

The first stop on the railroad was one week in a miniscule room in The North Beach Motel, secured with some cash and credit card help from our Revolutionary Donors and with the hands and arms of several of our poverty skolaz. Tragically, the first time seven of us poverty skolaz of color, accompanied by 52 paper and plastic bags and a large dog, walked through the front door of the trying-to-be-booshie North Beach Hotel, the desk clerk took an immediate disliking to us all. This caused an anxiety reaction from Betty, who proceeded to alternately shed hair and pee in the room, causing the North Beach Hotel to only last a week for Ms. Galves and Betty.

The next stop on the railroad was our Uncle Joseph Bolden. Joe is a founding member of POOR, PNN reporter, POOR Press published author, and teacher. He is also a disabled, formerly houseless African Descendent elder who has been living, barely, in one tiny room with no bathroom or kitchen in the San Cristina Hotel (SRO) in the heart of the Tenderloin District of San Francisco for over 16 years. Due to the way that all of us po' folk are treated in all of these plantation housing units, Betty and Ms. Galves were required to show ID's coming in and out of the building, and must always be accompanied by Joe, who had no cell phone, to go into the room to sleep at night.

This resulted in Ms. Galves and Betty having to wander aimlessly on the very busy and loud Market Street sometimes for hours in the cold night until Joe returned home. Suffice it to say, a room barely large enough for one man was not nearly large enough for two disabled elders and a large dog and the whole experience was difficult at best for Joe who had no bed as he graciously gave it up to accommodate his guests and Ms. Galves, who got bronchitis from the cold nights outside.

The next stop was more complicated because it required several more acts of deep revolutionary advocacy from all of us poverty skolaz, but to keep the train on the railroad, it had to be done. Our Uncle Bruce, an elder, disabled, and formerly houseless poverty skola is a very power-FUL revolutionary, PNN reporter, and organizer. He suffered from serious trauma as a veteran of the US Military Industrial Complex, from being discriminated and hated on for his learning disability, and from living Po' in this capitalist society. So although he was now housed in a fairly decent one room SRO with a kitchen (which is truly luxury from us Po' Folks perspective) he was unable to keep it clean. From the kitchen to the bathrooms there was mess, dirt, food, and the remnants of a depressed elder who was also physically ill. There was no one to call, no social service agency that could "help," no government crumb or slice of government cheese to be applied for. There was just us: his fellow poor people, his family of over-tired, always working-but-never-giving-up poverty skolaz who lead with our hearts and move with our hands and feet, inter-dependently, in a society that teaches you that you only must worry about your own personal success.

The first thing was to acquire some cleanser, a toilet brush, compostable trash bags, sponges, gloves, facemasks, and a vacuum. Thanks to cash and a vacuum from solidarity sisters and brothers, as well as a car and time from solidarity sister Sandra, we launched into the Community Clean. With revolutionary worker and son of a janitor, poet/PNN-TV and Manilatown nephew Tony Robles leading the bathroom project, myself, youth skola Tiburcio and Joseph Bolden launched into the rest of the house. The second day we had the help of Solidarity sister and Diasporic Daughter Sandra and within two days and six tons of elbow grease we did it. The toilet and walls were sparkling, the bathtub was returned to its original soap-white, the floors were clean, the old pee-stained bed was discarded and a new bed was brought in.

The next day with more cash help from solidarity family for POOR Magazine van gas and the hands and backs and time of us poverty skolaz, we moved all of Ms. Galves's belongings into the newly spotless stop on the Underground, Off-plantation SRO Railroad.

I have called it the Underground SRO Railroad to honor the power-FUL revolutionary Harriet Tubman who led the By Any Means necessary movement of the Underground Railroad to free enslaved Afrikan warriors and families from the bondage of chattel slavery. I am not being so bold as to say that there is a comparison to chattel slavery to describe the position of post-foreclosed, bank-gangstered, real estate snakkked, disabled Afrikan elders like Ms. Galves. But I will venture to say that there is a comparison with the By Any Means Necessary resistance to Non-profiteerism, Poverty Pimpologists, akkkademiks and most journalists, who would say, "there is nothing we can do" to a disabled elder like Ms. Galves when she is about to start sleeping on the street, when perhaps their NPIC has no rooms at the inn. Yet they, the NPIC worker who profit off of our misery, are receiving a paycheck, which they could simply share. They, the NPIC worker, have a car, which they could simply use to transport an elder's belongings. They, the government or NPIC worker, have a bed and a roof, which they could simply offer. And there is a comparison I am making in the way that our elders and families are being destroyed by this capitalism, this gangsterism, this separation, and these non-profiteering industries that use us for grant guidelines, for research studies, for science experiments and Big Pharma treatment. How these industries use us for interesting stories and photo essays but do nothing to actually, physically, financially, emotionally share with, be with, love with, live with us, Po' folks in crisis.

Now calmly ensconced, albeit in too small a space for three, with Bruce graciously sleeping on an air mattress on the kitchen floor to free up the one bed in the house for Ms. Galves who struggles with kidney failure, the three of them live.

Daily, just like before, Ms. Galves wakes up early and walks across the City of San Francisco attempting to get on every housing wait-list there is that will accept her. She also makes fresh food for her friend and roommate, Bruce Allison. The last time I was there to do a small clean-up day with Tiburcio, Dog Betty greeted me with a characteristic growl. Her eyes met mine, and for a second they flashed anxiety, assuming I was there to broker another move of her tired body. But then Uncle Bruce walked over and without even looking up, dog Betty calmly licked his hand and went to sleep.

We Are Healing and Care-Giving,
We Have Been Healing and Care-Giving

Indigenous healers have been doing healing work for hundreds of years. Many therapists of color tried it in the past with detrimental repercussions but many are still practicing this now, using drum, smoke, prayer, and other ritual and ceremony practices and ways of our ancestors to heal. In that way they are bringing back our ancestral healing methods into these systems and institutions.

Luz Calvo, Healing through Decolonizing Our Diets: Through the "Decolonial Cooking Club," Luz Calvo seeks to reclaim collective ancestral knowledge about food, recipes, and culture among people and communities of color. Calvo shares and disseminates healthy recipes and cooking tips with people of color, based on their own families' and cultures' traditional cooking.

Vivian Flaherty, System Infiltrator: While we are decolonizing, some of us poverty skolaz are successfully infiltrating the helping industry. POOR's own

Vivian Flaherty works for Homeless Action Center, "banging on the System" to acquire urgently needed welfare, social security crumbs and health-care.

The Peoples Community Medics of Oakland: a grassroots organization that teaches basic emergency first aid skills free of charge. Founders Sharena Curley and Lesley Phillips write, "As members of the Oscar Grant Committee, we learned that the BART police refused to call an ambulance for 20 minutes for fatally wounded Oscar Grant, despite the passionate pleas for medical help from his friends who were detained at the Fruitvale station by the police. That experience as well as our knowledge that 911 calls often do not result in an ambulance arriving in a timely manner to Black, Brown and poor neighborhoods largely inspired us to teach our people basic emergency first aid so that we can help one another until an ambulance arrives."

Native Youth Sexual Health Network from Toronto, Canada, which was launched to "reclaim and revitalize traditional knowledge about people's fundamental human rights over their bodies and spaces, intersected with present-day realities is fundamental to our work. We are a peer-based network of individuals, families, communities, and Indigenous peoples at large."

Maggie's Toronto, the first sex-worker-run education project in Canada, whose mission is to "provide education and support to assist sex workers in their efforts to live and work with safety and dignity. The organization provides information about health promotion, AIDS and STI prevention, Canadian law, and dangerous clients to sex workers. The only organization of its kind in Canada, Maggie's has been a model for sex worker peer-education projects, internationally."

The Idriss Stelly Foundation, launched by an indigenous mother, Mesha Irizarry, who lost her son to Po'Lice murder over a 911 call for help. She then began an all-out effort to train po'lice in how to handle a mental health crisis that didn't include guns. She and the foundation remain one of the most revolutionary in the nation and recently succeeded in stopping the SF Po'Lice from bringing more death weaponry to kill more poor peoples, youth of color, and disabled peoples needing help, while also providing counseling services to peoples in crisis with systems abuse and police harassment.

The Kenneth Harding Foundation provides healthy food, medicine, and love on the same block where Kenny Harding Jr. was shot by Po'Lice in 2010.

In resistance to the lack of bone marrow donors in the African-American community *Kevin Weston and Lateefah Simon* launched their own project to increase awareness and bring more donors in from communities of color.

HEAALS (Healing from Addiction thru Art, Liberation and Spirituality), Healing the Hood and *Healing Summer* are POOR Magazine programs that teach indigenous healing practices, food, movement, and spiritual traditions.

"No Po'Lice Calls Ever" Project, started by POOR. As poor and indigenous peoples of color we could not invite the perpetrator into our lives when we have mental, physical, and community struggles. When we have problems come up (which we do ALL the time as poor peoples in struggle) we convene a Family Council based on a model taught by our indigenous ancestors. The Family Council convenes for as long as it takes to resolve issues that require self-accountability and ownership to the problem and a series of commitments to actions, change, and healing to the situation from each person who is responsible for the problem. It also requires commitment from the participants, elders, folks who are in community with that person, and POOR Magazine.

We also do not participate in the western CPS concept of mandated reporter. And yet we take the lives and safety of the bodies of children and all of us VERY seriously, and so we rely on a body of decision-makers and elders to guide us through all of this colonization: the Grandmothers/Mamaz, Grandfathers/Uncles Elephant Council.

There are no simple answers to healing. There is no simple cure, Big Pharma shot, or laser therapy. One of the first steps for peoples who have the privilege to learn the wite-science is to share it. If you are a health practitioner, do street-level clinics like Michele S. in Oakland, who provides herbs and tinctures to community members at a sliding scale, starting at free. Or if you have a private medical practice start seeing at least one patient for free. Provide free dental help like they do at the Berkeley Free Clinic (and not just pulling teeth, but root canals, caps and surgeries). Or if you are a person who has the drive to learn it, decolonize the science from the institution with free downloadable medical books like *Where There is No Doctor* and begin to practice your own community health care like we plan to do at Homefulness.

Re-learn what colonization told you to lose, to forget, to give up, because it took too long, was too hard, too messy, or too complicated. Tap into your ancestral memories, deep structures and herstories. Re-engage with your pre-diasporic souls, seek out your herstories and histories, re-write your stories, decolonize your diets and your minds, and then truly begin the hard work of understanding what healing really means, which for us poor folks might just begin with clearing up who is the healer, and what and who is causing our sickness.

Colorful hearts chalked on the sidewalk are drawn under the words LOVED ONES LOST TO POLICE VIOLENCE. Roxsana Hernandez 5-25-2018. Asa B Sullivan 6-6-2006. Vaneesa Hopson 2-7-2018. Charlie Salinas 6-15-2012. Claudia Patricia Gómez Gonzalez 5-23-2018. The words LOVED ONE are written with love for those not named here. This art was created at the home Lisa Ganser rents, on their SSI dollars, with address privilege, from house arrest. Lisa is a white Disabled genderqueer artist and activist living in Olympia, WA on stolen Squaxin, Chehalis and Nisqually land. They are a sidewalk chalker, a copwatcher, a poverty scholar and the Daughter of a Momma named Sam. Lisa is a writer at POOR Magazine and chalks the names of Loved Ones lost to poLice terror in hearts.

We are not just Bag Ladies and Men

*We are not just people pushing
a buggy filled with belongings*

*We are not just faceless people,
panhandling with a cup stuck out*

*We are people in America,
sleeping out doors*

*Rain or Shine, disabled, displaced teens,
the elderly, ex-convicts,*

*Unemployed, mothers
with children*

In God we Trust!

—A FAYE HICKS, PO' POET LAUREATE
OF POOR MAGAZINE

7

Underground Economic Strategies, Unrecognized Work, and Survival Work

Our lives as poor peoples are filled with the work of survival: a full-time job with no overtime or benefits. Finding food by stealing, foraging, or waiting (for shelter giveaways, food banks, or food stamp navigations). Creating or finding shelter (blankets, cardboard, dry, secluded, non-policed areas to park or sleep, squats, money for a motel room). And/or the 52-hour work-week, navigating massive amounts of paperwork and scarcity models at agencies across the city—welfare, SSI, Medi-hell and the shelter system—just to receive tiny crumbs. Our poor people survival work is rife with sorrow and desperation. We are taught to be ashamed of our work, and told we are lazy, stupid and unnecessary. This is how capitalism is promoted.

What is work, and who defines it? In Yoruba tradition, work is an integral part of life. So how did a corporate-defined, wite supremacy-owned definition of work become the worldwide norm that it is?

Our notions of work are defined by the people who stole the land and then stole us. Over hundreds of years of systematic and strategic theft, rape, genocide, slavery, and incarceration, the hook of the kkkapitalists has been the lie of advancement and its temptations to be faster, smarter, prettier, thinner, and to live an easier life. Separating billions from their lands, customs, and beliefs with a promise of simplicity, happiness, and comfort. Sadly, the ones to profit from this lie are the people who launched the lie and the institutions that sustain it.

Through this lie, they have been able to convince indigenous peoples with cultures rooted in interdependence and collective work to embrace independence, greed, individualism, and the most bizarre and inhuman value of all: the hoarding of blud-stained Amerikkklan dollaz.

Desiring, hoarding, and even killing for the dollaz themselves, or things attained with the hoarded dollaz, enables the corporate, kkkapitalist, killer dominance of our bodies and minds through the plantation systems of labor.

What a brilliant scam. Stealing a peoples' means of production, making them work for your benefit, and then convincing them that yours is the best way so successfully that the victims of the theft begin to believe in it and then desire it for it themselves.

None of these lies would have been successful without the forced desperation of stolen peoples in diaspora, robbed of their natural resources, land, and traditional cultures through a complicated system of paper, words, and laws. The stolen peoples had no choice but to work for the peoples who stole it all. Peoples who had survived and thrived in agrarian societies with their own sources of food, clothing, and home production. From Africa to Argentina, from Peru to the Philippines, we made our own clothes, grew and created our own fabric and food, taught our own children and built our own houses. This was work. Self-determined, off-plantation and un-pimped.

For My Uncles, Father, and All the Workers

TONY ROBLES
REPRINTED WITH PERMISSION FROM POOR MAGAZINE
30 NOVEMBER 2011

I grew up seeing them, workers. They were uncles and friends of uncles—guys whose names were "Ant", "Booze", "Herman", "So-Deep", "Dave"—and so many others. They were janitors or hospital porters—mostly janitors. They worked and told me to stay in school, to study hard, to hit the books and never mind the ladies—the ladies will come, they'd say. They told me that they didn't want to see me grow up to be like them. I was going to be different...I *was* different. I looked at my uncles, checked out the way they walked, talked. They exuded confidence and spirit—not in the university or academic sense, but in the true sense. They knew who they were as men of color—young men who had seen men like themselves excluded from academia, had seen good young men and women with potential relegated to their "place in society." They had fire in their bones, they didn't forget who they were as Filipino and Black people.

They spoke with tongues stained with soy sauce, hot chili, fish sauce, and roast pig, which was our ancestral struggle that accented the words they spoke, gave true meaning to their sounds—their marginalized and excluded syllables formed from church claps, the thundering drum, the boiling rice pot and broken English their parents spoke around the kitchen table.

They would tell me that there was nothing free in this life, that if you wanted anything you had to get off your ass and get it. "You don't want to swing a mop like me," they'd say, "You don't want to clean toilets do you?" And so I went to school, was a fairly decent student—I was, as my uncles would say, "an educated brown boy." I ended up with an educated brown boy job—an office job—and my uncle would visit me and behold my desk with the collection of paper clips that fitted into a nice chain that kept me tethered to the chair. "You're an executive!" he'd exclaim. I would get a little embarrassed and reply, "I'm a customer service rep...*any fool can do this job*"—which was true. All I did was answer the phone or make calls—asking very probing questions such as the whereabouts of one's colonoscopy report. The guy on the other end would try to remember that colonoscopy, the where and when and why—who was that Doctor, hold on, I wrote his name on a napkin, etc. etc.—oh, what memories. My uncle would look at me like a gem in a pawn shop. "You're an executive!" he would exclaim again. I threw up my hands... "*Ok, ok I'm an executive!*" Then we'd take the elevator and go the hamburger place across the street.

He'd treat me to a burger. "Let me pay," I'd protest but he'd pay, pushing the bills I pulled out back into my pocket. "You'll pay it off eventually."

We'd sit and talk about the faces of our people, our elders, their voices. My uncle is a born storyteller. And as he speaks I see the workers, the migrants picking up trays, sweeping floors, wiping tables. What stories do they hold in their hands? I listen to my uncle and hear his voice and the voice of all workers who want to free their stories but never get the chance.

I look at his face and taste his words — his laughter is still there, it rises like fire. The workers hear it. It takes them to another place for a moment — an area of pause, where we can be ourselves, can take back our lives. We're all laughing together. Then, it's time to get back to work.

Organized Resistance of the People: Unions

Through kkkapitalism, all bodies outside of the owning/pimping class have been exploited, making interdependent family-based or village-based means of production very difficult. After so many years of genocidal theft of human capital, the people began to organize. Eventually they began to form unions, which were a desperate, necessary reaction to deadly kkkapitalism.

Often labor struggle discussions begin and end with labor unions. Unions are extremely powerful and important bodies, if un-pimped, for workers of all types. But this book is written by poor workers and unrecognized workers and is dedicated to workers who are not even viewed as worthwhile members of organized unions.

Sometimes through the herstory of the US workers' struggle, the original structure of non-corporate work is buried under a narrative that only talks about our fight for rights within the corporate-dominant system. This means that our indigenous structures of work are never recognized, and that triumphs for unions perpetuate capitalist models as long as they offer "fair" working conditions. Capitalist, separatist models of ghettoization, such as age-segregated schools, child care centers, and homes to care for our elders are normalized as positive ways to function. This keeps up the necessary "mobile workforce," a crucial part of capitalism's machinery.

Take one of the pages of labor herstory that bring a warm and fuzzy feeling to the minds of labor unionists, organizers, and liberals everywhere: the misunderstood case of child labor. From the beginning of pre-colonial time, agrarian and non-agrarian communities relied on their children to help the family, in the fields picking or tending to animals, or vending or making products to sell. Children as young as 4 or 5 were working in whatever capacity made sense for their small bodies. The labor of children in a village is not only essential to family and community economic survival and thrival, it is important for children to feel essential to the family's survival. Child labor is not essentially the problem: the problem is the corporate ownership of the labor.

Our poor bodies of color are not valued unless we are producing for the benefit of the kolonizer class. In this process of colonization, our backs, our production, our children, and our time have been stolen. Before, we worked together as families to survive and thrive.

The kkkapitalist system separates elders from children, mothers and fathers from their babies so the need for consuming, alone-living individuals is embedded in their souls. This acts as the perfect brainwashing ground for kkkapitalist belief systems of hoarding and stealing, as well as the feeling of uselessness that children themselves have. Hours upon hours of time spent alone, isolated, in front of computers or televisions, never being told that they are necessary to the family's survival, is a sure way to lead to a young person getting into trouble, feeling "bored" or unnecessary.

Child labor and family interdependence still exists in most indigenous communities and underground communities. It's just that in the western, Eurocentric, owning-class-defined world, the labor of our children is criminalized and pathologized. Street vending communities and families in all parts of the world rely on their youngest members to create, produce, and sell. I was selling and creating to support my mama and myself when I was as young as 12 years old. Without my labor, we would not have eaten, paid rent, or stayed alive.

Poor People for Other Poor People: The Underpaid, Unsafe Work of In-Home Support Services Workers

BRUCE ALLISON / POOR MAGAZINE POVERTY,
ELDER AND DISABILITY SKOLA

In 1980 I started my home care career. My first client was a transgender revolutionary and one of my sheroes, who was 420 pounds and tended to prefer appearing in mumus. She was the sixth grand duchess of San Francisco. She was the welfare fund for the AIDS Foundation before there was the AIDS Foundation. She helped provide funding for aides for very poor AIDS patients if they couldn't get funding from another source. My duties were to cook and prepare meals, wash dishes, give her a bath, and go shopping with her.

I had other clients too. I was earning $2.50 an hour. I had to do nursing duties like give injections and run respirators and other medical equipment with only one day of training (or less) to each item.

One day somebody from local 250 SEIU knocked on my door and invited me to the union hall to talk about our wages. I was polite, I went to the meeting. I wasn't a dyed-in-the-wool union member, but I wanted to hear what they had to say. As a low-wage worker, I had been burned by other unions. I went and heard what they had to say. I heard more about this union. At this time they were talking about a raise and giving us dignity, something I never heard from any union before.

During the day I would do my home care work and at night I would go and solicit more members to join the union. On other days I would go into meetings with City agencies to set up the public authority. They were as exciting as watching crabs walking across the street. We also had to go to Sacramento for rallies for the whole state. I've been up in Sacramento so many times that I knew each tree by the first name.

Doing home care work I had no life of my own, going to the Board of Supervisors explaining to them why San Francisco needed the Public Authority. Supervisors and State assemblymen were dumbfounded to hear of our conditions—carrying people up and down stairs in buildings without elevators for such a low wage, doing technical work that nurses assistants cannot do. We finally got the law to say that we could be represented by a union. The Public Authority was our equivalent of a company. Picked up another skill. Negotiations with a union. Went to negotiations training school in San Francisco. After all this hard work and negotiating skills I did not know I had, San Francisco had the first Public Authority with a union contract. The members voted it in with a 97% yes vote well above the required 50%.

While also doing home care work in the year 2000 I helped form the San Francisco Living Wage Law. The last night of the law we negotiated with Willie Brown. We were on two tracks at the same time. We had a ballot measure that we worked on as well as negotiating with Willie Brown. We were negotiating and if the Mayor didn't sign the Living Wage thing we would have put it on the ballot. The negotiations dragged on, but the Mayor caved in 5 minutes before midnight. We made some changes to the original idea that would have been on the ballot. This came out as giving all contract employees of the City of San Francisco a minimum of $10.00 per hour, where most of them were making minimum wage. Also a cost of living adjustment and health care.

My first client died in 1990. Other poor people clients I had were not the nicest people in the universe. Wouldn't know what the word thank you was even when it was written on a piece of paper. In 2001 I had to retire due to a back injury with no pension and no health benefits. This will be up to my successors to work into the contract. And good luck fighting the tightwads of our present system.

Underground Economic Strategies: Street Sales, Drug Sales, Art Sales, Survival Sex Work, Panhandling

Lots of akademiks have written about poor people's work, calling us the "underground economy." Politricksters and police have criminalized and legislated against us, and our own communities often hate us for the work we do to survive. From unions to business owners to fellow poor folks who work as slave-wage workers, we are never respected for our work. Over the years at POOR, us poverty skolaz, street skolaz, sex workers, vendors, and low-level drug dealers have begun referring to ourselves as micro-business people or Underground Economic Strategists. This re-naming is not meant to glamorize these forms of labor but rather to recognize them as the real work they are.

From sex-work to drug sales, there are many aspects of the ways we do business and use money that evoke judgment. And yet why is it that CEOs at Chevron, Bechtel, Monsanto, and Dow bring death, toxins, and environmental racism on our world and no one questions what they do with "their money"? No one asks whether they use their money to buy drugs or alcohol. The police aren't profiling them, following them, or incarcerating them for the constant violence they perpetrate on our communities.

This is not meant as a rationalization, but rather to bring some equanimity to judgments about whether one should "support a panhandler's habit" or use the services of a professional sex-worker. Discussions of drug sales and sex work and panhandling are filled with racist and classist hypocrisy. We are quick to say these are bad, crazy, criminal people, or sad people who must be "saved" if they are standing on the street, living and working in poor communities of color, or panhandling/soliciting for change instead of soliciting for donations to politrickster campaigns or for the United Way.

Underground Survival con drogas

ANGEL GARCIA
PNN RACE, POVERTY AND IMMIGRANT SCHOLAR
REPRINTED WITH PERMISSION FROM POOR MAGAZINE
02 OCTOBER 2007

As a gang member and a teenager growing up in the Mission, drugs were rampant. I, myself, have had many experiences in the barrio and calles dealing with my own addiction. I have been addicted to drugs and lived on the streets, sleeping under the freeway, cold and hungry. I have been clean for over a year now, but many times drugs helped me to survive homelessness and poverty.

Like all businesses functioning in the underground economy there is more risk than money. The money you make is barely enough to survive on.

Yo crecí in a rough barrio and saw many cosas going on all the time. When I started selling drugs in my neighborhood, I began mixing with junkies, drug dealers, and working people. En mi barrio, everything was brown, la gente and las drogas.

When we talk about the criminalization of drogas in our barrios we have to remember prohibition. From 1920 to 1933 the sale and consumption of alcohol in the U.S. was illegal and it was sold on the black market. Many people do not consider alcohol a droga, but alcohol does the same damage as other drugs. It breaks our comunidades apart. Alcohol was my first droga, and soon after I became addicted to drugs, the ones I would be criminalized for.

In the 1990's when I was just a teenager, only 14, many of the vatos and the regular gente raza got addicted to coca. I was a patojito (a little kid) with the junkies all around me smoking coca and Cristina (crystal meth). I saw this everyday, and then it became my life.

I used to see some vatos in the hood doing crazy things when they were locos (high) like talking to Satan. When I saw someone itching and scratching I knew they were high on some good heroin.

Para la gente que estaban addictas (for people who are addicted), your purpose is always the same, to find where you are going to get your next high. The question in my mind when I was addicted was how am I going to survive another day and not feel sick with the malias (the cravings). No one wants to wake up feeling sick with the cravings for your drugs.

I started smoking marijuana when I was 14. When I started selling drugs, I had never tried any harder drugs. I did not know how it was to be addicted to heroin, cocaine, or crystal. Then I got addicted to the drogas and knew the feelings of addiction that the vatos (guys) and jaínas (girls) from the barrio went through when they used to ask me for drogas. Then everything changed because I lost my friends and I had to keep on selling drogas para mantener my own addiction. Yo sabía that I was matando my own gente in the barrio of la Mission by selling and using drugs, and I wanted to stop. So sometimes instead of drogas, I would buy them food or even ropa (clothes). But I was still on my own, fighting against the drogas.

I became homeless sleeping at the bottom of the freeway; it was my casa pobre. I was sleeping in a space muy pequeño. It was like a jail cell, solamente 2 feet by 4 feet and filled with the smell of dirty socks. Mi único amigo was the grey hard slab that covered my head. For a long time, the nights were lonely. Fría and dark, se sentía like a refrigerator full of hielo.

Selling and using drogas was just another way to survive the long winters. Drogas helped me keep warm and to ward off hunger. My drug use and addiction was another way to survive the system in the U.S.

After much struggle I got myself into a rehabilitation program in Oakland. I have been clean now for a year and a half. I am currently writing a book about my life in the barrio de la Mission called, *Gangs, Drugs, and Denial.*

POOR News Network race, poverty, and immigration scholar Angel García sits outside, leaning against a fence.

Is Panhandling Work? A POOR Magazine WeSearch Investigation

DEE GRAY AND RICHARD X
REPRINTED WITH PERMISSION FROM POOR MAGAZINE
25 MAY 2001

At *POOR Magazine*, we consider panhandling/spare-changing to be work. The following is a transcript from the ongoing writer-facilitation dialogue between Dee Gray, co-editor of POOR and Richard X at his work site, located near Stockton and O'Farrell Streets in downtown San Francisco.

Dee: How many days per week do you work?

RX: Seven.

Dee: And what are your hours of business each day?

RX: I normally start anywhere from six to eight in the morning and go all the way through to nine or ten o'clock at night, with a couple of breaks in between of maybe an hour each.

Dee: What happens at your work when it rains, or in very cold weather?

RX: It's just another day...I'm still out here...rain or shine.

Dee: How does this job affect your health?

RX: It affects my health very seriously in that I have what's called venous stasis ulcers, which are skin ulcers caused by poor circulation in the lower extremities, the legs. Ulcers are sores, if you didn't know. And the fact that I'm on my feet for so many hours a day aggravates them.

Dee: I understand you also have emphysema?

RX: Yes.

Dee: Okay, so when your health gets really bad, where do you go for health care?

RX: General Hospital, basically.

Dee: How long do you usually wait?

RX: Anywhere from 2 to 4 hours.

Dee: Are you well treated, would you say?

RX: That's relative to who's treating me.

Dee: I heard that (laughter)...I know what you mean. Have there been times that you've...been out here with active emphysema and feeling really bad?

RX: Well, there have been times I've been out here and not wanted to be out here, but my needs necessitate that I be out here. In other words, my health takes a back seat.

Dee: Let's talk about harassment on the job. Can you tell us a little about that?

RX: There is a group, or should I say a team, of people called the Ambassadors, whose job was primarily designed to help tourists out, by way of giving direction, just helpful hints about where to go, where not to go, who to talk to, who not to talk to.

But in fact, in my understanding, they are contracted by different stores, different companies, to keep undesirables - I guess I would be listed as an undesirable - panhandlers and drunks and so forth, off of their property, which brings about some interesting situations. For some reason, I have become the number one priority with this group of Ambassadors. And I can say honestly that I have brought some of this on in that this one particular

*Original art by Art Hazelwood. Hand-drawn image of
Poverty Skola/Panhandler Skola Richard X — panhandler
by day, superhero by night.*

company, the Ellis-O'Farrell garage, which is one of their contractees, I have
been on their building site a number of times, because the flow of traffic
into the garage is where I get my money. People are more apt to give money
if they don't have to change the direction that they're walking.

Dee: So, that's your work site?

RX: One of my work sites, one of my best work sites…I have a good rapport
with the police officers in the area. They can attest to the fact that I have
never been aggressive…. Okay, I came to the conclusion that because these
people were hell bent on, to my way of thinking, destroying my livelihood,
I said I'm going to get off their property, get on the curb side, city property,
and continue my work…. As you can see behind you, there's a No Trespassing sign. That was put up primarily for me. So that they would have me or

have the tools to hopefully get me arrested and out of the way. This is the way I look at it, and I believe that's the way it is.

Dee: Here comes an Ambassador talking into her walkie-talkie.

RX: Oh, yeah, she's letting them know that I'm talking to somebody with a microphone. It all started when the director of the Ambassadors instructed her workers to take pictures of all the panhandlers and to label them as to what they either know or think that they do with their money. That is to say, if a person is a drunk, under his picture he's labeled "Joe Blow, Drunk" or "Joe Blow, Drug User." The lady had the unmitigated gall to come up to me one day and ask me what I did with my money. I in turn asked her what she did with her money. She didn't take too kindly to this, obviously. But this is the extent that these people go to.

Dee: Do you think panhandling is a job, self-employment?

RX: I most definitely do. It's probably one of the hardest jobs you can do.

Dee: What are your job duties? In other words, either you have to ask people to give you money or they just give it to you...or?

RX: There are different approaches...each panhandler has his own method, but there are a couple of things that have to be true if you're going to be successful and not violate any laws. Number one, you have to be courteous, because nobody's obliged to give you a dime. And myself, I try to have a kind word for everybody that passes, even if I'm under the impression that I might not get a dime today. If I'm courteous to this person, somewhere down the line I'm going to get something.

Dee: It's a sales technique...but what's going on with panhandling? Would you say it's guilt? What are the dynamics?

RX: I think it's any number of things. I think with some people it's guilt. I think with others it's a genuine concern. I think with some people it's a "here, look at me" thing: I'm giving to this down and out person.

Dee: Do you think you should get benefits for all your hard work, like the regular City worker's comp benefits?

RX: Sure.

Dee: With your permission, let's cover a little bit of your history. Did you go to college? What kinds of jobs have you held in the past?

RX: Before my health got bad, I was a dry cleaner, presser, and tailor. I worked with clothes...I was employed by Brooks Brothers for about eight years. I've worked at cleaners around the Bay Area. I have a year of college.

Dee: Were you a Union member?

RX: Yeah.

Dee: ...and then your health got bad?

RX: Yeah, my health got bad, I got laid off, my wife came down with cancer. I kind of went off the deep end, which kind of led me to where I am now.

Dee: So, it's an emotional and a physical kind of breakdown?

RX: Right, right.

Dee: So maybe self-employment or being an entrepreneur, if we look at it this way, is a way that you can access employment. It's your own hours, but you work really hard; I can attest to that fact.

Two days after this dialogue, Richard was arrested in Union Square and told by a San Francisco police officer that, based on a letter received from the Ambassadors, "he should not come within 100 yards of Union Square" (a downtown SF shopping district). This police officer had no stay away order or Temporary Restraining Order. But a very intimidated Mr. X has now moved his work site to a low visibility area of Market Street where he hardly makes enough money for his lunch every day. POOR Magazine's advocacy project is desperately attempting to attain pro-bono legal representation for Mr. X.

Workin' Hard for the Money

MICHAEL FORDHAM, WITH JEAN AND DENNIS,
RESEARCH ASSISTANT: MICHAEL ADAMS
REPRINTED WITH PERMISSION FROM POOR MAGAZINE
VOLUME 3: WORK (PRINT EDITION)

It's 7:00 am. Soft moist air lingers in the corners of benches and under sleeping vehicles parked in the Embarcadero parking lot. Through the mist I see our co-authors Jean and Dennis. They're pushing a shopping cart full of garbage bags. Jean and Dennis are recyclers.

Poor Magazine: Dennis, how long have you been in the recycling business?

Dennis: I've only been in it a little while, about three years, but it's been three years of daily recycling, all day long. When you're recycling hours and hours and hours of time, you feel like you know every dumpster, and everything that's in it.

PM: This seems to take a certain amount of skill or strategy. Do you consider recycling similar to having your own business?

D: Yes, definitely. I go at my own pace, and I know what I want to make. I make as much as I want and stop.

PM: How do you plan your work schedule?

D: I do spots where they actually save the bottles for me to be there at a certain time, so I've got them set up one after the other.

PM: What other jobs have you had in your life?

D: I've worked for Chevrolet, I've worked for Mazda. I drove in garbage trucks...I did recycling, actually, before, at a labor pool in Florida. I'm a detailer by trade.

PM: Do you consider this more or less difficult than those jobs?

D: I would consider this more difficult, because this involves more laboring. When I'm picking up bottles I walk probably 4 or 5 miles looking for them, and then I've got to do another 4 or 5 miles to get them back. And once I'm loaded, like now, I've got 700 pounds here. That's why I try to stay on the flat land.

PM: Can you give us a brief bio of your life before recycling?

D: I had a lot of problems when I was a kid. I got into a lot of trouble. And my parents and family kind of shunned me. They still love me. I can call them and stuff like that, but I choose not to because of all the stuff that I put them through. I felt like I was on the run for a long time. And I got married and that didn't work out. And that was when I had my jobs, with Budget and all that stuff. Once I got divorced, I ended up riding trains for 4 or 5 years, going state to state, city to city. I've been to at least 36 or 37 states in the last 5 years. I don't know how many cities. But that led me to here...I was just hopping freights here and there and I got over here and ended up getting a check from the General Assistance system, and food stamps. I got in trouble when I first got here with drugs, and I knew that wasn't my thing anymore, so I just quit that.

PM: How did you get started in recycling?

D: I did it before, like a can or two, in the state where I am from, but they don't pay like they pay here. But then I seen the guys doing it, pushing shopping carts, and so I just decided one day I needed some money. I didn't want to steal because I been in the penitentiary and all that before. I never want to go back. I went out and tried for myself one time. I think the first time I worked a couple hours, and it was really hot. I made like 8 dollars, and I sweated to make it, but I felt kind of good that I made that little 8 dollars. So the next day I did it again, I made more and more.

PM: Are you homeless, living outside?

D: Yes. I've been living with this woman here for 3 years outside.

PM: Are you constantly outside or do you raise enough money sometimes to get a place to stay?

D: Sometimes we raise enough money to get a place to stay, but most generally we live outside. We got a locker that we keep our stuff in.

PM: We've now arrived at the recycling center and this seems to be a really interesting little operation here along the Bay. The coincidence is that it's not a block from the shelter where I stay, the New Mission Rock Shelter. There seems to be a really viable operation going on here. Now they're taking each bottle individually and throwing it into a trash bin. Their work isn't done yet. Their scale weight was 594 pounds. There is considerable care taken to separate the bottles from the cans and the plastic bottles. Each one was weighed separately. Dennis, how much do you make on different items?

D: To be honest, usually you're only supposed to make $4.50, but I just gave her a couple of those extra Marlboro miles, with those right there, these guys give me an extra $1.50 on every 100 pounds that I've got. So, I have 500 pounds, so that's going to be $7.50 extra. That's just on the bottles. On the cans, it's all the same. The cans are 85 cents a pound, and the plastics... I'm not sure what the price is on that, but I do know that it's 5 cents each if you count them.

PM: What would you say about recycling as a micro-business?

D: It's a pretty good business. The only part about it that I see as bad is that people tend to feel like...for instance, I had a lady once when I was down off Embarcadero, she thought that I was going through the garbage looking at their bills trying to get numbers of their credit cards or something. Also because people throw a lot of trash everywhere, it just makes it kind of hard. I don't really think that it's profitable for a person on foot. In a vehicle that's a whole different thing.

PM: Thank you very much, Dennis, and Jean, too. They made $28.72 on bottles, $4.66 on plastic, and $1.27 on cans.

***

The hate and disrespect of recyclers is not purely a western phenomenon. Across the globe it is the poorest peoples, the lowest "caste" and usually women or children that rely on recycling or waste-picking. And most of these, the hardest workers of all, are criminalized and hated for the work they do.[17]

In 2007, poverty skola Sam Drew and I came up with a proposal for recyclers to take back some of our unrecognized labor: recyclers as independent contractors. We wrote:

All independent recyclers should hold the same rights as all the major recycling companies. Independent recycling should be decriminalized, recognized, and appreciated for the meticulous work it is. POOR's proposal for independent contractors should include not only decriminalization but remuneration and benefits for the independent contractors. …If the recyclers were able to obtain vendor cards, that would allow them to acquire their recyclable products without being harassed… These cards do not need to be too complex: just a simple card with their name, address and photo should be sufficient. Two cross streets could be used as a valid address if the recycler is houseless. The cards should also provide free medical care for the holder.

***

From South Africa to Nicaragua, poor peoples sell things we make, grow, find, and steal including food, clothing, pots and pans, chewing gum, dental floss, our own misery, and our own bodies on the street. In these businesses we can risk everything from harassment to incarceration.

People in the US usually think this form of money-making is associated with so-called "developing" countries, but actually people sell everywhere. It is one of the oldest forms of business and did not begin with the exchange of the colonizers' monetary system.

Several thousands of years before there was a United Snakkkes of Amerikkka or a blud-stained Dollar or Euro there were markets selling everything from medicine to food, many rooted in a barter economy. Before the gentrification food truck movement swept in, selling food outdoors was mostly a micro-business run by poor folks.

It has been years since I've been on the streets selling art and products made by my mama and me, in our underground, criminalized (read: illegal) micro-business, which I had been working in since I was eleven when my mama became too ill to work. Our never-licensed business was the only way we paid for nightly motel rooms, gas, food and the occasional apartment, if we sold enough that day or week or month.

Day after month, month after year, me and my mama stood on the streets of LA, Oakland, Berkeley, and San Francisco selling art, clothes, jewelry, and more alongside mothers and sons and daughters and uncles and fathers stuck in Amerikkka, lost in the criminalized diaspora of false borders across the globe. We stood together, selling watches, ties, sunglasses, always watching for Po'Lice officers/immigration, rain, or customers, whichever came first.

When we were selling on the street we had the same day as our fellow micro-business partners. If we sold a lot, Richard the panhandler would do well; if he did well, the street performer did well; and if he did well so did

A woman wearing a purple shirt and purple pants walks away from the camera, carrying a wooden pole across her shoulders with a large black trash bag hanging from either end. This photo of Mrs. Wong, a recycler/worker and designer, is from the back page of the WORK issue of POOR Magazine *Volume 3.*

the sex worker; and if she or he did well so did the day laborer soliciting work on the corner from contractors driving by.

We were all entwined in a street-based economy. We all supported each other and we all respected each other. And depending on the day, time and politrick-nology at work, we were all arrested with each other, because in Amerikkka you are always at risk of harassment, arrest, and confiscation if you don't own or pay rent on the land you are standing on. In the US this is more real than many other parts of Mama Earth where there are histories of street based economies and outdoor markets.

Us underground economic strategists, recyclers, street vendors, day laborers/trabajadores, and sex-workers don't need to be "saved" as much we don't need to be incarcerated. Peoples engaged in these different forms of micro-business need to be simply supported for the work we do, for the product, action, or information we are supplying, even if it's our own tragedy or struggles. We don't need the clean-up campaigns, BID's, neighborhood watches, security guards, and Po'Lice abuse. In many ways this was the point of AB5 in California, the Homeless Persons Bill of Rights and Fairness Act. Unfortunately, the bill was killed in the California Assembly in 2013, notwithstanding all of the work and time spent on it by WRAP poverty skolaz and Senator Tom Ammiano.

Consider the way people approach sex-work and trafficking. Sex work is rife with complexities, but it is also a valid form of labor. Sex-worker skolaz need to set the tone, the protections, and the legislations for their form of labor, not hyper-saviour feminists and fundamentalist Christians. Similarly, laws about the sale of substances are consistently written by people trying to profit off it as a multi-million dollar business or put more people in jail rather than the consumers or micro-business people. Instead of trying to save us, support us in the ways we are asking to be supported.

Criminalized, Labeled, and Thrown in Cold Cells

PHOENIX KAT/PNN — MAGGIE'S TORONTO SEX WORKERS ACTION PROJECT
REPRINTED WITH PERMISSION FROM POOR MAGAZINE
30 AUGUST 2012

Editor's Note: Phoenix Kat created this first piece for PNN Toronto, in a POOR Magazine revolutionary journalism workshop held at Maggie's Sex Worker Organizing Project in Toronto.

Tap tap. . . . I didn't hear the door as my mind was swimming some deep stinky muck. All I could think was: where I was gunna go, what was going to happen to me, and the events that had transpired a week before. I was a stone statue eating a BLT sandwich sitting on my friend Derick's couch while his mom vacuumed around me.

Tap tap. . . . Derick must have answered the door because he was calling me to the front hallway. As I turned the corner I saw two stuck up bananas standing in the hall outside of Derick's apartment. Both tall, one female, and they were both wearing ugly grey suits.

They identified them selves as detectives from 23 Division. My heart fell into my stomach, the room began to spin. I thought really? After all that. . . . After all the hiding, the running, after everything, this is how it was going to end — and I wasn't even gunna to get to finish my BLT sandwich.

"Can you come outside so we can arrest you?" the female banana said. Being 14, I didn't know that I could refuse and demand they bring a warrant, so I complied. Yes, I stepped outside. Outside of the last place I had to hide, outside of the refuge I sought for myself after frantically running and hiding in parks for 7 days, and outside away from my freedom so that two overdressed bananas could cuff me and drag me away to the next year and a half cycle of bullshit that I was about to face. . . .

Every day young people are harassed, profiled, arrested, and thrown in jail. Specifically young black and indigenous youth, youth who trade sex for money, panhandlers, ones that ran away from bullshit homes or foster care, and youth just trying to survive.

Being poor, indigenous, a person of color and criminalized means that you will continue to be sucked into the prison system where it is almost impossible to get out and get ahead. Many of the young women I met in Juvie were charged and held in custody for what they called an "AWOL charge." What this means is that they had run away — "AWOLed" — from their foster care home or group home. So to be clear, first your parent(s) are thrown in jail, then you are taken from the only family/community you know and forced into a bullshit home (if you can call it that), then you are criminalized and thrown in jail yourself for choosing to leave and live independently.

Moved around from foster home to foster home, left in group homes for months, often facing sexual and physical violence from the people or workers who are supposed to be caring for you until you are forced to run away and face criminal charges, thrown in cold cells for wanting to be free and define your own life. For wanting to leave an abusive and oppressive place. For wanting to go off into the world and figure out who you really are, create your own home, and choose your own family. This is not a crime, it's a right. Why does society, our government, and the court want to continue this cycle of institutionalization and criminalization of young people instead of providing the supports young people need to live independently and care for their children?

As I look back and remember my experiences with jail, knowing it's getting worse for youth who face the same bullshit, I fuckin worry.

Jumping Through the Hoops of "Micro-Lending"

Before the World Bank co-opted Muhammad Yunis and the Grameen Bank and got their grimy hands on the practice of "micro-lending," communities from Morocco, Egypt, Africa, Korea, China, and India were doing this process for thousands of years, supporting poorer family business enterprises with a community pot of support matching a small savings.

It began simply enough. The Grameen Bank launched a micro-lending program that truly helped very small savings circles started by poor women in India and Haiti. The women could launch micro-businesses and help themselves out of the deep poverty conceived by the wealthy class. And then the bottom-feeder bankkksters like Bank of America and Chase, looking for some way to clean their filthy records of exploitation, realized they could co-opt micro-lending. They launched the Individual Devil-opment Accounts and the International Devil-opment Association, more global, multi-national programs to make money off of poor people by feeding off their micro-businesses.

That said, no disrespect to any and all poor folks reading this who got sum blud-stained dollaz, Euros, or Gourdes from these multinational fools. But in my and my Mama Dee's case we first found out about this project because we thought we as poor women in micro-business could use it as a self-determined liberation strategy for us to support each other. Then as we looked deeper, we found that the "matched" money was controlled by some non-profit industrial complexes. We jumped through multiple hoops like business plans, weekly groups talking through our "obstacles to wealth management," reference letters from "established people," and bank statements. They were all humiliating, racist, classist ways of framing poverty and blaming the poor person without EVER talking about institutional racism, owning class hierarchy, and the deep lies of capitalism. But we jumped through ALL the hoops, no matter how high they seemed to hold them. And then at the end of it all we "lost" the contest to get the tiny micro-loan of $2,000. They said our business plan—based on what we'd been doing for over 10 years—wasn't "logical enough." "Another little murder of the soul," my mama said, and then cried.

"I'm a Venduh, It's What I Do:" An Interview with Marty G.

TINY AKA LISA GRAY-GARCIA
REPRINTED WITH PERMISSION FROM POOR MAGAZINE
PRINT EDITION VOL. 3, WORK, 1998

It was 9:30 am on Sunday. Somewhere in the center of the Tenderloin, a white yellow river of sun opened the street, cleaning mist, scattering fog, awakening small bugs, enveloping nearby breakfasts of Vietnamese donuts, cheap coffee, sausage, and pancakes. . . .

I don't care anyplace . . . anywhere . . . just as long as we're together ba-by . . . together ba-by . . . The chocolate syrup sounds of The Intruders and last night, and all the best Saturday nights, squirmed out of a scuffed boombox, and lingered on each link of a chain link fence, surrounding a parking lot where Marty Gonzalez was creating a product display on the dusty sidewalk.

Extra care was taken with a battered pair of Doc Martens, placed at an angle, just so, on a duct-taped end table. Then the clothes: first the dresses, how to fasten the sleeves of the dress to the fence without clothes pins so they wouldn't fly away in the San Francisco wind, then pants...how to hold up one leg so as to show the cut of the leg... "Hey brother-man... how's business?" a loud voice broke Marty's careful concentration, he turned to see his friend walking the rhythm.

"Well man, nothing yet... so you know, I took my usual shopping trip to the dump—some of the stuff is ok, but check out the microwave. It was almost new—the only thing wrong with it was a shorted plug, I re-threaded it, and now it's a fine-tuned frying machine."

"Alright, so now you sold me... what you want for it?"

"I'm tryin' to get ten dollars, but I'll take five—all I need is five and I can afford the flea market entrance fee. I got to work today or no lunch..."

"Well you just keep on tryin, that's a little rich for me, but I feel you brother."

"Never say never, maybe you'd be interested in this toaster?"

I remember...remember...when we used to play shoot em up, baby...

"I'll keep it in mind . . . it sure is a beautiful day — see any cops yet?"

"So far, no heat but the sun . . . "

. . . just as long as we're together ba-by . . . And then they came...rolling down the street . . . close to the ground, slicing through the sunny river . . . ripping life and hope in their wake . . . "ALL SELLING MUST STOP NOW . . . NOW!!" The mechanical eyes peering through the morning mist . . . the flashing red and blue signaling the end, the dresses were pulled . . . the pants torn off their careful display...

"What you gonna do now?"

"I don't know man . . . I just don't know . . ."

Somewhere in Manhattan . . .

> *"If we could get rid of the peddlers, panhandlers and prostitutes we'd have a clean city."* —RUDOLPH GIULIANI

On a sunny day in May, Rudolph Giuliani, Mayor of New York City, and amateur photographer, opened an art exhibit of his "work" at a posh Manhattan gallery. Outside, there was a large protest of citizens of the "peddler" persuasion, i.e. artists who have been known to exercise their First Amendment rights to free speech and display their art on public sidewalks or (egads!) actually attempt to sell their art in the parks or on the sidewalks of New York City.

Giuliani has waged battle against the micro-entrepreneurs, artists, and newspaper and book vendors of New York. His most recent plan involves restricting all sales or free speech by licensed and non-licensed vendors from 144 New York City blocks.

This unconstitutional legislation, fueled by Business Improvement Districts, corporations, and real estate interests are focused on reducing licenses issued to food carts, which are micro-businesses owned by primarily immigrant populations, and changing the location of the existing carts from the prominent well-traveled locations to infrequently traveled side streets where they will be sure not to be seen, not turn a profit, and be forced to shut down.

> *"Paintings, photographs, print and sculptures, such as those the appellants seek to display and sell in public areas of the City, always communicate some idea or concept to those who view it, and as such, are entitled to full first amendment protection... The City's requirement that appellants be licensed in order to sell their artwork in public spaces constitutes an unconstitutional infringement on their First Amendment rights..."*
>
> — 1996 U.S. SUPREME COURT RULING

Trabajadores migrantes/Immigrant Laborers
INGRID DELEON / VOCES DE INMIGRANTES EN RESISTENCIA

The perspective of an immigrant day laborer on multimillion condo project 8 Washington.

It seems like every week they are approving a new condo project for rich people in San Francisco. As a poor, single mama migrante/immigrant worker these will never benefit me or my family, so I thought it was interesting when the construction company claimed that a new multi-million dollar condo would benefit poor workers in San Francisco. I went to City Hall to find out more.

I found out that the condos will cost about two million dollars each. When I asked the spokesman for the project how this is beneficial to the people, he responded that it is because they work with the unions and are creating more jobs with insurance for the workers.

When I asked him what would happen with the workers that aren't here legally, he smiled and said that they would start somewhere. Perhaps cleaning rooms or making beds. In my opinion, this project wouldn't help poor immigrant workers like me at all. The construction workers that would benefit are all documented, and no poor person would be able to afford the condos being built. In reality, even though they say it's not for rich people, it is. As the rich rise, the poor are lowered - especially the immigrants.

Corporate Criminalization of Migrante Labor

GLORIA ESTEVA / VOCES DE INMIGRANTES EN RESISTENCIA

Day laborers made history today. Supported by several community organizations including the San Francisco Living Wage Coalition, POWER, Women's Collective, Day Labor Program, Catalyst, MUA, POOR Magazine, La Raza Centro Legal and others, hundreds of workers marched, spoke truth to power, and resisted the criminalization of day laborers by the managers of U-Haul. This march and protest happened after multiple failed attempts to negotiate through letters sent to the central directors running these companies explaining the workers' situation.

"I am here because the manager that just started working at U-Haul does not allow us to seek work outside the building and threatens that if we talk to people who approach us to give us work he will call the police. On occasions during the time that we were being hired he interfered with us even getting the job," said Jose Figueroa, day laborer.

Jose explained that the manager made his own list (of day laborers) and although they often begin waiting at 5 in the morning to get a customer, he still only gives the jobs to the people he likes even if they arrive late in the morning.

Another worker named Roberto said, "I have been here looking for work for over 3 years and we had no problem. We started having problems six months ago after this manager began working at U-Haul. He harasses us, disrespects us and yells at us and calls the police."

Sam, a jornalero activist, said: "We want him to stop humiliating us. All our problems started with this manager - we want him to let us work freely. He calls the police on the pretext that we shout but that's not true."

Maria Luna was leading members of the organization Mujeres Unidos y Activas who were showing their solidarity with the workers. She said, "We will not allow the laborers to be insulted. We will fight with them to achieve victory."

Donaji, representative of People Organized to Win Employment Rights, or POWER, appeared at this protest even in the rain and the cold and said that they felt the indignation of their neighbors: "This company (U-Haul) is in our community and their economy earns money from us and we can not allow this injustice to the laborers who seek work here. Therefore we demand that this injustice stop if they want to be in our neighborhood."

Secure Communities Unsafe for Migrant Laborers
JULIO CHAVEZ / VOCES DE INMIGRANTES EN RESISTENCIA

In the name of so-called "Secure Communities," legislators have created a new law that has a direct and very serious impact on all of us migrant peoples in the United States.

The law states that if an immigrant is arrested, the police will be required to share the information of the person detained with ICE (Immigration and Customs Enforcement), who acts quickly to detain and deport that person.

This law makes immigrant workers more vulnerable to rights abuses and exploitation, allowing employers to threaten to report them to police if they demand fair compensation and working conditions. Secure Communities is a plan that will negatively affect those people that are most unprotected.

21st-Century Plantation Slavitude (PRISON LABOR)

As more and more people become incarcerated for poverty crimes/survival crimes and criminalized underground work, as more of our black and brown children are shuttled through the special ed to prison pipeline, the giant apartheid corporate plantations known as prisons get more plentiful and powerful than ever.

Large corporate non-profit and for profit organizations set up to "help" or "rehabilitate" humans enslaved in these plantations have names like PRIDE (Prison Rehabilitative Industries and Diversified Enterprises), Third Generation, and Second Chance. Hundreds more "work programs" provide corporations like JC Penney and Victoria's Secret, IKEA and KMART with products. While the profiteering off the backs of our incarcerated brothers and sisters increases, the actual rehabilitation services, education opportunities, libraries, quality of life, and access to information decreases.

Prison is about loss—loss of freedom, loss of control, loss of family and friends, of life. Prison is about punishment, and loss of freedom is the punishment. But, that is no longer enough. Now prisons are slave camps and warehouses.

Big Business has moved in to combine with the California Department of Corrections and has set up work forces nicknamed P.I.A. (Prison Industry Authority). This has become a thriving business where the inmate is forced to work for pennies, often in unsafe conditions, while the prison system grows and prospers. Politicians have come up with fancy names like "war on crime," "war on drugs," "three strikes you're out," and "the crisis of public order." At the same time words like "high infant mortality," "horrible housing," "lack of food," "poor education," and "lack of jobs" are forgotten. Our court system is rushing those who are unable to retain private legal representation through the "proper channels" into the prison system and into big business' hands.

There are many akademiks and theoreticians who have never spent any time inside the walls of the plantation prison system other than to "research" their stories, who write about the injustice of the plantation prison system who we could cite. But it is the goal of this, the PeoplesText, to hear from the insiders, the survivors.

Decolonizing Work

> *"To The Patriarchy, Indigenous peoples are a threat. Indigenous people, so many of them are still free. Free to live as their Ancestors did, seeing themselves merely as part of the whole picture, not in charge of it.*
> *They are under grave threat from The Sociopaths, who want not only their land, their resources, but for them to become like us, controlled, beaten into a way of life that is making so many people feel so *wrong* inside, because it is so utterly unnatural.*
>
> *Fight with The Indigenous Peoples of the world, for they ARE standing up to OUR Masters...refusing to give in, to roll over, to just accept the Unacceptable.*
>
> *For WAY too long they have been hidden away by the Controlling Media, out of sight, out of most people's minds!*
>
> *THIS IS HOW YOUR PEOPLE ONCE WERE TOO, FREE!*
>
> *Wake Up, World, become proud of your Roots, of your Indigenous Relatives, all around Mother Earth."* —CHIEF RAONI[18]

What if you could create your work based on what is needed in your community? What if the work you did, the labor you contributed, was based on your natural abilities, your spirit, your soul, your culture, your land, your children? What if we took back our own backs, our own labor, stopped the system in mid-tracks and re-created our own systems of work?

In this capitalist plantation there is A LOT of decolonizing to do on work.

Our poor peoples' work—which can be anything from a hustle to raising a child—needs to be recognized. But this decolonizing is different from the rich-wite "reclaiming" of whatever they define as work: mothering, designing, art-making, reading, thinking. It's because of wite-supremacy values about legitimacy, whose ideas and movements are valued and "trusted," that peoples with class or skin privilege can choose what they want to do and call it what they want to call it.

In the 60's & 70's, hippies modeled communal living after indigenous peoples that their ancestors had colonized. They raised their own animals and grew their own food. Some of them lasted, some of them disbanded or progressed into co-housing communities working hard against the grain of capitalist separatism to build community. I don't mean to critique these movements for the sole purpose of critiquing them, but there are many embedded hypocrisies that need to be spoken about. The free-farm, community farm, and free food movement tends to operate in a middle-class savior complex bubble, providing anarchist-esque "volunteerism" and communal living to mostly wite people right on top of stolen indigenous land. They may "serve" poor people while existing on trust funds or other stolen resources, and yet never actually speak about reparations, financial remuneration, or all of the money and resources required to do this kind of work.

In 2012, POOR Magazine launched the Pachamama Garden at Homefulness and discovered the intense amount of blood-stained dollaz necessary to run a community garden. This is NEVER spoken about by the plethora of white, privileged community gardeners across the US.

As poor, urban indigenous peoples, landless peoples of color we can take these principles/actions back and conscious wite peoples can support this movement with their land, sharing, and reparations and create companion communities. Together we need to act on the fact that work really has nothing to do with the fake monetary system created by the original stealers (colonizers). Rather it needs to be centered on our collective, interdependent survival and thrival.

Take back action, education, art-making, and care-giving as part of our integral life. Grow food and animals as part of life, not part of a commercial enterprise. Formally introduce bartering back into economies and our lives. And most of all, define work ourselves, for our interdependent and humble thrival.

This means we don't have to rape land, steal resources, and exploit our and our communities' bodies and pain for profit, but instead see life as integrated with work and work integrated with life.

Doctors, dentists, optometrists don't go to school to start a business doctoring or optometristing, but rather to heal each other and their communities. Engineers don't go to school to learn to engineer drones and zones and build devil-opments we don't need but rather to build a water system to support a community. Or better yet, don't feed the akkkademik machine:

don't go to school at all but change the way we raise our children, teach and care for each other, and base it in humble care-giving for the land and spirit.

Corporations are eating their own tails. There are increasingly less resources to steal. It is up to the few of us that are conscious, oppressed peoples to not let them keep destroying our communities and colonizing our minds. To take back our labor, our children, and our backs and invest them in the protection of our Mama Earth before there is nothing more to protect.

Change Wont Come from A Savior, Pimp or institution

Change will only come from a poor people-led revolution

—TINY AND PO' POETS

8

Default Colonizers, 21st-Century Missionaries, and Our Own Poor People-Led Movements

A tiny brown house with a small porch. In Atlanta, Mad Housers build huts for other houseless folks as an alternative to big, state-sponsored shelters.

Mad Housers

JOANNA LETZ
REPRINTED WITH PERMISSION FROM POOR MAGAZINE
6 JANUARY 2008

"This used to be an amusement park. We've nicknamed it Fun Town," Joe said with a smile and pointed over to the old pool. "Martin Luther King Jr. drove past with his daughter when it was still the park. His daughter asked if they could go. But that was when the park was segregated. Now sometimes I sit here and play speeches by MLK Jr."

On the last day of the U.S. Social Forum in Atlanta a crew of POOR Magazine's Poverty Scholars and Digital Resisters climbed into POOR's rented van and escaped from the walls of the Civic Center. Led by Keif one of Mad Housers architects we rode toward Fun Town. We passed parts of Atlanta we wouldn't have otherwise seen. I felt like we had entered a different world. We passed the gates into one of Atlanta's largest Universities and we went quickly off road down a dirt path to Joe Agana's hut.

Joe Agana welcomed POOR Magazine into his hut and onto the land he has been living on for nine years. Nine other people live on the land, each with their own hut. Mad Housers build huts for houseless folks in Atlanta. Each hut costs Mad Housers four hundred dollars and with a team of people a hut can be constructed in a weekend.

The heat swelled as we all stepped out of the van. The cracked cement ground reflected the sun. Joe's hut is only a stones throw away from the highway and from the university with its tennis courts and large buildings. Most people probably have no idea he is living there, hidden amidst the trees. Up above us, a billboard loomed, reminding us we were not far from luxury. The billboard read, "Georgia Tech Tickets on Sale." The cement ground, what was left of Fun Town, proved good land for the Mad Housers huts. Joe explained the land also at one point was a land-fill of some sort. The land is privately owned. Joe retold stories of police helicopters circling above their huts.

Mad Housers huts provide a better alternative for shelter and security than big state sponsored shelters. Keif said, "Give me a task force to write grants, instead of building a 1.3 million dollar shelter." The huts provide a level of autonomy that big shelters do not. Each hut has its own lock. Joe said, "This place beats the shelters. You can go and come as you please."

To even just walk in Downtown Atlanta you must have papers, state issued Identification. Keif explained Mad Housers are making their own ID's.

We stood around Joe's hut as he walked us through some of his life. I listened steadily to Joe as I held one kitten in my hand. The cats and kittens were everywhere, "to keep away the snakes and rats," Joe told us. Around the huts mosquitos swarmed. Joe seeing our attempts at swatting the bugs walked away for a moment and came back with a can of bug spray.

Joe pulled his stove out for us to see. "I just finished making lunch," he explained. Joe makes his own charcoal to heat his hut and cook his food. Mad Housers builds the huts and provides each person with a stove. Keif described how the stoves are made. Lifting up the stove Keif said, "The stoves are made from paint buckets. The paint is taken off and the buckets screwed together. At the bottom the screws can be taken out to act like a thermostat. Mad Housers gets donations of wood that is used to heat the stoves."

Joe walked us through his garden. A tall tomato plant grew up from between the cement blocks. The soil Joe fertilizes with his own compost pile. Mustard greens, and swiss chard were ready to eat. Chickens and their little ones were scuttling about.

"There is no electricity or running water." Keif explained, "the city cracked the fire hydrant just down the road. We got a friend somewhere." Sanitation services, water, and power are difficult for Mad Housers to obtain. The billboard shines at night where Fun Town remains without power.

Joe Agana left Bolgotanga, Ghana for the U.S. in 1975. Joe said, "I didn't live like this in Ghana. I had to learn all this. What I don't have I live without." Joe has two huts, one he sleeps in and the other one is his library. On Joe's porch his battery powered radio sat waiting to be turned on.

Mad Housers is trying to forge relationships. Mad Housers has a relationship with the university where Joe just received his forklift certification. He is OSHA certified and he was the top of his class, but without papers Joe cannot find work. POOR Magazine is looking to find Joe a lawyer to help him get legal status.

Before leaving Joe's we made contributions to his library, some POOR Press publications and POOR Magazine's own poverty scholarship.

We piled back into the van and drove the short distance down the dirt road, past the fire hydrant, past the entrance to the college, and drove onto the highway. We drove back to the Civic Center and the US Social Forum walls. We drove past the McMansions, also known as the infills that have replaced bungalows, past condemned houses, past what POOR Magazine's Poverty scholar Vivian Hain nicknamed "Legoland Condos."

Poverty exists here in the U.S. as it does everywhere, only the U.S. likes to deny that poverty exists. The U.S. calls itself a "developed" country, a "first world" country, and relegates the use of "third world" and "developing" for those other countries south of here. But as Jewnbug, one of POOR's poverty scholars explained, "I come from a third-world economy right here."

The Mad Houser huts are not the end all of end alls. But as Joe said it beats living in a shelter. At community newsroom the issue of the huts is one of contestation. As Laure McElroy related, "We are fighting to keep the projects but no one really wants to live there. It is a thin line."

As Tiny said, "What isn't talked about is the criminalization of poverty. If you are houseless in Atlanta you go to jail. I was standing outside, a few blocks from the Civic Center two patrol cars came and asked me what I was doing. The other element of the Mad Housers is the huts provide a safe place away from being put in jail."

As Tiny also recalled, when poor folks get together to create communes and alternative lifestyles, they are criminalized. Such is the case with Mad Housers and was the case in the MOVE house in Philadelphia. But when white folks create communes, they are not forced to go underground. The lifestyle is equated with going back to the land, the agrarian dream.

Poverty Scholar Jewnbug related her experiences growing up in a camp in Castro Valley. "I lived for a few years with my family camping with other homeless families on private land. These places exist, but people don't talk about it. We moved back to San Francisco to a one-room apartment, my mom, my brother and I. I heard the police broke up the campsite."

Joe Agana and the Mad Houser huts have to remain unseen and hidden so as not to be criminalized and hounded by police.

Poor People's Movements

There are thousands of organizing efforts across the globe trying to help us. Us: poor, the underserved, the so-called voiceless, the wretched, hungry, the sick, the criminals, the disabled, immigrant, indigenous, refugee, homeless, and incarcerated. But very few of these efforts are visioned, organized, run, and maintained by poor and oppressed peoples. Instead there are parachute liberals, 21st-century missionaries, peace kkkorporations, Red kkkross and (I aint feelin' you) FEMA. And so often in the "helping" comes the profiting.

Non-profiteers often set up organizing agendas far too time-, meeting-, or commitment-heavy to include poor and working-class people actually suffering from the problems they aim to address.

They also tend to set up colonized emulations of turf wars for members. Collaboration is only available if you are part of their in-club, are working towards their agenda, or fit into their fundraising goals or grants.

Poor people-led efforts can be as small as one person creating a community garden in the front yard of their housing project unit in one of our neighborhoods, which is intentionally bereft of fresh food. This is what Matthew Robeson is doing in the Sunnydale Housing Projects of San Francisco. The Marcus Garvey Liberation Garden started behind a church in Houston, Texas, and then moved to a front yard to become a fresh farm stand/micro-business for the community.

Supporting, Standing With, Not Researching, Studying or Pimping

How do you support truly different models? Not through a devil-oper or a non-profiteer. Not by gentriFUKing (read "cleaning up") our neighborhoods.

You do it through listening and giving credit to the peoples' movements already here. Let the tenants in public housing take ownership of their own units, invite healthy young college students to come in and help teach us skolaz how to do plumbing, roofing, and other repairs, and also stay there to continue support. Give us a budget to take care of our own neighborhoods. STOP SAVING US, REHABILITATING US AND CLEANING US UP. Stand in solidarity with us, make things possible and help our young people help themselves and us.

Poverty and indigenous skolaz can go back to our own leadership skills, our own science, our own forms of accountability. Stop working off all these colonized plantation models. Start neighborhood elder councils, give our elders back their own leadership, and honor people for the knowledge and skills they already possess.

Living consciously as poor peoples, as indigenous peoples is organizing. Living while poor, black, brown, red and/or disabled in the US is organizing. Organizing for us folks under attack can be just staying alive and keeping our families safe and fed.

Just getting thru the day, your head, heart, and body filled with pain, depression, memories, flashbacks, hunger, exhaustion, anxiety, and fear is an act of resistance. Just not getting killed by Po'Lice, criminalized or profited on by NPICs is an act of power. Just paying rent, not getting evicted, gentrified, or displaced, not being incarcerated, profiled, is an organizing triumph.

Off-plantation, self-determined, poor and indigenous organizing among youth, elders, and families in struggle is a different kind of battle. Its EX-TREMELY hard for us to stay alive, run the hustles we have to do to feed ourselves and our families, struggle through our hellthcare, our unrecognized, underpaid work and the many different little murders of the soul, much less get along with each other, trust each other and love each other long enough to fight the oppressors on our neck and join movements.

So in this way, in a good way, with a clear gaze, and all this medicine we as fellow poor and indigenous peoples in struggle and resistance can begin to truly decolonize our souls, our land, our minds, our stories, and most of all our actions for all the peoples already here and for all of those still to come.

Letter from Shamans and Young Guarani People of Brazil
LETTER TO POOR MAGAZINE

We, the Shaman of the Guarani Kaiowá and Guarani Ñandeva are no longer known as Ñanderu and Ñandesy. We rediscover an ancient term and we are now called again the Tekoa'ruvixa, the ones who give life to the children.

What worries us the most is not being able to fulfill our dream of dying in our traditional Tekoha land. We want to come to our land and die in our land. This is our dream and we cannot wait any longer.

We have our own way of life. We deal with matters our own way. Each of our prayers serves a purpose: for good crops, for health, to avoid storms and their widespread destruction. We pray for solar eclipses. It is our custom to boil Cedar woodchips and drink it to help us pray. We also use it to bathe the young and heal the wounded.

We need the earth to keep our culture alive. Our culture is bound to the earth. We should not have to live by the side of the road or left at the corner of a farm. While we are landless, we cannot live.

Many white folk believe that we all we seek is land. But what we really need is the earth, our lives depend on it. We have been landless, without our Tekoha, for far too long; our young have grown not knowing what that is and they have grown traumatised. Consequently, our young often shun us the Sha-man, they do not know about us, they are far from nature, from nature's medi-cine, from our rituals and from the forest. It is our land that provides all that.

We have always had our health. But without the earth, we do not have the resources that kept us healthy for a long time. Without those resources we require government's health resources. We had everything we needed to survive in the forest, the forest fed us, but it has been destroyed, it has been taken from us, so we depend on government's staple food baskets.

The earth means the survival of our culture, or our nation. This is our life, but we fear that, for the white folk, this means nothing.

Our prayer house cannot be relocated. Our medicine is only obtained at our Tekoha. We have our own traditional education system and in order for that to continue to exist, we need our culture to exist as whole, so our young continue to be indigenous people.

The older Tekoa'ruvixa are aging and dying and wish they were back at our Tekoha. They want to go back to our land still alive, they wish to die there, where our ancestors died. We cannot wait any longer.

— ATY GUASU ÑANDERU MO MBARETE, JULY 27, 2013
TEKOHA JAGUAPIRU, DOURADOS, MATO GROSSO DO SUL

Transubstantive Errors/21st-Century Missionaries

One of the errors mentioned in previous chapters are the transubstantive errors of wite-supremacist arrogance practiced so often by what I affectionately call 21st-century missionaries, trying to "save" us.

Even revolutionaries, activists, and eager media producers make transubstantive errors. One of the most famous examples is Che Guevara. I do not want to take away from his tireless work to facilitate the important Cuban Revolution, which stands as a beautiful example of the success of anti-capitalist revolutions across Pachamama. But as an individual he was a privileged man, raised with owning class-akademia-infused cultural values about education, poverty, and healthcare. On one hand this was positive because he leveraged his class and race privilege to critique and fight against his own class and to share wite-science doctoring skills with poor communities across Mama earth. On the other hand this locked him to a rigid belief system about "what the people needed" which did not include a pan-indigenous understanding that valued the traditions, values, spirit, medicine, and scholarship already existing in indigenous peoples living on their lands of origin.

The most specific way this played out was his dominant class, or colonizer class, concept of literacy. To fight in Che's armies you had to be able to read and write. I understand this on one hand, to read instructions on the weapons, etc., but the linguistic dominance of the Western language does not make sense in a framework of language reclamation, land reclamation, and indigenous self-determination.

In some senses this made sense for the mestizo population of Cuba, filled with so many Africans in diaspora as well as other migrants who had been oppressed and enslaved by the owning class and had no access to their indigenous lands, but in deeply indigenous communities like Bolivia and the Congo I believe that European-organized political agendas like Marxism and Communism are over-simplified and don't speak to indigenous land use, interdependence, prayer or spirit-led, horizontal self-determination.

Not to say that our children should not learn these colonizers languages, but it should be placed in the context of learning the language of our oppressors to understand them and be able to trade, speak, relate, negotiate horizontally, but we also need to hold up our own strength, power, agency, beliefs, language and spirit first and foremost and never try to become, transform, adapt, or aspire to be them.

Mama used to say, "I ain't part of no 'ist' (Marxist, Communist, Leninist, Capitalist). I'm just a poor Black-Indian woman, without a pot to piss in or a roof to sleep under."

In this chapter we face one of the most difficult parts of poor people-led/indigenous people-led organizing itself: the reason POOR Magazine started, the reason we continue, the reason our revolution is silenced and co-opted, the reason our self-determination is consistently undermined and disrespected.

These boundaries are very nuanced and very distinct all at the same time. It allows the same people to profit from our pain and the same people to remain in pain. It allows gentrification to happen while organizers work on gentriFUKation.

How many times have I heard people who have not suffered, struggled with poverty, racism, ableism say blithely, "We need to get more poor folks, POC folks in this movement," or "Why don't more poor people, migrante, disabled, African descendent, Filipino, indigenous, elders show up to these demonstrations, marches, rallies?"

The first mistake is that we, the impacted, the hated, the criminalized, the bordered, the oppressed are not the ones leading the group. Because if we were we would already know why more of us weren't in the room. Perhaps, ironically, it's because of the impact of the very conditions, issues, struggles the movement is set against.

Just because we aren't in their room, led by their dusty wite or clean brown agenda, doesn't mean we aren't working toward liberation.

Many times for indigenous peoples in diaspora our ways of can be maintaining healthy relationships, raising strong, conscious children, feeding our bodies and communities healthy food, owning our own economies, liberating our bodies from the environmental terrorism waged on us.

It is also through coming back to each other, to our souls, to our deep structures, to our creation stories, to our prayers, to our ancestors and our traditions. Ujaama Villages in Oakland state clearly that their movement is by and for Afrikan peoples and works daily for self-determination of Afrikan peoples. The Black Riders Liberation Party teaches, organizes, and presents in the community on our own Afrikan peoples' liberation from all the oppressors' systems. The Vakas are Pacific Islander Canoe builders, traversing the oceans following their ancestors' stories, their creation stories, not the colonizers' maps, re-writing herstory as their own and addressing healing of our poisoned oceans and islands, global climate change and rising waters from their own deep structures, without an akademik, a middle-man of the institution making things clean, safe, or "understandable."

Dignity Village

In Portland in the late 1990s, like in so many post-gentriFUKed cities, houseless people were pushed from place to place, forced to migrate around town as the devil-opers and the Po'Lice created new rules to push them out of sight. In August 2001, the City Council finally "permitted" a group of houseless folks to camp at a lot called Sunderland Yard—far away from downtown, but still a place to stay. The City Council has resisted efforts to close down the campsite over the years. It is still intact today.

From Dignity Village poverty skolaz:

When people find themselves living on the streets, either in doorways, or under bridges, or the wooded areas along roads. There comes a time when it takes its toll on them. They start standing out, instead of blending in. Trying to maintain that blend is lost. The best they can do is survive.

Getting back to a standard normal way of life is simply a dream now. Someday I will have this and that. Reality of the real world brings them back to disappointment.

This is where Dignity Village comes in. The village offers many ways for people to get back on their feet again. The standard shelters systems just can't provide all the things one needs to get back up on there feet again all in one place. It is to broken up and spread out. Sometimes you have stand in a line half the day to get a shower and the other half of the day to get a bed to sleep on. You pretty much wait in line for everything. It don't leave you any time to go out and find a job.

Dignity Village provides all these needs and offers services like computers for online job search, and a phone center, where employers can reach them 24/7 for work.

Dignity village was built by homeless people that simply wanted change. They wanted their Dignity and self-respect back.

Dignity Village started in the year 2000. They went from tents, and tarp covered two by four huts, to small houses, which you can see today.

Dignity Village is one place that takes people off the streets and gives them a place to rebuild their lives. Some people need short-term help, others may need a lifetime. They took what they had and combined their efforts to helping each other, with support without shame.

***

This so-called "resilience" that is so often spoken about us po folks' "ability" to survive is over-simplified crap. It is so many things that keeps us going, holding on, fighting for life, love, crums and shelter, but what it's not is some mythical innate ability. Rather it's the refusal to give-up, give-in, or give-out. It's anger, it's stubbornness, it's rage.

Our movements are ambitious, they come from our heart, our prayers, our oppression, our pain. Our movements are enmeshed with our souls, they are not an intellectual exercise. They are not meant as a study or a research project; they are real. We protest because we can't sleep, we demonstrate because our children are murdered, our stomachs are hungry, our mother earth is crying, our ancestors are desecrated, our schools are closed, our homes are stolen. We protest, we organize because we are arrested for being poor, for living while black, brown, or disabled in Amerikkka.

Sometimes we are just one mama showing up to every kkkourt hearing for their profiled or murdered child,[19] or a few dozen houseless folks living under a freeway off-ramp whose camp was smashed by Po'Lice. Or young people of color dancing to respond to violence, or artists who use their art to teach, fight, and resist colonization—sometimes only to get killed by Po'Lice or community violence.[20] Sometimes it's just one elder like bringing medicine and action to care for Mama Earth, or the person who won't stop, can't stop fighting the corporations that continue to steal our land and poison our water.[21] Or one poverty skola who holds the herstory, the spirit, and the art that the kolonizers tried to kill about our gente.[22]

Poor people-led movements are migrante-led, worker-led movements fighting for the rights of migrant domestic workers,[23] transgender warriors walking and talking their poverty skolaship and decolonizing/educating wherever they go,[24] indigenous young people fighting for self-determination,[25] and sex worker skolaz fighting for own rights to work and live un-criminalized and recognized.[26]

All of us building, learning, and inspired by revolutionaries like Fred Hampton, Hugo Pinell, Leonard Peltier, Mumia Abu Jamal, and George Jackson. Inspired by movements like MOVE 9 who organized in the poor people of color neighborhood of West Philly who were focused on a self-determined, African-centered, humble vision of collective, anti-capitalist, hunter-gatherer living. Refusing to adhere to politrickster-led, lying legislators and Po'Lice controlled communities they were ruthlessly attacked by the mayor and Po'Lice of Philadelphia. MOVE is one of the models that we look to at POOR Magazine's Homefulness Project. The eight members of the original MOVE 9 — Debbie Sims Africa, Janet Hollaway Africa, Janine Philips Africa, Williams Philips Africa, Delbert Orr Africa, Michael Davis Africa, Charles Sims Africa, and Edward Goodman Africa remain in the plantation (prison) to this day.[27]

African peoples in diaspora are constantly creating, growing, and manifesting black-led power in our own neighborhoods outside the systems of control and oppression.[28] Our movements resist all the cages the colonizers try to keep us in,[29] fighting for land reclamation while living on government crumbs.[30]

We look to Las Patronas ("female bosses") from Mexico: women who give food to migrants who are on a train called THE BEAST (because many people die or lose limbs on the train) that transports folks illegally from Cen-

Underground street based dance crew Turf Feinz in the rainy streets of Oakland. Three young Black men look on while a fourth dances. The Turf Feinz came out in 2010 in response to the shooting of so many Black and Brown men in their East Oakland neighborhood.

tral America through Mexico into the USA. They are small groups of women who collect small donations from folks & local markets & recycle plastic bottles. They then stand next to train tracks & throw food to the migrants on the moving train. They do this as an offering to the Virgin of Guadalupe. They do not take government money, and they're not associated with any big org. If college students want to help they can donate shit like a kitchen or food but that is it. They don't do big shit donations cuz Virgen don't like that apparently.[31]

Indigenous warriors in traditional dress from North and South Turtle Island have their backs to the camera, in front of large university arches. They lead a prayer ceremony at University of California–Berkeley to reclaim stolen artifacts and ascestral remains of the Ohlone people.

The Revolution Can't Be Melted in a Pot

A ceremony took place on the UC Berkeley Campus to honor & remember the remains that are kept in the Anthropology dept. Bancroft Library & the clock tower are where over 11,000 remains are kept. The remains are housed in a very disrespectful manner, in the basement of the Library in school style lockers and in some cases in plastic grocery bags and amongst rat droppings. These are Our Ancestors. The school is objectifying and dehumanizing Native people. The local Mexica Danza capulli, with the help of other capullis and California tribal members, hosted this ceremony. Thru NAGPRA we can request for the return of Our Ancestors but the process is full of political red tape & remains difficult to pursue.

So we use the power of ceremony to pray for the return of Our Ancestors as well as other methods.

It is only the western, wite-supremacist, hetero-patriarchal values that would suppress prayer in political action, as it doesn't "fit" with a Marxist, atheist values system and therefore must not be part of a revolution.

Humility

One current that runs through our poor people-led, indigenous people-led movements is that we are humble. We don't claim to be everything, to answer all issues, or create a new world. In this way humility is key.

Organizing by wite-peoples with class privilege is bereft of humility because they hold the belief that they can go anywhere, do anything, save everything, fix everything, take care of everything, and be a part of everything. This is not entirely their fault because they have been told from their parents and their world that this is true. "You can do anything you want," says the constant stream of media and ad campaigns trying to sell you on this kolonizer informed arrogance. Their world is run by them, the colonizers who long ago believed they could go anywhere, take anything, be anyone and steal everything, under the guise of fixing, advancing, succeeding, helping. But really all they wanted to perpetuate was greed.

Humility dictates our poor and indigenous led movements. Constraining peoples' actions to move "in a good way" softly on Pachamama, thinking first about others who live there, are there, fight there, are from there. Who have already done this work, spoken about these issues, fought for these rights.

At its most benign, this arrogance of pseudo-corporate non-profiteer or NGO or Poverty industry movements fuels the movement of peoples with class privilege into neighborhoods they aren't from (gentriFUKation) or to launch teaching programs in poor, indigenous communities without asking. At its most deadly it creates media, art, and messages about worlds and peoples who haven't given their permission to be media subjects, the multimillion dollar tourism movement, constant and incessant "devil-opment." We are constantly told that this is what we as poor people need to get up and out of poverty. We are told this by the people who want to excavate our resources, sell us useless products, poison our land, our air, our water and our bodies. Perhaps, if we began to decolonize all of this so-called economic development, help, crumbs, programs, and services we could begin to speak about land, language, and resource reclamation. We could begin to lead ourselves, our families, and our communities out from under the heel of the oppressor.

Occupy Was Never 4 Me (1 year later)

TINY AKA LISA GRAY-GARCIA
REPRINTED WITH PERMISSION FROM POOR MAGAZINE
16 SEPTEMBER 2012

I am the .00025- the smallest number u can think of in yer mind —
Didn't even make it to the 99-
love to all of yer awakeninig consciousnessness –
but try to walk in mine . . .

—EXCERPT FROM *I AM .00025*

Occupy was never for me. I'm poor, I'm a mother, I'm disabled, I'm home-less, I'm indigenous, I am on welfare, I never graduated from a formal institution of learning, I have never had a house to be foreclosed on, I am a recycler, panhandler, I am broken, I am humble, I have been Po'Lice profiled and my mind is occupied with broken teeth and a broken me. And I am a revolutionary who has fought everyday to decolonize this already occupied indigenous land of Turtle Island in Amerikkka.

I'm not hating. I am glad, like I said when it all first got started, that thousands more people got conscious. I am glad that folks woke up and began to get active. What I am not glad about is that in that waking up there was a weird tunnel vision by so many "occupiers" of the multiple struggles, revolutions, pain, and deep struggle of so many who came be-fore you, upon whose shoulders and already "occupied" native lands you are standing on. This is what I have now come to realize is a strange form of political gentrification.

Like any form of gentrification there is a belief by the gentrifiers/colonizers that their movement is a different, new form, that it has little or no historical contextual connection to the ones before it. And that it owes little or nothing to the movements and/or communities already there, creating, struggling, barely making it.

And yes, race, class, and educational access matter. I have heard from elders that a similar thing happened in the 60's with the poor people of color movements raging on like Black Panthers and Young Lords then suddenly the "anti-war movement" sprung up, driven by white middle-class college students and the political climate suddenly got large.

This ironic disconnect was never clearer than the way that houseless people, people with psychological disabilities existing outside, were treated, spoken about, problematized, and "dealt with" in the occupations across the United Snakkkes this last year.

"We are very excited because the police agreed to come every night and patrol our "camp" because we have been having so many problems with the 'homeless

people' coming into our camp," said an occupier from Atlanta, Georgia.

City after city, occupation to occupation, these so-called conscious and political spaces which were allegedly challenging the use of public space and land use and bank control over our resources and naming the struggle of the 99% versus the 1%, were playing out the same dynamics of the increasingly Po'Liced urban and suburban neighborhoods across the US.

The lie of "security": who it is for? The notion of "illegal" people, and how some people are supposed to be here and some are not. Our reliance on police as the only way to ensure our community security. The veneer

Tiny walks away from the camera, carrying a large handmade sign with words like "Home," "land," and "shopping cart."

of racism and classism, alive and well in every part of this United Snakkkes reared its ugly head in all of these Occupations. In many cases the "occupiers" gentrified the outside locations of the houseless people in these cities. Taking away the sort-of-safe places where houseless people were dwelling outside. And yet no accountability was ever even considered by the "occupiers."

Perhaps it's because the majority of the "occupiers" were from the police-using neighborhoods, and/or currently or recently had those homes and student debt and credit and cars and mortgages and stocks and bonds and jobs. Perhaps it's because Occupy was never for me or people like me.

In Oakland and San Francisco, the alleged "bastions" of consciousness there was a slightly different perspective. Many of the houseless people were in fact part of the organizing and then eventually, due to deep class and race differences, were intentionally left out or self-segregated themselves from the main "Occupy" groups. They began their own revolutions or groups or cliques, or just defeated huddles around the camp.

Several of the large and well-funded non-profit organizations in the Bay Area re-harnessed Occupy into their own agendas and helped to launch some of the huge general strikes and marches to support labor movements, migrant/immigrant struggles, prison abolitionist movements, and economic justice.

In the case of the poor, indigenous, im/migrant, and indigenous skolaz at POOR Magazine we felt we could perhaps insert some education, herstory, and information into this very homogenous, very white, and very ahistorical narrative and to the empirical notion of occupation itself, so we created the *Decolonizers Guide to a Humble Revolution* book and curriculum. With this book and study guide and our poverty scholarship and cultural art we supported other indigenous and conscious peoples of color in Oakland who began to frame this entire movement as Decolonize Oakland, challenging the political gentrifying aspects of Occupy itself.

POOR Magazine in an attempt to harness some of the energy and minds of this time towards the very real issues of poverty and criminalization and racism in the US, created "The Poor Peoples Decolonization (Occupation)," traveling to both sides of the Bay (Oakland to SF), to the welfare offices, public housing, the Po'Lice department (where all of us black, brown and po folks get incarcerated, profiled and harassed every day, not just when we "occupy"), and Immigration and Customs Enforcement.

But in the end a small turn-out showed up for our march. I guess our poor people-led occupations weren't as "sexy" as other 99% issues.

Finally, in Oakland there was a powerful push to re-think the arrogant notion of Occupy itself on already stolen and occupied native lands, and became one of the clearest examples of the hypocritical irony of occupy.

After at least a five-hour testimony from indigenous leaders and people of color supporters at a herstoric Oakland General Assembly, to officially change the name of Occupy Oakland to Decolonize Oakland, with first nations warriors like Corrina Gould and Morning Star, Krea Gomez, artists Jesus Barraza and Melanie Cervantes and so many more powerful peoples of color supporters presenting testifying and reading a beautiful statement on decolonization and occupation, it was still voted on that in Oakland, the stolen and occupied territory of Ohlone peoples, the name would remain Occupy Oakland.

So as the "Occupy" people celebrate 1 year of existence, I feel nothing. I am glad that elders are being helped to not lose their homes through foreclosure, but truthfully, that work was already being done by so many of us already on the front line of eviction, tenants rights, and elders advocacy.

So one year after Occupy was launched, while lots of exciting media was generated, massive resources were spent, a great number of people were supposedly politicized and the world started to listen to the concept of the

99%, the same number of black, brown, poor, disabled, and migrant folks are being incarcerated, policed, and deported in the US. The racist and classist Sit-lie laws, gang injunctions and Stop and Frisk ordinances still rage on and we are still being pushed out of our communities of color by the forces of gentriFUKation and poverty. So, I wonder, how have these political gentrifiers changed things for black and brown and poor people? Not at all, actually, but then again, Occupy was never really for us.

Mama / Family-Led Organizing Against Po'Lice Violence

Poor people-led organizing can be revolutionary mamaz refusing to take the state-sponsored murder of their sons. We will continue to fight for our youth and the community to uplift it and bring forth some much needed change.

Mesha Irizarry's son, who was mentally ill, was shot 28 times by San Francisco Police. Mesha Irizarry launched a legal challenge to the culture of Po'Lice violence that encourages the shoot-first mentality that pervades these occupying armies in our poor communities of color. She stands as a role model for all mamaz resisting police murder today.

Denika, mother of Kenneth Harding Jr., and Monique Duenez, niece of Ernesto Duenez, have also taken action to counter Po'Lice terror and remember the legacy of their loved ones.

Along with these nieces and mamas, there is the power of Oscar Grant's Uncle Bobby who, along with his wife Beechie Keeton and the Oscar Grant Committee, has become a several thousand-family strong force marching in Anahiem, Oakland, Florida, New York, San Francisco, Texas, and Los Angeles against the crimes of Po'Lice against our black, brown and disabled and poor youth in Amerikkka. Ase-O, Rahiem Brown, Ramarley Graham, Amadou Diallo, Oscar Grant, Trayvon Martin, Alan Blueford Jr., John Williams, Derrik Gaines Jr., Manuel Angel Diaz.

Kenneth Harding Jr.
DENIKA, MAMA—LEADER OF
THE KENNETH HARDING JR. FOUNDATION

Since my son's murder by San Francisco police on July 16, 2011, over a $2 Muni transit fare, my life has drastically changed. I have left my hometown of Seattle, Washington, and my livelihood and relocated to the Bay Area with my daughter who had just turned four at the time, Mi'Neika, to stand for righteousness while seeking justice for the murder of my son. I have started the Kenneth Harding Jr. Foundation. I have become an activist, an active protester, and a public speaker. My life purpose now is to prevent another child from experiencing such a heinous death. I have been active within the BayView / Hunters Point community. I have been going into the high schools, colleges, and universities reaching out to the youth and building awareness that this is happening and trying to create prevention so that no other parent has to experience what I have. I have spoken out publically against police brutality at several events. We also feed the community on the third Sunday of every month at the exact spot where the ground is still stained with my son's blood. Because the Kenneth Harding Jr. Foundation and various other organizations such as Power and ANSWER Coalition continued to fight against the MUNI transit system in San Francisco, to date over eighty thousand low income youth have been approved for free transit.

Ernesto Duenez Jr.
MONIQUE DUENEZ

Monique Duenez is the niece of Ernesto Duenez, who was killed by Manteca Police. She organizes with her family and thousands of other families across the state to fight the endless attacks on our black and brown youth. The family holds vigil every Sunday outside the Manteca Police station.

When my Tio Ernest Duenez Jr.was murdered by John Moody of the Manteca Police Department on June 8 2011, a big chunk of happiness and heart was taken from my family as well as myself. We have been fighting every Sunday since then at the Manteca Police Department. As a part of my Tio's fight for justice I have met a lot of families along the way who I have gained so much love and respect for. I see what these families are going through and I know why they fight so hard and never give up. I do it because of the love and respect and pain in my heart I have to go through to see my family in pain and relive that event over and over each time we go to protest or a march, so I stand on that street in front of MPD with my sign raised high, reading JAIL FOR MOODY to support my family in this FIGHT. This is my passion, where my heart is at and I want to do the same for each and every other family going through the same, because I see my grandmother and grandfather in pain, with anger and a fire within them and having to remember why they are out there fighting each Sunday. That is the same pain, anger fire and love-driven emotion I see these families going through. I am driven with the same emotions to help and fight alongside each family including my own, to show them all "I am here. I feel your pain, and I am with you all the way!" When my family has events and marches and we have supporters coming from far and wide, the feeling in our hearts of support and solidarity is also what helps us keep pushing and fighting, support is everything in the fight for justice to all families because we all need each other and we are all feeling the same way.

My Tio Jr ALWAYS had my back, he NEVER left me hanging. He was one of my best friends and he always gave me his best advice. I don't speak much about my pain I usually just put it into the fight but the reason I go so hard for my uncle, the reason I am the warrior I've become is because I know for a fact, if roles were reversed he would have me in a minute, he would have never given up on me so I am never giving up on him! When I'm out fighting for justice even if it's at another family march or protest, I feel him with me more than any other day, giving me the motivation to fight with my fist up in the air yelling "no justice no peace." And my heart feels at ease for the moment. His son Dominic is my godson, and I made a promise to my Tio Jr that I will always have his baby boy's back, just like he had mine. I see my godson and know he will never get the chance to know who his father is and that puts drive into me even more and makes me want to fight for John Moody to be behind bars like he is supposed to be, so I also fight for the children of these victims of police brutality. My Tio Jr is putting this drive in me, I feel him every day and each time I'm fighting I can feel him standing with us all, so proud to know his family isn't giving upon him. That's what makes me fight.

Community Safety / Po'Lice Violence

At POOR Magazine we have practiced a "No Po'Lice calls" mandate since our inception. We believe this is one of the ways to activate liberation off the grid of control of wite-supremacy. Our comrades in the Black Riders Liberation Party also practice "Watch a Pig" and "Watch a kkkourt." Along with several allies, we hope to create a Po'Lice Free Zone in East Oakland.[32]

BLACK RIDERS LIBERATION PARTY OAKLAND CHAPTER
BLACK RIDERS LIBERATION PARTY

THE BLACK RIDERS LIBERATION PARTY IS THE NEW GENERATION OF THE BLACK PANTHER PARTY FOR SELF-DEFENSE. THE BRLP BEGAN IN A Y.T.S. GANG PRISON IN CALIFORNIA WHEN GENERAL T.A.C.O. (TAKING ALL CAPITALISTS OUT) AND OTHER BLOODS AND CRIPS BEGAN LEARNING ABOUT THEIR HISTORY, OF HOW THEY WERE CREATED AS UP AND COMING SOLDIERS OF THE BLACK PANTHER PARTY AND THE BLACK LIBERATION MOVEMENT....WHEN THEY LEARNED OF THIS AND HOW THE RACIST UNITED SNAKKKES GOVERNMENT HAS BEEN MURDERING AND USING BLACK PEOPLE SINCE THE FIRST AFRIKAN SLAVES WERE BROUGHT HERE, THEY DECIDED TO STOP COMMITTING GENOCIDE AGAINST EACH OTHER AND TO STAND UP AGAINST WHITE SUPREMACY AND KKKAPITALIST OPPRESSION....BLACK RIDERS LIBERATION PARTY'S MAIN FOCUS SINCE ITS INCEPTION IN 1996 HAS BEEN ORGANIZING TO EDUCATE THE MASSES OF AFRIKAN PEOPLE IN THIS COUNTRY AND ALL THROUGHOUT THE DIASPORA TO STOP BEGGING THIS SYSTEM FOR FREEDOM AND JUST TAKE IT!!!!THROUGH THE PHILOSOPHY OF REVOLUTIONARY AFRIKAN INTERCOMMUNALISM BY ALL MEANS NECESSARY!![33]

The T.A.Z. Foundation, Inc.
THE T.A.Z. FOUNDATION

The T.A.Z. Foundation, Inc. is 3 brothers, Torian, Amir, Ziair, born to Audrey "Candycorn," a West Oakland native.

We are proud to present "Ishy-mi Stranger Danger Saga." This book was created to create awareness of eradicating hatred, violence, and bullying in Oakland. The boys also have T.A.Z. Foundation, Inc. apparel, anti-bullying gear. This trendy urban wear was inspired by the "Ishy-mi Stanger Danger Saga" storybook.

T.A.Z. Foundation came to life in 2008. In 2015 Torian was murdered by community violence. In 2016 T.A.Z. Foundation, Inc. helped with the adopting of Oakland's new city motto, "LOVE LIFE," voted in by the people. In 2018, T.A.Z. Foundation helped build a play structure in West Oakland with Project Kaboom and Blue Shield. In the summer of 2018 we will be opening our very first Healing Dance Camp.

Currently, Ishy-mi aka Ziair and Amir are street reporters and youth poverty scholars with POOR Magazine, students at Deecolonize Academy, and are part of Youth Poverty Skolaz Radio on PNN-KEXU 96.1 FM radio and television. Mama Audrey Candy Corn is a poverty scholar, journalist, and the host of KEXU radio Sista Save A Soul.

Mayan Resistance to Police Terror

TINY AKA LISA GRAY-GARCIA
REPRINTED WITH PERMISSION FROM *SF BAY VIEW*
29 JUNE 2016

Editor's Note: Adante Pointer represents the family of Luis Góngora Pat

"Get on the ground! Get on the ground!" Moving in slowly like they were on a hunt, high-powered weapons pointed down, the descendants of slave-catchers aka police stalk an indigenous man crouching on Shotwell Street holding a soccer ball. They shout disgustedly and dismissively in English from the video screen; my heart stops.

I try to keep watching, reminding myself I need to wear my reporter hat instead of my trauma-filled police-terror-from-my-life-of-houselessness blanket. We are watching the extrajudicial murder of Luis Demetrio Góngora Pat by San Francisco police.

This is a press conference. I need to remain sane. My body is shaking; my eyes turn back to the horrific video. They keep approaching—robotic, murderous minds already made up to kill, their bodies tense yet arrogant, as if they were the aggressor and he their prey. "Get on the ground!" Then the sounds of genocide fill the room: pop pop pop pop pop pop pop ...

"Mr. Góngora Pat was already down on the ground when the third officer decided to pump three more shots into his body," said Adante Pointer, one of four members of the John Burris legal team who spoke at a press conference held Friday, June 17, to announce their filing against the city for the unjust murder of Luis Demetrio Góngora Pat. "And, contrary to the police claims, they were speaking English, a language Mr. Góngora didn't even understand," concluded Pointer.

"When he tried to get up and move like anyone would do, he was shot, shot, shot, shot, shot, shot—in the side, back, shoulder, and head. That shouldn't have happened. It is why we are here today to vindicate this unjust murder," said attorney John Burris to the small crowd of media and family gathered at the Episcopal Church of Saint John the Evangelist in San Francisco's Mission District.

"He had a knife."

"He was acting erratic."

"He was a homeless man."

After the violent murder of innocent Mayan father, brother, uncle, husband Luis Demetrio Góngora Pat, just like after the violent, horrific murders of innocent sons and brothers Mario Woods, Alex Nieto, Amilcar Perez Lopez, O'Shaine Evans and almost all the other victims of police terror, the police and their corporate media stenographers perpetuate a message of the police terror victims' perceived violence and "criminal" behavior.

Not only is this racist and classist, it is an outright lie. In Mario's case just like Luis's, there was no knife danger, aggressive, or allegedly criminal behavior. As a matter of fact, the police released the same stock photo of a random knife both Luis and Mario allegedly were brandishing when they were killed in cold blood by the police in the now gentrified neighborhoods of the Bayview and the Mission in San Francisco.

"This is the fourth shooting in San Francisco, a pattern of deadly force that goes unchecked and unmonitored. What we want is the shootings to stop," Burris declared. "The witnesses do not support in any way, shape, or form the claims by the police that Luis was acting in a threatening manner. Essentially, they say he was a non-aggressive person. He was sitting there on the street minding his own business, and his life was taken unnecessarily."

Both Luis and Mario were known as easy-going, kind people doing nothing but being alive in Gentrification City. They were unarmed and never dangerous. Both, however, were men of color and, in Luis's case, also un-housed, living in one of the richest cities in the world, with rampant and overt displacement efforts and increased police harassment and occupation of their communities.

"Our husband, father, brother Luis will never be forgotten," said Luis's daughter, Rossana Poot May, calling in from Mexico to the press conference. We thank all the people who are working for justice for him in San Francisco. It means a lot to us," Rosanna concluded.

"He was our friend. Anyone who needed anything only needed to ask Luis and he would help out," said Marty X, one of the unhoused neighbors of Luis on Shotwell Street. Marty was one of over a dozen housed and unhoused San Franciscans who knew their unhoused, peaceful neighbor, Luis Góngora Pat. "He always peacefully kicked his ball, never bothering anyone or anything."

POOR Magazine's PeopleSkool and Revolutionary Social Work project, with our own poverty scholarship, have been working with the unhoused witnesses to Luis' murder. All of us unhoused and formerly unhoused mamas, uncles, poets, artists, and cultural workers teach and write our own stories to make sure our lives are not narrated by only the hater ruling class.

As we have done for our entire organizational life in poor and unhoused communities, we have launched a new series of street newsrooms and writing workshops to chronicle the stories of police murder and harassment in the tent city encampments in San Francisco and Oakland. We have also released a series of WeSearch results to make sure that people's belongings being stolen by the Department of Public Works are chronicled as belongings, not trash.

As unhoused people, we face an onslaught of focused hate coming from corporate media, corporate politricksters and the capitalist business class, with a healthy dose of hate from society at large for our exposed, roofless bodies. Luis, like the most recent police murder victim, Jessica Nelson Williams, were fundamentally seen as a "problem" by the landlord class who direct the agenda of the police because they were unhoused in a city being remade, redeveloped, and rebranded as a city for the very rich and mostly white.

And because our unhoused bodies are no longer considered human and our belongings are no longer seen as belongings, we no longer have basic human rights and are constantly at the mercy of more and more ancient, re-branded settler-colonizer laws like the recent tent city removal laws being proposed by San Francisco Supervisor Mark Farrell, which are just like the ones created by Scott Weiner before him and Ed Lee before him and Gavin Newsom before him.

They come up with odd, Kafkaesque ideas like the Department of Home-lessness, which does a whole other form of rebranding and remaking to make it seem like new stuff is being done to solve an intentional capitalist problem.

"We are here to support and fight for justice for our brother," said José Góngora Pat, brother of Luis Góngora Pat, at the press conference, translated by the amazing artist and community caregiver Adriana Camerena.

In actuality one of the most powerful things happening now is the resis-tance of Black and Brown communities to the ongoing police terror across Amerikkka and, in the case of Luis' family, who are indigenous Mayans, they are bringing their own pre-colonizer controlled indigeneity in the form of their language, culture, spirit, and consciousness into the white supremacist halls of injustice.

"We are here in support of the legislation written by John Avalos" was the beginning of testimony given in the language of the Maya at the budget hearing on Monday by José Góngora Pat, while the Justice and Honor for Luis Góngora Pat Coalition stood with them in the Board of Supervisors chambers.

They brought into City Hall the spirit of the Maya, the spirit of Mama Earth and ancestors from all four corners, all of the things never respected in this stolen Yelamu Ohlone territory the colonizers called San Francisco. With every pre-colonized word, Luis' family crossed and unhinged false colonizer borders built with hate and stood up for honor and justice for their peaceful father, brother, uncle, husband Luis Demetrio Góngora Pat.

Indigenous resistance

For First Nations peoples, prayer, ancestor honoring, and our creation stories, teaching our indigenous languages, songs, and prayers to our children, and honoring our ancestors and our Mama Earth are at the core of organizing.

And organizing isn't linear: it's often in a circle, launched with a dance and always with prayers for Ancestor, Creator, and Mama Earth. These values run through powerful, indigenous people-led movements like Idle No More, which was launched by aboriginal resistors in Canada, but brought to the world stage through the hunger strike of Chief Theresa Spence of Attawapis-kat First Nation. She went on a hunger strike to pressure the prime minister and other government officials to hold a meeting with her to talk about the treaty rights of First Nations people. People around the world heard about her strike and acted in solidarity with her and Idle No More. "Idle No More calls on all people to join in a peaceful revolution, to honour Indigenous sovereignty, and to protect the land and water. INM has and will continue to help build sovereignty & resurgence of nationhood. INM will continue to pressure government and industry to protect the environment."[34]

Land and Housing

There are many revolutionary models for poor people-led, self-determined housing/land control across the globe. In the US, many that are truly revolutionary like MOVE 9, the Albany Bulb, Dignity Village, and Right 2 Survive get attacked, harassed, hated, and with few exceptions eventually destroyed.

There is also a long herstory of squats in the US. I make the distinction as many of the squatting movements are led and peopled by 20-something, wite-middle-class trust-funders who often become "disillusioned" as they grow older and fall back into their race and class privilege. That said, one of the most famous examples of this movement that POOR Magazine reported on in our 1996 issue, *Homefulness*, was the fact that we have homesteading laws on the books in the US, which means if you take possession of a property and pay the property taxes for a period of time (varies in every state) you have the right to "own" that property. Again, this is complicated, as conscious lawyers need to kick down bro-bono time, aka skill-share, to make sure the massive paperwork is completed and the politricksters and devil-opers can't take it away. Revolutionary jail-house lawyers outside of jail without a degree can also do this, but it's a lot of work and time.

In *Between Torture and Resistance,* Luis Nieves Falcon describes Oscar Lopez Rivera and the Spanish Coalition fighting for housing for self-determined housing for poor people: "In the same spirit, Oscar also helped organize the Spanish Coalition for housing to improve housing conditions for Puerto Ricans and free them from the rat- and cockroach- infested basements in which many were living. This involved direct confrontation with the (often absentee) landlords who collected excessive rents while pocketing the money and refusing to make the pigsties they rented to Puerto Ricans even remotely inhabitable. Protests in luxurious neighborhoods, in front of the homes of the exploitative landlords, acquired a dramatic character when rats and cockroaches 'collected' from the apartments the landlords refused to clean up were released in front of the landlords' own mansions."

There were some power-FUL people of color housing/squatting and anti-gentriFUKation resistance movements in New York's Lower East Side and Brooklyn led by folk like Chino Garcia and Armando Perez, as well as many powerful Puerto Rican activists of the '60s and '70s who staged the first building takeovers and created gardens, tenants associations, an arts revival, and community and environmental organizations. These institutions are oddly or intentionally green-washed or white-washed by wite artists and non-profit art movements led by art school graduates. To be clear it's not that these often "conscious" wite-artists are bad people, it's just that there is never a conversation about race, class, and/or education privilege and who should be leading art and movement work in a poor/indigenous community like the Lower East Side. The white-washing just enables the gentriFUKers to move in with ease.

Groups like Homes Not Jails are often times led by working class wite people but then seem to be quickly co-opted, taken over by middle-class folks who have absolutely no poverty skolaship, and things go quickly sideways. What is rarely said about squatting is it is very hard for single parent families with young children, elders, and disabled folks to function within these rather ableist, ageist models. There have been some powerful movements to take back foreclosed houses in Florida and California by the former residents. In Oakland and the Bay View district of San Francisco, displaced peoples have worked in tandem with ACCE, Occupy the Foreclosure Auctions and Right To a City to take back homes. These aren't for everyone and some of the groups tend to create NPIC cliques, only open and availed to some peoples, but resisting real estate snakkkeing nonetheless.[35]

Picture the Homeless: NYC

We were founded by two homeless men in the Fall of 1999, Anthony Williams and Lewis Haggins, Jr. The catalyst for our founding was an urgent need to respond to the Giuliani administration's policy of criminalizing homeless people, broadly supported by the media. The co-founders of Picture the Homeless (PTH) began reaching out to allies for support, a place to meet and to figure out strategies to create an organization of homeless people that could carry out this work. In January 2000, PTH held its first organizing meeting. Picture the Homeless has since worked to develop an organization directed and run by homeless people by building an infrastructure that keeps organizational decision-making in the hands of homeless people.

We are a citywide, multiracial, bilingual organization and our constituency includes homeless people living in shelters as well as those living on the streets and in other public places. We serve a broad population of people because homelessness cuts across all boundaries: race, ethnicity, culture, gender, family composition, age, sexual orientation, language, etc., but what all homeless people have in common as a community is extreme poverty and social stigmatization. The vast majority of people in the NYC shelter system are Black and Latino/a, and many of them are women and children. There are currently nearly 40,000 people in the New York City shelter system, including over 9,000 families with over 18,000 children. These numbers do not include street-dwelling homeless people, or the hundreds of families waiting for placement in a shelter, or the estimated 350,000 doubled-up households throughout the city. Our outreach targets individuals from within the shelter system, as well as those who are unable/unwilling to live within it.

War on the Poor from San Francisco to South Africa:
Poor People of South Africa Resist the Amerikkklan Style Slums Act

TINY AKA LISA GRAY-GARCIA / PNN
REPRINTED WITH PERMISSION FROM *SF BAY VIEW*
1 JANUARY 2010

"I conclude that section 16 of the Slums Act is inconsistent with the Constitution and invalid . . ."

— STATEMENT FROM THE CONSTITUTIONAL COURT OF SOUTH AFRICA

When I heard about the revolutionary resistance of our South African brothers and sisters in Abahlai base Mjondolo (The Shack Dwellers Union) in South Africa, a revolutionary group of landless folks in Capetown and Durban, South Africa, who successfully overturned the deadly Amerikkklan style criminalizing legislation called The Slums Act which would have given South African Po'Lice the ability to legally demolish, destroy, and evict poor peoples from their shacks without notice, I cried.

As a person whose life has been rife with the terror of eviction, displacement, landlessness, and criminalization, I was devastated by the stories of destruction of poor peoples in South Africa and equally inspired by the resistance of the young people who organized, hit the streets, chanted, danced and sung for freedom for post-apartheid Amandla in 2009 and eventually overcome that terror and Won!

I remembered the power of the poverty scholars I had met from the Shack-Dwellers Union. Scholars who protested, organized and led resistance from the grass-roots. Scholars like Maswi, a young revolutionary care-giving brother and visionary.

In his soft voice he related the struggle of his family and community to deal with the deadly war on the poor that was raging in the post-apartheid South Africa.

The new struggle in South Africa according to Maswi and his fellow freedom fighters is over the rights of poor people to be housed, to be listened to, to not be incarcerated. "It's not racism anymore, it's poverty," he had told me in an interview in August of this year. From The Bayview to Bayou, poor folks of color across the globe struggle with Amerikkklan style gentrification and criminalization. For the last few years Shack-Dwellers in South Africa come home from work and school only to find their homes have been demolished and then if they fight back the government turns guns on them.

This current push of deadly destruction by the South African government has been fueled by the transnational corporate interests in South Africa trying to build the world cup stadium for the 2010 world cup.

When I spoke with Maswi he explained how the South African constitution stated that no-one can be evicted once they have lived in a place for over 24 hours without due process, but that in the push to be the new corporate Amerikkklan-style clean city, there is no room for poor people, for the slums, and so no-one follows the constitution. The Slums Act was the going to be the final tool to push poor folks into the streets, the jails, or death.

Currently if poor children are found living on the streets they are put in jail for weeks at a time, if tourists are expected to come to Durban. Mazwi's stories of removal and criminalization reminded me of the ways that en-campments of landless folks in the Bay Area are arrested and washed away with high pressure power washers when they are found in settlements under the freeways, under the bridges, in doorways, and other outside residences.

But mostly what I learned from Maswi and his fellow revolutionaries is that we, the poor, the disabled, the indigenous, the migrant, the silenced, the incarcerated, the profiled, the displaced, must Not give up! That we do have power, and that we will, if we are truly working in coalition with each other, triumph![36]

A protest sign reading "stop the war on the poor" leans against concrete steps, under a Prensa Pobre banner. These signs are from a PNN protest of the Ellis Act, which is used to evict elders and poor folks in the Bay Area.

The Shackdwellers Movement in South Africa

"A man who called himself a documentary filmmaker came into one of our meetings and began filming us. We told him no, if anyone was going to film us it would be one of us." — MASWI

I met Maswi, a humble member of the powerful, poor people-led Shack-dwellers Union of South Africa, in 2010.

The Abahlali base Mjondolo (Shack Dwellers) Movement began in Durban, South Africa, in early 2005. Although it is overwhelmingly located in and around the large port city of Durban it is, in terms of the numbers of people mobilised, the largest organisation of the militant poor in post-apartheid South Africa. Its originary event was a road blockade organised from the Kennedy Road settlement in protest at the sale, to a local industrialist, of a piece of nearby land long promised by the local municipal councillor to shack dwellers for housing.

The movement that began with the road blockade grew quickly and now has tens of thousands of supporters from more than 30 settlements. In the last year and a half the movement has suffered more than a hundred arrests, regular police assault and ongoing death threats and other forms of intimidation from local party goons. It has developed a sustained voice for shack dwellers in subaltern and elite publics and occupied and marched on the offices of local councillors, police stations, municipal offices, newspaper offices, and the City Hall in actions that have put thousands of people on the streets. The movement also organised a highly contentious but very successful boycott of the March 2006 local government elections under the slogan 'No Land, No House, No Vote'. Amongst other victories the Abahlali have democratised the governance of many settlements, stopped evictions in a number of settlements, won access to schools, stopped the industrial development of the land promised to Kennedy Road, forced numerous government officials, offices and projects to 'come down to the people' and mounted vigorous challenges to the uncritical assumption of a right to lead the local struggles of the poor in the name of a privileged access to the 'global' (i.e. Northern donors, academics, and NGOs) that remains typical of most of the NGO based left. The movement's key demand is for 'Land & Housing in the City' but it has also successfully politicised and fought for an end to forced removals and for access to education and the provision of water, electricity, sanitation, health care and refuse removal as well as bottom up popular democracy. In some settlements the movement has also successfully set up projects like crèches, gardens, sewing collectives, support for people living with and orphaned by AIDS and so on. It has also organised a 16 team football league and quarterly all night multi genre music competitions.

We are the Third Force

S'BU ZIKODE

REPRINTED WITH AUTHOR'S PERMISSION
ORIGINALLY PUBLISHED ON ABAHLALI BASEMJONDOLO (ABAHLALI.ORG)
19 OCTOBER 2006

This journalistic intervention by S'bu Zikode, the chairperson of Abahlali baseMjondolo, caused a national sensation when it was first published in November 2005 and then rapidly translated into Afrikaans, Xhosa and Zulu and widely republished in newspapers and popular magazines. It is quite probably the most widely republished piece of journalism in post-apartheid South Africa. The term Third Force became part of the national imagination in South Africa after it was used to describe the apartheid security agents who offered covert military support to Zulu nationalists waging a war against the ANC in the last years of apartheid. It is highly pejorative, implies covert white manipulation towards evil ends and, in its contemporary avatar, assumes an absolute inability for poor black people to exercise historical agency on their own. From the road blockade that birthed this movement until now numerous and very often contradictory variations of the Third Force argument have been deployed by the state in an increasingly neurotic and at times outrightly hysterical mode. It is an unfortunate fact that a section of the NGO left, a section that chooses not to attend the meetings of, or to in any way engage in serious discussions with the people it assumes a natural right to lead, is increasingly also resorting to the racism of the white agitator thesis to try and explain away the fact that a large movement of the militant poor is uncompromisingly asserting the right to speak for and to represent itself. It seems that everyone in the business of speaking for the poor, in the state or on the left, is equally disturbed by the assumption by the poor of the right to speak and act for themselves. In this article Zikode offers a startling and now classic response to claims that the Third Force is behind the mass mobilisations organised by Abahlali baseMjondolo.

The Third Force

The shack dwellers' movement that has given hope to thousands of people in Durban is always being accused of being part of the Third Force. In newspapers and in all kinds of meetings this is said over and over again. They even waste money investigating the Third Force. We need to address this question of the Third Force so that people don't become confused.

It is time for us to speak out and to say this is who we are, this is where we are and this how we live. The life that we are living makes our communities the Third Force. Most of us are not working and have to spend all day struggling for small money. AIDS is worse in the shack settlements than anywhere else. Without proper houses, water, electric-

A row of people—children and adults—stand in a line, their right hands in the air. They are part of the Shackdwellers Movement in Durban, South Africa.

ity, refuse removal and toilets all kinds of diseases breed. The causes are clearly visible and every Dick, Tom and Harry can understand. Our bodies itch every day because of the insects. If it is raining everything is wet—blankets and floors. If it is hot the mosquitoes and flies are always there. There is no holiday in the shacks. When the evening comes—it is always a challenge. The night is supposed to be for relaxing and getting rest. But it doesn't happen like that in the jondolos. People stay awake worrying about their lives. You must see how big the rats are that will run across the small babies in the night. You must see how people have to sleep under the bridges when it rains because their floors are so wet. The rain comes right inside people's houses. Some people just stand up all night.

Those in power are blind to our suffering. This is because they have not seen what we see, they have not felt what we are feeling every second, every day. My appeal is that leaders who are concerned about peoples' lives must come and stay at least one week in the jondolos. They must feel the mud. They must share 6 toilets with 6 000 people. They must dispose of their own refuse while living next to the dump. They must come with us while we look for work. They must chase away the rats and keep the children from knocking the candles. They must care for the sick when there are long queues for the tap. They must have a turn to explain to the children why they can't attend the Technical College down the hill. They must be there when we bury our children who have passed on in the fires, from diarrhoea or AIDS.

For us the most important struggle is to be recognised as human beings. During the struggle prior to 1994 there were only two levels, two classes—the rich and the poor. Now after the election there are three classes—the

A group walks up a hill carrying a banner that reads "University of Abahlali baseMjondolo."

poor, the middle class and the rich. The poor have been isolated from the middle class. We are becoming more poor and the rest are becoming more rich. We are on our own. We are completely on our own.

We discovered that our municipality does not listen to us when we speak to them in Zulu. We tried English. Now we realise that they won't understood Xhosa or Sotho either. The only language that they understand is when we put thousands of people on the street. We have seen the results of this and we have been encouraged. It works very well. It is the only tool that we have to emancipate our people. Why should we stop it?

The 16th of February 2005 was the dawn of our struggle. On that day the Kennedy Road committee had a very successful meeting with the chair of the housing portfolio of the executive committee of the municipality, the director of housing and the ward councillor. They all promised us the vacant land on the Clare Estate for housing. The land on Elf Road was one of the identified areas. But then we were betrayed by the most trusted people in our city. Just one month later, without any warning or explanation, bulldozers began digging the land. People were excited. They went to see what was happening and were shocked to be told that a brick factory was being built there. More people went down to see. There were so many of us that we were blocking the road. The man building the factory called the police and our local councillor, a man put into power by our votes and holding our trust and hopes. The councillor told the police "Arrest these people they are criminals." The police beat us, their dogs bit us and they arrested 14 of us. We asked what happened to the promised land. We were told "Who the hell are you people to demand this land?" This betrayal mobilised the people. The people who betrayed us are responsible for this movement. Those people are the second force.

Our movement started with 14 arrests – we called them the 14 heroes. Now we have 14 settlements united together as abahlali base mjondolo [shack dwellers]. Each settlement meets once a week and the leaders of all the settlements meet once a week. We are prepared to talk but if that doesn't work we are prepared to use our strength. We will do what ever it costs us to get what we need to live safely.

We have learnt from our experience that when you want to achieve what you want, when you want to achieve what is legitimate by peaceful negotiations, by humbleness, by respecting those in authority your plea becomes criminal. You will be deceived for more than ten years, you will be fooled and undermined. This is why we have resorted to the streets. When we stand there in our thousands we are taken seriously.

The struggle that started in Kennedy Road was the beginning of a new era. We are aware of the strategies that the police are coming with to demoralise and threaten the poor. We don't mind them building the jails for us and hiring more security if they are not prepared to listen to what we are saying. It is important for every shack dwellers to know that we are aware of what is happening in Alexander in Johannesburg, in P.E., in Cape Town. We know that our struggle is not by itself. We have sent our solidarity. We will not rest in peace until there is justice for the poor – not only in Kennedy Road there are many Kennedy Roads, many Mhlengis, many poor voices that are not heard and not understood. But we have discovered the language that works. We will stick with it. The victims have spoken. We have said enough is enough.

RIGHT 2 SURVIVE: Portland, Oregon
RIGHT 2 SURVIVE MEMBERS

RIGHT 2 SURVIVE is a member of Western Regional Advocacy Project

Right 2 Survive was founded in 2009 and is a direct action group that educates both houseless and housed people on their civil, human, and constitutional rights. We also work to bridge the gap between housed and un-housed people by clearing away misconceptions and stigmas associated with houselessness and empower houseless people to stand up for them selves when their rights are violated.

Every day right here in the United States, millions of houseless individuals are being denied access to adequate shelter, sanitary restrooms in which to perform basic human functions, the ability to congregate into larger groups for safety while they sleep, and many other things that should be basic human rights. The shelter system is overburdened and there are not enough shelter beds to accommodate the houseless population, yet there are laws being passed daily which prohibit people from having a tent or even a tarp to protect them from the elements as they sleep on the street or under bridges. Here in Portland, there is a sit/lie ordinance in effect that prohibits people from sleeping on the sidewalk, in doorways, and even under bridges. We at Right 2 Survive believe sleep and affordable housing are basic human rights and should be treated as such.

ain't no denying we each have

a RIGHT 2 survive

a right 2 sleep

a right 2 shelter

a right 2 safety

a right 2 self support

a right 2 sustainability

a right 2 simple living

a right 2 share and barter

a right to sit and lie

and

a right 2 say so
our goal is to empower the un-sheltered, the disenfranchised, those
of color, oppressed minorities, those who are being treated like
criminals because of their poverty.

our goal is to use the legal process as much as possible to obtain use
of public lands, buildings and resources for the purpose of helping
people (not corporations and the politically favored).
our goal is to proclaim and protect the rights of the those who
capitalism has left behind.

our goal is to facilitate creative use of under-utilized private spaces
and resources for the purpose of getting people off the streets.

our goal is to shine a light on the abuses of police as they abuse
the homeless and poor

Water Is Life: A Poem for Standing Rock

TINY AKA LISA GRAY-GARCIA
REPRINTED WITH PERMISSION FROM *DECOLONEWS* AND *SF BAY VIEW*

Editor's Note: Written for a journey Poor Magazine made to Standing Rock.

Dedicated to all water protectors

Water is life
but not to the colonized
who have lost their eyes
to dollar signs
deep in dark corners with bankkksters
mama earth hoarders
& blood-stained money lovers
covering our ancestors with
colonizer bricks & colonizer mortar
Water is life to us
the people who drink, love, & hold water
instead of blood-soaked dollars
—think love instead of kolonizer borders
who have mamaz & babies we care for
not merchandise we order
Water is life and
blue suits with dollar signs for heads say
"Not without a price"
We say water is life—
they say
it's water or your life
we drink poison—& eat oil
& pray to corporations
& rub ourselves in your toil
& dream of how much more and more of mama earth
we can destroy
& people we can kill
& mama's lands we can drill

Water is life—
and for those of us outside
drinking the man's poison wine
trying to hide in doorways, cardboard boxes and streetsides
on stolen land called public but not for us house-less
we beg for water on days so hot we might not make it
hoping someone might give us a break
overstanding that for ALL of us
water is life—
water is sacred

Herstory was made on April 1, 2016 when the Sacred Stone Camp was established by 1st Nations leaders, Indigenous prayer-bringers and water protectors as a center of spiritual and cultural opposition to the Dakota Access pipeline, and is determined to stop construction through prayer and non-violent direct action until adequate tribal consultation and environmental review are conducted. The spirit camp was located in between the pipeline's proposed crossing of the Missouri River and the water intake valves for the Standing Rock Sioux Tribe, just over a mile downstream. The power of prayer, ceremony, resistance and indigenous leadership lasted for over a year. After the occupation of the Wite Peoples House by Donald Trump — the pipeline was approved and the powerFULL resistance camp was dismantled in February of 2017.

Standing Rock in the snow. A massive resistance camp filled with tipis, pickup trucks, trailers, and tents on snow-covered ground.

From Port-au-Prince to Puebla: Poor People of Color Resist!

MUTEADO SILENCIO
REPRINTED WITH PERMISSION FROM POOR MAGAZINE
3 MAY 2012

My heart is the drum that makes my feet dance to the beat... I sing my poetry in Spanglish... I love... fight... struggle... with knowledge... I pick the drum as my weapon to fight for liberation... and revolution... My brain is from Mexico y America. My feet are from Africa.

Our faces Black & Dark Brown like mama Africa, our noses round beautiful like the mountains of the Americas, our pyramids and temples from Egypt to Yucatan, Mexico can't lie of the connection between my black and brown brothers and sisters.

In high School my teacher once told me that my people were savages, I was taught to hate the color of my skin and the shape of my nose.

Until One day I found myself in the Legion of Honor museum in San Francisco, who was built by the descendants of the people who slave us and stole our land. I was there to witness an exposition of Aztec and Mayan artifacts, when I seen my nose and face engrave in those great artifacts I knew my people were not savages.

To witness the Olmec head, to see the traits of my African people, I knew we have more in common than the suffering our ancestors share under colonialism.

To learn about Yanga the first African slave people who free them self's from Spanish rule in Veracruz, Mexico and created families with indigenous people from the area.

More than 500 years and we are still here breathing and thriving by any means necessary, and is time we celebrate our resistance and our people.

EXCERPT | **Living Pimp-Free**

TINY AKA LISA GRAY-GARCIA

REPRINTED WITH PERMISSION FROM POOR MAGAZINE

25 JANUARY 2012

And to live pimp free—

To really be truly free—

Is to redesign systems based on eldership, ancestors, Pachamama

And We

> To deconstruct all the simple answers of why
>
> we kill each other,
>
> starve our mothers,
>
> shoot and kill our black and brown brothers
>
> incarcerate so many others

***

In POOR Magazine we destruct and speak about the separation done by systems within capitalism that are use to separate us by race, gender, class, and struggles, for the benefit of this system to keep functioning. We also see the importance to keep building those bridges among communities of color, that many sheroes & heroes have done in the past and present.

It was beautiful and powerful to read the letter from Sub-comandante Marcos from the Zapatistas EZLN to Mumia Abu-Jamal to congratulate on his birthday and to stand in solidarity with all political prisoners in Amerikkka.

Sub-comandante Marcos wrote:

"We are also 'people of color' (the same color as our brothers who have Mexican blood and live and struggle in the American Union). Our color is 'brown,' the color of the earth, the color from which we take our history, our strength, our wisdom, and our hope. But in order to struggle we add the color black to our brown. We use black ski-masks to show our faces, only then can we be seen and heard. Following the advice of an indigenous Mayan elder, who explained to us the meaning of the color black, we chose this color. Old Don Antonio used to tell us that from black came light and from there came the stars which light up the sky around the world. He recounted a story of a long time ago (in the times when time was not measured)."

Through the Americas black and brown people were used to build this civilization where we are found ourselves captives under capitalism or kill daily, persecuted. More than 500 years of genocide to our people, have failed to exterminate us, and on May 4, 2012, we will celebrate our ancestors and that we are still here fighting and resisting.

The people of Haiti and the people of Puebla share a common bond—in Puebla, mestizo soldiers were outnumbered two to one while Black Haitians faced Napoleon's heavily armed military—but both oppressed peoples prevailed in what many refer to as two David and Goliath victories.

We hope this celebration of community can inspire us to begin to form the strength in what is possibly the most insidious Goliath to date—the United States of America. Only united can people of color be the most powerful David we can be.

Altar at Homefulness for victims of poLice terror, racism, poverty, gentriFUKation, war and community violence. Photo: Al Osorio.

We walk back and forth in a jail-house everyday —
it's called your doorways, tent cities
Bus benches
Metal chairs in the emergency room waiting to be seen

its main street outside the razor wire plantation in a cell
called houselessness and poverty
Teetering on a colonized definition of safety
from scofflaws to stop and risk laws
we can barely survive one day without the violence
of hate and poLice brutality

me daughter of a houseless, single mama—
sleeping on street corners, cars and not really public parks
in this stolen indigenous territory
its enough to drive anyone completely craz-eee
it took my mama—
unable to unhinge from that deep well of trauma

So whats the answer—
you don't want to see me
You would like to walk down the street cloaked in
your amerikkklan lie that doesn't include me

Yes we are political prisoners—
outside the razor wire plantations
us Po folks are NEVER free
not free from our mind demons
the abuse we can't get out our mind no matter
the quantity of psycho-pharma-cology

I hold my mama in this space
rolling over her torture
daily
"My life is political
my prison is personal," she would always say

My struggle / our struggle is poetry
and i can't escape these walls inside my mind
I can't ever be free
No Matter what
i can't ever be free

— TINY EXCERPT FROM
"THE POORHOUSE TO THE JAILHOUSE"

—9—

Homefulness: A Poor People-Led Solution to Homelessness

Houseless

TIBURCIO GARCIA, 12, YOUTH SKOLA WITH DEECOLONIZE ACADEMY AT POOR MAGAZINE (ON THE SACRED LAND WE LANDLESS PEOPLES CALL HOMEFULNESS)

On the sidewalk the pounding of feet passing by. We holding up cardboard signs and all we usually get a wary eye. Always moving. People think we looting. We are treated like criminals for sleeping on the street even though America is the one who made sure we had nothing to eat. This country left us jobless, friendless, loveless, and most of all houseless.

Beyond

DEE ALLEN

Three homes stand
Amidst this lush
Garden so far.
Two in back,
One in front,
Soon to be seven
With four straw bale
Dwellings added to
The liberated land.
A cafe,
A library,
A radio station,
A media centre
Where the destitute,
Evicted, displaced, gentrified out
Can write their own
Tales from their own
Standpoint, reaching digital
Streets, live on wi-fi,
A school to decolonise
Poor children from the
Ways of genocide masters
And re-learn ancestors' knowledge
Thought to be lost to history,
A barnyard with livestock
Supplying families' needs,
Milk & cheese from goats,
Eggs from chickens.
None of these

Are utopian dreams.
They're what this
Lush garden produces everyday,
Aside from vegetables & vines
Scaling up the chainlink steel fence.
All of these
Began with a dream.
Somewhere in 1990s Oakland,
A self-determination
Vision was discussed between
Mother and daughter inside
A parked car they
Both slept in.
Their ambition
Was a solution
To extreme poverty.
Their words contained an alternative
To sleeping in cars, owning scraps of lives,
Living nowhere, deemed undesirable to the eyes.
From homelessness
To homefulness.
Flash-forward: 2012.
When the right place was found,
The smothering asphalt
Covering the land
Had to be broken, lifted, hauled away.
The dream had to live
Beyond two homeless females.
The dust had long cleared.
The construction tools, long in storage.
The asphalt, long removed.
The land, long mended, seeded, planted
And flourishing still.
Homefulness means
"Everyone has a home.
Even plants & animals."
It also means
"There's nothing this
One-way system
Can offer us
That we couldn't

Teach, build or farm ourselves."
Each passing day
Each new project
On this land
Are overtures
Movements conducted
From Oakland's,
Deep East,
Long blighted
On purpose, towards lives
Without undue
Hardship, beyond
Just ideas, movements toward
The growing green future
Beyond this lush garden
And the comfortable lie of Capitalism.

***

For Dee Garcia (1945–2006)

Mama put her best black pants and matching sweater on. Mama was ghetto fabulous and from LA, so that meant some Adidas, sweat pants, matching sweatshirt, and the seldom-worn almost-new overpriced running athletic shoes she reserved for special occasions.

The concrete and steel of the Federal building where Housing and Urban Development (HUD) was located went so far up into the sky that you couldn't see the top of it. For years all of us poverty, indigenous skolaz had gone there to report and support, protest and organize constitutional challenges for migrant peoples and against killer cops. We had even walked in the building to face off with Nancy Pelosi about several battles for indigenous land rights and for justice. And yet going in to actually meet with someone felt different. Menacing and foreboding, like the silence that happens before someone in a horror movie gets killed.

The ghost-like eyes and hideously fake smile of George Bush greeted us at every turn. They seemed to move with each of our moves and it wasn't just one picture, he was all over that building, meeting us at every steel, wood, glass, post-modern-institution artery. We went to the elevator, getting lost at the options (there are two different elevators, one leading to the top-secret-Mission impossible CIA-co-intel-pro area and one for the rest of us).

We reached the 16th floor, slowly de-barking the muted lights of the sub-quiet elevator. We were shuttled into a room with a giant conference table, which was shiny and slippery enough to skate on to meet with the HUD representative.

He came in, all bureaucrat-quiet, in a yellow sweater vest and Banana Republic khakis. He spoke almost in hushed tones, immediately launching into a carefully prepared narrative.

"We are so sorry that it didn't work out." He proceeded to tell us that we had written a budget that would give us a whopping $35.00 dollars a month to support the Homefulness project. There is really nothing we could do at this point but maybe in the next funding cycle (2 years later) we could try it again.

"You son of a BITCH-MUTHAH-FUCKER." In the middle of one of his bullshit sentences which explained nothing and took no accountability for the politrickster-bureaucrat abuse that just happened to us, my mama jumped up from her chair and started going ghetto-crazy: screaming at the top of her lungs about how they knew this was going to happen, how they were responsible, and this is why indigenous and poor folks never trust the government politricksters and the fake temptation of "working inside the system."

Within seconds security guards were in the room. I was trying to stop my mama from screaming and attacking the guy. We were wrestled to the ground and eventually dragged out in handcuffs while my mama continued to scream, "You lying, fake, colonizing muthafucking Son of A Bitch. You and your fake-azz departments and fake-azz funding was never for people like us."

And then it was over. Another little murder of the soul was in. The dream of Homefulness, a poor people-led/indigenous people-dreamed solution to houselessness was shot down, AGAIN.

Since the inception of Volume 1: The Homefulness Issue, my poor, houseless, single-parent-isolated mama and me had dreamed, worked, manifested and begged so hard for this people-led dream to manifest. And by any means necessary we did manifest versions of it, like re-purposing tiny grants that were workshops for homeless mothers and children to include housing for mothers and children.

Us poor and indigenous mamaz, elders, and youth met for hours, days, months, and years conceptualizing the dream of Homefulness. We made manifestos and declarations, we slogged through tons of possible "funding streams" and grants, workshops on "capital campaigns" and politricksters, and then one day a small part of the government funding process appeared to be opened up to folks, real peoples, not just NPICs and housing devil-opers. It was through a body created by pushback from poor folks at the

Coalition on Homelessness and other groups called the Local Homeless Coordinating Board, which could vote on HUD projects that would impact homeless people of San Francisco.

Ever-optimistic goofballs, we high-fived each other and launched into one of the most gut-wrenching grant-dances we had faced to date. We slogged through a several-hundred page HUD application to make Homefulness a HUD-funded project. Me and my mama and other POOR Magazine skolaz did our best, staying up nights and wrangling in all of our scant linguistic domination skills. I taught myself Excel overnight and we proceeded to propose Homefulness to HUD before the extremely-soon deadline. By any means necessary we got it before the local Homeless Coordinating Board, peopled by other community skolaz and poverty skolaz who approved it hands down, ranking it second in the competitive process.

We left and cheered, thinking it was finally possible. We would be able to fund the dream that was Homefulness. Three months later we received the budget. Without knowing what we were doing, we had painstakingly created a budget that granted us approximately $35.00 dollars a month as an operating budget for something that would take at least $200,000 to launch and at least $60,000 to run. Our proposal was solid, it was based on the experience of us po mamaz and daddys, uncles and aunties and real-time experience of the Mamahouses before and since. It included leasing a flat or house with at least four bedrooms, art/community meals, shared child care, and revolutionary case management (poor people-led support by any means necessary as described in the Hellthcare chapter), sliding scale sweat-equity to pay for rent, (i.e. a non-ableist, concept of what ever you are able to do based on your time, energy, physical challenges, etc., which sometimes means cooking meals, helping with child care, or paper-work, admin, rides, etc.).

These were humble and solid ideas and plans, tested and tried but our goals weren't attached to so-called "legitimate entities" like million-dollar shelters and underfunded public housing. Instead what were approved were more contracts for the devil-opers who already got millions of dollars for politricked approved housing projects like "Master leases for Single Room Occupancy" Hotels, or shelter plus care transitional housing projects.[37]

We were shot to the ground: our dreams had ended. We were beyond depressed, and as usual my mama decided to let the poltricksters know how she felt. This led to the fateful day at HUD. And to put it simply, she said what needed to be said. For all of us.

We didn't understand until afterwards what really went down. They in fact have no technical support for poor peoples, "lay" people outside the channels of access to apply for these government dollars. Yet if you have a full-time administration staff with people who know how to do all that stuff like it's the back of their hand, you can get those dollars. Little guys like us are intentionally kept out. After the pain subsided, we got back on the trail and shopped the proposal around to both progressive and middle of the road legislators and community organizations, only to be told, "You need to collaborate with a known and accepted (read, well-funded) non-profiteer housing devil-oper." So we sought out non-profiteer after non-profiteer, endlessly hearing a nice or terse "No." Eventually, over 10 years from its original conception, we gave up and realized we had no choice but to do it ourselves, by any means necessary. And the rest is her-story.

Fast Forward twelve years. . . .

RAD Public Housing Privatization:
Stealing Our Last Acre and Our One Remaining Mule

TINY AKA LISA GRAY-GARCIA
REPRINTED WITH PERMISSION FROM THE *SF BAY VIEW*
23 SEPTEMBER 2013

"Can you guarantee there will be housing for low, low income people, cause many of our folks are low, low income?" the inquiry from SF Public Housing Commissioner Patricia Thomas was tentative, her voice building power with each word.

"RAD is an integrated model that preserves affordable housing," replied Olson Lee in a careful monotone, representative of the Mayor's office of Housing.

"Mr. Lee, you are not answering my question, is the Mayor's office guaranteeing that there will be housing for low, low-income people, or like one of the public commenters said, we will we be gentrified out of our own communities?"

The San Francisco Housing Commission meeting of September 4th on a new acronym called Rental Assistance Demonstration (RAD), code for selling public housing to private investors, was still. Still like a grave. A grave for all us poor peoples' destruction from the massive privatization of our public housing. Us unprioritized and barely housed, the holding-on-by-our-fingernails-families, the forgotten elders, the un-remembered disabled folks, the very poor, the displaced, now houseless and rarely remembered.

I was the public commenter Ms. Thomas referenced who brought the deadly "G" word (Gentrification — or what we at POOR affectionately call GentriFUKation) into the tomb-like room. After listening to an onslaught of thinly veiled lies presented by the Mayors Office of Housing (MOH), cloaked in feel-good titles like SFHA Re-visioning, projected onto PowerPoint presentations using confusing terms like outcomes and clusters, and littered with acronyms, my body was shaking with fury and betrayal. Sadly, this was nothing new. POOR Magazine poverty skolaz have been writing, WeSearch-ing and protesting this mess since our inception. There was just a deeper arrogance about the theft than we have seen before.

"He (Olson Lee) can't guarantee it. They are selling public housing stocks off to private investors as mortgages, so of course they can't guarantee what private investors do with their investments," said Paul Boden. I called Paul from Western Regional Advocacy Project (WRAP), who has done extensive research on the destruction of public housing for poor peoples in the US, to get some truth beyond the acronyms.

One of the statements that is continually used by politricksters about public housing is the "obvious need for a solution to the problem of public housing." The truth is, according to (WRAP)'s *Without Housing* report, beginning as far back as the 1960's when President Nixon put a federal moratorium on the building of HUD's affordable housing (aka poor people housing) the government sponsored gentriFUKation plans have been rolling out one brutal slice at a time, making sure that the New Deal idea of public housing for all became a "failure."

Throw in rampant re-development across the nation that has hit the Black community more deeply than any other folks, the implementation of the paper-based mythology of the Section 8 program which has never been a guarantee to housing and has already lost over 300,000 units to foreclosure and opt-outs since the 90's, and is currently barely surviving the so-called sequester hits, combined with the demolition of over 200,000 units of public housing, you have a planned government-baked recipe for the end of public housing.

Shuttled in with the benign title of Rental Assistance Development or acronym of RAD, a series of last minute, so-called "community" meetings are being held in the public housing projects that will be bought and sold right under us, claiming they will be improving our lives and communities by displacing us, just like every redevil-opment project has done since its inception such as Fill-no-more/Western Addition in San Francisco to the Brooklyn gentriFUKation of the 70's to Phoenix, Arizona's Joe Arpaio-funded destruction of poor people hotels downtown in the 90's to almost any city you can name in Amerikkka.

But the reality is, the devil-opers are running out of communities to gentriFUK so the next frontier is turning all of our public housing into private so-called "affordable" housing, with the complicit involvement of corporate government forces like the Jerry Brown, Gavin Newsom, Lee, Jean Quan, Villagarosa, Michael Bloomberg, administrations of San Francisco, Oakland, LA, New York and beyond.

"In the last four months, over a hundred representatives from 72 different organizations including residents, non-profit service providers, affordable housing developers, local labor unions and private sector development experts along with 20 city departments and representatives from HUD have met a total of 18 times."

— SFHA REVISIONING PROCESS RECOMMENDATIONS

"We have had multiple meetings in the communities leading up to this application," said Naomi Kelly, Mayors Office of Housing representative.

That's funny, I thought, neither myself nor any of our POOR Magazine family who are currently living in public housing units have got notices of these so-called tenant meetings, or any meetings about this for that matter.

The City of San Francisco has a deadline of September 30th to "apply" for RAD and we are all caught up in a wave we barely understand. This false urgency set by politricknologists have launched a whole slew of meetings scheduled with little or no notice ensuring that hardly any poor, disabled, elder, or working folks can make it to them. This take-down in the night is also possible cause so many of our backs, souls, and spirits are broken by years of race and poverty hits, Post-traumatic slave syndrome and the lie of capitalism in Amerikkka.

The other glaringly obvious part of these private devil-opments is their colonizer work crews who are flown in like the 21st century carpetbaggers they are to "work" on the construction sites.

"These developments are in our communities, why aren't they hiring us in the community," said Fly Benzo, Hip Hop Youth Skola, Media producer, and revolutionary Bayview son of Claude Carpenter, a leader in the building trades based in the Bay View. Fly, Claude, Mary, and Willie Ratcliff and many others have been speaking truth to this colonizer situation for years, and yet the construction bids keep magically going to anyone but local folks. (Fly's powerful statements were caught in the new movie, *Let em Hear Ya Comin*, by revolutionary comrades Black Riders Liberation Party.)

"My family has been living in the Fillmore public housing projects for over 5 generations, where is our equity?" said Queennandi XSheba, fellow poverty skola reporter, poet, and welfareQUEEN at POOR Magazine.

In the end it is up to us family, to take back our 1/16th of an acre and half of a hoof of a mule. Like Queennandi, so many of us have lived in these devil-oped and intentionally destroyed communities so long, po'lice harassed, contained, redlined, gentriFUKed, under-employed, incarcerated, and never respected and yet as my strong black/Indian Mama Dee would always say, "What do we have to show for it?"

This is why us Po' folks/evicted, landless/houseless peoples (some of us living in so-called "public housing") at POOR Magazine launched the Homefulness project. Un-philathro-pimped and never devil-oper controlled, it puts the equity, decisions, power in the hands of all us peoples who are usually only told what and where we can go and do.

We have a 10-point plan to teach/share with any and all public housing tenants who want to fight for their own control. You have equity, you have the ability to stop this take-down and take back your own stolen resources, rooted in thousands of plantation lies that go back into generations of Amerikkklan/Colonizer lies.

Capitalism Killed Mamahouse

Community of poor mothers and children in San Francisco's Mission district is gone due to $700 dollar rent increase fueled by gentrification

"What is the moon saying tonight, Mama?" My son looks into my face as I gaze into the face of the moon. The moon's voice travels like a whisper into my heart.

It was bedtime and my son and I were going through our nightly ritual of gazing at the moon, talking-story, reading, and naming our blessings and spirits from the rectangle window in our tiny bedroom. As someone who grew up houseless, rarely sheltered by a roof, much less a window, these moments were filled with gratitude, love, and humility, always certain that our impending houselessness lurked silently around the next shaky rental agreement.

I no longer live within the soft wood frame of that house. I was served with a rent increase of $700 dollars two months ago. But of course, the house never belonged to me. I only rented it. Lingered with trepidation within its bright long walls.

And so me, my son, and the other poor mamas and countless children that co-habitated together in that house we dubbed Mamahouse, sharing food, stories, resources, art, support, liberation, and social justice consciousness in the Mission district of San Francisco, no longer dream, think, rest or live there.

The Herstory of Mamahouse

Mamahouse, the rented, smaller vision of the sweat-equity co-housing dream that is Homefulness. Mamahouse, the revolutionary concept and project launched by my Mama Dee and me so many years ago, as a collective for mothers and children in poverty. A place to live and resist the deep isolation that kills the spirits of so many people in a capitalist society, combat the discrimination that impacts poor single parents of color, and provide peer support and scholarship for the struggle of raising a child in this society that never supports poor parents and has effectively separated our elders and ancestors from our young folks.

A group of poverty skolaz — adults and children — stands in front of Mamahouse, a few of them with their fists in the air. Tiny holds a sign that says "No more evictions."

Mamahouse has always worked, even as capitalism hasn't. In its first incarnation Mamahouse existed within a tiny one-bedroom apartment in the Tenderloin District, launched by a revolutionary slice of philanthro-pimped dollars, meant solely for a series of writing workshops with youth, adults and elders in poverty and the publication of Volume 1 of POOR Magazine, which was called HOMEFULNESS. The workshops and publication were done with great success, at which point my revolutionary, community-driven, always tortured by capitalism, indigenous Taino, single mama of color in poverty, Dee, announced in an act of change-By-Any-Means-Necessary!, "let's realize the dream of Homefulness beyond the pages, otherwise we may never see it happen."

My beautiful and sad mama, tortured as an unwanted child of color in Amerikkka foster homes and orphanages, stripped, separated, and devoid of her indigenous family, culture, language and community, never took anything for granted. She always knew, like all us po' folks know, that if you ever have any access, or money, that there is absolutely no guarantee that it will continue to be there, or continue to flow, no matter how hard you pull up your bootstraps, or dream the only-in-sleep-Amerikkklan Dream.

Me and my mama struggled in and out of homelessness throughout my child-hood and into my young adult-hood. And as soon as we had a few resources to realize any dreams of counter-capitalism-separate-ness, we did.

It was never easy, we were never supported in our efforts, but we knew if we were to infiltrate the destruction of capitalist separatism in real time, in our own lives, as a poor single mama of color and daughter, with no extended family or community, it was necessary that we act fast and act revolutionarily.

I lived as a "good daughter" with my ghetto-fabulous mama creating art, revolution, and as much community as our resource-poor POOR Magazine family could cobble together, until she passed on her spirit journey in March of 2006.

I work so hard in my mind and heart everyday to not take my son through the sorrow of loneliness, desperation, and poverty that me and my mama felt for so many years. Isolation kills. Capitalism promotes isolation and the cult of independence and separation. Our barometer for sanity is based on how "happy" we can be while being alone, separate from others and at peace with our solitude.

The Tenderloin Mamahouse circa 1998 successfully housed two landless indigenous families, ran beautiful community dinners and art events, and silly moments of love and indigenous justice in real time.

We had to end it one year later, due to no more funding. Sadly, capital campaigns (property acquisitions) are usually only launched and realized by already-wealthy organizations and individuals who have access to long ago stolen-from indigenous peoples U.S. resources.

In 2005, after a series of very serious organizational and personal losses at POOR Magazine, (organizational and personal lives are naturally enmeshed as a natural part of revolutionary poor people-led/indigenous people-led organizations like ours), I founded the next series of Mamahouses, this one in a substandard house in the Mission District, shared with many non-paying tenants with tails and feathers and wings and antennae, these un-seen tenants facilitated the only truly affordable market rate housing in the brutally gentrified Mission District of San Francisco.

In 2007, the slumlord from hell of this Mamahouse actually set fire to her own property to rid her building of "problem tenants" like us mamas and children (in other words, tenants that tried to get her to fix the plumbing and rid the house of the serious rat, roach, and pigeon infestation). It proved one of my other theories, that poor folks who want/need to stay have to take sub-standard dangerous conditions like mold, insect infestation and asbestos, even if it kills us, just to remain housed.

Which brought us to Mama-house — the Gentrification Palace — an unbelievably beautiful place with shining floors and spacious rooms and a backyard out of the pages of a glossy magazine, only affordable to us poor mamaz, because one of the mamaz had a housing subsidy.

"Mama can we stay here forever?" My son would say while we lived within its serene structure with multiple other mamaz in and out of crisis, several children, a houseless family member or two and birds, cats, and even a little dog, sharing stories, dreams, ideas, and equity, crafting complex future plans for Homefulness's truly shared equity and food localization and a micro-business economic self-sustainability model.

And then one day it was over. The slice of paper hung flimsily from the grand blue oak door. "60-Day Notice." Its words, slashing across the page, dripped with ancient blood of conquistadors, missionaries, real estate speculators, mortgage brokers, developers, and benevolent landlords. My relationship with its beauty, its never-really mine- stability, its community with other mamaz and families, life-breathing support and love, was gone.

On our last day at Mamahouse, all of us indigenous mamaz, brothers, sons, daughters, uncles, aunties, grandmothers, and grandfathers huddled together, our abuelita pictures, icons, and spirits from our mama altars, our clothing, stuffies, beds, desks, chairs, wastebaskets, feathers, icons, beads, shoes, and toys strewn across the sidewalk, scattered from the wind-less hurricane of deadly gentrification and displacement, while default gentrify-ers raced by to get $4.00 fair-trade, organic, coffee and raw, vegan donuts at the plethora of blond wood filled cafes and $100 artist/designer dresses at the new, "underground" clothing stores beginning to fill up all the store-fronts in our inner-Mission neighborhood.

My eyes cry tears of untold evictions and displacement of communities—of children and elders—faces that are left in faded murals to be covered in sheets of cold white paint or brushed over by the whimsical brush strokes of hipster/artists that have no respect for the neighborhoods they gentrify.

As the rays of warm Mission sun began to slip away through our beloved, no longer-ours, front yard tree, all us mamas and children were still pulling thing after tragic thing out of unseen crevasses in the house.

All of sudden, my son, perched on a box full of his complete collection of legos, looked up at me, tilting his head to the side and holding back tears, "Mama, it's ok, I just figured it out, we are going to move to Homefulness after this, and then we will all be ok."

To this day my son and I are still houseless, we have bounced in and out of different temporary living situations all over the Bay. Although I no longer live in the neighborhood, I still inhabit it on the margins, driving past my street, glancing at the just-painted front steps, the newly planted flowers in the front yard, dreaming of the sounds, the love, the times spent in community there, lingering within its inside-ness. Remembering, always recollecting the words of the Po' Poet Laureate of POOR Magazine, A. Faye Hicks, "When us po folk are evicted we don't always leave the neighborhood, we just move into the sidewalk hotels, the card-board hotels, the street.

"In our communities, the earth that was used to fatten the cattle of ranchers and landlords is now used to produce the maize, beans, and the vegetables that brighten our tables." EZLN (Zapatistas in Chiapas)

From Houselessness to HOMEFULNESS…in Oakland!!!

The first resting place/creation space of Homefulness is located at 8032 MacArthur Blvd in Oakland.

How did this finally happen?

Revolutionary Change Session Launches True Change…. Crumbling the Myth of The Gift — Deconstructing Donor Denial & Dismantling The Non–Profit Industrial Complex….One Outcome at a Time

Launched on Juneteenth of 2009, the POOR Magazine Revolutionary Change Session was a moment in herstory, a poor people-led/indigenous people-led teach-in for conscious folk with race, class, and/or education privilege who were interested in exploring, implementing, and practicing truly revolutionary expressions of giving, equity sharing, and change.

At this herstoric event poverty, in/migrante, race, elder, youth, disability, and indigenous skolaz presented curriculum on the kkkriminalization of poor peoples and public space, local and global poverty, ableism, welfare, border fascism/false borders, systems abuse, underground economic strategies, po'lice brutality, profiling, globalization, gentriFUKation, indigenous removal, and more.

At the culmination of the Change Session we launched the Declaration of Interdependence and the Manifesto for Change – two documents birthed in the hearts, minds, and revolutionary eyes of Mama Dee, Tiny, Ken Moshesh, Joseph Bolden, Lauren X, Maria Lopez, Kimo Akaha and other indigenous, landless poverty scholars existing in doorways, on street corners, in welfare offices, in SRO hotels, in shelters, in HUD housing, and in cars.

The Revolutionary Change Session birthed POOR Magazine's Solidarity Board

POOR Magazine's Solidarity Board was formed by conscious young folks with different forms of race, class, and/or akkkademik privilege whose perspectives were skooled by Poverty Scholarship at the Revolutionary Change Session. From this skooling, each became interested in POOR Magazine's analysis of reparations and resistance and began to work on decolonizing their resources.

Two years later, POOR Magazine's Solidarity Board gathered enough blood-stained Amerikkklan Dollaz to facilitate a "purchase" of stolen land on Turtle Island to begin the healing of Pachamama, to begin the healing of our communities, our children and our families, ancestors, and elders through equity redistribution, decolonization, prayer, and ceremony.

To be clear, POOR Magazine the organization, is still Po', we only barely get by on donations by you, our families, and ancestors and friends support to do the revolutionary poor people-led education, media, and art. But for the first time in our herstory we have the access to create/realize a poor people-led/indigenous people-led take back of stolen land to move off these grids of plantations, po'lice, poverty pimps, corporate and government control to true liberation.

To ask permission, to cleanse, to pray, to meet, to heal...

In the ways of our ancestors first we must walk softly on our (Pacha) Mama and in this East Oakland community, where many of POOR Magazine's family members have been gentrified out of, or currently dwell houselessly or in different forms of at-risk housing. We must introduce ourselves to the land and the peoples of this intentionally blighted, scandalously speculated on, po'lice brutalized, and long ago forgotten community in poverty and ask permission in ceremony to build the Revolution that is HOMEFULNESS.

The first HOMEFULNESS site includes sweat-equity co-housing for 4-10 landless, houseless/landless families in poverty, as well as a site for PeopleSkool, a multigenerational, multi-lingual school based on an indigenous model of teaching and learning, POOR Magazine peoples media center, Uncle Al & Mama Dee's Social Justice and Arts Cafe and Tierra Madre Garden where we will hopefully grow food for the whole community.

The process to dream and build HOMEFULNESS will be a community-led one with indigenous scholars and formally edukkkated scholars respecting and working together to create a re-mix of design, sustainability, and off-grid self-determination.

Otro Mundo Es Posible y se esta Construyendo /
Another World is Possible and is Already Being Built

MUTEADO SILENCIO
REPRINTED WITH PERMISSION FROM POOR MAGAZINE
16 MAY 2013

Like thousands of people, I have worked, cultivated and planted seeds, never to see or enjoy the fruits of my labor.

We have made and cleaned the most beautiful gardens that I have seen in my life in the mountains of Berkeley for people with money. Earning $10 an hour, we have built and managed houses with immense beauty, only to never see them again.

We have silently obeyed the orders of the stewards, managers, and company owners (the owners of the house, the owners of our checks, the owners of our lives). We have been forced into "obeying always in silence," but it does not always have to be this way.

In January 1994 a group called the Zapatistas (EZLN: the Zapatista National Liberation Army) emerged from silence. They came forth from the silence that uses politicians, butlers, and carries the cries of injustice against indigenous people and workers.

The Zapatistas began using a language that speaks of justice, land and freedom, always talking and working with each other. They do not use Twitter or Facebook, newspaper or television. They do it face to face, people to people, village to village.

In the early hours of December 21, 2012 the EZLN came out of the shadow of injustice and corruption that still lives and breathes in Mexico today. It was rumored that they left five *caracoles* (villages). In total there were over 40,000 Zapatistas in the streets of Chiapas.

The Zapatistas left a Press release:
http://enlacezapatista.ezln.org.mx/2012/12/30/el-ezln-anuncia-sus-pasos-siguientes-comunicado-del-30-de-diciembre-del-2012/

"Another world is possible, and is being constructed"

The press release of the Zapatistas said that little by little they are creating a world that we romanticize here in the United Snakes of Amerikkka. The Zapatistas have stopped believing in the lies of all politicians, political parties, and non-profit organizations that only bring misery and injustice.

"The Lands Belongs to those who worked the Land" is not only a saying in Chiapas; it is an action in Zapatista communities.

Other communities have taken steps similar to those of the Zapatistas. In Cheran, Michoacan, the P'urepecha people took up arms after the Mexican Government could not ensure the safety of the people, and where organized crime had plundered the forests that the people of the region depended on for survival.

In Oakland, California, people are taking a stand too. In 29 years of life, I've always had to respond and obey to my teachers, my employer, the people who sign my checks, to the bad governments, the nonprofit organizations and other authorities. But in June 2011 a group of workers, dreamers, displaced Poor folks, Migrants, Mothers, uncles, aunts, grand-mothers, and grandparents of different social classes took up a piece of land in East Oakland called Homefulness. The land originally belonged to the Ohlone people, the Natives of this Land, and so with permission and humility the dream of Homefulness became a reality.

With the help and support of the community we tore up the concrete and released *Tonanzin*, Mother Earth to plant seeds of hope and resis-tance. We created a garden of herbs and vegetables called Pachamama Garden in East Oakland. The Pachamama garden was a real community effort. With the help of groups like Take Back the Land, ROOTS, Decolonize Oakland, Phat Beets and through the efforts of volunteers and community members, we planted carrots, cilantro, lettuce, oregano, and other herbs. We did it all without the help of Foundations, Non-profits, or pimps. The project was completed only with the help of the community and a Grass-roots organization called POOR Magazine, *Prensa Pobre*.

POOR Magazine is creating, developing and spreading hope and strength for the community of Homefulness. In these times when it is difficult get a plate of food, Homefulness offers and shares food with our community, including fruits and vegetables from the Pachamama garden.

In the not too distant future POOR Magazine plans to build a housing center, media center, and cultural center for our community at Homeful-ness, following our principles as a very Grassroots organization, without asking the Poverty Pimps, foundations, or non-profit for their Crumbs.

Homefulness

"From Removal to Reparations...From Houselessness to HOMEFULNESS*...*
From indigenous lands stolen to budget crumbs throw-en-
From affordable housing in name only to rights to a roof by any means necessary...
From the cult of independence to the Revolution of inter-dependence...
From poverty-pimped housing po-lice to
Revolutionary equity for all Realized...!!!!"

After 500 years of removal, GentriFUKation, Anthro-Wrong-ology, akkka-demik studies, and philanthro-pimped capitalist compromises, and consum-erist destruction POOR Magazine's family of landless, indigenous elders, ancestors, mamas, aunties, uncles, fathers and abuelitos, daughters and sons will be realizing the revolution that is Homefulness.

I pulled each torn lace a little more tightly through their broken shoelace holes. Leo brushed back his dread-locks with one hard push of his muscled hand. Muteado tightened the hair-tie that held his thick black braid in place. We were ready.

We had spent the last several weeks, months, years, and centuries preparing.

Our steps quicken, our breath gets heavier. The ancestors are with us now holding 520 years of genocide. Downtown Oakland was quiet, there was a stillness in the corporate nature landscape of Oscar Grant Plaza. Even the pigeons knew.

We, the evicted, incarcerated, bums, hobos, trash, domestic workers, day laborers/trabajadores, street husslaz, medicine people, mamaz, youth of color, elders, disabled, criminalized, profiled and crazy were walking into a battle to liberate stolen indigenous Ohlone land By Any Means Necessary.

We slowly climbed the marble steps of the colonizer's mansion, passing countless blood-stained file cabinets, computers, and locked rooms holding our stolen stories and the micro-fiche memories of genocidal treaties and the coordinated lines running across our poor bodies of color, our indigenous souls, our ancestors' spirits.

When we arrived there were no guns, or shouts or screams or machetes, only a soft weapon held to our throats, masked as a hand-shake, a smiling introduction hovering over a shiny conference tables.

Our weapon was heavy in our hands. The corners sharp and crisp. We shifted our feet to not drop them.

We had a 2pm appointment with our local councilperson.

The violence of a landless peoples' land liberation movement waged within a wite-supremacist system created with kolonizer HIS-Stories and

A red, black, and green print of the POOR Magazine family in front of Homefulness. Poster by Dignidad Rebelde. It reads: "Homefulness: A self-determined landless people's movement."

values, rules, and laws based in clock-time, paper-theft, corporate law, and above all blood-stained Amerikkkklan dollars is a different kind of revolution.

In the tradition of MOVE 9 meets the Zapatistas, the indigenous/poverty, migrante, disability, elder, youth, and mama skolaz at POOR Magazine/Prensa POBRE have been working steadfastly for the last 520 (indigenous peoples genocide), 220 years (chattel slavery's metaphorical end in Amerikkka), and 16 years (the life of POOR Magazine) to manifest a landless peoples land liberation movement in the over-priced, gentrified streets of the Bay Area.

Like our hermano@s in Chiapas we are indigenous peoples in struggle but with an added oppression, we are urban, landless, indigenous peoples in diaspora, removed, displaced, separated, stolen, immigrated, from our tribal lands of origin, with no hope of re-couping them in struggle to stay alive and work in humility with our Ohlone brothers and sisters who are the 1st nations people of this stolen land.

Like our sheroes and heroes in MOVE 9 we are located in a majority African descendent intentionally blighted and gentriFUKed neighborhood, but unlike them we are attempting to work within the city constraints of land use and real estate snakkkeing and politricksterism.

And like the Shackdwellers Union we are poor, we are landless, we are Po'Lice harassed, and we are always under attack by Po'Lice, politricksters, and land-LORD hustlers.

From the beginning we have been guided by our landless, poor, indigenous, multi-tribal elders and ancestors, our many spiritual guides, Orixas, Mama Earth's whispers, and Creators prayers.

Similar to our sheroes and heroes from the Black Panthers, we follow the Black Commune and most importantly we believe that The Revolution Will Not Be Melted in a Pot. We diligently work to honor the multiple languages, traditions, spirits, religions, and practices, both pre- and post-colonial of our many different family members, of our ancestral memories, of ourselves.

We work in solidarity with young people with race, class, and/or educational privilege. These young people humbly understand that their role is not to save us or lead us, but only to stand with us — and support visions for us and by us as they activate clear-headed reparations of wealth and access they have easy but unjust access to. They learn this through a constant process of learning and teaching and guiding by us as poverty skolaz.

The Homefulness project like the POOR Magazine revolution began with an indigenous, houseless mother and daughter. Our revolution began in the back seat of a car. Our revolution began with a poem, as we walk humbly through so much pain and with a story, and continue to operate always in a story.

One of the things that corporate-simulated non-profits demand is the separation of self and state. This is to ensure that when the philanthro-pimps tire of your work, they can handily drop you on your baby-heads and it isn't exactly genocide, because its only the death of an "organization," not a people, not a spirit, a dream, or a hope for a neighborhood.

So as poor people-led, indigenous people-led organizations we are very clear that our issues, our struggles, our resistance, and our healing are entwined with us as people-always.

People worked together for... the bountiful welfare of everybody, and everybody prospered together. So there was no fighting among themselves to gain power or gain wealth or anything like that; that was unheard of. And the worship in the creator was something that they lived on. It was religion based on nature; they believed that the Great Spirit was in their people, in the trees and in the earth and in everything else. It was a civilization that worked quite well. I don't think that at this point in time you could reinvent that kind of thinking among the people, or re-instill it, because we are so corrupted by the European God that was imported into the Americas and that is greed. Greed is something that is very destructive and our people were doomed because they had no concept of what greed was, they couldn't understand it. Chief Sitting Bull [made] a statement that if North America had been twice as large as it is, it still wouldn't have been large enough for the Europeans, they still would have wanted it all.

— DR. DANIEL PAU, AN ELDER WITH THE MI'KMAQ NATION

10

Community Reparations and Revolutionary Giving: Moving Away from Philanthro-Pimping and the Non-Profit Industrial Complex

Mama Dee's Manifesto on Race and Class Privilege:
A Letter from Mama Dee to the Poverty, Race, and Media Justice Interns at POOR Magazine

DEE GRAY
REPRINTED WITH PERMISSION FROM POOR MAGAZINE
6 SEPTEMBER 2010

We have read all of your résumés. Many of you have had access and privilege beyond anything we, and many of the people we work with, have ever known.

Many of you have had exciting extracurricular and postgraduate volunteer work. Exciting is the operative word here. Some of you have had well-paying and interesting jobs as well.

When I see that kind of race and class privilege experienced by people, some still in their twenties, and contrast it with some of the people with whom we work, in their thirties, forties, fifties, and more, who have never had the opportunities most of you have had, I am almost at a loss for words and thoughts.

You owe so much and yet I do not want to see people helping others out of guilt because it often becomes nothing more than positivism, something you can forget when you go back to the next interesting job or advanced education program.

We, the originators of POOR, have come from poverty, and only because of our intelligence and ability to organize our thoughts — itself a form of privilege — have we been able to take these experiences from poverty, racism, and suffering and be at one with them, to create this grassroots organization that hopefully gives opportunity to others who have experienced similar backgrounds.

Do you have the ability, I wonder, to understand the nuances of your access and privilege? Your health, your optimism, your dental care, and on and on and on.

We need people who have the ability to understand the subtle and not-so-subtle differences between yourselves and the people with whom we work.

I wasn't impressed by your insights on your applications. I didn't get the feeling that you were in touch with what I'm talking about.

It is possible for you to learn. However, places like Global Exchange that provide exciting volunteer work for people with privilege, to keep them stimulated and excited, is not what we are about here at POOR.

There is a lot, a lot, a lot of drudgery in poverty—very little intellectual or creative stimulation. Much sadness and much, much frustration and isolation.

What can you do about this?

Beyond all else, you need to see those tiny differences that occur between yourself and those that exist in poverty. That is the beginning.

We at POOR need people like yourselves that can do the frustrating tedious chores like grant writing and other types of fundraising, as well as other administrative work. You need to pay your dues with work that is not very exciting. Working with the political events and assisting impoverished and disenfranchised people in writing from their voice and their experience is the exciting part. Even copyediting for these folks is more interesting than some of the day-to-day frustrations of maintaining our vision.

If you are interested in being here at POOR, you will be required to help with both, whether or not you are bored, annoyed, or frustrated. It is part of running a grassroots organization and it is what we do.

You can benefit by using your strength and optimism and abilities that have come to you from privilege and access to help us, and I hope that, at least in part, you experience some of the boredom and frustration that we have experienced. That, in fact, you do not feel intellectually stimulated. That you are annoyed and have a pervasive sense of hopelessness from feeling overwhelmed, like us and the people with whom we work.

From these feelings, you will learn about poverty. Be thankful if this happens to you. Include that in your résumé. Those feelings are more meaningful than any travels in India, Africa, or other faraway places with strange-sounding names, Ivy League college degrees, or honors from the dean's list, Phi Beta Kappa or Magna Cum Laude, stimulating and informative college classes, books with new and edgy thinking, or any of the cumulative warm and happy holidays that you've experienced with family and friends.

I did not see any mention of this kind of experience on your résumés. I did see a lot of near clichés about wanting to "help" people.

I suppose you have gotten in the habit of writing this kind of résumé because it is what graduate schools and good jobs require, but if you work here at POOR, I would want you to rewrite your résumé including these feelings based on your experience here — and then convince future employers that this is, in fact, the way a résumé should be written.

If you want to work at POOR you can let us know in writing how you understand what we expect of you. Do tell us what you think you can learn here as well.

EXCERPT | **Writings on Reparations**
THE POOR MAGAZINE SOLIDARITY FAMILY

Editor's note: This is a never-before-published series of anonymous writings by people with race and class privilege. It is a collection of short excerpts by various authors. Each writer's work is separated by a "***."

Land-grabs from Indigenous People, that's literally where the root of my money is. White European settlers in the fifteenth and sixteenth centuries. The captors of Pocahontas, Mr. Founding Father Thomas Jefferson himself - this is my blood, passed down and down, but still in mine, trickling directly through the centuries of a family tree to the present day. Milking capitalism, too - taking part in the rat race and winning. Using privilege to make more privilege - a tip-off before the great stock market crash of 1929 saved my great-grandmother's bank account. Privilege begets privilege.

I think my family — the whole extended networks of ancestral aristocrats — doesn't oft remember this. In fact I think they choose to forget (sometimes I do too). The past is in the past. True to the WASP form, there is little emotion, even little attachment. What's done is done, that's what they say. We can only do what we do now. it's a learned pattern, so I've learned to forgive them. It's not their fault - it's not my fault.

Thinking of all the resources I have overwhelms me - a trust fund, a savings account, a stable job, healthcare, an apartment, my parents' house. A father in politics, a doctor for a mother. A lifetime of consistent (western) healthcare, vaccines, TLC, and ample time off when I'm ill. Always a multitude of vegetables, fruits, local foods, and wholesome options. Enough space and time in my life to cook food and enjoy it. Enough space and time in my life to sleep for 8 hours a night and enjoy it. Braces when my teeth were crooked, eye exams when my vision was questioned. Specialty therapists when I felt depressed, specialty therapists when I had an eating disorder. Uncles and grandfathers in high places at prestigious universities, who've hobnobbed with presidential candidates and their ilk. A network at Wesleyan and beyond, of professors, academic resources, bright-eyed young people with a college education and a background like mine. 40 hours a week (at least!) spent connecting with other young wealthy folks. Innumerable friends with apartments, innumerable family members and extended community members with homes with extra beds.

Parents who love me, whom I love fiercely right back. Who would take me in and hold me — emotionally and financially — for as long and as deeply as I ever needed.

***

Rich people traded pieces of earth among themselves as if they were theirs to trade, and one of my parents facilitated those transactions for a commission, and a small share of that share was passed along to me. But even that sliver of a sliver of huge dollar amounts is big enough that I have the safety net of knowing that whatever I might do, whatever choices I might make, through no work or effort of my own, and on the backs of people who have been displaced, gentrified out of their longtime homes, whose entire neighborhood, where their families in many cases had lived for generations, was completely changed without their consent, I will have a chunk of money coming to me that means I will never be without food or a home. On other people's backs, my basic needs, for the rest of my life, will be met.

What makes sense within the dominant economic system makes no sense when all the lives, people's and earth's included, are acknowledged. What seems to make sense within this system — that earth can be divided up and owned and traded, that people can profit off other people's housing and have so little responsibility to them — just doesn't. There are so many unacknowledged costs: stories upon stories of people who were shoved out, displaced, disrespected, disregarded, unacknowledged—the people buying and selling have to blame them or make them wrong when they manage to notice them at all in order to justify to themselves what they are doing — stories upon stories of land partitioned and owned, traded, with no regard for its life and needs and wholeness outside of its utility to whoever happens to "own" it at a given moment, then whoever comes next, with no regard for the people who live there without the entitlement ownership confers, whose payment for their housing enriches the very owners who are unaccountable to, unconcerned with them when the time comes for another trade.

I could consider as "mine" money that streams to me through an accident of birth in the context of white supremacy, colonialism, earth exploitation, and capitalism, but only if I shut my heart, spirit, and mind to huge pieces of the story, only if I am willing to not notice impacts, not register the whole. I could consider this money "mine" and use it as such only if I were willing to not be whole, and I am not.

To be whole, to even move or aspire toward wholeness within a context of thousands of years of violence enabled in part by fragmentation and disassociation, requires facing the fact that the entire earth is a whole, that each aspect of it is connected to each other. That it is all and we are all in some senses already whole, but we have been violently disassociated from that fact, and there is no true wealth or security or fulfillment in "benefiting" from violence and disassociation. I make reparations as part of dreaming for communities, for the earth, for the truth of interconnectedness, in waking life, in action.

***

In my life I have made money and not made money, sometimes living off the inherited stolen profits and wealth from my family. But class privilege and wealth is so much more than the material things. I have an effervescent positivity and optimism, generated by never having to worry about money. I have a sense of freedom in how I move about the world that lets me enjoy confidence, that is reinforced because people respond well to confident energy. I can afford to share resources, including time, with friends and acquaintances, and I get a lot of credit and praise for "being there" for people and being a "good friend" because I can afford to consistently prioritize people I care about, not needing to hold on to a job or save money on transportation to get places. My relationship to wealth, stolen capital, affects every relationship I have. It is direct access to often-invisibilized power, a power that is seductive to hold onto and that so many folks, even with tight anti-capitalist analysis, are also attracted to. It makes me feel and makes me get treated as superior, someone whose time actually is more valuable than other people's, just like I was told every day growing up that I was one of the "best and brightest."

Unlearning that lie can't happen just in the classroom. It's going to take practice. Living without direct access to wealth. It's going to take vulnerability, anxiety, disappointment, and loss. I need to let go of enough privilege that I can start experiencing my humanity. Asking for help. Not being the hero at the meeting who takes on huge tasks because I have limitless time. Disappointing friends that I can't see whenever we both want. Not being able to buy whatever I want whenever I want it, or live anywhere I want, or spend my time however I want. I am afraid to give these things up. But I know the cost of these privileges is a separation from what it is to be human in this world, and an allegiance, no matter how subtle, with capitalism.

***

My father and our family returned to the US from Turkey, and he got a degree at UC Santa Cruz. He was a member of the first graduating class at this experimental college. Like my Grandpa, he was the recipient of state-subsidized financial aid before the days of affirmative action, and got through school basically for free because he had traveled through Europe, Asia, and the US, accumulating experiences that signified his complex and unique perspective on the world. Inheriting my Grandpa's legacy as a world traveler, he was able to use the paths that US imperialism had carved before him to advance academic interests in obscure and exotic subject matter. He and his revolutionary ideas learned from time spent with Italian socialists took off for Cornell graduate school (Dad was a legacy now), where he became a scholar of Antonin Gramsci and socialist organizing. He didn't have a lot of spending money, but he was provided a stipend to cover food and housing through various fellowships and loans thru his Akkkademic networks. He got to travel to Italy and finished his dissertation, after which he was hired to teach politics at SUNY Albany, where he and my mom met. He was a professional now, living cheap in the de-industrialized city of Albany.

Through my ancestors' experiences of world cosmopolitan travel and research, I have inherited financial security directly tied to the U.S. caste/apartheid system and worldwide tourist and academic institutions. From my Jewish great-great grandparents, who could easily find jobs in the racially charged industrial economy of World War I; to my grandparents, who were eligible for loans to buy a house during the 1940s and 1950s white flight; to my dad, whose increasingly exclusive education had been financed by US military and academic imperialism....With each generation, my family's class ascendance has been subsidized by state institutions designed to support white families at the expense of everyone else. I have grown up caring deeply about my parents' stories of travel, study, and adventure, hoping to emulate their curiosity about the world and their wish to make it better. My head is filled with some very complex questions about how I can best transform the culture of imperialism and entitlement that my family has grown wealthy within. I need to repair the patterns of inheritance, to challenge ideas about what a rich life of knowledge might mean, and to heal some of the wounds that my family's extraction of resources have inflicted.

***

I don't really understand what my mom does, how her work fits into this economic system. The company she works for now, the company she's paid to legally protect, trades in things that aren't real, that I can't touch. Insurance, annuities, portfolios. These are ways to make rich people's money "grow," and to provide rich people with the feeling that Certain Financial Decisions will keep us safe until we die, without having to rely on anyone else. The company's website says: "How much is enough? How much would you need to accumulate over time to fund a 20-year retirement?"

Money "growing" means that people, somewhere, are working without being paid what their work is worth, and that that money is being siphoned into financial markets, which contain things like "annuities." Because capitalism is so violent to so many people, and because it doesn't make sense for the things our souls long for, it takes intense labor to keep it standing. So the kind of work that people in my family do, that help keep these enormous companies and structures intact and humming smoothly, is crucial to the system. And so my mom gets paid more than almost anyone else in the world.

Some of the reparations I owe are vague, enormous. It's the heart of this economic system, of people trading in non-tangibles, in things that don't help anyone meet their basic needs. Some are a little more specific: affirmative action, which brought my mom where she is today, grew from civil rights and freedom struggles that demanded something much bigger, and whose visions are still visions—visions that demand reparations from me and my family.

***

I think it's crucial to draw connections between media storytelling and the stories we tell in our families; between the racism of politicians and legislators and the insidious, institutionalized racism that affects us without our even realizing it; between the paternalism of philanthropy and the privilege that we as individuals unconsciously enact; between the oppression by obvious perpetrators like police, military, and sweatshop-owning, union-busting multinational corporations and the oppression underlying our personal family fortunes.

The "progressive philanthropy" world tends to take a stance that resists truly challenging capitalism and oppression in order to accommodate more moderate wealthy donors. Much of the landscape of social change philanthropy seems designed to make rich people feel better about ourselves and to channel some funds to progressive (or even radical) organizing without actually challenging the roots of inequality.

You don't have to look hard to find clear explanations of how capitalism is inextricably linked to multiple oppressions: racism, through (for example) slavery, imperialist acquisition of land and raw materials, and dividing white and POC workers to keep them from organizing; sexism, through exploiting the labor of women (who are already culturally devalued) and relying on women's unpaid and unrecognized labor; ableism, through laws allowing companies to hire people with disabilities at less than minimum wages; and so on.

For white folks with class privilege, the history that gets erased when we tell our simplistic "pulled-himself-up-by-his-bootstraps" money stories is the (continuing) history of explicit and institutionalized racism in the U.S. Some of us can trace our inherited wealth to slavery or other systems in which white people directly profited off of the stolen labor or land of people of color. Even for those of us with "new" money, previous generations of our families are more than likely to have benefited from racist policies and institutions that helped white people and discriminated against people of color (Homestead Act, G.I. Bill, land grants, New Deal, loans, jobs, contracts, unions...). Throughout U.S. history, people of color have been explicitly prohibited by racist government policy from building assets; and since the most important indicator of wealth is how much money your parents had, cultural myths about a "level playing field" start to look pretty empty.

For class-privileged people to be allies in social justice movements, we have to take responsibility for the bigger picture behind our own wealth. Our personal decisions about money and the stories we tell (to ourselves and others) have reflections and repercussions connected to our place in the larger class system. Challenging these decisions and narratives, and challenging ourselves to look deeper, is a good way to start shifting our participation in oppressive systems.

To People with Race and Class Privilege

All of that money, comfort, resources, connections, both seen and unseen, that you have always had unquestionable access to is not now and never has been yours. It is not yours to keep, to decide on, to cogitate over, to dream about, to worry about, to feel guilty for, or even to give away.

These ideas are not meant as a critique. You have always been told that you "deserved the best," that you are "special." Most of all, you were never asked to question your wealth and privilege. So these are just spoken real-nesses, told by the peoples your ancestors and your family and now you (by default) have exploited and profited off of.

This chapter presents a map for immediate, actual change—not intellectual or metaphorical change. There is no more time for thinking, dreaming, worrying, guilt, or strategic planning. This is a call to urgently needed movement.

If you have been reading this whole book and/or have been educated in well-funded formal institutions of learning, you probably already hold a vague herstorical account of whose stolen wealth, resources, lives, land, and/or bodies your family, your cultures, and your communities have benefited from to put you in this moment, with this trust fund, this BA, this over-priced apartment, condo, or room in a hipster enclave of a gentrified neighborhood, this job, and so forth.

You also should know that your life is based on so many lies that it's very hard to untangle them all, the first being the cult of independence that likely motivated you to leave your family home, your comfortable and completely livable room, so you could fit nicely into a trajectory of separation and independence and take up your role as an important and necessary part of the consumer culture, living "away from family" and buying blankets, furniture, cleaning products, and silverware (even if it was at Goodwill) and perpetuating gentrification and displacement of a working-class family of color with your very presence in an already-filled urban city.

You have been carefully sold, pimped, and played in ways you may already be conscious of. But what you may not know so clearly is that your decision-making processes, your painstaking, time-wasting cogitation over what to do with your stolen wealth, is killing people with every moment you continue it. So here is the template for immediate change.

Cut the Bullshit and Start Writing the Checks

Give all of your stolen wealth away to indigenous-people-led, poor-people-led movements. Please make the distinction. If a group is already heavily funded and entrenched in NPIC budgets and admin constraints, they are probably a corporate-simulated poverty-industry group (see below for more on the Non-Profit Industrial Complex, or NPIC). I am not telling you to not give them money; that's your decision. But be clear that they will be okay without your donation and are profiting off of poor people's backs. Reparations means giving to groups working toward self-determined liberation in the deepest way as dictated by their elders, ancestors, and communities.

Don't give away stolen wealth with the goal of "having something to do with your time" or feeling good about yourself. These lies of the "charity" industry continue to perpetuate the myth that this is your money or your family's money in the first place. As well, don't offer your "services" instead of giving away stolen money or to "leverage your knowledge" or give in "other ways." If you want to offer your "services" and they are actually necessary, like cleaning, or cooking, or fixing computers, or managing databases, doing taxes, or teaching about some software that a lot of us Po' Folks don't have access to, then offer it separately from your money, otherwise a lot of us Po' Folks will "let" you do something just because we are humble and kind-hearted and feel indebted to you because you have given away the stolen money.

Don't try to control where the money is going, or barrage the organization with any kinds of demands, except maybe a receipt for your IRS requirements. Don't try to get fame within the organization or praise for being a good person. You are not, anymore than a person who steals someone's backpack and then gives it back is a good person. Matter of fact, they should be ashamed of themselves for the original theft. It might not have been your original theft, so shame and guilt do not make sense. But humility is most definitely a feeling you should be moving with.

This idea of shame in terms of money is interesting, because those of us without it are actually taught in a capitalist society to be ashamed if we are poor. We live with the shame every time we can't afford to pay the over-priced theft-rent, the rising utility bills, or the cost of our children's back-pack, or when we take the government hand-out crumb like food stamps, welfare or SSI, and yet people who stole all our resources, wealth, and jobs and continue to profit off of our pain through non-profiteering are actually taught to feel nothing or to feel pride for all they have. It is quite bizarre, who in fact is holding this misplaced shame.

If you can make a donation to a group related to the original theft, that might make sense—like a person whose family made money in real estate making donations to houseless people taking back land or fighting the criminalization of homelessness, or a person whose inherited wealth came from stolen resources making a donation to indigenous peoples trying to fight fracking. But that kind of cogitation might take too long and again im-plies that you, the stolen-wealth inheritor, has some kind of special right to sit with that stolen wealth and obsess on it and work on it like it's a project when it is just an accident that you were born into it and you have already benefited countless times from it. Just start writing checks.

Poor Peoples Don't Have Presidents: RAD and Other Pre-Trump Anti-Black, Anti-Poor Laws and Demand for Reparations

TINY AKA LISA GRAY-GARCIA
REPRINTED WITH PERMISSION FROM THE *SF BAY VIEW*
24 NOVEMBER 2016

Poor, unhoused/barely housed, indigenous, disabled, Black, Brown, and Red peoples don't have presidents. We have prison wardens, police, sheriffs, anti-social workers, landlords, judges, bailiffs, poverty pimps, case manglers, ICE agents, CPS workers, and debt collectors. Under KKKlinton we lost wel-fare, institutionalized the criminalization and incarceration of young peo-ples. Under Reagan we got called welfareQUEENs and accused of stealing and were permanently kkkriminalized and racialized as poor single parents, and lost all mental hellth care. Under Bush working-class and poor folks lost the right to file foreclosure suits, the president began fake wars against all Muslim peoples locally and globally, we lost dental care and were told we had to get married. And under Obama more of our families were deported than ever, po'Lice terror against Black and Brown people and unhoused people continued and increased, and all of our public (poor people) hous-ing has been stolen.

Since the beginning of this kkkolonial theft our lives have been and are consistently consumed by an endless stream of people that feed off of us, profit off us, and "manage us," obstacles that we have to navigate just to get through a day, acquire a crumb of help, stay housed, sheltered, not beaten, not terrorized, not deported, not have our children, belongings, and lives seized, searched, harassed, or ended.

So where does this leave us in the face of this adult Chucky monster claiming some "control" over us? First of all, it is important for those of us holding on barely to the margins of this stolen land to understand and innerstand that our dribble-down experience of the monsterule is really just an intensified hate, oppression, and terror of what we are already experiencing. To preserve our human and mental bodies we need to stay sane and realize this is NOTHING new. Next we need to take action, and yes that's protest, but it's also offensive. This is the time to launch those reparations cases. Reparations for stolen lives, stolen profits, stolen land, stolen rights.

Three years ago when the horror of the privatization of all public housing as we know it was launched by an illegal, backroom deal between poverty pimps, non-profit and for-profiteering housing devil-opers, and HUD/Housing Authority, POOR Magazine and the *SF Bay View* launched a series of actions and a call out to a revolutionary law firm who would represent Black, Brown, and poor peoples living in public housing for generations who were now facing eviction from their neighborhoods, barrios, towns because the stolen Ohlone land that their housing was built on was considered too valuable for mere poor Black and Brown families to live on. This "program" is called RAD and began under Demicans Obama, Ed Lie, and was written by another Demican, Julian Castro

As reported in multiple stories by POOR Magazine and the Bay View Newspaper since 2013, the RAD program will mean the mass displacement and houselessness of literally thousands of very poor families across these United Snakkkes.

Last week, our Demican "mayor," Ed Lie, who has consistently navigated stolen Ohlone (San Francisco) land, resources housing, and dollars to the very rich, causing the mass eviction and displacement of elders like 100-year-old Iris Canada and the Po'Lice death of Luis Demetrio Góngora Pat, Amilcar Perez Lopez, Mario Woods, and Alex Nieto, proudly announced again that he "successfully transferred all the public housing to private devil-opers."

"*Bank of America Merrill Lynch is pleased to continue its work with the City of San Francisco and the San Francisco Housing Authority on the second phase of SF-RAD,*" said Maria Barry, Bank of America Merrill Lynch community development executive.

This announcement is yet another example of the blatant theft of resources from the people and specifically from very poor people who will have nowhere to live once we lose our housing. This is when we have the backdrop of ballot measures in cities across Amerikkklan that make it more illegal than it already was to be unhoused. And all of this is under a so-called "Democrat." Neo-liberalism is killing us. Who needs ChuckyTrump?

So once again, I hope people move offensively. If we can't stop this evil from being inaugurated and even if we can, revolutionary lawyers help us launch those reparations and equity cases, disengage from the lie of "capitalist success," institutional skool debt, private ownership, nuclear families, age-grade separated lives, education and Po'Lice, and the belief that if we just get the right poltrickster we will be ok.

This is also why POOR Magazine, Krip Hop Nation, and the Sogorea Te Land Trust launched the Stolen Land/Hoarded Resources Tour this year in Ohlone and Tongva Lands and will be touring and offering the medicine of redistribution to land-stealers and wealth-hoarders in New York, Philly, and beyond in 2017 with the solutions of poor, indigenous, and Black-led self-determination projects like Sogorea Te Land Trust, Homefulness, and the Auntie Frances Self-Help Program.

Poor people don't have presidents or governors or mayors. We have ourselves.

"Change Wont Come from a Savior, a Pimp or an Institution. Change Will Only Come from a Poor People-led Revolution." —PO' POETS PROJECT

Poor People Help "Rich" People Redistribute Stolen Inherited and Hoarded Wealth Across Mama Earth

VIVIAN FLAHERTY

On Earth Day, April 22nd, 2016, the 'Stolen Land & Hoarded Resources Redistribution, Decolonization & Community Reparations Tour for Mama Earth and its Earth Peoples' was launched by POOR Magazine, led by "Poverty Skola" Lisa "Tiny" Gray-Garcia of POOR Magazine/Prensa POBRE, and fellow race, disability, and indigenous scholars, Leroy Moore from Krip Hop Nation, and First Nations Ohlone warrior Corrina Gould of the Sogorea Te Land Trust.

Along with many local Bay Area community allies, this nation-wide tour kicked off in the wealthy Pacific Heights neighborhood in San Francisco (Yelamu), later followed by a second tour on May 20th in the wealthy neighborhoods of Trestle Glen in Oakland (Huichin) and in nearby Piedmont. Houseless, working-class, privileged-class, Black, Brown and indigenous communities walked in humility and prayer with guidance from ancestors from all four corners of Mama Earth in an effort to seek monetary reparations through healing the sickness of 'hoarded wealth.'

With the increasing epidemic of wrongful displacement of long-time residents, both poor and working-poor, and the increasing houselessness of communities under attack from high-speed gentrification, environmental racism, hyper-apartheid incarceration, and police terror, this tour is embarking on a mass movement to reclaim stolen land, practice decolonization, and seek reparations across the United States in an effort to heal Mama Earth and all of her Earth Peoples.

During both walks, the community humbly and peacefully walk into "wealthy" neighborhoods door-knocking, offering wealthy land- and stolen-resource-hoarders a chance to begin the very serious work of 'decolonization' by redistributing one or more of their hoarded and bordered stolen indigenous territories, buildings, homes, stocks, bonds, cash, extra pleasure boats, and/or trust funds to landless and indigenous people in the form of what POOR Magazine calls "Community Reparations."

A group of poverty skolaz stands in front of large letters that say "Beverly Hills." A group of kids stand on the left; in the center Tiny is wearing an orange jumpsuit with her arm around her son, Tiburcio. Adult skolaz hold signs for the stolen land tour on the right.

Alternatively, if people are unwilling or unable to redistribute their stolen or hoarded wealth, these land-stealers and/or wealth-hoarders were then asked if they could begin an active dialogue with the community on the concept of "Community Reparations" for those most adversely impacted such as landless, very poor, and colonized communities.

"Its important for Ohlone People to be part of this movement, as we are unrecognized in our own land, and suffered the first form of gentrification: colonization. We had our languages and cultures stolen and are now displaced in our own ancestral lands," said Corrina Gould, Ohlone land warrior and co-founder of the 'Sogorea Te Land Trust,' the only Native woman-owned land trust in the United States.

The first walk in San Francisco (Yelamu) began on top of a hill in very cold and windy rain, and the prayer was powerful. Present were members of POOR Magazine, Krip Hop Project, and the Sogorea Te Land Trust, standing strong in unity with several local San Francisco organizations and well-known community members. They held it down in song and chant while speaking truth with a deep and powerful vibration that sailed in the damp wind as words, poetry, and song, led by the beautiful spirit of the ancestors. This drew a lot of curiosity from those peering out from their perfectly clean windows of greedy grandeur.

The walk ended in sunny Potrero Hill, where several community members with economic privilege read their amazing written pieces about how they were going to 'redistribute' their trust fund savings in an effort to 'redistribute the wealth.' This was truly the beginning of 'herstory' making indeed!

The second walks in Oakland/Piedmont (Huichin) began with song and prayer, like the first, on a very windy and blustery sunny day. Many community members from all parts of Oakland (Huichin) were present, including Auntie Frances of North Oakland who is working with POOR Magazine to build a second Homefulness in North Oakland for displaced, gentrified, unhoused, African descendent residents of that community who are struggling with racist, classist criminalization from the "new" members of that neighborhood. The Huichin Stolen Land Tour also included members of the powerful group Resource Generation, who committed to collaborate with POOR Magazine on future acts of decolonization and redistribution for unhoused and 1st Nations peoples' movements.

As several community members door-knocked on the lush and beautiful houses in Trestle Glen (the same area where Hipster mayor Libby Schaaf lives), most people didn't answer. But amazingly...one person did! Clad in his neatly pressed wealthy attire, a man opened his front door and intently listened to the community pitch the antidote for the disease of wealth

Poverty skolaz in front of Oakland City Hall at an action called "Where can we pee?" We were fighting the criminalization of poor peoples and our basic needs alongside a fellow poor, Black self-determination project led by Aunti Frances Moore, called the Self-Help Hunger Program in North Oakland. This area is ground zero of gentriFUKation in the Bay Area, and the post-gentriFUKed black residents of the neighborhood are criminalized in their own hood for just being there ... and God forbid they pee or even get a port-a pottie.

hoarding: redistributing their stolen wealth to houseless people and First Nations movements. This man said: "What a beautiful idea...yes, I'm interested." He then took an information flier. Amazingly the following day, he emailed POOR Magazine, saying that he was interested in finding out more info about redistributing wealth to the Sogorea Te Land trust!

The tour is planned to travel through other cities across Turtle Island (US) where the descendents of settler colonizers will be asked to redistribute their excess wealth or stolen land to First Nations people of the city/town where they live, or to support the launching of Homefulness models in that city/town for houseless people.

From Trump Tower to the Tenderloin:
The Hoarding Cluttering of the 1%

"Mr. A, Mr. A, this is your case-mangler, we are here for your daily, weekly, hourly room inspection." Covered in face mask, latex gloves and waving a mock pesticide spray bottle, playing a character I created called The Case-Mangler in POOR Magazine's 2017 production of Theatre of the POOR, I yelled through the "door" on the stage at poverty, disability, elder skola Bruce. This play, like all of the Theatre of the POOR productions at PeopleSkool, is based on our real lives, our real experience, our real trauma. This is what happened to Bruce when after years of homelessness and languishing on endless groups of waitlists he got a tiny 5 x 5 room in a Single Room Occupancy Hotel (SRO) in the tenderloin district of San Francisco. And although it was billed as "housing" it was really a kinder, gentler, poor people jail. With ID checks, no guests after a certain time and an endless list of rules to contain the rowdy poor "residents." But above all, one of the worst "rules" was and continues to be the constant and unbridled room and apartment inspections of his not-at-all private space.

Privacy is a Privilege
Any of us houseless and formerly houseless folks who have lived in publicly or privately "funded" poor people housing (or any kind of aid for that matter) have been subjected to incessant inspections of our yards, our rooms, our cars, our bodies and our children. In the SRO or project-based section 8 units, these inspections are constant and focused mainly on the "disease" as it is called, of "hoarding." It actually has a number attached to it and is listed in the encyclopedia of the empire, the DSM (Diagnostic and Statistical Manual), which has created an official diagnosis for this "disorder," and, like all of the disorders listed in the DSM, is now used to criminalize, fund, organize and stereotype poor people who supposedly "suffer" from it. The mere act of poor people having access to privacy is seen as a privilege we are not deserving of.

The odd part of all this is there are literally millions of people all over the world struggling with the CONfusion, violence, isolation, poverty, structural racism and classism, greed and resulting trauma of a global post-colonial reality, and even more specifically the disease of Western hetero-patriarchal capitalism. In other words, there are a lot of people with this "disease" but most of them don't get called sick. It is a class- and race-based "illness," and us poor folks are the ones who get "diagnosed" with it.

From the "Stolen Land and Hoarded Resources Tour" by POOR Magazine and Krip Hop Nation in Hartford, CT, on Pequot lands.

The Rich are Called Collectors

Rich people are called archivists, collectors, stock-pilers, museum curators, buyers and owners. Having two or three or nine homes, condominiums, vacation getaways, more pictures than you can fit on your wall, in your home, or in your office, four, five or 15 luxury vehicles, planes or boats, designer shoes you never wear, clothes you never try on, equipment you never use and/or literally billions of dollars you could never possibly need to survive. Rich people are rarely, if ever, called out for their capitalist sickness of hoarding, never forced out of their housing, threatened, inspected or harassed, but rather they get complimented on their ability to archive, or collect, or buy more and more things, and dollars, and stolen land. They are held up as examples of capitalist success and their class-based sickness remains hyper-normalized.

Conversely, if you are poor, you do not have the privilege or the "right" to have "too" many things, or actually pretty much anything. No matter how important our things even are. Once our lives are deemed dependent on the state, we have no right to the precious. How dare we collect mementos, art, archives, papers, or anything deemed not absolutely necessary by a litany of people now "responsible" for our lives, housing, and survival, or as I affectionately call the army of our saviors: the case-manglers, poverty pimps, anti-social workers, or Po'Lice, who believe they are necessary for our daily survival.

Now it's true that sanitation and cleanliness are an important part of health and safety, and it's also true that many of us poverty skolaz who are "saved" by the system from our lives of homelessness suffer from extreme depression, struggle with serious trauma, psychological disabilities and the long-term effects of post-traumatic slave syndrome, capitalism, and colonization. We sometimes keep or get things to replace all the people, family, loved ones and/or children we have lost or who have been stolen from us. Normal things like mementos, family photos, cards or old toys were long ago lost to the multiple evictions, displacements, foreclosures and/or incarcerations people like me and my mama suffered throughout my childhood. So we might begin to collect picture frames or batteries, or like my tortured, traumatized mama, literally hundreds of pairs of socks and pill bottles. Due to our trauma, we lack organizational skills, so we just make piles of things on top of more piles of things. This is part of what is happening to a lot of us at POOR Magazine like Bruce and his beautiful partner Kathy, in their "affordable" housing units in GentriFUKation City. Both are disabled elders, with trauma around homelessness, ableism and endless harassing inspections.

The insane hypocritical cycle of this process is that the few of us who get off the street into housing, end up facing homelessness again, almost immediately once we are in housing. This is due to the poison cocktail of DSM-fueled pathologizing and criminalizing of our behavior, actions, and living spaces, and the battery of anti-poor people laws that support the criminalizing. Even the so-called "advocates," who more often than not encourage folks to sign stipulated judgments to vacate, thereby supporting the non-profit housing developers they work with. All of which results in us being on the street. Again.

Hoarding When You Have No Roof at All
The collections, belongings, products of poor workers, recyclers, unhoused folks who haven't been lucky enough to get access to a roof (or who are back outside again), don't even get the "privilege" of an inspection. Rather, our belongings and our bodies are constantly and immediately viewed as trash, blight, a mess, dirty, unsanitary, dangerous and unsightly, and whisked away daily, weekly, monthly, hourly by a society and a system that refuses to allow poor people to even be seen, much less be human. Hence the constant "sweeps" and the use of the word "sweep" to describe the removal of unhoused peoples from so-called public streets. These violent acts of race- and class-based removal happens every day in San Francisco, Oakland, and everywhere this lie of public and private space, and use of this already occupied indigenous land, rules.

Touring the Real Blighted Hoods
This is why POOR Magazine and the Sogorea Te Land Trust launched the "Stolen Land and Hoarded Resources Tours," through the other kind of

"Blight," the other hoarders, the rich. Sharing the medicine of redistribution, and something I developed called Community Reparations, with people never seen as suffering from a disease. Lifting up and sharing a different way of being with people whose actions are never questioned, whose choices to keep hoarding, exploiting, acquiring, and owning are not only unquestioned and un-pathologized, but complemented, enabled and encouraged. From gated communities in Pacific Heights to the Shinnecock Nation in Eastern Turtle Island (The Hamptons), where the extreme wealth-hoarders acquire acres and acres of stolen indigenous territory only to put a house on it. No food is grown, no peoples are housed, no ancestors are honored. This is the blight of poverty and scarcity and capitalism. And the shared belief that this is ok, that this is normal, that this is success, is actually frightening to me.

Trauma Support Healing Groups at Homefulness

For us unhoused and formerly unhoused poverty, disability, migrant and indigenous skolaz at POOR Magazine barely surviving the loss and trauma of so much, we hold each other in ongoing healing as we try to build a poor people-led movement for land liberation and housing. In this process one of the most important parts of this movement work has been the creation of the People's Agreement, which each member of the Homefulness and POOR Magazine Family co-created over a three year period, a document which remains a living document, moving and changing each time we see another manifestation of our collective trauma. One of the many innovative ways we try to build in the healing is through the creation of a trauma support therapy healing group, to process the collection of belongings and its relation to our collective living. We will also eventually launch a redistribution store, for all the things we might acquire that we don't actually need.

As the daughter, granddaughter, and descendent of so many broken poor, indigenous, and colonized women, who collected little tiny broken things to fill the places of so much brokenness and things stolen from them, I do this work and teach this medicine to heal through a new, non-punitive framework towards our collective healing. I don't blame the wealth-hoarding 1%-ers anymore than I blame myself or my family of unhoused poverty skolaz for accumulating, collecting, desiring of collecting, or desperation with the stuckness of it all. This is the lie we are all taught in a capitalist system. And it might take 530 years to unlearn. But toward this end, I share this framework to change the way folks view the process of accumulation, and its class-based criminalization, with the idea that there is another way to be.

We all suffer from this disease called capitalism. Let's all heal together.

Move Back Home

One of the most revolutionary things you can do in a capitalist society is to move back home with your "difficult" parents — who by the way probably love you immensely and worry about you every day.

In doing this, you are launching your own inter-class revolution because you will be educating your elders, siblings, friends, and community in their own decolonization. This will not be easy or hipster-exciting like a demonstration over some issue that has a lot of media attention or community love. It won't be an Occupy or sit-in or policy meeting; but it will be *extremely revolutionary* because it will be challenging wite-supremacy at its core, in its own home and with its own perpetuators.

No one will praise you for this move. It will be hard and sad and fun and soft and easy and confusing. And that is what makes it powerful and deeply revolutionary.

There is an urgency to all of this as the world's resources become more and more scarce and your people continue to take more and more of it while you think that you are working on change.

Humility is missing from organizing by wite peoples with class privilege because they hold the innate belief that they can go anywhere, do anything, save everything, fix everything, take care of everything, and be a part of everything, This is not entirely their fault because they have been told by their parents and their world that this is true. "You can do anything you want," says the constant stream of media and ad campaigns trying to sell you on this arrogance. The world is run by the descendants of colonizers who long ago believed they could go anywhere, take anything, be anyone, and steal everything, under the guise of "bettering," fixing, advancing, succeeding, helping.

Humility dictates the opposite: constraining people's actions to move softly on Pachamama, thinking first about others who live in any given place—who are there, fight there, are from there. At its most benign, arrogance about movement through the world fuels the movement of people with class privilege into neighborhoods they aren't from (gentriFUKation); or teaching jobs in poor, indigenous communities in programs that don't include the perspectives or leadership of the people already there; or into "helping" missions in the Global South. At its most deadly, this arrogance creates media, art, and messages about places and peoples who haven't given their permission to be media subjects, which is hardly better than the multi-million-dollar tourist industry, which profits off stolen land and resources, and gives tours of sacred sites of indigenous and poor peoples without seeking permission or paying reparations.

Moving back home is a humble move that counters all of this.

Once in your family home, you can start respectable and humbly waged organizing efforts launched with eldership, because one of your revolutions is to treat and speak to your parents without wite-supremacist angst, disgust or attitudes, or annoyance. You can start change movements in your own suburbs, towns, and communities: teach on reparations, invite poverty skolaz in to teach on reparations, un-gate gated communities, un-po'Lice heavily po'Liced areas, un-injunct gang injunctions, unNIMBY nimby hate against day laborers and food giveaways, un-gentrify gentrifying neighborhoods, redistribute stolen indigenous land (including the land your family's homes are located on) and un-lock locked public bathrooms and doorways and begin sharing and reparating through land-redistribution campaigns in your family's churches, jobs, community centers, and elsewhere. This will not be easy. It will be full of contradictions and confusing moments, terror, hate, love, and fear. And in that confusion, in those gray areas and soft resistance, lurks the deepest challenge to wite-supremacist domination.

For Peoples with Formal Education and / or Skin Privilege but No Access to Stolen Wealth

Having formal-educational and/or skin privilege but no access to stolen wealth is complicated for many layered reasons. If you got the paper from the institution by any means necessary (scholarships, loans, bankkk debt) to please your parents, you have to be very careful to recognize, honor, and love them for loving you enough to help you through the oppressor's gate. As well, if you are supporting yourself, your parents, elders, family, extended family, or your own children with the money you are now making from a non-profiteer job, as most of us poor folks are doing with these plantation non-profits, this process is slower and harder and must be incremental. But that's not the end of the conversation.

Are you going for a hipster, Obamita-esque POC role, or the old story of "I'm re-making the image of wite-male CEO into a strong woman or LGBTQ person of color CEO to prove it can happen, to smash racism with my life and my role modeling"? By stepping into a plantation-prescribed role—the ED, the social-justice coordinator, the case manager, the social worker, the corporate lawyer, etc.—you are emulating, creating, *being* a capitalist idea of productive success, and the perpetuation of the plantation continues.

It is one thing to get the formal-education paper; it is another thing entirely what you do with it. If you had the strength, access, organization, time, housing, energy, and health to get through those gates, use the paper for the community.

And if you are thinking, "Well, I need to survive," I say: yes you do, but do you need to hoard money and perpetuate the endless "taking, benefiting/profiting off of" poor and indigenous peoples that is often disguised as "giving back." Many of your ancestors never hoarded wealth the way they do here: buying a house so one person or one family can live in it, a new car 'cause you like the way it looks, a new outfit, and on and on – living for the sole act of living, not caring, giving, sharing. Forget the disembodied charity nation. Join the fully in-spirit sharing nation. Who in your family, town, community, life, street corner needs their rent paid, needs a ride to the doctor or dentist? Help with moving, sitting with, or skill-sharing.

If you had the calmness, order, help, housing, time, and/or linguistic-domination skills to get the paper to become a lawyer, para-legal, doctor, nurse, medical assistant, dentist, or dental tech, figure out how you can donate 5, 10 or 50 percent of your time to offer these services for free to the community. It can be by donating your time to neighbors, elders, or friends who are poverty skolaz; to a poor-people-led, indigenous-people-led grassroots doing front-line work; or to an already existent, under-staffed, over-worked community medical health clinic. Or straight up offer 1, 2, 3 or 30 percent of your private practice for free. Let local poverty skolaz know you are doing this by distributing flyers to community clinics, shelters, government-project housing, street corners, and/or among underground economic strategists on the street, as well as creating on-site care in locations where people work, convene, or dwell. For the techs: redistribute medical supplies to grassroots organizations locally and globally whenever possible. For the lawyers: we lose our housing, our possible government crumbs, and the tiny chance to win in the wite man's kkkourts when we have no access to legal representation. Offer that representation.

There are several revolutionary, grassroots efforts across the country like the Suitcase Clinic, Eviction Defense Center, Housing Rights Committee, and Berkeley Free Clinic that are overwhelmed and under-staffed and desperately need dentists, lawyers, doctors, and paralegals. When they are faced with serious budget genocide (cuts), they often have to completely stop free care. The Berkeley Free Clinic stopped providing dental care at a lottery because there were no more dental students willing to take some of their precious time out to give to poor people losing their teeth.

Connect the dots from the current perpetration of capitalist, consumerist lies and plantation politricks through all of the lies that originally brought your own people down: the lies of borders, chattel slavery, real-estate snakkkeing, gentriFUKation, the NPIC.

If you have followed the lies of capitalist separation, realize that now you are operating outside of your natural deep structural values. In essence, you have followed the ways of the wite-man, even if you think you haven't. Practice humility, and live and be change.

So Many Grant-Pimp Lies, So Little Time: Philanthropy and The Non-Profit Industrial Complex

In the '90s, when POOR started receiving government funds to teach journalism to people coming off welfare via the "welfare to work" program, at first we felt high off getting the money and moving our po azzes off the street hustle. But then we began to rely on it. And the government money inspired some foundation-pimp loooove and we relied on that. And then came the donor-advised-fund love and we relied on that. And finally, with all of this money (which still wasn't that much—our total budget was no more than $120,000), we had piled up a ton of administrative work: pages upon pages of paper, excel sheets, outcome forms, budgets and pre-budgets and pre-pre budgets, which we could not have accomplished but for the love of a nice man who leveraged his race, class, and education privilege and did it pro-bono for us.

So for two beautiful years we ghetto skolaz proceeded to do beautiful revolutionary things, and then the ball dropped. The city began to pick away at us because we refused to "report" on people—i.e., the bureaucratic money requires reporting on poor people if they don't show up. And then because our admin wasn't good enough, and on and on with the reasons, eventually they took all of our money away. And the minute that government money went away, all of the private foundations slipped away, and as the foundation and government money left, the donor-advised money shamelessly came to an abrupt halt even though we were in the middle of a project, already planning dates and enrolling young people. They took all the money away. . . .

After this we got and then lost money from the US Department of Housing and Urban Development. And then we got Catholic money and lived on it and did great things with it (even though they required that we sign a 30-page agreement about never mentioning the word "abortion" in any of our media material – we were ghetto and this was just another hoop; people needed to be paid so we signed the agreement), and then we started relying on that, and then the revolutionary pope died and that money went away....

All along we were required to do what I call the step-n-fetch-it grant dance: telling the funders anything they needed to hear, creating new titles and new projects for the same necessary work we were already doing cuz the old ones weren't "sexy" enough, juggling funds from one bill or project to another, filling out an endless amount of paperwork, parsing our struggles into separate "outcome" categories, putting up with questions like "I know you bring art, culture, change work, and media to poor communities, but how does this change the world?"

20 Million Dollars??!!!

DEVI PEACOCK

INCITE!'s book *The Revolution Will Not Be Funded* breaks it down: It's not a "non-profit sector," it's a non-profit industrial complex (or NPIC): as Dylan Rodríguez puts it, "the managed control of dissent." A.k.a. a spider-web of strings that catch activists who'd otherwise be flying around trying to bring a revolution that could overthrow the people (/spiders?) in power and end poverty for real.

The web traps us into shitty jobs at non-profits where (usually, white) upper middle-class folks with masters degrees that teach us how to dance for our cookie, become the (usually, under-paid, overworked) salaried boss-es of (almost always, *way* overworked and under-paid) poor and working-class folks who do front-lines work with the people we're supposed to be serving, and get pimped out (along with some token folx who use the organization's services) when a funder visits, to make the nonprofit's work seem legit.

There's supposed to be a lot of oversight of non-profits. It isn't over-sight, it's surveillance, through the IRS, grant reports to bullshit funders, etc. And they're modeled after giant for-profit corporations: a board of directors, hierarchy, stock-holders (a.k.a. "funders" and "donors"...not all donors, just rich ones), rules that block the deeper work of transforming society to actu-ally get equality, fairness, justice... But unlike a lot of for-profit corporations, non-profits tend to be chronically under-funded, on purpose.

I think the big goal of the NPIC is to give just enough people just enough money and power (just enough supposed agency) to get by — if we con-stantly scramble, and if we beg.

If we're so busy scrambling, we don't have the time or the space to look at the big picture, to work together to change the system as a whole.

I learned this right away at my first fancy non-profit job.

Fresh out of college, I moved to Washington, DC, to be a Big-Time Pro-fessional Activist, working for a social justice organization founded by one of my idols. Our goal was to bring 3,000 people from across the country to a big, one million-person march on Washington for reproductive rights. We said we were prioritizing the leadership of poor and working-class young women of color. Except I, an upper middle-class man of color, was the boss of ten women "field organizers" across the U.S. I never even applied for the job; I applied to be an unpaid intern. But I'd gone through non-profit "leadership development" and "community organizing" training, so they made me the boss. Hmm...

To make it accessible, bus tickets were supposed to cost $5. But my boss totally under-estimated the cost of renting buses to get people to DC. Our budget was so small (/unrealistic) that her boss expected march-goers to just pay more to come; bus tickets went up to $75. There was no childcare, we didn't set up meals or proper housing for all those people...They were just expected to take off from work or school or the rest of their lives and spend a cold rainy Sunday marching on Washington. Meanwhile, the rumor behind the scenes was that one of the four main non-profits organizing the march got $20 million in funding just to work on the march. Twenty. Million. Dollars. How much of that went to groups working on getting pre-natal vitamins to mothers in prison (or, shit, to closing prisons so families can stay together?)? How much of that went to services for poor and working-class folks of color? The four big groups sucked up a ton of money for that march. In the end, what changed?

Surprise—my organization had a hard time selling $75 bus tickets in spots like rural Oklahoma. So my boss's boss started secretly listening in on calls I'd have with our regional staff. Once, when one of them started crying that she was having a hard time selling tickets, the big boss took herself off of mute and started screaming that my co-worker wasn't trying hard enough. Seriously?

So, our process of getting people to and from the march was a disorganized mess. People (our "members") were pissed. I was pissed. And my bosses blamed me for just barely pulling it together...by which I mean, hiring, training, and supervising ten staff; booking 50+ buses and all the travel, housing, and other logistics; planning and attending events in ten states; and getting 3,000 people to the march...in twelve weeks. I was working from the time I woke up till the time I went to bed. No wonder people burn out of non-profits so fast...

I've been researching activist burn-out and the NPIC ever since that first non-profit job. I collected the stories of hundreds of people. Then, through a day job as a fundraising trainer working with thousands of people, I heard just about every non-profit horror story. (When shit goes down, it always affects the non-profit's fundraising...). I started noticing patterns; the same patterns of burn-out, power, and control, the ultra-rich deciding what is and what isn't an acceptable/worthy type of social change, etc., talked about in *The Revolution Will Not Be Funded*.

Some friends and I turned those stories and others into a cabaret show called Agen(c)y: Nonprofit Dreams + Disasters, that POOR, INCITE and other dope folx co-sponsored. 400 people came to the show; tons of others wanted to come but we sold out of tickets (because hello, tons of burnt-out non-profit workers out there, trying to heal from all the bullshit). So we're doing it again. We have to. We have to keep talking about this shit. Even if it means we never get a foundation grant that would help pay some bills. Even if it shuts me out of some jobs (which it did). Especially because of that. Because of the backlash. Because the backlash means we're doing something right. We're shaking shit up, exposing the spider-web for what it is.

***

You have to read the book *The Revolution Will Not Be Funded: Beyond the Non-Profit Industrial Complex* by INCITE! Women of Color Against Violence, which breaks down and gives numerous examples of the exploitative, insidious, oppressive reality of the non-profit system.

Slave Owners, Philathro-pimps and the NPIC

Here's my (brief) take on philanthro-pimping and the NPIC. During the theft of indigenous peoples' land, destruction of resources, and genocide known as European colonization in the US, the missionary ideals and practices of Christian Charity were replaced by the capitalist and patriarchal pattern of philanthropy. One of the earliest examples of philanthropists were benevolent slave owners who took care of their slaves. From that frightening template of patriarchal domination, philanthropy was implemented by corporate moguls like John D. Rockefeller, Leland Stanford, and Andrew Carnegie, who gave away money to appear as though they cared about people while they sponsored studies, endowments, grants, and entire institutions around eugenics, a terrifying fascist and racist pseudoscience eventually adopted by Hitler to rationalize Nazi beliefs.

Philanthropy is rooted in Euro-centric, western values of capitalism. These values directly impact the programming decisions and priorities of organizations, transforming the agendas of well-meaning and sometimes even revolutionary organizations rooted in poor communities of color into programs that harm indigenous, multi-generational, care-giving communities.

For example, there are organizations that create youth-only programming for indigenous youth whose cultures value eldership and family. And funding guidelines or narrow thinking promote de-linking of naturally linked cross-movements such as an organization working for tenants rights and organizations advocating for homeless families. In another internalization of capitalist values, non-profit organizations are forced to pursue funding based on that year's "sexy" initiatives.

Non-Profit — Can't Get No Profit
LEROY MOORE

Non-profit can't get no profit 9 to 5 can't get no time

Do you ever wonder?

Why non-profits go under
Just like domestic violence

We have to break this unhealthy, unrealistic cycle

Bulldoze the government fence
Picking from activists' garden
The Black Panthers to the US Social Forum

Leaving us starving

Writing grant proposals at 12 midnight
Run Executive Director run make that deadline
Got us hypnotize

Nonprofit can't get no profit 9 to 5 can't get no time!

Putting Raw Onion Juice on the Whip.....
QUEENNANDI XSHEBA
REPRINTED WITH PERMISSION FROM POOR MAGAZINE
19 FEBRUARY 2008

The state of Virginia is voting on whether or not to "officially apologize" for slavery, a race and poverty scholar responds.

You want to apologize for slavery?
Why don't you just put raw onion juice on the whip
and hit me again?
What a slap in the face to the afrikan!

Other nations that were victims of Amerikkklan atrocities got reparations, regardless of those tragic events happening on Amerikkklan soil, or not. What's due to the poor slave and his/her descendants, whom for centuries by force shedded blood, sweat, and tears? Families were sacrificed, names, language, culture, manhood, womanhood- lives were lost, just to primarily profit the Europeans and their descendants.

So what's in it for the afrikan slave? An apology? Try again!!! The damage has been done and recycled, upgrading to a terrible level that resulted in my people being psychologically murdered, full of self-hatred, but yet still willing to kill one another to protect massa's plantations (ghettos, sets), or to protect massa himself.

After hundreds of years of intentionally destroying a people and their land, you apologize? You want us to forget-just like that? Your apology to me is like a rapist violating his victim, apologizing to her, then returns to violate her again! Plain insane!

Even if you apologize today, a descendant of a slave is still going to die tomorrow, due to Amerikkklanization, and the Willie Lynch Syndrome, just to name a few ailments my people suffer from.

If you are truly sorry for the inhumane, brutal conditioning that was inflicted upon blacks (especially), then why are you (the powers that be for now) repeating this psychotic, bloodthirsty behavior? Why are nooses being tied to trees as constant reminders to slave descendants? Why are the perpetrators left unpunished and powerful? Why the offspring of slaves are still being railroaded, framed, and blamed in the kourt systems? Why such vicious attacks on all peoples of color around the globe? You even sacrifice your own children if they dare challenge your sickly plans of world domination and war.

So as for your Apology?? Not accepted. But cash, checks, money orders, lumber, land, liberation, equality- write it out to:

Descendants of Stolen People?
P.O. Box R.E.P.A.R.A.T.I.O.N.S

To all people of color, misplaced and scattered in the lands
    That WILL be accepted!

Community Reparations & Revolutionary Giving

So what would it look like to redefine development and fundraising? To practice what we at POOR Magazine call revolutionary giving? It would begin with the recognition that just because people have money and con- nections, they don't inherently have knowledge to distribute that money. Further, it would require understanding that people who have struggled to raise children in poverty, take care of elders, keep multiple low-wage jobs, or navigate systems like welfare, education, social security, and/or project housing hold a deep scholarship about the use and distribution of resources. Similarly, that values of caring, interdependence and eldership as defined by indigenous folks and folks of color aren't just nice ideas but actually need to drive organizational development and funding initiatives for poor communities of color. Finally, to even consider a new form of philanthropy and giving, it must be cleansed of its eugenicist, racist past and redefined as a form of reparations that centers giving within the concept of redistribution of the wealth, resources and land that were stolen from indigenous communities and poor communities of color locally and globally—the people who in the beginning of time were the stewards of the now very sick earth, who remain invested in its thrival and growth and who survive directly on its gifts and harvests.

In 2009, POOR hosted the first Revolutionary Change Session, where people with race, class, and/or educational privilege, most of whom were enmeshed in academia and the NPIC, spent the weekend in POOR's space being educated on the lies and destruction of philanthropy and the non-profit industrial complex. They were schooled by poverty, race, disability, youth, migrant, and indigenous scholars. That weekend, we introduced a new kind of philanthropy—community reparations. Several participants with privilege formed the now continually growing POOR Solidarity Family, which practices community reparations and is guided by the Manifesto for Change, a new vision for thrival and the taking back of and control of resources by indigenous and landless peoples all across the globe!

Revolutionary Giving

POOR Magazine's solution to the Non-Profit Industrial Complex and the exclusionary hierarchy of U.S. philanthropy is Revolutionary Giving. We believe that giving and donating is not a privilege, an option, or a nice idea for the donor; rather, it is a duty of people with class and/or race privilege, to give their time, their surplus income, their equity, and/or their support toward change for people struggling with poverty in the U.S. and across the globe.

Poverty Scholars as Co-Funders

Philanthropy, which has its roots in the Slave/Master "plantation" model, operates from the premise that people with money and/or resources inherently hold more knowledge about money than people without money. On the contrary, we believe that people who have struggled to survive, feed, and clothe multiple family members and themselves in fact hold deep scholarship about the use and distribution of resources.

Another mythology is rooted in the notion that a person receiving funding must be in a dire state of need to "deserve" the money. We believe that the root of oppression and poverty is separateness from our fellow humans, the oppression of one people by another people, the theft of land and resources of indigenous peoples, and the harmful cult of independence (bootstraps) that informs the western/US experience.

Poor folks, African peoples, Raza, and indigenous peoples need to self-determine our own futures. The role of peoples with privilege is not to save us, or create a non-profit for us, or a study to prove something to us, but rather to support us in our own poor and indigenous-led movements.

Change can only come from the inclusion of all voices and the collective leadership of poverty scholars working collaboratively with donors to create a different and truly inclusive process that doesn't perpetuate the historical oppression of people of color living in poverty.

Petition to Demand Afrodescendants
Be Given Reparations for Slavery
NORTH AMERICAN REPARATIONS TASKFORCE
REPRINTED WITH PERMISSION FROM POOR MAGAZINE

Afrodescendants, slave descendants of the Transatlantic Slave Trade, deserve reparations as a result of 400 years chattel slavery.

As "minorities" in the western hemisphere, we do not enjoy full equality before the law due to the total destruction of our essence, our identity, which, as we have seen, is the loss of our identity internationally.

By reuniting ourselves to the human family through having our human rights recognized and restored, we believe reparations, emancipation, and repatriation can be achieved.

Our continued effort will be the catalyst that brings us together as a Nation.

This means — no matter what religion we now practice, no matter what organization we belong to, no matter where we live – we have a common bond.

As a result of the aforementioned, our goal is to submit a petition with 50,000 signatures in support of reparations for Afrodescendants.

The Honorable Silis Muhammad, Chief Executive Officer of the Lost Found Afrodescendant Nation of Islam, will then take the signed petitions to the appropriate body within the United Nations to move our demands forward.

Homefulness Becomes Reality

Long yellow rays of morning sun shone through Oakland City Hall as seven poverty and indigenous skolaz floated in with building plans, standing shoulder to shoulder with revolutionary architects Dunya Alwan and Bob Theis. After three years, countless false starts, community love, asphalt removal, dreams, hopes, prayers to ancestors, mama earth, Creator, desperate and constant fundraising, humility, lost hopes, harvests, more plans, and more prayers and dreams, in we went clutching giant pieces of paper with lines and calculations, names and things we couldn't begin to pronounce. These were the plans for the recent manifestation of the landless peoples movement we call Homefulness, which we hoped would soon be built on land purchased with the help of community-reparations dollars in East Oakland.

We were gifted with the referral of our architect who, although a wite man with race and class privilege, walked with humility and generosity and came to us after deep prayer over the direction of our dream and then a referral by First Nations leader Corrina Gould, one of our spiritual guides.

We were racing the clock and the Gregorian calendar on this the next-to-last day of December 2013. We had just finished an endless litany of required tests, forms, and inspections. We had planned from the beginning that although we were poor, we would work in solidarity with our brothers and sisters who had access to race and class privilege, from revolutionary donors to architects to realtors, who would help us infiltrate a capitalist system that intentionally keeps landless peoples like us landless.

We would do all of their required papers, hit all of their points, follow all of their paper trails leading nowhere. And we would do it right, so they could never take this away from us, and so we could officially free this land from real-estate snakes and the lie of ownership forever.

There were so many expensive and difficult documents it would spin your head. But this is where our solidarity family came in, harnessing their family connections, their generations of peoples who knew peoples, from akademiks to developers to city planners to zoning officials to lawyers.

The city was quiet as our dreams and histories of oppression sat quietly in the hands of a disinterested zoning department assistant. We sat uncomfortably in our city-issued chairs.

We were all on edge because we had lost an important letter that was granted due to the race and class connections of Architects for Humanity, who came to help us through a solidarity family member because of who her family knew. They had opened the City of Oakland's door to us in the first place, nine wite architects being treated very differently from what they would have normally done with POOR Magazine ghetto skolaz, closing the door on us, leaving us outside, as usual.

We lost the letter because POOR Magazine has no admin staff; we are all holding on by a thread to organization and logical thinking.

And then she said it what we were all terrified she would say: "I can't take this application. It's missing a document (the letter) and it's just not complete."

NOoOOOOOOOOOOOOOOOOOOO.

We were there on that last day of December because we needed to get the application in before the end of year. If we had to re-apply it would mean another several thousand dollars, more time we didn't have, more work by more over-tired volunteers. And worse of all, it would mean more time before any of us desperate, houseless, to-up folks would be housed.

And then he came in. Traveling on a tiny, unseen magic carpet. He was a small man, soft-spoken. He had slipped into the chair behind the lady who just said no and looked quietly into the shining computer screen. And then suddenly his tiny finger rose up, as if guided by the hand of God herself, hovering above the return key.

"Oh no, this is ok, we can... (mumbling something)" and then his tiny finger clicked the return key. Before we even knew exactly what happened, he was gliding effortlessly out of the room. Before he reached the doorway, he said, "You are the friends of Ro Siedelman right?"

"Yes," we tentatively replied in unison.

"I am their uncle, tell them I said hello," and then he turned and added. "This is their mama's hand-made cup I am drinking out of." And then he was gone.

Ro is one of our solidarity family members, the first one who had actually put their feet on the sacred ground that is Homefulness. Unsure of what their ancestors need to repair for, Ro is a beautiful sibling who has thrown down in the deepest ways to support this project, and like all of our beautiful and humble solidarity family, walks with humility and love always, carrying their own privilege with the deepest understanding.

Their uncle was the reason our plans were accepted, and moments like this must NOT be underestimated or misunderstood. It is not just the blood-stained dollaz that lead to positions of access and privilege, it is all of the other stuff, the peoples and places of unseen privilege that open doors to other privileges, the intangibles of access.

Bank of Community Reparations

My whole village is ok, because I have a job.

—MASWI, MALAWI

All across Mama Earth people walk, talk, and live inter-dependence. No one has to explain or un-pack the basic tenets of sharing, love and mutual respect for each other. We as peoples are intrinsically connected to each other more than we are un-connected to each other. We must be there for each other rather than the insane opposite we are taught by capitalist theory: to only care about our own success, or the success of our immediate family.

Time banks are a beautiful beginning of a conversation and perhaps a radical notion in a US or UK framework of either elitist volunteerism or self-centered capitalism. The roots of this notion are often credited to Ed Cahn. But indigenous peoples all over the world who have not slipped into the bottomless pit of hegemony and capitalism understand and actively practice something like time banking, not stopping at one hour of care for an elder, or washing cars for a school fundraiser, but doing whatever a family or community member needs to survive. Many of us know that our "success" is linked to everyone's success, that hoarding wealth is actually sick and pathological and does nothing for anyone, not even the money hoarder.

One of the many things we are visioning right now at POOR Magazine/ Homefulness is the creation of a Bank of Community Reparations. It will be a redistribution station for hoarded and stolen wealth, so that blud-stained dollaz will go to anyone who needs them. This would be a way to help all decolonized suns and daughters of wealth hoarders or wealth hoarders themselves redistribute their blud-stained dollaz directly to po folks in struggle and/or to poor-people-led, indigenous-people-led movements.

It will have nothing to do with wite-supremacist bankkking institutions or philanthro-pimped grants. Just peoples getting over humps, po folks getting food, shelter, hellthcare. Decisions for support will be made in our inter-generational council meetings for as long as we continue to have to suffer under this lie of a wite-supremacist dollar ekkkonomy.

Concurrent to this POOR Magazine will be launching Po folk interdependence bartering systems to move us completely off the lie of capitalism. These would be based on trading economies of our ancestors and not defined by capitalist values of worthiness.

Sister Ping aka SnakeHead: The Poor Peoples Banker

I was exhausted from a very long day of souljahing for the peoples, working in my underground hustle of caring for elders, running a class for POOR Magazine Poor Peoples Journalism, cleaning to get ready for the next day of life Homefulness, when I sat down to some mindless corporate TV.

Yes, with all this revolutionary liberation work in my head and heart, this poverty skola hunkered down for a good dose of stupid kkkorporate media: a cable TV show called *Gangsters* which was full of wite supremacist, hollywood-babylonian POV's of who is "bad" and who is good and who is a gangster. In other words, never in this show did they include the likes of corporate gangsters and banksters like Dick Cheney, Donald Trump, or Jack Abramoff. But still I found myself glued to the TV show watching my own peoples, poverty skolaz, getting the only media we ever get: criminalizing stereotypes about all the "crimes" we have supposedly done, created through the gaze of the ruling broadcast class.

Tonite's show was different though. Instead of the usual Italian "mafia" figures they trotted out, this episode focused on a woman of color, an immigrant, a poverty skola, a mother, a micro-business person, an underground economic skola who came from one of the poorest parts of China, the village of Shengmei in the northern Fujian province of China. She had been part of Mao Zedong's Cultural Revolution and a member of the Red Guard, which made her a target of criminalizing, racist amerikkklan media, and the US Department of Justice, who painted her as an evil criminal and a murderer no matter how much good she did for thousands of poor immigrants.

"Without Sister Ping, I could never have dreamed of coming here," said Zhang Yuanjing, 69, a Chinatown resident, whose passage to New York from Fujian province in 1989 was financed and arranged by an (in)famous poverty skola known as Snakehead, aka Sister Ping.

She was made famous because of a tragic accident known as the Golden Venture, which was a boat transporting refugees from China that capsized killing 10 passengers. She was condemned as the party responsible for the entire accident due to her negligence, even though in the end it came out that she was only responsible for two of the passengers in the whole voyage.

Her involvement with "smuggling" people from China to the US (which is called "smuggling" when poor people do it, and "asylum," "moving," "migration," or "a journey" when rich people do it) happened because that's the "help" that poor people needed, and she, as a fellow poverty skola, helped folks in the way they needed help. It was not some NGO-inspired poverty pimpology.

But one of the most important things that Sister Ping did, which was rarely considered or talked about was create a truly underground, off-grid bank. This poor peoples' bank is a perfect example for all of us poverty skolaz to emulate, and the template for the future Bank of Reparations.

As most people know who have investigated US bankkking, all of the money-handling, from banks to credit unions to the corner sto check-cashing places to the remittance deliverers for out of country wire transfers, including the so -called conscious or progressive ones, are somehow involved in the same sleazy pot of money. From the use of Chek Systems to check credit scores to the same Federal Insurer, to shared board members, they are all in the same parasite-filled bed and no one is the wiser.

Which is why in this case Sister Ping was such a banking revolutionary. Her community of immigrant poverty skolaz who worked in underground economic industries needed to send, store, and cash money and checks all the time — after all, the main reason they were here was to send remittances home to support their families. Her micro-bank, run out of a dollar-store basement in Chinatown, did all the services a person needed for a mere 2% — not the 5, 8, 10 or 20% charged by most corner stores or remittance places or even banks.

Sister Ping's many services were always urgently needed, and they threatened industries and institutions that relied on the dependency, criminalization, and ignorance of the poor, which is why I think the DOJ worked so hard to destroy her reputation like they did all powerful outlaws. Her work was rooted in her poverty scholarship as early on she had developed a class consciousness witnessed in a statement she made to her biographer Patrick Radden Keefe-Ping:

> . . . *as a girl of 12 years old she survived the capsizing of a rowboat in which she had been traveling to another village to cut wood for kindling. She recalled of the incident that all of the people in the boat who had been rowing and had been holding an oar when the boat turned over managed to survive, while "the two people who were lazy and sat back while others worked ended up dead."*

I was always personally heartbroken by lie of "microfinance," so it was so beautiful to be sent this message by Sister Ping — my new sheroe — aka The Snakehead. What we learn from Sister Ping is everything, even money-handling, can be done by ourselves, for ourselves.

A Rich man asked the African Jewish Arab revolutionary known as Jesus Christ how he could enter the kingdom of heaven. Jesus said, give all of your possessions to the poor and follow me. The rich man walked away disappointed.

One of the best traditions (of Indigenous peoples) is that of transforming tradition in a traditional way. They know that they cannot exist without a vision of the future, but they do not pretend to control that future: instead of the arrogant expectations of modern man, based on the assumption that the future is programmable, they maintain hopes, well aware that these may or not be fulfilled: they nourish them to keep them alive but without holding onto them. They have not been able to avoid the experience of modernity, but they have not become rooted in it.

— GUSTAVO ESTEVO, MEXICAN ACTIVIST,
"DEPROFESSIONALIZED INTELLECTUAL" AND
FOUNDER OF THE UNIVERSIDAD DE LA TIERRA
IN THE MEXICAN CITY OF OAXACA

11

Liberation, Decolonization, and Building Poor People-Led Self-DetermiNATIONS

The Poverty Industrial Complex and the Great Lie of Civilization

Poverty is not real. Poverty is a construction of the Great Lie of Civilization. It is supported, funded, researched, pondered, and cognitated on as an act of control to keep us poor people in our placated, confused, and/or ashamed mindset and keep the great lie going and the huge poverty industry built around it continuing so that ultimately we are all collectively paralyzed by its enormity, its impossibility, and its seeming unsolveability.

The poverty industry keeps us pathologized, segregated, criminalized, researchable, strange, separate, and most of all deeply enmeshed in shame and self-hate. It keeps us weak, and not asking the real questions or making the real demands. People make money on us, write about us, study us, make art about us, but never stop to own their own role in keeping us poor.

Pre-colonized, pre-stolen indigenous peoples all over the world had an abundance of natural resources and land and water and skills and time and love and accountability systems and humble, respectful relationships with Mama Earth. And we still do. We poor folks can decolonize our own bodies, minds, and hearts out of the lie.

From the colonizer clock time we are all set to so our bodies can run the machines and do the jobs that keep the rich people rich to the one or two colonizer's languages we are forced to speak to the endless amount of asphalt and concrete beneath our feet.

From Po'Lice to schools, from housing to land use, from labor to business to economy to media to art—our minds, souls, and actions need to be collectively decolonized. For us so-called "civilized peoples" living in this post-colonized owning-land-class-controlled reality, this seems hard if not impossible. For us poor and barely holding on folks, survival is most important, our minds toiling on basic day-to-day depression and struggle, much less liberation. But we must activate this change work if any of us hope to survive, much less our children and grandchildren and most of all our great mama earth as she is increasingly destroyed and less and less of her exists. We must end this brutal and self-centered cult of capitalistic independence and learn back our true spirits of inter-dependence.

The first thing to do is to realize that every message you have received, every lesson you were taught, has been tainted by the derivative messages of wealth-hoarding, corporate-loving, genocidal, land-stealing wite-supremacists. This means that the so-called comfort and "wealth" we are taught to desire is a well-crafted lie, a rationale for all they took, all they continue to take, to perpetrate and to destroy. It is so entrenched in our souls and lives that decolonization seems odd, impossible, or just plain confusing.

The next lie we as indigenous, people of color, and Po' folks must get clear on is the definitions that the politricksters and po'Lice and rich peoples give us. They say that our barrios, hoods, unincorporated neighborhoods, towns, projects, ghettos, and calles are bad, ugly, dirty, and in need of cleaning up as well as that our poor, brown, black, red, and yellow bodies are dangerous, pathological, crazy, criminal, and stupid. They are the exact opposite of that: they are ours, and must be reclaimed by us, redefined by us, taken back by us, and loved by us. To do this we must decolonize our minds and spirits off of their lying, soul-sucking, criminalizing narratives, the ones they use to endlessly re-devilop us out of our own neighborhoods, incarcerate us out of our own homes, and take us out of our own families. This is not easy and yet it is very easy. It means looking at the neighborhood recyclers and houseless elders as the wise peoples they are. It means looking at the pre-corporatized, pre-sanitized, and pre-gentriFUKed storefronts and corner sto's, funky homes and unused parks and loving them, listening to them, using them, honoring them, and most important of all, not changing them, but rather humbly cleaning, caring, planting, art-making. It means re-defining our young peoples as the leaders, the creative and intellectual peoples they already are.

A poster from the Jackson Educational Cadre out of the PROUDjects in Los Angeles.

If we do this we can actually prevent the continued theft of our neighborhoods, families, cultures, and selves.

Afro-centric skolaz have been taking back their spirits and cultural deep structures through journeys back to the Motherland. Aztec and Mayan peoples and the peoples of island nations have been re-indigenous-izing themselves. Native Turtle Islanders are taking back their sacred sites and ancestral remains.

Us Ghetto skolaz are rarely seen as the innovators we are. Pre-corporate Hip Hop was innovation. So are the 12:00 o'clock boyz and other urban dirt-bike groups who resist the po'lice and redefine their own community power. There is also the Jackson Educational Cadre out of the PROUDjects in Los Angeles, the Grace Lee Boggs Institute in Detroit, and Tyree Guyton's neighborhood-as-art movement.

Tyree Guyton, an actual sun of his Detroit neighborhood, didn't "clean" up his neighborhood or redevil-op it or raze it or leave it. Instead, with his own hands and the hands of the elders and young people still there, they fixed some broken pieces and left some broken pieces just like they were. They wrote a story on every corner and created a piece of art from every old, to'-up and discarded piece of the neighborhood. Most importantly, this neighborhood sun really didn't change his neighborhood at all: he transformed it.

Art house, also called The Heidleberg Project, by Tyree Guyton, an artist and poverty scholar in Detroit. We took this photo on the poverty scholars' journey to the Detroit Social Forum. His work and life and beautiful mission, which we love, are featured in "Homefulness" Vol.1 of POOR Magazine (Print Edition).

Change won't come from a savior — a pimp or an institution.

Change will only come from our own poor-people-led revolution

We don't need to go anywhere or to get anything. We don't need money or institutional, elitist schooling. We don't need missionaries or case managers. We only need to look inside ourselves and to each other to find our love, our pre-colonized spirit, our skillz, our knowledge, our beauty, and our self-determined liberation.

The Undocubus, painted colorfully with butterflies and the words "Sin Papeles Sin Miedo" (No Papers No Fear). The bus carries "undocumented" migrante revolutionaries who crossed the stolen indigenous country to speak the truth about immigration, deportation and the lies of these racist borders. POOR Magazine's own Gloria Esteva was part of this powerful journey for justice.

Resisting Contact and Colonization

But what if they never came? What if the colonizers were NEVER let in? What if their lie of "discovery" was never believed, funded, or sanctioned?

What if we as indigenous peoples acted like the Sentinelese, who throw poison spears at intruders when they approach their sacred lands, refusing to enter into any part of the lie of "discovery" which leads so nicely into the truth of destruction.

If we, the original peoples, the displaced, the lost and the stolen, were in control, we wouldn't be running things on neoliberal scarcity models of hate, disrespect, loss, and incarceration—that is, the way they do things. This is why our world has become the sorrow-filled place we are at now. We would run our communities and societies in the ways we have always done, with values of respect and self-determination, love, and inter-dependence.

So now, post-colonization, we have scarcity models of care, scarcity models of knowledge, land, food and resource distribution, poverty industries that hand out poisoned food while profiting off the food delivery, prison industries that criminalize and incarcerate poor people while making money off their criminalization and incarceration, Wite Medical industries that provide appropriated and stolen indigenous medicine and then make money off their scarcity distribution.

Now to be clear for folks who have unwittingly entered into institutions of formal learning, or folks who are working in the poverty industry with a beautiful full heart: I am not critiquing your love or time or work. You knew no better. It's what the neoliberal, wite-supremacist system sets up for people to do who want to "help" or be good peoples. We are given no alternative. And our parents are also brainwashed into thinking that, if we go to college and learn the colonizers' ways and industries and institutions, if we pass their colonizer tests and get their colonizer jobs in their colonizer corporations, we have in fact, made it. We have all been carefully trained into believing this, and any and everything outside of these colonizer models becomes, as wite-science calls it, "dissonance."

Un-Contacted = Un-kkkolonized: The Story of the Sentinelese

Theory after akkkademik theory has been written, researched, lectured, and funded about the impact of colonization. This, like most of the industries of profit and theft, means that the people who stole everything from you now set up a ponzie scheme to "study" the impact of what stealing from you, forcing you into slavery, and not allowing you to practice your spiritual traditions or speak your languages felt like.

This is all part of the colonial hustle we have spoken about in this book. Which is why the ultimate heroes of this book are the First Peoples who have fiercely resisted the colonial hustle for centuries and continue to to this day, teaching us all how possible it really is to live without their lies.

Perhaps no people on Earth remain more genuinely isolated than the Sentinelese. They are thought to be directly descended from the first human populations to emerge from Africa, and have probably lived in the Andaman Islands for up to 60,000 years. The fact that their language is so different even from other Andaman islanders suggests that they have had little contact with other people for thousands of years.

The Sentinelese live on an island in the Indian Ocean and continue to resist all "contact," including so-called "friendly" contact, with nearby governments and outsiders. This does not mean, however, that they live just as they did 60,000 years ago. Though they are commonly described as belonging to the 'Stone Age,' they do in fact make tools and weapons from metal, which they recover from ships wrecked on the island's reefs.

The colonizer myth is that "pre-contact" means ignorance. But this is just another aspect of the colonial hustle that needs to stay in place so 21st century missionaries, NGO-colonizers can sell the ideas that they will help us all, the idea that anyone who hasn't received the "blessing" of the colonizer education is inherently lacking in knowledge.

The real story is that the Sentinelese are geniuses with advanced skills in science, medicine, architecture, math, and design, who managed to survive the 2004 tsunami unscathed when no one else in the region did. They are also one of the healthiest peoples on Mama Earth. They have created powerful weapons that shoot directly into meddling colonizer helicopters. And these are just the knowledges we can see from the outside.

In 1879, a couple of their village elders and 5 children were taken by force and brought to the nearby town of Port Blair. The colonial officer in charge of the kidnapping wrote that the entire group, "sickened rapidly, and the old man and his wife died, so the four children were sent back to their home with quantities of presents." This was obviously the only experience the Sentinelese needed with the colonizers. So the Sentinelese simply did not LET any more of these colonizer murderers in, so they never had to face the fate of millions of us indigenous peoples barely alive on the fringes and the crumbs of the colonizers.

There are over 100 known "uncontacted" peoples across Mama Earth, and who knows how many unknown nations refusing the lie of colonization. But it is not our right as post-colonized peoples to romanticize any of these fierce resistors. They know everything about us, and that is exactly why they choose to refuse any contact with us. The lesson for us poor and indigenous peoples lost in the colonial hustle struggle in our life-long quest to decolonize is to stop believing and stop depending on the man who wants us dead for help. We have the resources and the choice of building our own un-pimped and decolonized solutions, our own ancestral visions of post-colonial communities, love, and thrival.

To Parents

> *"We are here to awaken from the illusion of our separateness."*
> —THICH NHAT HANH

The first touch of capitalist destruction begins when we condition our children into the cult of independence and away from their natural spirits of Inter-dependence. This isn't only the institutions' fault; it's now become part of us, as though we believed in everything that has killed us and our peoples for centuries.

As single parents we are left alone to fend for ourselves, slogging through our loneliness, PTSD, trauma, and poverty. We are constantly juggling the lie of capitalist productivity, nuclear-family happiness and the deep, painful experience of alone-ness and isolation in this alone-ness-honoring culture. I speak to my fellow mamaz 'cause that is me: the first thing you must do is to stop, by any means necessary, believing in the lies of independence. As quick as possible please begin to de-isolate yourselves with Mamahouses (like the project I started for low-income single mamaz). Un-hinge yourselves from the dis-respecting wite culture and re-connect with your elders. If you are coming from positions of struggle, your elders might be angry and not always user-friendly. But that doesn't mean you follow the throw-away culture demanded by capitalism. Rather, you are there because of them. They are you and you are them. And they are your community.

> *"We went to the garden of Ms. Sherena Thomas. There, all the plants were big. There was broccoli, tomatoes, strawberries, squash, and plums that were pruning. "The more we water them, the juicier they will be," says 13 year old Dante Curley in his mother's backyard gardens. Afterwards we came back to our own garden and said, "I'm glad to be back." Me and my mom and dad live in a lot of mold in a very small place, this was after me and my mama were homeless, and we are really poor, my mom had a hard life but managed to have me...."* —TIBURCIO, 9 YEARS OLD, YOUTH SKOLA

It is also important for us conscious mamaz and daddyz to stop believing the capitalist lie of productivity and so-called success. The most successful thing to you can do it to raise your young people. The most productive thing you can do is to hold them close all the time. The hardest, most unappreciated and valuable work you can do is to raise your babies up right. To teach them, be with them, work with them. Learn with them. If you aren't striving for the capitalist notion of more and more blud-stained dollaz you might already have enough to accomplish this. Use the welfare/food stamp crumbs to pay your rent. Start small, home-based hustles to bring in small bits of more cash. Care for elders or do other jobs that you can take your children along to and have them work with you. Start little or big gardens depending on your space and grow your own food and have them work alongside you. Make sure from the beginning you tell them how important they are to your collective survival. Mama used to say, the reason we have all these young people killing young peoples is they have nothing to do, way too much free time to do nothing, no one has told them they are important, that their work and contribution are dire and necessary. THIS IS NOT EASY. But nothing is easy. Death, suicidal tendencies, substance use, and random violence—all outgrowths of capitalist separatist realities—are not easy.

This is what I have done with my sun, and as a poor woman, this is EXTREMELY hard. I'm struggling all the time to keep us alive. But I have a good dedicated partner, my sun. It's what my mama did with me. And I was not easy to deal with. I had to drop out of the man's skoo to help my mama and me survive. Not so I could survive alone, so we could thrive together. It's what many indigenous, Afrikan, and conscious peoples already do.

The whole culture of man's age-grade skools, warehouses for elders, overpriced child care and elder care, and false notions of success are what we are taught to perpetuate the culture of away-ness. To keep making more and more capitalist jobs to keep taking us away from our children, from our elders, from our souls. Children, just like our elders, are smart and capable of working with you together, to keep you alive. You don't need that new pair of shoes. You can start fixing, repairing, and maybe making shoes as a side business. You don't need that big ridiculous house with all those rooms; all us Indigenous and Po' folks been sharing rooms and space for years. You don't need that new car or boat or some other ridiculous product. Matter of fact, what you need is to realize how little we really need to be ok.

The Legacy of Colonization, Movements of Resistance

For centuries colonization has been shuttled in through organized religion. We have been forced out of our indigenous spirits, aboriginal languages, traditions, lands, clothing, dances, music, and natural resources through the myth of "Sin" and the lies of "savage" and "civilization." These crimes were called discovery and were perpetrated with guns and reading from the Bible. Under this sacrilegious reading of Jesus' revolution, actual sins were committed, including the destruction and selling of our indigenous bodies for work and profit, and, perhaps worst of all, the raping of our children. The legacy of rape under the guise of religion continues through today – and arguably this rape is not just of our bodies but our whole spirit. But the key piece is the relationship of sexual abuse, rape, and colonization to poverty. Our communities' use of substances, violence, and rage are often casually associated with poor communities of color without looking at the systemic ways they are rooted in child sexual abuse and colonization.

Pre-colonial communities had ways of protecting, raising, loving, and leading our young peoples in to adult-hood. With the rape of our traditions these ways were lost with all of the other things that were lost in colonization.

Then the colonizers began a 520-year legacy of rape of our bodies and we began to rely on their poison to exist, just to wipe out the depth of pain of this trauma that is left in our heads. That becomes our alcohol, that becomes our drug abuse, that builds our obesity, and our violence.

Before there was ever any alcohol abuse or domestic violence among the indigenous Inuit peoples of Alaska, there were priests sent there. Two remote Alaska villages are still reeling from a Catholic volunteer's sojourn three decades ago, in 1968, when he allegedly molested nearly every Eskimo boy in the parishes. The accusers, now men, are scarred. Many of them turned to alcohol and drugs. Some attempted or committed suicide. One expressed his rage by assaulting fellow villagers, including his own children. The international attention to the Catholic Church molestation scandal in the mid-2000s prompted some of the survivors to finally speak up. By 2005, Alaska natives from 13 villages have now filed claims against the church for abuse. "The flood of allegations has led to speculation that the Eskimo settlements were a 'dumping ground' for abusive priests and lay workers," wrote William Lobdell in the *LA Times* in 2005.

It is urgent that we as harmed peoples begin healing. We don't need the colonizers' religion, languages, and institutions to do this. We need to bring back our own. To take care of our children, to love each other and Mama Earth as we always did. This is the ultimate healing, not just for us but for future generations of us.

For indigenous peoples forcibly removed from our lands of origin, we can take inspiration from nations like the Wiyot people who 150 years after a brutal slaughter by settler colonizers returned home after buying back their sacred land. Or the Paiute Nation who are teaching themselves their own ancestral knowledge with their food system one garden at a time. Or inter-ethnic people-led movements like The Black Mesa Water Coalition who work within and from the Navajo and Dine Nations to break our collective dependency on the fossil-fuel industry.

For stolen peoples in diaspora from the Mother land of Africa we can work to rebuild communities based on African deep structure such as Ujaama Villages in Oakland, Detroit Summer, Homefulness, and Marcus Garvey Liberation Garden in Texas.

For poor peoples in public housing projects we can work to organize and take back your equity (see the 10-point plan later in this chapter). Houseless folks can work to take back stolen public spaces like Right-2survive and Project Dignity in Oregon. This is very risky and usually is squashed, as with the attempt of several people to reside in California's Albany Bulb, but the concept of public land for the public must be continually surfaced in this great lie of wite-supremacist domination that would rather put us in jail than honor our self-determination.

Poor peoples in lands of origin across Mama Earth can work collectively to organize like the Shack-Dwellers Union in South Africa, the Zapatistas in Chiapas, and people in Hawaiian, Maori, and other Pacific Island nations who are taking back lands and control of what is already theirs.

All of these movements must move off the lie of the great Charity Nation. Work with your communities to create your own manifestos for change, to center your work in your herstorical and present trauma, your resistance in your healing and reclaiming of your own cultures, land, and resources. Begin to teach your donor base and your communities how to re-frame donations as redistribution of stolen or hoarded wealth and/or reparations.

Because many of us poverty skolaz are not reading this, are currently in deep struggle and are deeply and seriously damaged, our pain and memories beyond what we can move through, many of us are actively hurting each other and/or ourselves. We are in so many stages of trauma and so many positions of need. Maybe we seek the man's poison to self-medicate ourselves out of thinking. Many of us must live in different ways to go on living at all.

So the other act of decolonization is to move off the cult of rehabilitation. Everyone doesn't need to be fixed or changed but rather respected, listened to, and fought in solidarity with. If people need to sleep outside, in parks, under bridges, or on empty land, let's fight along with them for their right to live outside, to use public spaces that are for the public! If people need financial support, government crumbs like public housing, SSI, welfare, or food stamps to survive because they can no longer work in the corporate-crafted jobs centered on colonizer clock time, let's do whatever we can to get them this support. If you have the access to make this happen, then activate: leverage your privilege like Osha Neuman did for me, like we do for people as revolutionary case managers and underground railroad social workers at POOR Magazine. And if people just need a dollar for a street newspaper or for themselves, and you have one, give it to them.

Korporate civilization is a dangerous and hurtful myth. Due to all of the destruction we have all collectively caused, our great mama earth through corporate mining for an endless stream of energy and products and natural resources, we must urgently begin sharing Everything. From our over-sized backyards to our empty rooms. From our water systems to our over-farmed, vegan, raw, and organic food. We must get smaller, humbler, leaner, and more careful, in every step we softly walk on mama earth. We must open our communities, towns, neighborhoods, and homes to our families, extended families, and uprooted island nations and other communities in the global south who are suffering from the impact of corporate domination and empire theft.

We must look to our hunter-gatherer, bartering, sharing and collectivizing, thriving ancestors who only grew, built, and killed as much as they needed, ate and lived under.

Our movements are here. Decolonization is happening. Here are some examples.

EXCERPT | **Response to the Doctrine of Discovery**
NATIVE YOUTH SEXUAL HEALTH NETWORK, AT THE UNITED NATIONS /
INDIGENOUS PEOPLES MEDIA PROJECT

The Native Youth Sexual Health Network affirms the importance of taking a culturally safe, rights-based approach of sexual and reproductive health as an integral part of ending violence against Indigenous women and girls. We reclaim healthy sexuality as a central part of ending sexual violence, as well as all other forms of violence. As taught by Mohawk midwife Katsi Cook, "Woman Is The First Environment."

We wish to remind those present that the ongoing, widespread shaming and blaming of sexuality today is directly linked to the underlying philosophy and legal framework of the Doctrine of Discovery, which in turn creates the structural conditions that lead to violence against Indigenous women and girls. Instead, we call for the reclamation of Indigenous understandings of gender and sexuality fluidity. Such understandings are rooted in self-determination and cultural practices; including coming of age ceremonies and rites of passage, which affirm the traditional knowledge of Indigenous peoples over our own bodies and related control of our own reproductive health.

In accordance with Article 7 of the UN Declaration on the Rights of Indigenous Peoples and as recommended by the Report of the Expert Group Meeting on combating Violence against Indigenous Women and Girls, we call for greater investigation of the links between increasing rates of suicide and inadequate supports given to young women facing situations of violence. Supporting self-determination in experiences of violence means empowering women to make their own decisions. We also recommend particular focus be given to the high rates of suicide among young Two-Spirit and transgendered women as forms of violence that are currently being overlooked. The self-determined gender expression of Indigenous Peoples, for example, the freedom to identify as Two-Spirit, is something to be celebrated—not criminalized.

Incarceration of Indigenous women in the prison system is a particular threat to the foundation of reproductive health and justice for Indigenous women and girls. The incarceration of our bodies is the incarceration of our reproductive health, such as the unacceptable practice of shackling women who are incarcerated during pregnancy, labor, and birth. Such control sets the stage for the further violations of the rights of Indigenous women....

We also call for recognition of the need for a broader definition of the expansion of what is considered 'violence' pertaining to Indigenous peoples.

For example, a central driving force of the HIV epidemic for Indigenous women includes new forms of colonial manifestations of violence. As identified in paragraph 25 of the Expert Group Meeting, there is a need to address disproportionately higher rates of HIV/AIDS and other sexually transmitted infections in women and girls. In fact, there is minimal culturally specific HIV/AIDS support and resources for Indigenous women and youth that supports a harm reduction approach. There is still a need to reduce stigma and fear; while the global epidemic of HIV/AIDS rates are decreasing, these rates are increasing for Indigenous peoples, specifically Indigenous women....

[We also have] particular concerns around environmental violence and how it relates to increased sexual violence and the overall assault to our Mother Earth through resource extractive industries.

One particular aspect of environmental violence that affects the overall health and well-being of Indigenous women and future generations is inadequate access and culturally unsafe reproductive health services and resources for Indigenous women. Due to the lack of appropriate options, conditions are created for increased experiences of violence within the industrialized medical system. This can include a lack of access to traditional and ceremonial services such as traditional midwifery.

. . . We call upon UN agencies, states and Indigenous peoples to advance the sexual and reproductive health, rights, and justice of Indigenous peoples — this is not an issue that is the sole responsibility of Indigenous women and girls. If woman is indeed the first environment, then this is everyone's responsibility.

About this photo, photographer Georgianne Nienaber writes in "Haitian Women: Rea Dol vs. the Republic of NGOs" in the Huffington Post: "Looking over the broken courtyard wall of the SO-PUDEP school one sees the familiar sign of Save the Children dominating an undamaged rock wall with a blue metal gate in the center. It is less than 30 yards away. At least 10 cars and trucks sit idly in the extensive courtyard that is locked to the surrounding community. While we are watching, a man who looks like he stepped out of the pages of GQ, bluetooth in ear and briefcase in hand, strolls up to the gate, shiny watch visible on his left wrist, and calls to the guard to let him in."

Women's Movement-Building and Creating Community in Haiti

SOKARI EKINE
DECEMBER 14, 2010

Thousands of words have been written about Haiti in the past 12 months covering everything from the NGOization of the country, the politics of humanitarian aid, endless questions and discussion on what happened to the millions of dollars donated by individuals and countries, the horrendous conditions in the camps, where some 1.2 million internally displaced people are forced to live and, particularly for women and children, hundreds of whom have been raped, trafficked to the Dominican Republic and forced into prostitution to survive. In addition to the earthquake, Haitians have had to live through another devastating hurricane and now cholera, which as of today has affected 30,000 people.

And to add to the frustration and anger, an election, which by all independent accounts was fraudulent and farcical. There have been continuous protests since the elections on Nov. 28 and if one is to judge from the many radio phone-ins, people are angry and concerned that the much hated Preval will announce his preferred candidate, Jude Celestine, as the new leader. This despite the fact that so far the majority votes appear to be for Michel "Sweet Micky" Martelly and Madame Mirlande Manigat – but all of this can change in a moment.

Nonetheless, for women activists and the masses of poor women who struggle on so many fronts, feeding, and educating their children, eking out a living wherever possible, protecting themselves from cholera and searching for clean water, the elections are a distraction. From the women I spoke with, there was no single candidate they felt would in reality make a difference to their lives.

One of the stories least reported has been the one about Haitians organizing for themselves, particularly stories presented within a framework of feminist organizing and movement building. This is one woman's story of how she, her family, and the people in the various communities in which she works came together collectively to care for each other's needs and how that struggle has become the foundation of a new movement of the poor for change in education and the material lives of women and men – a struggle for dignity.

Their personal and collective humanitarian response was completely off the radar of NGOs, international institutions, and the Haitian government. Even Save the Children, whose office is located right next to her school, did nothing to help SOPUDEP (Society of Providence United for the Economic Development of Petion-Ville). However, ultimately this was an aside for Rea Dol, who heads the school. What was important was that those who needed help of whatever kind received it and, beyond that, the struggle for dignity and self-determination for the poor people of Haiti was able to continue.

A mere five minutes passed between the death of one of the school teachers and the life given to Rea and her teenage daughter — one of three children.

On Jan. 12, when the earthquake hit Haiti – the first in 200 years – a mere five minutes passed between the death of one of SOPUDEP's school teachers and a new life for Rea and her teenage daughter – one of her three children.

"I was in the school when it happened and I cannot describe the horror around me," Rea said. "The school was empty and did not fall, but the neighborhood collapsed. Five people were crushed to death just meters from me when one of the outer walls of the school grounds collapsed. My first responsibility was to my family, so I had to get home, but the streets were chaotic. People were panicking and screaming. I had to run home 10 kilometers through those streets to find my family. The phones weren't working. It was horrible."

Once it was established Rea's family were all safe – a house just five minutes' walk from Rea's own home collapsed – she set about caring for the many in her community and wherever she was needed. Everyone was in shock, but there was no time to think about what had happened, as people were injured. Many people – students, families knowing about her community work – flocked to Rea's home and at one point there were some 60 people in her home. People feared to sleep indoors so they removed all the mattresses, blankets, pillows, whatever they could find, and spread them outside.

It was January and freezing cold during the night but anything was preferable to being inside. Rea said it took her months before she stopped waking up with nightmares of being crushed. Even now one wakes up and gives thanks for making it through the night. I too find myself staring at the ceiling every night and wondering which part would collapse first and how I would get out.

The first day after the quake, Rea went to the shop where she usually bought the school supplies and asked if they would give her credit as she needed to buy food. They told her to take whatever she needed and not to worry. As much food as possible was collected and everyone in the house, the children, students, guests, neighbors, set about making food packs. They worked all night making the packs, which they then distributed to anyone on the streets during the day.

As donations from friends of SOPUDEP, the school Rea Dol heads, and organizations such as the Haiti Emergency Relief Fund (HERF), the Haiti Action Committee and Sawatzky Family Foundation (SFF) began to arrive, Rea was able to buy more food and medical supplies and continue the distribution. Food, which was being given only to women, and mostly bags of rice were available for those prepared to queue for up to four hours.

Rea said she did not have the time to queue for 25 pounds of rice and preferred to go and buy it with whatever money she had on hand. Besides, fights often broke out with people tired and hungry and everyone trying to push their way forward. The military would then beat the women and children. In total, food and water were distributed to 31 centers by Rea's team.

In addition to financial donations, SOPUDEP received a lot of medical supplies, which were taken to the various mobile clinics which had been set up in camps and other locations. Though the number of recipients decreased over time, the food collection and distribution lasted for three months. At a point in time Rea realized this dependency created out of a crisis could not continue. They would forever be in a state of oppression and remain in the clutches of NGOs, beggars in their own land.

No one ever knew when money would arrive, which meant any kind of systematic planning was impossible. It was like waiting for the tooth fairy to arrive. And besides, what humanitarian aid was being distributed was not reaching Rea's community. It was all too ad hoc to be sustainable.

The next money she received was a sum of $3,000 and she began to think of another way. Instead of buying food, she would deposit the money in the bank and start a small micro-credit-saving program. It took courage and was a huge risk because people were hungry but determined to create some degree of sustainability and stability. In a moment she made up her mind.

A meeting was called and the idea put to the 21 women with whom she had been working over the past months and, though there were doubts, they trusted Rea. The micro-credit scheme, Fanm SOPUDEP an Aksyon (SOPUDEP Women in Action), begun with $3,000 and 21 women.

I was surprised when I heard Rea had started a micro-credit scheme, as there were so many negative reports on schemes which rather than enhance and empower women, ended up impoverishing them even more. So I was interested to find out more about the SOPUDEP scheme, whether it was working and why it worked. I will write about this later after meeting with the various women's groups.

Rea's philosophy is that each individual has to take responsibility for herself and the notion of something for free is neither healthy nor sustainable. Both the school and the women's project are framed within the idea of personal and collective responsibility.

Education in Haiti must be available for all. Everyone is encouraged to attend and no one is turned away from SOPUDEP because they cannot pay.

However, everyone is asked to try to contribute something when they can, even if it is 5 gouds (40 gouds equals about $1), or to help in the school somehow. The school operates two sessions – the main one in the morning and an afternoon session for those who have never attended schools, both older children and adults.

The elections are a distraction. Leaders have the power to bring change, but no one believes any leader will do anything for the poor. Everyone I asked about Aristide wanted him back because they believed he was one leader who could change their lives for the better. Right now the only way is for communities to reach out to each other and create alliances, which is what SOPUDEP is beginning to do.

Rea's vision is one I share. We cannot fix Haiti, but we can fix our community and help others fix theirs. Eventually, as all these communities build alliances amongst themselves, they will become strong and then maybe begin to fix Haiti.

Family Council

One of the crucial things to decolonize are the systems of control that keep us in place, keep us incarcerated, and maintain the great wite lie of safety.

At POOR Magazine we have instituted a No Po'Lice Calls and No Mandated Reporter promise. To deal with the many very serious problems us post-colonized peoples do to hurt ourselves and each other, we have developed a Family Council. This is a multi-racial, inter-tribal, inter-generational council to deal with our most serious problems modeled after the ways of our ancestors.

Our "No Po'Lice calls Ever" mandate begins with an agreement between each POOR family member, student, and/or leader to follow our "Rules of Respect," and whenever we face a breech of the rules of respect, including violence, aggressive behavior, substance use/abuse, etc., we call for a Family Council. The Family Council meetings are peopled by family elders who have already been guiding us with prayer and scholarship, as well as family members who have been working with us for at least a year and graduated from at least one semester of PeopleSkool.

The Family Council we are hoping to build at Homefulness would be an extension of that original idea and would also help us to make decisions about the ongoing, self-determined movement and progression of Homefulness.

We also envision this Family Council as the first step to bring eldership, leadership, and council back to our indigenous/POC communities like Deep East Oakland to help us move off of our dependency on Capitalist systems of oppression like Po'Lice, CPS, Jails, Poverty pimps, philanthro-pimps and kkkourts to a self-determined, indigenous-people-led system of account-ability. We hope to eventually collaborate with our other revolutionary comrades in the neighborhood like BLRP and launch a Po'Lice-Free Zone in this block.

Herstory of No Po'Lice Engagement at POOR

For the 16 years we have been practicing the Family Council at POOR — it has NEVER been easy. We are colonized/decolonizing/Stolen peoples on stolen land with our hearts, souls, and minds in many places of struggle. Our souls, our lands, our ancestors, and our bodies are constantly under attack. And we often perpetrate pain on each other.

We are a multi-generational family with our children's safety in our hearts first and foremost, so this challenge is important. Recently, our dedi-cation to this way of being was tested, and we have had to re-assess and begin thinking through the steps that people have to do before they ever come in to our circle in the interest of protecting our children.

We are trying our best to move humbly and walk softly with respect to bring positivity and healing to our families and communities. We might make mistakes, we might not move quickly or perfectly right, but we are

A pile of blankets sitting on a park bench, in a beautiful example of Revolutionary Social Work. The Washington, D.C. Department of Public Works found a pile of wet, soiled blankets on the ground of a park at the foot of this bench and picked them up in trash bags, ostensibly to discard them. Instead, later that same day, one of the city workers laundered and carefully folded them and brought them back, placing them back on the bench where they were found.

doing our best and always trying to bring it in a good way. We hope this council will become a template for change for all of us seeking to return to our ancestral memories of pre-colonial accountability.

We are inspired by the examples of people like the Maori in New Zealand who, faced with high rates of incarceration of their young peoples, started to resist the imposed western system of justice. Instead, they started using an accountability process that involved the whole community, and that focused on repair and healing instead of punishment.

NOT Calling the Kkkops — EVER

"I'm going to hurt you." One of our long-time POOR Magazine family members stood in the doorway of our humble office. It was a Wednesday. POOR Magazine has no programming on Wednesdays, so there were only four of us present: our brother, who was under the influence of possibly many substances twisting his already trauma-filled brain into places he could not control; one of our disabled, houseless elders; my own houseless and under-severe-stress self; and another family member who struggled with multiple mental disabilities. The scenario that ensued had nothing to do with our 18-year long-agreed to, co-created rules of respect, which guides us through our mandate to never call the po'Lice. He did not stop; substances like that don't disappear or subside quickly from your bloodstream or psyche. Instead, they tend to get worse by the second. Violent words were exchanged, followed by a move by the three of us who were sober to circle around him and guide him slowly back out of the front door.

Not calling the po'lice is hard, so hard that most people aren't ready to do it. Relying on the white supremacist notion of "security" which was set up hundreds of years ago to protect the stolen indigenous territory and the settler colonizers that stole it, modeled after the "slavecatchers," is what comes easy. Not calling them, EVER, is the deep, hard, frightening, and ultimately most revolutionary work.

From Betty Jones in Chicago to Cau Bich Tran in San Jose – it's not just the evil white supremacists or the benevolent gentrifiers that call the kkkops, it's often us calling these paid killers on each other. In the case of many of the most tragic stories of death at the hands of the police, it is us, the poorest, working-class, trauma-filled, and most vulnerable among us that make a 911 call on each other because we often say to each other "what else can I do?"

So what else can we do? Our ancient ways of protecting and loving each other, circling around each others' children and mothers, listening and being guided by our elders and ancestors, and walking more slowly with intention, prayer, and purpose have long been left in the road of hamster-wheel driven success, survival, displacement, and the ache of what we have been told we must have but can't seem to attain.

So the first answer is to do everything this white-supremacist society has told you not to do. This requires a deep mental and spiritual process of decolonization, prayer, and intention, which does not happen overnight. This requires you to very likely "give up" the things that you have been taught will provide you with safety.

U.S. Independence Kills

Then unpack and discard what I call the cult of independence, "bootstraps," and individualism. Resist the capitalist push to own things as a measure of happiness like cars, mama earth, clothes, and jewelry.

The third answer is to move back home. If your home is safe, if your families and your communities of origin are alive, help them and yourself resist the idea that you should be as far away as you can from the people who made you, who love you, and who depend on you. The isolation caused by capitalism-inspired individualism can lead to mental health crises and personally unsafe lives. Your families need you and your young self and your strength and love and connectedness to help them prevent mental health crises. American-style independence kills. Your families are your elders, they can support you in moments with partners who get abusive. (If your families are unsafe, then the intention of creating and being a part of a chosen family is extremely important for you to survive and thrive.)

The fourth answer is not so much to give up personal safety, which for women (including trans women) and children is not a possibility, but to understand deeply and spiritually that the "safety-bringers" aren't safe. This will prompt you to speak, collaborate, and coalesce with your neighbors, community, friends, and/or families of origin or chosen families to begin accountability circles, i.e., spaces where we hold each other accountable for our actions. This is a much harder step and requires a long journey with your families and/or communities.

This idea is nothing new. It is actually very old and it's what we did before we had slave-catchers to "take care" of everything that scared us. This is how we walk and live as a poor and indigenous people-led organization at POOR Magazine/Prensa POBRE, following and learning from the Black Panthers and MOVE Africa before us who refused to engage with the state agencies in place to kill and incarcerate us.

We launched POOR Magazine's No Po'Lice/CPS calls mandate when we poverty and disability skolaz began fighting for justice with La Mesha Irizarry over 15 years ago on the case of her sun who was killed by San Francisco

Po'Lice after a 911 call for help. POOR Magazine family member and race and disability scholar Leroy Moore, Mesha, myself, and many more folks worked for years on mental health training for po'Lice, but lo and behold as we see now with the tragic case of Mario Woods, mental health training doesn't really stop the paid murderers who are trained to kill us from killing us. So many layers of settler laws and post-settler protections continue to support them in their murderous ways. And then the kkkourts support them once they kill, as in the horrible cases of gentrification-inspired murders of Alex Nieto and Amilcar Perez Lopez. Once you are in their jails, prisons, and behind their razor wires you face more chances at their hands of murder such as the murder of Sandra Bland and so many in San Francisco County jail.

This is why we, as a group of displaced, po'Lice harassed, colonized, incarcerated and profiled, disabled poor peoples of many nations, colors, and cultures knew we could NEVER engage with the people who see us as the people to test, arrest, incarcerate, and evict. We realized that we needed to create a way to hold each other with love but also discipline. My strong Afro-Boriken mama launched this discipline: she took no mess from no one and held us together as poor people because she could smell a threat, an issue, a struggle a mile away, coming from a long line of curanderas and ancestor talkers.

After my mama passed we launched a series of circles. Our elephant circle is where we poor mamas, daddys, uncles, and aunties decide core issues at POOR. It is also where we tweak and re-tweak our rules of respect which we all created and are all accountable to as it demands respect of and from all of us, no matter what nation, generation, or spiritual tradition we walk from. We also launched our Family elders council and Inter-generational councils which holds our family to our core values determined in our Manifesto for Change, Declaration of Interdependence, and Peoples Agreement which we crafted at Homefulness to hold us to our values and principles at this sacred landless peoples movement we have created in Deep East Huichin Ohlone land with the permission of Ohlone Peoples. There are many nuances to these circles. Age alone does not mean someone is an elder.

We are not just challenged by land-stealers and the family members we love, but by our fellow community, poverty, and disability skolaz who have threatened us with all manners of abuse which would lead most people and organizations to the man's kkkorts and killers. We are constantly tweaking and re-tweaking what it means to be people in trauma facing our own trauma and other people in trauma, who don't solve things by dialing those three frightening numbers or ever stepping into those kkkourts to "resolve" our conflicts.

There are other organizations like Critical Resistance who are working on this same issue with powerful anti-state movement building and a

373

group of folks in Oakland working on a first responders "app," which is a powerful idea.

As revolutionary mamaz and survivors of po-Lice, case manglers, non-profiteers, prisons, and government crumbs we also work as revolutionary social workers with each other to help, protect, care for, heal, support, and peer educate our fellow mamaz, babies, and elders, not ever calling CPS or APS (Child Protective Services and Adult Protective Services), no matter how much the system would encourage us to. This is VERY complicated and takes both poverty skolaship and strength to realize but we believe this is necessary to truly realize the often spoken but rarely understood concept of the "village."

We are still working on a way to support our fellow sisters and brothers from domestic violence trauma and crisis, and this is in progress.

Not Kkkop calling isn't easy, it seems so much "easier" to dial 911. But then again, it's not "easy" to die either.

The People Reclaim the Land

There are multiple land reclamation efforts going on right now across Mama Earth by indigenous leaders. Here are some that have recently triumphed.

In 2012, Pataxó Native peoples in Brazil gave all of us Indians in struggle for land some hope. The Pataxó, a native nation of Bahia state with a population of about 2,700 peoples, endured a decades-long violent conflict with ranchers occupying their territory. Brazil's constitution and international law guaranteed them what they wanted—to simply live undisturbed on their ancestral land—but it took a long judicial battle to make that right a reality. Finally, in May 2012, Brazil's Supreme Court ruled that the ranchers must leave the area. The Pataxó celebrated the decision with song and dance. One of them said, "Today our damaged heart is crying with happiness."

In 2013, the Wiyot tribe performed a healing renewal ceremony at their ancestral home of Indian Island in California's Humboldt Bay. The tribe lived on the island until 1860, when a massacre by white settlers nearly extinguished them. They were displaced to other locations and faced generations of post-traumatic struggle. But in the late 1990s, part of the land came up for sale, and the community came together to raise the funds to purchase it in 2000. In 2006, they convinced the nearby city of Eureka to return additional Indian Island land to the Wiyot. But by that time, it was a toxic-waste dump. The Wiyot spent the next years cleaning it up, partly with funding from the Environmental Protection Agency and the National Park Service. Today, the tribe has 645 members, for whom the 2013 renewal ceremony on their ancestral land was a crucial sign of survival and endur-

A flyer for the Revolutionary Legal Advocacy Project, launched by Marlon Crump and Tiny in 2007 at POOR Magazine and re-launched by Leo Stegman and Tiny in 2014, helps poor peoples caught up in the US in-Justice system who do not have the money for a lawyer. Our motto is "jailhouse lawyers, outside of jail, without a degree." This model can and should be replicated by lawyers or other para-legals or peoples who have learned enough about the law through their own experience of struggle to become advocates to help other folks help themselves.

ance. One member said the ceremonial dances will help "to heal the world of all the wars we're having now, all the atrocities — to make everything fall into place."

Sometimes there are government solutions that actually have revolutionary possibilities. In Mississippi, Chokwe Lumumba, former vice-president of the Republic of New Afrika, ran a grassroots campaign rooted in Afro-centric values to become mayor of Jackson from 2013 until his death in 2014.

Gayle McLaughlin is the Green Party mayor of Richmond, California. She has consistently stood up for poor peoples of color and challenged the stranglehold of the corporation that thinks it owns that town: Chevron, which has a refinery there. And then there is Socialist Seattle City Council member Kshama Sawant; Cynthia McKinney, who served six terms in the U.S. House of Representatives, always serving the people; and author, poet, peace-bringer, and father Luis Rodriguez, who is running for governor of California on the vision of the people.

U.S. states such as Rhode Island and Illinois have actually passed a Homeless Bill of Rights, and in Utah they have implemented a human-based policy where you get a house if you are homeless. What a beautiful and simple idea.

Indigenous Resistance: Models of Revolution

The MOVE Organization is a family of African, White, Boricua, Chinese, strong, serious, deeply committed revolutionaries who moved off of the grid of utilities, government, and private systems in West Philadelphia in the 1970s. MOVE members lived community and as an active alternative to dominant U.S. colonized ways of living until police literally bombed them in 1985.

Since 2003, a group of Indigenous food producers and their communities have collaborated to create the Great Lakes Indigenous Farming Conference, for the purpose of nurturing, restoring and creating Indigenous farming and food economies as well as food sovereignty in the Great Lakes region.

In Mexico, since 1994 the Zapatistas have been in a revolutionary struggle for "work, land, housing, food, health care, education, independence, freedom, democracy, justice, and peace." They have built their own schools, health clinics, and fair trade initiatives, creating political autonomy and growing their self-determined economic prosperity.

Giving Public Housing Back to Us (Members of) the Public

As tenants we have resided in public housing units for years, maybe generations; we have suffered in sometimes dangerous living conditions that go unrepaired for generations, which also might have put us and our families at risk of cancer, asthma, lung disease, high blood pressure, and more.

We have paid rent depending on your income, paid utilities and made small repairs, and/or lived in a space in disrepair.

Rather than continued removal and devil-opment, gentriFUKation and meager "buy-outs" which amount to a few months' rent in market-rate housing, our families' time, love, work, herstory, and struggle in a community, in a neighborhood, in a home should be seen as the building of equity.

Since the 1960s with Nixon thru to the 80s when they started destroying housing and giving people pieces of paper (Section 8, which was never meant to be guaranteed housing) there has been a slow move to end public housing as we know it.

In the late 90s it morphed into the lie of HOPE VI, which effectively began the inclusion of privatization under the guise of "improvement."

And now we have RAD (Rental Assistance Demonstration), which will sell off the public housing buildings to private devil-opers.

The Following proposal is dependent on two main issues:

The point of this precedent-setting proposal is before the government pimps, poltricksters, and devil-opers sell them out from under us, AGAIN. We need to take them back. Our lives, Our struggles and our herstories are our Equity. And these buildings in our neighborhoods are our last remaining acre and our 1 remaining mule.

Building a poor-people-led, self-determined movement: this is a humble draft document, which should/could change depending on the cultures, spirit, resources, ideas, language, and beliefs of each group that uses this. It is a media-based, very grassroots-based plan that is rooted in our values as poor and indigenous, landless peoples at POOR Magazine who have done organizing over our 16 years as poor people organizers.

A black and white photo of a billboard that says, "It takes the hood to save the hood." It's a billboard for the organization United Playaz, launched by poverty and indigenous skola Rudy Corpuz, which is a group of beautiful ghetto skolaz who walk self-determined liberation. This is one of its mottos.

Organizing Housin' 101

1. Core group of leaders. To activate a movement and help move it along, you need at least a couple of folks as a core group, it can be as small as two people and they can be in the same family, but who are willing to commit time to a project of self-determined, off-plantation power-building.

2. Plan a first time informational meeting on a night or weekend afternoon that works for your core group.

3. "Lets Take Back Our Land," "Got Equity?" Create a simple flyer stating one or two lines about your goal. (If you can also get the flyer translated with the help of a local librarian, friend or teacher into Russian, Chinese, and Spanish, please do and then ask that person to also be at the meeting to do on-site translation, but if not, then this can happen later in the movement.)

4. OUT REACH — OUTREACH aka Talk wit folks! Take your flyer door to door to talk to fellow residents in your building and as many buildings as you have the energy to hit up.

5. Speak with your son or daughter's teacher about what you are doing and see if they are willing to help you in different ways — the first one is to distribute it to other parents who live in your public housing,

6. Multi-generational/indigenous organizing. We were colonized away from our own children by this cult of independence system. Poor-people-led movements who are not poverty pimped and philanthro-pimped need our young folks' strength and health and energy to be part of our movement. We can't do this movement separate from our families and elders and children. Sit down with your son or daughter or granddaughter, grandson, niece, nephew, or any family member under 21 along with any elders or other family members in the home and explain to them what you are doing and why, and tell them that to do this we are going to need to work together.

    The tasks they will be expected to lead/help you with vary depending on their age and ability, anywhere from painting signs to walking in marches or showing up with their family at protests to leading a social media and on-line promotion.

    Tell them they are important leaders too and without their help this movement will not be possible.

    For youth 12-25 their first task will need to be to put the flyer out on social media, Facebook as an event, Instagram as a picture, a short video on YouTube and/or a tweet- multiple times per week leading up to the event and any other ideas for promotion they might have.

7. Cotact the local revolutionary media: radio, public TV, or newspaper, and deliver your flyer to them and ask them to publish the notice and/or put it out on the air.

8. To prepare for your first meeting, print out the Without Housing Report by Western Regional Advocacy Report (WRAP) and the PNN article *Stealing Our Last Acre and Our One Remaining Mule*.

9. If you are in the Bay Area, invite POOR Magazine into your first meeting.

10. REPAIRS/IMPROVEMENTS OF SEVERELY SUBSTANDARD HOUSING WITHOUT THE PIMPS. One of the ways that the poverty pimps and devil-opers continue to rationalize their endless and monstrous lie about our "needed devil-opment" is that they say that is the only way we can get "the resources needed to fix the broken housing. "How else are we going to fix the broken elevator?"

    So one of the most important parts of our self-determination take-back of our resources is to believe that we can, like our ancestors before us, fix our own shit, and of course, because we have been colonized for so many years away from the hammer, and the shovel, our hands and our arms, our strength and our own skillz to repair and renew, we may have to be re-taught and assisted. SO this where we borrow from principles from the Cuban revolution of the 1960s, where healthy, strong young people with different forms of race, class, formal education privilege came into the campos (farms) and helped to farm the land, fix the roofs, repair the plumbing, and on and on.

This would include creating an Equity-Building Internship.

11. Class Action Suit for Equity/Legal/Lawyers help: To activate this entire project we need to build a legal precedent which will act as the touchstone for the entire movement across the US. POOR Magazine is seeking this for the 1st test case in the Bay Area, and we already have the beginning of a "class." This is necessary so we can trump the Devil-opers' move to steal our equity and continue to make profit on our backs.

Once we have established legal precedence in one case, this will be pretty easy to do nationwide.

After the case is won, equity/collective ownership agreements will have to be created as well as an organizational body to steward the land and the buildings. This is a long-term agreement that can emulate housing trusts or POOR Magazine's idea that no-one owns the land. It would be a decision that would be up to the residents to decide collectively.

12. At your first or second meeting agree to a structure for your group. For example:

- Implement rules of respect in terms of listening, aggressive behavior, use of violence, respect of body and children and the group facilitator

- Roles: Based on the skills of people in your group and the family members of people in your group decide who will handle meeting dates, outreach, admin, building/repair supervision, lawyer contact, etc. (this limited list will expand if you end up with a full-throttle project)

- Engage one or more of the older children/youth/adults in the group to lead the social media campaign. Assign one of these leaders to document every meeting and post it on YouTube or Vimeo and beyond as well as create a Facebook, Twitter, and Instagram page where it gets shared and uploaded.

- Create a timeline and goals. Decide as a group what you want to accomplish by what date. This is estimated but will help move you along.

- Create your next meeting date and dispatch everyone with specific outreach tasks: who will you reach out to, who you will try to bring to the next meeting, etc.

- Make a list of what repairs need to get done in each unit in each building of all of the members of your group.

Youth skolaz at Deecolonize Academy / Homefulness Summer Revolutionary Youth Media Camp.

- Have one of the members of your group create a quick survey of repairs needed so even if folks don't attend meetings their issues can be included in the long-term project.

- Contact local lawyers and law schools to find a lawyer willing to take on your reparations/equity lawsuit.

- "Help a Poor People-led Movement" "Do Meaningful Work in Your Community to Create Change." Create a simple flyer and an ad seeking interns. Post it on Craigslist and distribute it to local high schools, your children's high school teachers, community colleges, universities, Americorp, volunteer bureau, to engage their student body as volunteers/interns for your repair team.

- In the next meeting, create a new time-line of repairs and work and start doing the repairs. Make sure you document with video, pictures, and in writing ALL repairs you and/or the volunteers do, including how much it cost to do them, and how long it took.

The Manifesto for Change

This Manifesto for Change was written, agreed and prayed upon in multiple ceremonies and POOR Magazine elephant circles and includes the agreement that we as poverty, houseless, criminalized and displaced poverty skolaz form POOR Magazine agree to take the small piece of Mama Earth known as Homefulness off the extractive industry of real estate devil-opment and speculation. We will do this both legally and spiritually so this small part of Mama Earth will never be sold, flipped, devil-oped or destroyed. And will always be here to house, educate, liberate and heal youth, adults and elders in struggle.

The Manifesto for Change is a truly "green" model for housing, art, micro-business, spirituality, interdependence, self-accountability, care-giving, and community that incorporates the teaching of our elders, ancestors, and spiritual leaders in harmony with Mother Earth. It can be launched in any city in the U.S. with a Revolutionary Giving Ally.

The Manifesto for Change was created in a 16-year process by a multi-lingual, multi-racial, multi-generational group of landless, indigenous elders, children, families, and folks engaged in a life-long struggle with poverty, racism, incarceration, welfare systems, white supremacy, mis-education, landlessness, ableism, Non-Profit-Profiteering, and violence.

To build power, to take your movement into action and activation, you need to write your story and her-story. From the earliest beginnings of POOR Magazine, when it was just my mama, me, Joe Bolden, Ken Moshesh, and A. Faye Hicks, and a few other poverty and indigenous skolaz, we launched poor-people-led solutions through writing each of our stories of houselessness, incarceration, eviction, and racism.

It was from these earliest meetings that we began to create our goals and ideas, which ultimately became the earliest version of our Manifesto for Change. The first thing we were very clear on is that we as poor and oppressed peoples needed to manifest the solutions we held in our hearts and souls.

Fast forward to 2002 when we lost all of our foundation and government funding and then were evicted from our office and lost everything. We added to the Manifesto. In 2009 we went into a deep retreat to draft the final version of the Manifesto for Change and the Declaration of Interdependence. We see these as sacred documents, our cave paintings if you will. They are not meant to be digitally shared, face-cracked or tweeted, but rather to live on their own as sacred texts that guide us into the light.

To create these final, sacred texts we created a herstorical framework of our shared oppression as poor and indigenous, landless peoples in this stolen indigenous land. The following is that document. This is a document rooted in who we are.

Overall Premise/Who We Are

As Africans in diaspora whose ancestors' bodies were used as a form of profit for rich European-descent people who were already engaged in the theft of indigenous lands across the globe, we have a long-standing debt that has to date still not been paid.

As descendants of Indigenous peoples of Turtle Island (The Americas) and Island Nations, our lands were stolen through the lie of discovery, and your reparations and resources have never been returned.

As descendants of migrant/immigrant peoples of the Central and South Americas, Philippines, Bosnia, Africa, Syria, Iraq, South Asia, Palestine, Asia, or other lands our own resources in our own lands were stolen, mined, raped, devil-oped and/or destroyed, our peoples cultures were ruined by the lie of devil-opment and colonization and you were sold the lie of Amerikkklan comfort so we could become a cheap labor force in this stolen land, and we too deserve our reparations from this empire and other multinational conglomerates that have stolen and raped our Mother Earth.

Through a combination of Jim Crow/wite-supremacist laws, redlining, abuse, racism, profiling, re-devil-opment, gentrification, displacement, predatory lending discrimination, low-wage or underemployment/mis-educaton in schools, workforce, and housing market you were systematically shut out of access to home ownership, credit and residence in other neighborhoods, ghetto-ized into public housing devil-opments, sub-standard housing, unstable or unsecure housing, and/or houselessness.

Heretofore, in this liberation document we will refer to each other as landless peoples and we all deserve to be granted our resources and self-determination BACK.

Declaration of Interdpendence

The declaration of Inter-Dependence is a sacred text—not living on any digital streets. Created, written, dreamed, prayed, visioned and signed by poverty skolaz as a different way to walk, act, vision and manifest liberation for Mama Earth, ancestors, elders, children and all of us for generations to come. It was conceived through talk-story, love, pain and tears. It is the roots, spine and pact of the self-determined landless peoples land liberation movement us poor and houseless people call Homefulness. It is love, it is grief, it is loss. And so like any of the most sacred texts it is not meant to be excerpted, tweeted, instascammed or face-cracked. But rather just read, prayed, witnessed, lived, and dreamed. It lives on the wall behnid the altar for our ancestors in the liberation School us Po' mamaz and daddys built called Deecolonize Academy at the sacred part of Mama Earth us landless peoples call Homefulness.

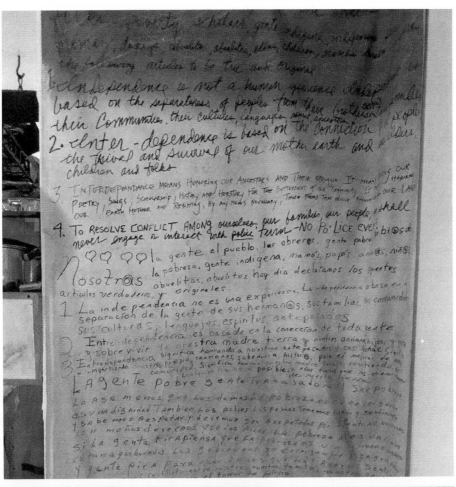

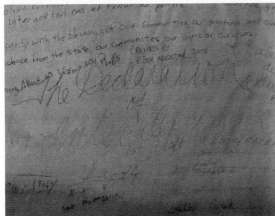

A long banner is covered in black handwriting against a yellow background: the POOR Magazine Declaration of Interdpendence.

THE PEOPLE'S GLOSSARY

TINY, MAMA DEE, AND 500 YEARS OF INDIGENOUS AND
POVERTY SKOLAZ IN STRUGGLE ACROSS PACHAMAMA

AnthroWrongOlogy: The theft, storage, display, removal, and displacement of indigenous ancestors for study, research, profit, entertainment or development without descendants inclusion, permission, leadership, direction, prayer protocol, and/or ceremony.

Anti-Social Work & Case Manglers: The angry at poor people, working for the man, believing in the "sys" hegemony-filled, people who often work in the Non-profit industrial complex as front-line staff or advocates, or in Social Security, welfare/Hellfare offices, shelters or drop-in centers and ascribe to the scarcity model of the "deserving vs. undeserving poor" notion that poor people are lazy, crazy, etc. —which is often translated/taught in training sessions, academia, and/or existent in a person who lacks poverty scholarship.

Blood-Stained Dollars: US Dollars or Euros (and all other empire monetary systems) gained off the exploitation, wars, removal and/or genocide of people.

Brother-Ship/Sister-Ship/Mama-Ship: The opposite of a "fellow-ship"— a designation, support for loving and care-giving for your family, community and village.

Comm-UNITY: A village of poor/indigenous and/or in-struggle folks operating interdependently.

Eldership: The active (as opposed to passive and in name only), non-capitalist practice of caring for, honoring, and showing deference to elders in your family and in society.

Fetishization: When folks in struggle are used, pimped, exploited, traded, capitalized on, spoken about, studied, researched, and theorized about because of our race, culture, gender, ability, and other aspects of our selves.

Folks in Struggle: We don't say "homeless people," as if "homeless" were our only identity just because we don't have access to a roof. "Homeless" is a grant-pimp guideline word/determination. We don't say "low-income"— because whose idea of low-income are we talking about within a capitalist society? And we don't even always say "in poverty," because that isn't the only way to describe the struggle of people who struggle with other oppressions like racism, ableism, gender oppression, border fascism, and more. So, as often as we can, we say "folks in struggle" instead, adding that folks are in struggle with poverty, ableism, houselessness, landlessness, and more.

GentriFUKation: Gentrification and displacement of poor peoples of color and indigenous peoples from their rooted communities, jobs, and land.

Hellthcare: The treatment received (or not received) by poor, unhoused, disabled, migrant/immigrant, indigenous and/or very low-income people.

Houseless/Landless/Unhoused: As poverty skolaz we resist the term "homeless." Like "youth"and "seniors," "homeless" is another way that nonprofit industrial complex organizations, philanthro-pimped grants, legislators, politicians, corporate governments, media, and akkkademics "separate" us from the tables of decision-making and power, so they can talk about us instead of talking with us. By claiming the term "landless," we align ourselves with landless peoples movements in Brazil, Kenya, South Africa, and Mexico. Our relationship to a roof does not define us as people - we are multi-layered, multi-generational, multi-cultural, multi-racial, multi-lingual we just don't have a roof - also many folks live outside in a neighborhood, community or town, that doesn't mean that we are any less residents than someone with access to a roof on this stolen, indigenous land.

Interdependence: The intentional connectedness of people, families, and community. Interdependence is the reliance on each other with an open acceptance that, as people, we need each other. It is a rejection of the bootstraps, capitalist ideal of separateness, isolation, and western, Euro-centric ideas of individuation and independence.

Landlessness: The state of people in poverty globally and locally who don't own the property where they stand, sleep, work, convene, and live.

Lie-gislators /Politricksters: The people known as legislators and politicians who use bloodstained and stolen dollars and power to abuse, criminalize and profit off of the backs of poor peoples and people of color. These folks should not be confused with conscious peoples who try to be in the race, classed and colonized space of politricks navigating the settler-colonizer laws for collective justice.

Linguistic Domination: Linguistic domination privileges the colonizers' languages and speech, which results in the exclusion, shame, silencing, segregation, disempowerment, and destruction of voices speaking their indigenous languages and tongues. Proficiency in the colonizers' tongues affords access, space, resources, and power to a small group of people with race, class, and/or educational privilege. Linguistic domination rewards people who can master not only the master's language but also the dominant way of thinking, forming ideas, and living. These institutionalized forms of silencing dictate which words and information are considered legitimate, who and what is funded to create media, and who is considered valid as an expert, a media maker, a communicator. The colonizers' languages have been afforded this legitimacy and "privilege" via access to stolen resources and imperialistic stability—e.g. libraries, endowments, institutions of academia, media corporations, and the like.

Media Missionary: Media missionaries do "exposés" on marginalized peoples and communities with the idea that by telling their stories they are "helping" them. Instead, by writing about them with no accountability to them or inclusion of their voices, a media missionary is silencing the peoples and communities they purport to help. Like all missionary work, media-missionary work is misguided; the "help" can be a form of genocide, telling a story that's not the media maker's to tell, leading to/enabling the destruction of a community. Media-missionary work is not specific to corporate media, but it started there.

Media Resistance: Media resistance occurs when people who are usually intentionally silenced by media channels create media for the purposes of change, resistance, and revolution.

Micro-Businesses: Micro-businesses have existed for thousands of years in places all over the globe. The practice was codified with this term by the World Bank, which co-opted the concept from the Bank of Grameen in India. Micro-businesses are very small businesses that are usually started with little or no capital, sometimes as little as five cents. They usually include the sale of goods or services in a public space or out of the family home. Micro art-businesses include the sale of some kind of art, like painting, t-shirts, or jewelry that the businessperson makes by hand.

Nonprofit Industrial Complex (NPIC): The NPIC is in the tradition of capitalist paper-theft projects like real estate, multinational corporations, hedge funds, and fake insurance policies based on "capital" earned on long-ago-stolen land. Nonprofit organizations are created as corporations, beginning with 501(c)3 papers that use language very similar to that of for-profit corporations. They are all created with capitalist, individualistic structures like boards, secretaries, and presidents who follow strict guidelines and codes of conduct meant to "keep everything in line." The organizations function in the same way corporations do—sometimes even worse, depending on what they do. Big poverty-pimped organizations like Goodwill an Salvation Army compete for government contracts to "provide" services to poverty, disability, youth, and migrant skolaz and then create large shelters that operate like jails, with piss tests and shut-down rules. Smaller organizations insist that we respect "boundaries" and create punitive requirements/actions if we don't follow the "rules"—which often means that we are punished for acting in the ways of our ancestors, with indigenous love and respect. Nonprofits within the NPIC create projects based on the "guidelines" of big philanthro-pimps, which leads to separatist, individualistic ways of allegedly providing services. In reality, though, they keep people sick, in the system, and out of control. See Chapter 10 for deeper explanation and examples.

Philanthro-Pimping: The industry of philanthropy includes a heavy pimping aspect with covert and overt ways of commodifying and exploiting people and their pain, struggle, and oppression. This process of commodification and exploitation often includes language about the "sexiness" of a project, initiative, or problem. See Chapter 10.

Po'Lice: Paid agents of the prison industrial complex (PIC) who protect property and provide customers for the PIC.

PO'groms: Describes the deliberate inflicting of suffering, harassment imprisonment, through homeless sweeps and displacement, experienced by the poor through neo-liberal policies that deny the right to exist for those who have been historically marginalized and presently living on the precipice of survival. (Note: This Re-Mixed word by POOR Magazine family-Bilal Mafundi Ali).

Poor Peoples Equity: Within a capitalist context, equity means the falsely bolstered property values of stolen land acquired through paper theft. Within a context of landless/houseless people, though, it can mean many things: fair access to a roof that we aren't at risk of being kicked out of due to non-payment or lack of access to blood-stained amerikkkan dollaz (which landless/houseless people never have, due to many racist and classist setups and paper thefts and boundaries and dominations that happen every day to poor people/indigenous peoples); the ability to walk into a store and not have a security guard follow you; access to mental-health services; the knowledge that someone is caring for you or will care for you if you are an elder; relationships, from academic networks to knowing there are people you can count on to provide a job or a place to stay, or anything else. Equity is covert, intangible, and at the root of race and class separation.

Poor Peoples Sweat Equity: Access to land, housing, and food security, not based on how many blood-stained amerikkkan dollaz we have or the over-used and oftentimes ableist, racist and classist concept of "sweat equity" based on how much physical labor humans can do. Poor peoples sweat equity" is based on "whatever we can do" as poor elders, youth, disabled and differently abled poor people, i.e., child care, media, chairing of meetings, cleaning, organizing, i.e., the time, love, sweat, labor, struggle, and spirit we put into caring for our mama, each other and Pachamama.

Poverty Pimps: Organizations, usually within the nonprofit industrial complex that earn money on the backs, problems, and struggles of people and communities in poverty.

Real Estate Snakes & Devil-opers: Real-estate snakkkes and developers are the people or organizations who imagine and oversee real-estate speculation, from conceptualizing new real-estate developments to buying land to financing and managing construction to selling and leasing. Most developers are devil-opers, key agents of community destruction and displacement. When a developer uses "redevelopment" of an area to destroy and displace a thriving community of color, they get statues and plazas named after them. For example, Justin Herman, head of San Francisco's Redevelopment Agency in the 1960s, oversaw the displacement of tens of thousands of people of color from a neighborhood that was once described as the nation's most diverse. That neighborhood now has a plaza named after him. See also gentriFUKation.

Underground Economic Strategies: Unrecognized ways of work, labor, and business such as selling products on the streets without a license or selling services not seen as "legal" or sanctioned by society. Underground economic strategists include recyclers, panhandlers, and unlicensed street vendors or artists.

United Snakkkes of Amerikkka /Amerikkklan: The Stolen indigenous territory of Turtle Island named after one of the colonizers who aided and abetted in the stealing of this land and building/creating the mythology of discovery.

We-Search: At POOR we launched the concept of We-Search because we don't believe in the akkkademic domination of research. Academic research uses philanthro-pimped and funded initiatives to study, deconstruct, and survey poor youth, adults, and elders in struggle. This research creates papers, thesis projects, and studies that talk about how poor we are, how much racism there is, and how bad our neighborhoods and schools are. We-Search is poor-people-led research and proactive media that deconstructs the lies told about our criminalized and mythologized communities.

Wite: Not to be confused with the "color" or the melanin in someone's skin, this relates to the system of "White supremacy" that rules of institutions of learning, housing, hellthcare and service provision in the US.

Wite-Science: Post-colonial science, medicine, biology, eugenics, rooted in/based on the study, experimentation, torture, exploitation and/or death of indigenous, Black, Brown, Disabled peoples stolen, disrespected, poisoned, incarcerated bodies.

FELT-NOTES

1. If you are sleeping in a late-model RV, parked in a rented RV stall, you won't be cited and arrested for sleeping in your car; but if you are a person of color or a white person who "looks" homeless sleeping in an old car in a suburban or gentrified urban neighborhood, people will call the Po'Lice on you and have you arrested and/or cited under "habitation laws." Similarly, if you are a person who looks "homeless" and you are sitting on the sidewalk or sleeping in the park, you will be cited and arrested under any number of vagrancy laws; but if you look like a "yuppie" and are sleeping in the park while watching a concert or at a picnic or just during your lunch break, you will not be cited, arrested, or even spoken to by Po'Lice. If you are a day laborer of color, you will be cited and/or harassed for seeking work while being poor and of color and not owning or renting the land you are standing on, whereas if you are a politician soliciting campaign contributions on street corners or door-to-door you won't be arrested or cited. And if you are a young person of color standing in a group, convening, or socializing on a street corner, you will be profiled for possibly being in a gang, or accused of causing trouble; but if you are a white jock celebrating a game win with public displays of loud noise while inebriated, you won't be cited, arrested, harassed, or treated as part of a "gang."

2. As poor people who do sex work and other forms of unrecognized and criminalized labor, we use the concept of "pimping" in an intentional alliance with sex workers. Sex work and underground economic strategies like panhandling are all ways that we as poor people handle an economy of exploitation. Many sex workers have powerfully taken back, or do not use, the word *pimp*, and many become independent contractors and businesspeople who are self-sustaining. But we use this language intentionally to make the connection between the exploitation of criminalized, marginalized, and silenced workers and the exploitation of poor people for the profit of people in power. People are used for profit within the nonprofit industrial complex—philanthro-pimping—just as people are used for profit in sex work.

3. Shane Bauer, Sarah Shourd, and Josh Fattal—hikers arrested in 2009 for allegedly crossing the border into Iran while hiking in Iraq—are conscious folk who were similarly highlighted and exceptionalized in the media.

4. Another poetry journalist/poverty scholar in residence at POOR Magazine is Byron Gafford, author of *Thru the Eyes of the Child*, who has written over 5,000 poems, five POOR Press books, and several poetry-journalism exposés on racism, child abuse, Child Protective Services (CPS), the violence of poverty, and the teachings of the Creator. Ruyata Akio McGlothlin, another poetry journalist, has launched several stories on racism, violence, and loss and has published five POOR Press publications focusing on addiction and recovery.

5. Dr. Wade Nobles and Pamela George.

6. Wade Nobles.

7. Western Regional Advocacy Project.

8. See Harriet Washington, *Medical Apartheid: The Dark History of Medical Experimentation on Black Americans from Colonial Times to the Present.*

9. http://postcolonialstudies.emory.edu/language/

10. Information shared and excerpted with love and respect from Jessica Davies, Amber Howard and Narco News.com- and our Zapatista brothers and sisters in resistance to education colonizers. For more information, see http://upsidedownworld.org/main/mexico-archives-79/3305-the-assault-on-autonomous-education-in-southeast-mexico and http://www.narconews.com/Issue44/article2487.html.

11. For more about some of these revolutionary peoples' schools across Pachamama, see http://schoolingtheworld.org/resources/get-involved/.

12. Mentee vs. Intern: We reject the exploitative notion of intern, as this is a lie based on corporate non-profit mythology. In fact these students, only "educated" in the man's skool, have nothing to "teach" us, but everything to learn from our institute of peoples' learning. And therefore, one of the first acts of learning and unlearning they need to practice is that this institute of poor people skolaz costs money too! This is always one of the hardest lessons to learn, as it challenges their institution-taught beliefs that learning is only "worth" a resource exchange if it is from the institution, accredited by the institution, and therefore is somehow vaguely therefore considered legitimate. It also challenges the idea that the "homeless people," the poor people, the disabled and un-formally educated have nothing to teach formally educated people.

13. But in the same breath, there are beautiful acts of resistance like the Pacific Island Skolaz who are using the plantation walls to grow new spaces and new dreams of their own Pacific Island liberation. See "We Are the Oceans," by POOR skolaz at http://poormagazine.org/node/4365.

14. The genocides disguised in language like "medical research" are massive. My poor Indian experimented-on mama exposed many of them throughout her life. Two in particular were the syphilis experiments on Tuskegee airmen and the horrible case of Henrietta Lacks, whose cancerous tumor cells were used for years, making countless millions of dollars on the research of her body without her permission while she was buried in a "pauper's grave."

15. Volume II of *POOR Magazine,* entitled HELLThcare, included a story from me entitled "A Healthy Mouth is a Wealthy Mouth" about my multiple struggles to attain dental care as a poor and houseless young adult with no health insurance.

16. Boundaries are the notion of "safe separation" from client to provider. They are put in place to ensure that the "care" one is given is not from a place of love or connection, friendship or kinship, but rather, a place of distance and "professionalism." Boundaries

are an adaptation to corporate-simulated environments of control. All advocacy needs to be meted out within highly constrained rules, regulations, and protocols dictating a precise amount of care and concern, not to be confused with your actual emotions or empathy or feelings. This is billed as the way to protect a worker's energy and resources but is tightly controlled by wite-science notions of therapy and distance. Like my mama, Tony Robles was also fired from lay counselor/advocate position for taking his clients off-site and having coffee with them because it endangered the "boundaries" put in place by the so-called helping institution. At POOR Magazine we say boundaries are bullshit. That isn't to say that we romanticize our relationship with folks in struggle, it is just to say that we are them and they are us, so how can we have boundaries from ourselves? To be led by each other, we are actually in collaboration with our fellow folks in struggle to achieve liberation from these multitude of pimps that rule our lives. We are clear that care-giving and advocating are not "safe" or separate or professional, any more than it is for the peoples seeking the care, advocacy, or help. In that way, we are changing the dynamics of industrial treatment to "however we are able to help folks."

17. http://www.theguardian.com/global-development-professionals-network/2013/jun/06/rummaging-through-rubbish

18. Chief Raoni and other Amazon Indians launched a many-year fight against the Belo Monte Dam. The dam required the devil-opment and destruction of the Brazilian rainforests and was sold to the people of Brazil as a "job-creator."

19. Like Mesha Irizarry, Yolanda Banks, or Sala Haquiyah.

20. Like the Turf Feinz, Caspar Banjo, Isreal "reefa" Hernandez, John Williams, Mike Dream Francisco, Herbie, Mel Veracruz, Melanie Cervantes, Jesus Barraza, Daniel Cruz Mayan, Tyree Guyton, and Dignidad Rebelde.

21. Like Gerry Randal from West Virginia who led a one man fight against mountain-top removal by Massey Coal.

22. Like Jose Lopez from East Oakland.

23. Domestic Workers Alliance, Mujeres Unidas y Activas, La Colectiva de Mujer, Angeles Sin Fronteras, and the Day Labor Program from La Raza Centro Legal in the Bay Area.

24. Organizations like El/La, by and for revolutionary Trans-Latinas, or individual warriors like CeCe McDonald, Alexandra Rodriguez de Ruiz, Jazzie Collins, and Bo Brown.

25. 67 Suenos, 50-50 cru, Native Youth Sexual Health Network.

26. Maggie's Toronto and Ashodaya Academy (an NGO based in Mysore that is run by sex workers and provides HIV-AIDS Services and supports sex workers in other areas to launch similar organizations to defend themselves and their rights).

27. Other self-determination projects include Little Earth of United Tribes in Minnesota,

The Black Panthers, the Brown Berets and the Xican@ Moratorium, the Young Lords, and the Peoples Coalition of Coney Island — who worked across class, race, and culture along with the Amethyst Women's Project to help teach organizing and raise up leaders among all the folks struggling with life post-Hurricane Sandy.

28. The Hip Hop Congress, the Unemployed Peoples Congress of Zimbabwe, the Black Riders Liberation Party, the Peoples Community Medics.

29. Prison Hunger Strike Movement.

30. Little Earth in Minneapolis.

31. Another important community self-determination project is the Primer Hospital Garifuna, providing people-led (not wite-science or colonizer-provided) healthcare to the people in the community of Ciriboya, Colon, Honduras.

32. See also Black August Committee, Afrikan revolutionaries, current and former prisoners, and resisting genocide behind prison walls (http://www.dragonspeaks.org/baoc%20website/history1.htm); Onyx Organizing Committee: "ONYX is committed to raising the consciousness of Black people to facilitate the healing of our bodies' minds and spirits in order to create sustainable, just, equitable, and thriving Black communities" (http://onyxbrief.blogspot.com/2011/11/what-is-onyx.html); and peoples in resistance in Michoacán, Mexico who have created an armed self-defense group to protect their families from organized crime operations (http://www.proceso.com.mx/?p=323893).

33. http://2servethapeople.wix.com/brlp.

34. Other indigenous-led struggles often center around the protection of sacred sites from development, like the Save the Peaks campaign to fight the corporate development of the Arizona Snowbowl; the shutdown of Whiteclay near Pine Ridge; resistance by the Houma Nation in New Orleans to protect their ancestors' graves; and UPOEG and CRAC, indigenous and community self-defense projects in Mexico.

35. For an account of farmers in mainland China taking back land that had been held in their families for generations and then illegally seized, see *No Enemies, No Hatred* by Liu Xiaobo.

36. The Shackdwellers Union has a university, University of Abahlali baseMjondolo, which was founded in 2005. It has been dismissed by many so-called progressive intellectuals as "criminal."

37. Fast Forward 10 years, a drastically un-funded housing Authority in SF and across the nation boards up their units, smoking the tenants out, one poverty skola at a time so the politricksters can come swooping in like the Mayor of San Francisco and prove "blight" claiming that see, public housing doesn't work so let's give it over the private devil-opers who are salivating in the wings like Lennar and John Stewart so they can Save the day.

About the Authors

The principal writer and visionary of this book is Lisa "Tiny" Gray-Garcia, a formerly unhoused, incarcerated poverty skola, revolutionary journalist, lecturer, poet, visionary, teacher and single mama of Tiburcio, and daughter of a houseless, disabled artist, visionary, revolutionary mama Dee Garcia. Dee and Tiny co-created the original theory of Poverty Scholarship, and co-founded the organization, magazine, and poor and indigenous movement known as POOR Magazine/Prensa POBRE/PoorNewsNetwork. Tiny has authored over 200 stories, blogs, and podcasts on issues such as poverty, racism, criminalization, homelessness, reparations and displacement. With her Mama Dee, she co-founded Escuela de la gente/PeopleSkool — a poor and indigenous people-led skool — as well as several cultural projects such as the Po' Poets Project/Poetas POBREs Proyecto, welfareQUEENs, the Theatre of the POOR/Teatro de los pobres, and Hotel Voices, to name a few. She is also the author of *Criminal of Poverty: Growing Up Homeless in America*, and co-editor of several books, including *Decolonizers Guide to a Humble Revolution*, *Born N' Raised in Frisco*, *Los Viajes — the Journeys*, and *Trabajador Fuerte / The Hard Worker* — a revolutionary children's book and curriculum. In 2011, she and fellow poverty and indigenous skolaz who contributed to this book co-launched The Homefulness Project, a landless peoples self-determined land liberation movement, as well as Deecolonize Academy, a liberation school for children, in the Ohlone/Lisjan/Huchuin territory known as Deep East Oakland.

One of the lived theories discussed in this book is the concept of interdependence, and how it is necessary for this value to undergird everything, even a "by-line." This concept is practiced in all of our revolutionary media, art and movement projects at POOR Magazine, and in media and writing Tiny calls this "publishing access." So in keeping with that practice, this book is released as a by-line shared with the POOR Magazine family of poverty skolas, writers, poets and teachers, Leroy Moore, Muteado Silencio, Laure McElroy, Corrina Gould, Tony Robles, Ingrid DeLeon, Aunti Frances Moore, Vivian Flaherty, Queennandi XSheba, Bruce Allison, Bilal Mafundi Ali, Joey Villareal, Dee Allen, and many more who contributed, wrote, spoke, lived and created work that is included in this text.

51073678R00236

Made in the USA
Columbia, SC
15 February 2019